Inferno

Inferno

An Anatomy of American Punishment

Robert A. Ferguson

HARVARD UNIVERSITY PRESS

Cambridge, Massachusetts

London, England

2014

Library of Congress Cataloging-in-Publication Data

Ferguson, Robert A., author.
    Inferno : an anatomy of American punishment / Robert A. Ferguson.
        pages   cm
    Includes bibliographical references and index.
    ISBN 978-0-674-72868-4 (cloth : alk. paper)
        1. Punishment—Philosophy.   2. Punishment—United States.
I. Title.

    K5103.F47   2014
    364.601—dc23   2013034386

For Kenji Yoshino

Deliberate cruelty is not forgivable.

—Tennessee Williams,
A Streetcar Named Desire

Contents

Acknowledgments

There are no experts on punishment—at least, none whom you would want to meet. I am instead indebted to many people for counsel on discrete aspects of this complicated subject. Debra Livingston put me onto an essential plan of reading about police work. Vince Blasi stoked my interest in nineteenth-century philosophy. Susan Sturm furnished information on reentry plans for prisoners. Elizabeth Emens suggested initiatives in restorative justice. Jim Liebman gave me his scholarship on death-penalty issues. Trevor Morrison lent me his expertise on the law of torture. An aside from Hal Edgar about the basis of desert in sentencing aided my thinking. David Pozen indicated a worthy comparative frame. A conversation with Gillian Metzger supplied rhetorical direction and confidence in the closing chapter. Brett Dignam, whose clinical expertise on prisons transcends that of anyone else I know, was a crucial resource on many particulars and my close and unstinting helper in a relevant classroom experience.

Four research assistants provided thought as well as information: Dina Hoffer, Alexander Lemann, Amy Conners, and Ian MacDougall. Kent McKeever and his law library staff have always been ready to step in with what was needed and with relevant works that I had not thought of. Here I owe special thanks to Dana Neascu, who went beyond the call of duty in tracking down material for me. My assistant Gabriel Soto encouraged all stages of the project in more ways than I can count.

All the individuals mentioned in the preceding paragraphs have been my colleagues at Columbia Law School, the most obliging environment for sharing ideas that I have found in academic life. I am beholden to many others there in our twice-weekly discussions of faculty research initiatives. This faculty makes the study of law an absorbing communal endeavor. The level of cooperation I have found among them in communicated thought is rare. It has been a constant inspiration, as well as a challenge.

If I owe so much to so many, it is because I could only write about this subject by surrounding it, entering into it from many different directions, taking it apart piece by piece, and then putting it all back together in a new way. John Paul Russo enriched the final Coda to the book. Doran Larson's work in prisons steered me in certain directions. Two expert readers for Harvard University Press, Nan Goodman and Lloyd Weinreb, gave extraordinary advice and valued correction on a penultimate draft. They were twin Virgils in my final descent, the last revision, and the book is a much better effort for their guidance. My editor, John Kulka, added direction and encouragement at various stages of the project. It is always vital to have someone who understands exactly what you are trying to do and knows how to assist that process, and John was that person. Heather Hughes answered all my many questions and guided the book expertly through production.

The dedication of this book speaks for itself, but it also points to a larger indebtedness. Kenji Yoshino offers the most profound philosophical grasp of what the law should be against what it is of those I have met in the legal profession. That grasp is also as graceful as it is profound, and he has shared it with me across many meals together. If it is possible to have a continual symposium between just two people, this has been one for me. His suggestions on various parts of the book have sustained me at difficult moments by making them suddenly bright and clear. No one is more important to how the law must be thought about in the pressures against it right now. Well beyond the support I have received, it has been a privilege to watch this mind in action.

A final recognition is similarly intellectual and emotional. I had no real idea how ugly the subject of punishment would become when I began this study, and it has been enough to bear me down at times. What people will do to other people is indeed a hell in our midst. In answer—with penetrating insight, sustaining comfort, corrections, and the happiness that life can provide—has been my companion, Priscilla Parkhurst Ferguson, in the pleasure, writing, and engagement that we have together.

Inferno

The Intractable Problem

The power of punishment is to *silence,* not to *confute.* . . . It can never promote the reception of truth.

Samuel Johnson, *Sermons, xxiii*

You are afraid all the time, and there is good reason to fear. You are alone with enemies all around you. No one cares about you. You can be attacked where you are, but it is more dangerous when you must move in the open. Groups roam the territory looking for victims. You cannot hide. Your only weapon is yourself. There is no authority to call on that you trust. Over and over you ask, "How did it come to this?" But it has come to this and for the foreseeable future.

Who are you? Where are you? You are not a soldier or a spy on some mission in a foreign land. You are not an undercover agent. You are not under siege. You are not a survivor of a civil war. You are not an explorer in some alien jungle, though in some ways you are. You are an inmate in an American prison. You belong to a peculiar version of hell, one that the American separation of church and state has imagined for you.

What did you do to get here? Perhaps you had too much dope on you when stopped or sold some of it to the wrong person to feed your habit. You have never been violent, but now you are surrounded by vicious inhabitants who enjoy hurting other people. Your chances of getting out of here in one piece are limited. They will depend on your wits and some luck, not the help of others, and if you do get out, there is nothing

1

waiting for you—no job, no family likely to help, no skill set for use in an economy that has passed you by and that will reject you anyway for what you have become. There is nothing to do where you are, but if you try to do something useful, predators will come after you. The lowest common denominator rules here. Most of all, you should not be the only person asking, "How did it come to this?"—a question with many answers.

The inspiration for this book came first in classrooms. At Columbia Law School, I can design scenarios in prosecutorial discretion that will lead seventy students to divide sharply over proposed sentences for a given crime. Their recommendations for punishment will extend from six months of house arrest all the way to twenty years in prison for the same offense. Arguments over the differences are intense, and the recommenders are budding lawyers who know some criminal law.

How can responsible citizens with that much knowledge come to such divergent views over the same facts? My answer to that question will figure prominently in coming chapters. Even educated Americans do not know what they are doing when they want to punish, but they nonetheless hold passionate views about it. The discrepancy is doubly important because the United States punishes more frequently and more heavily than other modern democracies. The incarceration rate in Europe is 1 out of 1,000; the United States imprisons 1 out of 143 and for longer periods under poorer conditions.[1] The richest country in the world is one of the worst in housing the people it punishes.

A dozen books in recent years have addressed this problem without having much impact on policy or practice even though the best account exposes "a criminal justice system long on degradation and short on mercy."[2] Some of the reasons given for severity include fear of crime, communal violence, gang activity, ethnic division, a democratic spirit that holds everyone to account, distrust of authority, political opportunism, economic inequality, demographic shifts, the legacy of slavery, the easy availability of firearms, and strict religiosity in assessing behavior and assigning blame.

Without quarreling with these assumptions or even with the possibility that together they have created an overly aggressive punitive impulse, I ask different kinds of questions. Why has identification of the problem had so little effect? What is it about punishment that confuses people? What can a deeper analysis of punishment tell us? Why does the average American citizen show little concern about prison systems that are harsher in practice than those in any but totalitarian countries? What does punishment as we now know it accomplish?

These questions point in a new direction. They also indicate an intractable problem that must be dealt with in some way. With 2.26 million people held in overcrowded and abusive prison systems as late as 2010, with one out of nine state workers employed in prisons, and with parts of the country spending more on incarceration than on education, the United States faces a dilemma of serious proportions and even of republican identity. The incarceration rate in the United States is the highest in the world today.

Penal institutions are also getting worse. They exact tremendous human and economic costs even as their size and vocational importance give them independent political power and an institutional momentum all their own. The sudden creation and rapid spread of private prisons, which are run for profit off the misery of others, indicate just how far penal policy has strayed from previous norms.

Those norms no longer control, if they ever did. Most debates over punishment turn on long-established reasons for it. Are we trying to deter, rehabilitate, incarcerate, satisfy victims, promote a safer society, restore loss, revenge a wrong, or limit the damage to all concerned? The conflicts in such theoretical preferences still drive debate, but they exist high above the grim reality of actual punishment, and acrimony over them reinforces the intractability of the problem by ignoring the obvious.

Punishment is punishment if you ask the punished. The recipient of it in an American prison endures violent discipline and repression under very loose administration. Exercises of penal authority go virtually unchecked. Rampant antagonisms and uncertainties determine the amount and kinds of punishment in ways that are often arbitrary. Yet, and typically, the primal scene of such infliction is rarely witnessed except by its participants; punishment is its own lonely problem. How does one record and comment on an absent presence that no inflicter wants known and most victims fear to reveal?

In response, writers who address the problem of harsh punishment usually reach for a particular readership. Directly or indirectly, books on this subject address the legal profession and law-enforcement institutions, but the logic in targeting these audiences has not worked well.

Two problems have left matters where they stand. First, the law is hardly ever reform minded on its own. It makes its decisions by turning to the past to solve the problems of the present, and punishment in America has outstripped previous perceptions. Legal systems are also invariably comfortable with where they are. They depend on the status quo and profit from it. Second, and not to be forgotten, the system thrives on a curious intellectual disjunction. Lawyers learn their trade in schools where the focus is on the punisher, not the punished. My own classes in prosecutorial discretion are a case in point.

The ability to deal with crime through law is a necessity in every well-ordered state. The law says to a wrongdoer, "We have proved that you have improperly injured another, and you must pay the consequences." A just society leaves the matter to this legal formula to restore order, and rightly so. Nonetheless, punishment involves other contingencies that should shape how transgressors are dealt with. In a truly effective democratic understanding, only the decision to punish should be left to the law. Its human impact is another matter and a large part of the issue to be faced here.

Long ago a reform-minded Jeremy Bentham needed a battering ram rather than a builder's trowel to answer the fixed ways of established law.[3] As in any intractable problem, some of the desire for change must come from outside the invested framework. The disciplines of philosophy, history, and imaginative literature will help serve that purpose here. Punishment is an interdisciplinary subject in both theory and practice. How we punish says how we think of ourselves generally.

Disciplines beyond the law are significant in this regard because they focus on the punished as much as the punisher. In their emphasis on relationships, they attack conventional views and offer more open appeals. The humanities, broadly speaking, make us look at the nature of our conduct. As such, they convey an intimacy of their own on the elusive subject of punishment.

Why is the subject so elusive? In the epigraph to this introduction, Dr. Johnson, the eighteenth-century man of letters, gets it right when he suggests that the power to punish silences in ways that do not promote truth. Moreover, the average person does not like to think about punishment at all, much less endure it or witness it. There are no normal pleasures here. Evasion, shame, secrecy, excess, division, intolerance, anger, and unseemly desires dominate much of its infliction.

Perhaps we also avoid consideration because we think we already know what it is. Hasn't everyone been punished and at some point punished another? Yes, but experience is an inadequate teacher on this subject. A parent who says to the erring child, "This hurts me more than it hurts you," mouths a lie. The truism skips past reality: pain administered is never pain endured. Even the language used is faulty. The concept of "hurt" has endless connotations, as do the many parallels to the word "punish"—"chastise," "castigate," "correct," "discipline," "restrain," "sequester," "inflict," "convict," "condemn," and on and on.

The main aberration or mystery in American punishment has to do with its severity, and this leads to question after question. Is severity a matter of communal apathy or design? The first punishers in America are its legislators, and they are elected by a people presumed to approve of what they do. Is the nation unaware, or confused, or indifferent, or misinformed about what happens in its prisons, or does it simply like things the way they are? This book tries to answer such questions, and it asks the country's citizens to respond to them.

How a culture punishes is part of its very meaning, and any explanation of its American forms must revisit that meaning in its parts and functions. An anatomy is accordingly the method of approach to be used here. The book begins by taking the subject apart, seeing it for what it is, and eliminating the many confusions about it. Only then can we assign the specific parts and levels and movements in punishment for how they have come together with such intensity. Only then can we comprehend institutional consequences that are now spiraling out of control in thought and action.

An anatomy also encourages the possibility of prescription. In this case, that means finding a way to cope with injustices that currently go unanswered even though they have been identified. Accountability must replace communal reluctance to engage—a reluctance born of how matters have gone so reflexively wrong without anyone quite realizing why. If we can detail how punitive intent and its applications have created such high levels of incarceration under conditions that humane sensibilities cannot justify, we can begin to think about the problems in new ways.

Seven graded steps will put the subject of punishment in sharper light and explain why the desire to punish has become so strong in American culture. Chapter 1 gives legal definitions that may be in need of revision. It then exposes veiled pleasures in the impulse to punish, eliminates basic confusions, and identifies the tendencies toward extremism that these pleasures and confusions breed.

Chapter 2 takes up punishment theory. Arguments flourish here but over hidden common ground. Room for severity exists in all theories of punishment, however benevolent. When rival theorists overlook this shared characteristic, they contribute to controversies that render current debates fruitless because they ignore the universal baseline that pushes all punitive practice toward darker alternatives. There are deep-seated reasons why retribution remains the calling card in punishment today.

Chapter 3 can then clarify the quality of infliction in punishment. Pain is a loose variable misunderstood when applied to the countervailing precisions in legal punishment. Controversy over the role of suffering in legal punishment is, in fact, a vexed subject in the twenty-first century, and that controversy can be traced back to the Latin concept of *poena*, the root word that conveniently conflates pain and punishment. That conflation is one way of easing the conscience of a punisher. The history of suffering is central here because the instrumentalism in modernity has radically changed the context and even the meaning of pain.

Three celebrated works of literature, each a different monody on punishment, inform these early chapters: Franz Kafka's story "In the Penal Colony," Fyodor Dostoevsky's internal sketch "The Grand Inquisitor" from *The Brothers Karamazov*, and Victor Hugo's novel *The Last Day of a Condemned Man*. They do not replace law in these chapters, but they tell us what the law cannot or will not say. They express the hidden characteristics of punishment regimes and the uncanny sources of their deterioration over time.

Chapters 4 and 5 convert the intellectual parameters just identified into the physical reality of the American punishment regime. Companion pieces, they dissect polar opposites on the ground of conflict. To examine incarceration is also to trace the intricate decisions and constructed procedures that hold so many people hopelessly in prison today. These chapters probe the ugly dynamic of imposer and imposed upon.

Institutional forces dominate these two middle chapters and have spawned a deepening harshness on both sides. Two classic works of imagination help to parse a growing sense of woe: James Gould Cozzens's famous novel *The Just and The Unjust* and Jack Henry Abbott's notorious autobiography *In the Belly of the Beast*. Punishment in these chapters erupts into an alienating thing full of insensitivities and hatreds that refuse to adjust to the problems of incarceration as we now know them.

With the degradations of incarceration fully rendered, Chapter 6 pulls us back outside legal institutions to the American people to ask why such horrors are so widely tolerated. The evolution of a punitive impulse owes much to habit in communal belief. Sociologists say "practice has a logic which is not that of the logician." Routine behavior works through dispositions "internalized as second nature" that take the world for granted instead of accommodating its realities.[4] The result in American thought has been a thrust toward incarceration beyond all verifiable need, but with just enough psychological room left over to challenge those controlling dispositions.

Chapter 7 uses all previous chapters to reintegrate law and society. It reveals the joint complicities that sustain a massive American punishment regime disguised in plain sight. Here, too, are some answers, though they run against some obvious cultural assumptions. Popular attitudes privilege retribution without much consideration of it. Against them are available ways of thought that challenge the amorphous assumptions in the punitive impulse. At issue is whether Americans can recover what was once called the better angels of our nature.[5]

Punishment, after all, is dictated as much by the character of the punisher as by that of the punished. Who are we? The question is appropriate at a time when innovative definitions of "the self" and "the people" have begun to dominate psychological and political discourse in a changing nation. New possibilities might now be available, if only because punishment depends on relatively inchoate conceptions about human nature and its needs. What are those conceptions, and how can they be used a different way?

A concluding "Coda: The Psychology of Punishment" accepts the challenge of new thought on punishment by turning to an original moment in consideration of it but with present purposes in mind. A masterwork at the beginning of the fourteenth century redefined the meaning of punishment. It could do so out of a desperate need to address human needs in a better way. There is, in other words, some proof that new thought can arise when the circumstances are right.

Are the circumstances right today? The story of American punishment is a troubling one, and it should worry the citizenry in a republic of laws. More than law-abidingness is at stake. Why should the average citizen know more about the dire conditions in legal punishment today? The answer is at once simple and complicated. How we treat others dictates how we might be treated in turn, and this time the devil lives in the abstractions as well as the details. Indeed, the abstractions have to be addressed as much as the details.

Citizens listen in a democracy. Then they speak about what they know—at the polls, in the newspapers, through electronic means, and during public association—and the need to know more is especially great on this subject. The people are the ultimate punishers. They should have a better idea of what they are doing.

Of course, the difficulties in knowing are just as great, but when punishment becomes too strict, there is a communal duty to evaluate it, and we can do that only by finding all its meanings. Even then we must leave room for externalities, other kinds of illumination. The impetus to punish works through covert combinations. The complicated values and passions involved cannot be gauged, as they often are, through narrow allegations of reproach. To comprehend the phenomenon requires a story of explanation, not of blame. Nor, for that matter, will explanation suffice.

Political, economic, historical, religious, philosophical, psychological, and legal implications have combined to create a perfect storm of punishment in American culture. Tactical policies will not alter that situation. Experience shows that tinkering with the rules only redirects blame. Change, if it is to come, will be through new understandings of punishment.

Punishment Misunderstood

In order that the happiness of the saints may be more delightful to them
and that they may render more copious thanks to God for it, they are
allowed to see perfectly the sufferings of the damned.

> Thomas Aquinas, *Summa Theologica,*
> *Supplement Third Part, Question 94, Article 1*

All punishment is in itself necessarily odious; if it were not dreaded, it
would not effect its purpose; it can never be contemplated with
approbation,

> Jeremy Bentham, "Chapter X: Popularity,"
> *The Rationale of Punishment*

The Puzzle

Must suffering make sense? It can make sense with either more or less
pain inflicted depending on the period in which you lived, and the question itself remains fundamental to many disciplines, especially theology, medicine, psychology, and political science. Pain, sometimes unbearable pain, comes to every life, and we tolerate it better if we have an
explanation of the reasons for it.

In religious understandings, the question turns on acceptance of a
divine plan. In medicine, diagnosis and mitigation are hallmarks. Psychology treats the mental anguish that we cause to ourselves and to
others. Political science studies collective levels of distress. Yet despite
the absolute centrality of the question in these fields, the answers offered
remain tentative and subject to alternative forms of measurement.

Law provides the great exception. It actually depends on the deliberate, affirmative, and calculated use of suffering. In most other professions, suffering occurs, and disciplines react provisionally to it. Law creates systematic anguish in the name of punishment, and instead of responding to the suffering involved, it must justify the deliberate infliction of it through highly structured rationales and definitions.

There is no more distinguishing characteristic in legal thought. The schemes needed to convince a people to submit to chastisement require rhetorical sophistication and aesthetic appeal. Holistic in intent and intricate in resolution, the legal justifications for inflicting pain should be studied for what they leave out as much as for what they include. The beauty of the law lies in form, and the underpinnings that make punishment such a complicated subject are a good place to find it. Few things are as intuitively unpleasant as punishment. The need to make its exaction a measured and agreeable system of control is therefore paramount.

Nigel Walker, a leading scholar in the field of penology, offers a typical, if crisp, example of what must be said and written. Walker is also useful because he has left out most of the obfuscations used to disguise the nastier aspects of the subject. In *Why Punish?* he presents "seven features of punishment" in a comprehensive legal definition. I abbreviate and paraphrase for purposes of brevity but keep Walker's language and structure.[1] Punishment is:

1. The infliction of something that is assumed to be unwelcome to the recipient.
2. The infliction is intentional and done for a reason.
3. Those who ordered it are regarded as having the right to do so.
4. The occasion for the infliction is an action or omission that infringes a law.
5. The person punished has played a voluntary part in the infringement.
6. The punisher must offer a justification. "It must not be mere sadism."
7. The belief or intention of the punisher, not of the punished, defines the act.

As simple as it sounds, this arrangement manages many variables while leaving out a few others without seeming to be incomplete. Seven, after all, is a lucky number. But lucky or not, there is no way around the fact that punishment diminishes the recipient of it, a fact obliquely noted in the euphemistic admission that infliction will be "unwelcome." Walker's emphasis remains fixed on the punisher, and there are reasons for that. Fairness requires first and foremost that punishers be held in check. Authority to punish must come from beyond the inflicting agent, it must address the breach of a particular known law, and it must target a proven and voluntary violation of that law.

Every point made is reasonable, fair, and necessary, and together they give shape to the enterprise in punishment, but can we trust the list? These seven characteristics say nothing about the limits of the pain that can be inflicted. The law likes to mask its problems in the language it chooses.[2]

Walker, to his credit, hints at one of those problems in his short quoted aside. What are we to make of the qualification in the sixth item of his list when he says punishment "must not be *mere* sadism"? Can it, then, involve some sadism, and if so, how much? Notice, as well, that only number five in the list comments directly on the volition of the punished over that of the punisher, and number seven appears to take that part of five back: "The belief or intention of the punisher, not of the punished, defines the act."

These interpolations are not picky ones. They point to facets of punishment that the legal process prefers to ignore. Left to the imagination are the boundary lines of suffering that the law will permit itself to employ and the nature of their impact on the recipient of it. In effect, the authority to punish sometimes hides elements of the definition even from itself! Rare is the formal definition, to take just one example, that acknowledges any animus in the act. Covering the anger in punishment is a presumed objectivity, but no legal framework holds back its negative feelings forever.

The emotionalism of the punisher will out, and it finds its place in most systems when punishment is announced. A judge at the moment of sentencing feels empowered to say what a community thinks of the newly named criminal. All recognize a legitimate shift in tone at this moment. The release of pent-up resentment—in tacit acknowledgment of feelings previously quashed—gratifies both the holder and the observers of it. We accept harsh words at sentencing as part of the righteous urge to punish. A judge says to the convicted person, "You are as bad as we thought you were, and I am now going to tell everyone why."

A sometimes related and uglier emotion is never far from punishment. In perhaps the most adept philosophical account, "Of Cruelty," Michel de Montaigne concludes that many people like to dominate other people when they can. Ten minutes in any crowded playground or five on a busy highway will confirm the point for anyone. Montaigne knew its extremes from the religious strife and civil wars of sixteenth-century France. With cruelty everywhere around him, he writes the main purpose of education is "to unlearn evil." There is "a natural propensity toward cruelty," and he calls it "the extreme of all vices." Montaigne locates vindictiveness in all of us and says it will always be hard to overcome. He dreads the worst. "Nature herself, I fear, attaches to man some instinct for inhumanity."[3]

Even less hopeful, Friedrich Nietzsche just assumes the worst. He explains that the negative insinuations in punishment are so strong because cruelty is the basis of it all. Infliction unleashes a "festival of cruelty," which reaches its most jubilant form when organized by the state. Nietzsche is at his canniest when he identifies a fundamental distortion in considerations of the subject. Punishers and their justifiers, he notes, fail to distinguish the origin of punishment (the pleasure it gives) from its purposes (revenge, deterrence, correction, etc.), and the conflation is as dangerous as it is convenient. By eliminating the distinction, a punisher can rest in the purpose, the rationale for the act, and forget the drive behind it. Lost is the unwarranted intensity that pleasure will give to infliction.[4]

Evasion of this truth leads to accusations of intellectual bankruptcy from Nietzsche. Cruelty is not only "one of the most ancient and basic substrata of culture"; it is so basic that it "cannot be imagined away."[5] The pleasure in punishing must not be forgotten because it is its own warning. "Whoever battles with monsters had better see that it does not turn him into one." Without the knowledge of what we are capable of doing, punishers lose the balance that legitimates their identity. "If you gaze long into an abyss," Nietzsche explains, "the abyss will gaze back into you."[6]

For a dramatic example, think of the suddenly false punisher in Shakespeare's *Measure for Measure*. As he gazes at what he has so unexpectedly become—a sexual harasser, intellectual bully, and torturer—the shaken Angelo can only exclaim, "O, fie, fie, fie! What dost thou, or what art thou, Angelo?"[7]

The point is not that Montaigne or Nietzsche or Shakespeare figures in American punishment regimes. They do not, but they pose subliminal problems that officialdom cannot afford to ignore and must handle in some way. The legal process in the United States responds through mechanisms that protect its functionaries from the dark side of punishment. The instruments of punishment are carefully divided. Legislatures create criminal statutes, police use them to arrest, prosecutors charge, juries decide, judges pronounce sentence, and prison officials carry out the sentence. The approach to punishment is multifaceted in the name of fairness and objectivity, but it serves an exculpatory purpose as well.

The separations in the function of punishment mean that no single official ever has to look directly into the abyss. No one punisher need feel the full burden of creating suffering. As a procedural safeguard and institutional relief, these divisions are as they should be, but, as we shall see in Chapter 4, the compartmentalization of perspectives also insulates each unit from the others. Everyone in the process of punishing has the courage of someone else's convictions to fall back on.

There is more. The mixed agency in punishment encourages a belief that all monstrosity, all blame, all loss of identity, all knowledge of the abyss, and all suffering belong to the erring recipient of punishment. Very few officials in the system actually have to *see* what they have done, and modern sensibilities add a special distance. The suffering of the convicted is carefully arranged to take place somewhere out of sight.

Powerful traditions in legal thought support the intellectual avoidances in punishment. Americans save their highest regard for judges, who are said to be free of rancor and in control of the mechanisms of punishment. The appellation "your honor" is more than a unique form of address. The epithet encompasses the entire legal system, guaranteeing its integrity. So strong are these communal attitudes, so generally do people believe that the convicted have gotten what they deserve in an objective forum, that modern criticisms questioning judicial objectivity have made little difference in popular understandings.

Assumptions about the honor of a judicially run system are all part of our need to believe in it. We forget that judges do not control the legal process anywhere near as much as is generally understood, and we overlook the fact that many problems in punishment are hidden from judicial view.[8] Even if we are willing to presume a Judge Hercules who will hand down perfect decisions with preternatural wisdom, the difficulties in punishment are significantly greater than the law will admit in the administration of it.[9]

Consider one of the simplest of current assertions about punishment. Every court in the country accepts the principle that punishment should be proportional to the crime, and the assumption holds whether the presumed goal of the punisher is retribution, deterrence, incarceration, rehabilitation, communal security, or social justice. An additional mantra used everywhere bolsters and protects this appeal in proportionality: "the same punishment for the same crime."[10] These joint claims are ones of basic fairness, and yet they tell us nothing about the length of a sentence to be imposed.

How, in the first instance, does one calculate the number of years to be served? In establishing proportionality and consistency as fairness, what is the gauge for measuring the gravity of a specific crime? Proportionality and the added notion of similar treatment for similar crimes are relational concepts. Together they are the virtue, the very legitimacy of punishment.[11] The logic is impeccable, but missing from it is the basis, the source that might tell us what the ideal sentence should be.

Any sentence of length by itself is an arbitrary measure. Its integrity exists as a variable fixed by legislative debate, determination, and statutory construction. The basis of a sentence for, say, the crime of assault and battery exists not in the number of years assigned but in what that number means in relation to other numbers or years in prison for more serious crimes, such as armed robbery, kidnapping, manslaughter, or murder.

The comparative gauge is what gives meaning to what would otherwise be an arbitrary sentence. The number of years assigned for a lesser crime sets the template for assigning higher sentences to greater crimes. But stop and realize what this also means. The longer the sentence for a crime like assault, the greater in the name of proportionality will be the number of years assigned for a more serious crime, such as armed robbery, and the harsher the punishment regime is likely to become. Everything gets decided under a banner of consistency where proportionality is fairness.

As the gradations in punishment climb for greater crimes, "fairness" turns into that which is "less severe" than the sentence for a worse crime. Whatever its virtues, proportionality thus gives limited assurance to the design of a punishment regime. The opposite may, in fact, come closer to the truth: the more crimes a legislature establishes under rubrics of proportionality and consistency, the greater is the likelihood of a more extended and harsher range of penalties at the top end of the scale.

Does the benchmark of a moderate or lower sentence for a lesser crime as a gauge for measuring a higher sentence for a greater crime eliminate the arbitrariness of the benchmark selected? Hardly. When the sentence assigned for assault or any other crime is legislatively chosen, it exists as a variable in the practice of punishment with a range of years left open, say, from one to three years in prison. The factors that might adjust the number of years in the actual sentence for that crime include the harm done, the intent, the motives for the crime, a previous record, and every other circumstance of mitigation or aggravation.[12]

Even a Judge Hercules will have his work cut out for him in this scene. The affirmations in statutory construction of a punishment regime do not begin to explain the hidden difficulties or variations in sentences that judges mete out. Differences in sentencing for the same crime occur all the time.[13]

Years actually served might seem to be a simpler concept to measure the meaning of punishment. We know what years are by our own experience, but can we know years in this context? Can any person at liberty really comprehend what confinement does to time? "One day in prison is longer than almost any day you and I have had to endure," Associate Justice of the Supreme Court Anthony M. Kennedy declares.[14] "Prison," explains one longtime convict, "is wanting to breathe with someone's fingers up your nose."[15] Time changes in jail.[16] Think about it by locking yourself in your bathroom for a day.

Can we know what the years actually mean to one serving them in prison? Judge Gerard Lynch, now on the Second Circuit of the United States Court of Appeals in New York, once asked his auditors to quantify in real-life terms a "short sentence" of seventy-eight months. "Imagine," he said, "being sent away from your family when your daughter is eleven, and returning on her eighteenth birthday."[17]

The Puzzle Recognized

The problems in punishment grow the closer we look at incarceration. Time served, a passive conception, does not describe the life of anyone in prison. The standard joke—inmates are in control of the asylum—is the reality that every prisoner must learn to live with today. Organized gangs, predatory inmates, endemic violence, simmering personal disputes, indifferent or abusive prison guards, insufficient surveillance, ethnic wars, dysfunctional cellmates, serious overcrowding, rampant disease, certifiable insanity, wretched physical circumstances, and a merciless pecking order make every jail sentence a daily ordeal of danger, humiliation, and insecurity.[18]

Nothing about these conditions makes the incarcerated any better than they were, and all of them contribute to more crime. Just as worrisome is the magnitude of the situation, a magnitude on such a scale that it begins to define the country itself. Imprisonment has reached proportions unprecedented in the history of the United States. In the last three decades of the twentieth century, incarceration rates rose by 500 percent.[19] Close to two million people are currently held behind bars in the American penal system. Seven million people are now under some form of penal supervision. To grasp what that means, you need only know that supervision now applies to one out of every thirty-two adults in the nation.[20]

Incarceration rates are five to twelve times the rates of imprisonment found in Europe and Japan.[21] Forty percent of the nation's prison population consists of impoverished African Americans who cannot afford private counsel and are thus ill equipped to handle an adversarial legal system geared to bargains between counsel.[22] True, too, it is easier to punish someone who is different from you and whom you have no desire to know or understand.[23]

The consequences of incarceration are, if anything, just as alarming. American jail sentences fail more than they succeed. The national recidivism rate for those who have been imprisoned has climbed to 67.5 percent.[24] The notion that prisons serve as "houses of correction" can no longer be maintained. They exist now as holding pens with incapacitation as the objective. Rehabilitation has been discredited, and resources for it have grown scarce.[25] The number of inmates serving life sentences has skyrocketed, as has the expense of maintaining such an elaborate system. The United States now spends more than $80 billion a year to keep its huge prison population in place.[26]

As hard as it is to grasp the meaning of such numbers, incarceration levels pose an even greater puzzle. What are we to make of the apparent indifference of the American people to high rates of imprisonment and levels of punishment in a penal system that is manifestly worse than that of any other liberal democracy one can name? Why hasn't a citizenry dedicated to freedom and individual rights rejected institutional horrors that begin to rival the gulags of Communist Europe and the former Soviet Union?[27]

One can imagine two answers to the puzzle of communal apathy. The first conceivable explanation, the one that will dominate this book, traces indifference to an unplumbed cultural configuration of ignorance, confusion, anger, and misunderstanding. The second possibility is more disturbing. Is the prison system this way because the body politic wants it that way? Complicating either answer has been lack of communal discourse on the issue. The prolonged and bitterly divided debates over national ills in the presidential campaign of 2012 nowhere addressed the need for prison reform.

No authority that one can name will take on this controversy and give a straight answer to it even though it is one of the gravest issues of our times. Nor is the reason for hesitation lack of awareness. No less a personage than Associate Justice Anthony M. Kennedy carefully straddles the two explanations for passivity in an uneasy account of the problem. Is it ignorance or a more knowing disregard that explains the deplorable conditions in our penal system? In an address to the American Bar Association in 2003, Justice Kennedy balanced the alternatives against each other without choosing between them.

The address begins with a revealing claim. "The inadequacies—and the injustices—in our prison and correctional systems" have to be read against "the continuing need to teach the principles of freedom" because "unbounded relativism as a civic philosophy soon becomes passivity and indifference."[28] Empirical data and legal doctrine bear out the inadequacies alluded to here, and Kennedy confirms that "our resources are misspent, our punishments too severe, our sentences too long" (4). Much in the system is "unwise and unjust" (4). Much more is literally intolerable. "It is no defense if our current prison system is more a product of neglect than of purpose" (7). But which is it, neglect or purpose? And whose passivity counts most? Shouldn't there be answers to these questions?

Justice Kennedy agrees that the current prison system actively seeks "to degrade and demean the prisoner," and he concludes "a purpose to degrade or demean individuals is not acceptable in a society founded on respect for the inalienable rights of the people" (7). This leads to another conclusion: "Out of sight, out of mind is an unacceptable excuse for a prison system that incarcerates over two million human beings in the United States" (7). The pivotal issue for Kennedy turns on forms of disregard, but whose disregard and at what level? Is it the people's disregard or the legal profession's or both, and if both, what is the connection that might respond to the unacceptable situation?

Always an adept compromiser, Kennedy heads for middle ground. "Even those of us who have specific professional responsibilities for the criminal justice system can be neglectful when it comes to the subject of corrections," he charges, turning first to the legal profession. "When someone has been judged guilty and the appellate and collateral review process has ended, the legal profession seems to lose all interest." But then this: "When the door is locked against the prisoner, we do not think about what is behind it." The broadened use of the pronominal "we" extends the puzzle. "We have a greater responsibility," Kennedy announces. "As a profession, and as a people, we should know what happens after the prisoner is taken away" (2–3).

The two-pronged assessment of responsibility, the legal profession and the people, holds with rhetorical finesse throughout the address, and it allows Kennedy to skirt an intellectual problem. Long ago Alexis de Tocqueville recognized a fundamental truth: "the stationary spirit of legal men and their prejudices in favor of existing institutions."[29] Law holds to the status quo. Justice Kennedy knows that he needs the people to effect change. There must be "a new public discussion about the prison system," and "it is the duty of the American people to begin that discussion at once" (7).

But how? An implied logic, often referred to as Occam's razor, hovers ambiguously over Kennedy's assertions. Yes, the people, depending on how you define them, come first in principle, but raising vague principles so that the simplest hypothesis should prevail does not decide who must take the lead in this case, the law or the people. Nothing is ever going to be that simple here.

A key sentence in Justice Kennedy's appeal presents another rhetorical evasion, but it is doubly important because the same words give the direction that this book must and will take. Again Kennedy refuses to choose between the law and the people as his subject. "Were we to enter the hidden world of punishment," he observes, "we should be startled by what we see" (3). The comment is helpful, but it does not go far enough. We should not be startled by the hidden world of punishment; we should be ashamed of it by knowing what we have seen.

The intellectual passivity or inability of both the legal profession and the people to react to the deprivations of a deteriorating prison system defy easy explanation without more basic recognitions. We have to know more about the theory and the reality of punishment in America if we are to come to grips with what Justice Kennedy rightly calls "an unacceptable excuse for a prison system" (7).

Looked at in this way, no one should be surprised that Justice Kennedy's eloquent legal appeal for reform has had little practical impact despite his leading role as the swing vote on the Supreme Court. His address to the American Bar Association presents the problem squarely and with the authority of one making legal decisions at the highest level, but if so, why hasn't his thorough account of the problem led toward a solution?

The best answer given anywhere to the communal passivity that Justice Kennedy describes comes from an obscure bureaucrat writing a story on the edge of the collapsing Austro-Hungarian Empire a century ago. Franz Kafka's bizarre account of unjust punishment, "In the Penal Colony," gives all the reasons why those who might resist penal injustice do not.

The Parameters in Doing Nothing

Completed in 1914, just as everyone intuits the horrors unfolding in World War I, "In the Penal Colony" is Kafka's most terrifying story.[30] There is no more explicit investigation of the vitality in punishment.[31] Hannah Arendt may have been the first critic to put it fully into words when, cognizant of the even greater horrors of World War II, she wrote, "Kafka's nightmare of a world . . . has actually come to pass."[32] To gauge the pumping heart of punishment and our passive reactions to it, we must realize what we are capable of becoming; Kafka knew how to tell it in the realm of story.

Most previous critiques have focused on the story's mesmerizing torments or allegorical significance.[33] Far less attention has been given to the writer's interest in punishment and the means by which people become inured to both the infliction and the receipt of it. Kafka delivers an arid message. "In the Penal Colony" announces what few want to face. Punishment, he says, fascinates through its pleasures, and those pleasures turn us against ourselves and paralyze our sensibilities.

The style and tone of "In the Penal Colony" are so ruthlessly neutral and spare that we can get the story in a few sentences. An explorer visits a penal colony that punishes every crime, however minor, with a slow, torturous death under a machine that inscribes the answer to the crime on the condemned man's naked body. The agonized victim dies only after realizing the ever more deeply tattooed message on his body. The purposes and success of this punishment regime are explained and demonstrated to the reluctant explorer by an officer who is in charge of the machine, but when the explorer indicates his disapproval, the officer tries to change his mind by having the machine needle the words "Be Just" on the officer's own body. The machine falls apart, killing the officer. The appalled explorer then hurries away, but not before preventing all others from leaving the colony with him.[34]

This summary does not do justice to Kafka's cold-blooded account of the torture engine, but it tells us what modern mechanisms have brought to punishment. Worship of the machine is the first thing noticed. "It is a remarkable piece of apparatus," exclaims the presiding officer in the first line of the story (140). Fascination with the machine adds wonder to punishment. Kafka proves that it is now easier, cleaner, and better entertainment to let a machine kill than to do it with one's own hands. World War I will dispatch fifteen million victims and wound another twenty million as the opening salvo in a century full of mechanized slaughter.

The officer in charge, the punisher, has gone insane from conducting so many executions with the machine he adores, but there is method in his madness, and Kafka spells out the details, using the sordid impulsions in all punishment. There is, first of all, satisfaction in killing before an admiring audience. Huge crowds have watched the machine at work, and the officer is proud of the uniform he wears for "the performance" (147). Second, the officer cares only about the execution going well. Victims are forgotten ciphers. Third, expertise enhances the enjoyment by giving the officer his own closed world of aesthetic appreciation. He gives pet names to the parts and plans of the machine; they are his "most precious possessions" (148). Fourth, "the technical problem," not the law, not the crime, not death itself, has become the rationale of punishment (147).[35]

Each of these gratifications distances the officer, an unnamed everyman, from the torture he inflicts, but Kafka adds a disgusting intimacy to the enterprise. The thing that every punisher tries to instill is acceptance of the punishment, no matter how cruel, by its victim. It does not matter that the original crime can be a negligible offense or one not fully articulated. Punishment alone conveys the message. Justice lies not in legal interpretation but in infliction. Thus, in the sixth hour, when the punished are finally too weak to scream, "enlightenment comes to the most dull-witted" through the inscription repeatedly stitched on the body. The victim deciphers his crime through his wounds (150).

Words, the prisoner's sentence, have become insufficient indicators of punishment by themselves. It is the body that records punishment, imbibes it to the fullest, and then tells the mind about it. So powerful is this reciprocal moment of recognition between punished and punisher that the officer enters the machine himself to prove it. The fact that the machine collapses when asked to inscribe the message "Be Just" underlines an obvious theme (161).

No machine, no matter how intricate or refined, can provide the meaning of justice. Punishment and the justice in it are relational concepts. Even so, as the story makes clear, machines can sustain a far more elaborate punishment regime. No one should forget that technological capability as much as policy has created the enormous size and highly structured security arrangements of the American punishment regime. It can be done because mechanism allows the possibility on an unprecedented scale.

A subtler issue drives the officer of "In the Penal Colony" from madness in thought to madness in action. The once-smooth punishment regime has fallen into decay through overload of the system and a failure in higher authority. Punishment has lost the perfection in performance that the officer identified as justice. Consumed by his own responsibility in the ceremony of infliction, the man for whom torture has become a habit gives way to despair over its imperfect manifestations. Justice has devolved into getting horrible particulars right.

Kafka offers several explanations for the disintegration of his punishment regime. A new commandant of the penal colony disapproves of the machine without having the active courage to resist it, but here, as always in Kafka, the story offers a darker possibility that is more powerful because it characterizes all punishment regimes.

No matter how enlightened punishment becomes, no matter what aspirations theorists use to justify what should be done, the institutional infliction of suffering will deteriorate into something worse than it was. The ideals of legal enforcement give way to the impetus in all punishment. Kafka's story foreshadows our own: American penology also had a plan, but its prisons have broken down under the weight of its claims about punishment.

A third explanation by Kafka offers a ray of hope, but perhaps only a ray. Critics misread "In the Penal Colony" when they downplay the role of the visiting explorer and argue that Kafka needed the explorer for "technical reasons" to get his story out.[36] The explorer *is* the story. How the explorer acts and does not act tells us what happens in the history of punishment regimes. This particular punishment regime collapses when an outsider says it is unjust (159–160). How much hope can we place in an outsider who announces that legal punishment, as justified, is actually unjust? That is a proposition to be tested in every chapter of this book.

Our knowledge of the explorer is limited but crucial. He arrives as a private citizen from an unnamed community. He is thought to have more influence than he has, but he is also our only moral guide. His name, "the explorer," implies more than a witness, and he moves from "indifference" through passivity and toward a more active appraisal of the torture mechanism (143). Notably, the punishing officer assigns the highest level of authority to this visitor and seeks his help, but it is an authority the explorer repeatedly disclaims. He is all or nothing.

How involved should this outsider be? "The explorer thought to himself: It's always a ticklish matter to intervene decisively in other people's affairs." He reminds himself instead that "he was neither a member of the penal colony nor a citizen of the state to which it belonged" (151). Yet he is "strangely tempted" to intervene, and the reason is clear. "The injustice of the procedure and the inhumanity of the execution were undeniable" (151). There is no moral uncertainty here. "I do not approve of your procedure," he says at last. "I was already wondering whether it would be my duty to intervene" (159–160).

What is anyone's obligation in such a situation? For a brief moment the explorer's hesitation gives way to a plan of action. "I shall tell the Commandant what I think of the procedure, certainly" (160). But this certainty immediately wavers, and the plan is never carried out. Given these vacillations, what are we to make of the explorer? We know that he has led a rich life of varied experience and that he is "fundamentally honorable and unafraid" (159). Fundamentally? For we also notice that the explorer does nothing. He does not contact the commandant. He does not intervene at any moment. He does not even bother to explain what happens to the officer. Instead, he rushes back to his ship ahead of schedule, pausing only to keep others from following him.

Semiofficial as an honored visitor but utterly private as an unaffiliated adventurer, the explorer is the puzzle in Kafka's story and ultimately the puzzle in the book you are reading. He stands for how anyone might hesitate between involvement and a simpler disengagement. Should the explorer have intervened or not? The point is that he does not. We are given a moral stance for engagement against a passive physical demeanor in response. He does nothing.

Inaction defies easy evaluation, but the explorer fails to intervene to prevent even the catastrophic death of the officer. "The explorer bit his lips and said nothing. He knew very well what was going to happen, but he had no right to obstruct the officer in anything" (163). Why not? Failure to intervene in the official punishment of the condemned prisoner can be construed as a bow to established authority. The incarcerated live under a legal fault to be paid for. The officer's spontaneous decision to punish himself requires no such explanation. Any moral agent might try to step in to prevent it, and again we are left with the question: What are we to make of the man of action who does not act?

Kafka does not help us with these problems after presenting them at length, but he wanted his account to be the lead story in a collection titled *Punishment*. The book was to give extended reflections on that theme, and although the idea was never carried out, the plan itself allows a larger comment.[37]

When the will to punish dominates, as it does in this story, all other relations dissolve. In one of Kafka's more nuanced touches, the guard who holds the condemned man to be executed treats his prisoner as the merest object on the end of a chain until the man is replaced by the officer. With that release, the two men suddenly become amiable competitors laughing with each other over food and other objects available to them. A dim spark of humanity exists in these minor figures, but punishment, the ordering device here, destroys its every possibility.

"In the Penal Colony" teaches that punishment will trump every other concern, including the meaning of crime, procedural integrity, verification of guilt, the rights of the punished, proportionality in punishment, and the mental balance of the punisher. Kafka proves that insensitivity in the punisher is a norm. Indifference to suffering follows logically from habitual infliction. Expertise in punishment may protect the punisher, but it displaces concern for the punished, and this means infliction will increase. Given enough time, severity will flourish in a punishment regime unless someone stops it.

Kafka's explorer tells us even more. He stands for the proposition that anyone looking at a punishment regime from outside of it must accept handicaps in perception. The punisher will always want the approval of this witness and will want it on the punisher's own narrow terms, and so the punisher is never going to be a reliable guide to what actually happens in prisons. Left to one's own devices but aware of limitations in what a punisher will allow to be seen, an outsider must read the situation through a mixture of attention (fascination over punishment), disgust (the observed manifestation of it), protest (recognition of what would be injustice in any other setting), and uncertainty (confusion over the trustworthiness of the enforcer, the rules that apply, and the unknown scope of the operation).

An outsider who briefly witnesses a punishment regime will not know what to do about it. The negative status of a prisoner eliminates the rights of the normal self. The incarcerated deserve some punishment; that is why they are there. Perhaps, though, they do not deserve the treatment at hand even though they are defined through fault. If they seem less at fault than the punishment administered, where should the line of interference be drawn? Legal punishment bespeaks a sovereign's assertion of integrity. When should an outsider challenge a legal response that is also a claim of order restored?[38]

Kafka's explorer epitomizes every uneasy public eye looking in. If he falters, it may be in the same way that an American citizenry remains passive in its limited knowledge of its own punishment regime. To the insider, punishment performs an intense set of necessary practices that outsiders are in no position to question; to the outsider, observation is a momentary act with little or no frame of comparison. Punishers and punished are enmeshed in the messy details of maintaining a prison. The outside observer naturally remains tentative about interfering where others appear so certain.[39]

The most hard-driving of rationalists among punishment theorists, Jeremy Bentham, comes closest to explaining the emotional state of our outsider. "All punishment is in itself necessarily odious," Bentham writes;

"if it were not dreaded, it would not effect its purpose; it can never be contemplated with approbation."[40]

Why should a discreet witness invest serious consideration in something so odious, where, in fact, approval can hardly be expected anyway? Why analyze feelings of dread, why challenge official approbation, why embroil oneself in an argument with an imperious authority of unknown dimensions? Most observers of punishment will act like the explorer. They will flee to their own safe ship in the harbor, and they will prevent anyone from escaping with them.

Punishment Out of Control

Punishment is misunderstood in part because examination of it rarely leads to agreement. Experts in criminology argue over it all the time. It may also be true that the only real experts are inside the issue. How does one measure and agree on an appropriate amount of punishment when the criteria for choosing are rational on the surface but deeply emotional in impact and very different in practice? Public debates are sharp out of ignorance, out of the inability to see what is really going on in prisons, but also out of recognition of a prison system that is too harsh and getting harsher.

Acrimony flourishes because the concepts used in argument do not reflect what the punished undergo. Which of several conventional ideas of punishment correctly justifies the appropriate length of a sentence to be served? Debate is as endless as it is intricate over ideas that are as irreconcilable as they are self-limiting.[41] Should retribution drive sentencing and other penal policies, or should the engine of concern be deterrence, rehabilitation, utilitarianism, incapacitation, or restoration?[42]

Abstract principles dominate these discussions and repeat the same intellectual fallacy that Friedrich Nietzsche rejected more than a hundred years ago. Arguments over the purposes of punishment ignore the practice of it.[43] Insofar as the length of a sentence can be justified, it provides a sanitized gauge for the punisher, not the punished. A sentence, short or long, ignores suffering that has little to do with time even though time always counts. The years assigned do not touch the reality that anyone confronting confinement endures in an American prison.

A governmentally commissioned bipartisan Ford Foundation report from 2006 using that very title, *Confronting Confinement,* captures the concreteness in American punishment. A summary of the report reads, "American prisons are dangerously overcrowded, unnecessarily violent, excessively reliant on physical segregation, breeding grounds of infectious disease, lacking in meaningful programs for inmates, and staffed by underpaid and under trained guards in a culture that promotes abuse."[44]

Prison practices outstrip all the theories. In the Rikers Island prison complex operated by the New York City Department of Corrections, class-action suits, one as late as 2013, have not prevented a pattern of "brutal and unlawful beatings" of inmates by uniformed guards. Organized groups of guards regularly take handcuffed inmates to unmonitored areas before attacking them. The results for inmates, according to court reports, have been broken jaws, facial fractures, major broken bones, perforated eardrums, permanent spinal damage, severe concussions, and life-threatening internal injuries that were diagnosed only because hospitalization was required. In a consummate irony, the video cameras used to ease guard surveillance have become a prisoner's best friends. They limit the locations for beatings and sometimes show the marks of injuries.[45]

Specificity conveys what generalization cannot capture in punishment. In the summer of 2013, nine correctional officers and supervisors at Rikers were arraigned on criminal charges after a security chief "ordered his subordinates to kick the inmate's teeth in" because "this guy thinks he's tough." The prisoner had dared to lock eyes with a supervisor. He was taken to a search pen "where five members from an elite correction unit were waiting for him." There, tackled to the floor, "he was repeatedly kicked with his body in a fetal position, covering his head." The legal defenses for such actions come tied to a cover-up and are always the same: "The officers did everything they were supposed to."[46]

Horrendous stories of prison abuse can now be found anywhere in the United States. A warden and a guard in North Carolina were suspended in 2012 for inmate abuse after allegations that "guards had forced them to rub hot sauce on their genitals, kiss deadly snakes, and imitate sex acts."[47] Prison gangs in Maryland run extortion rings, drug-trafficking operations, money-laundering schemes, and organized sexual liaisons in which correctional officers participate. Maryland prisons have one of the highest rape rates in the country.[48] In Mississippi prisons, "rapes, stabbings, beatings, and other acts of violence are rampant." Inmates claim that they have to set fires "to get medical attention in emergencies." Guards, as a matter of course, coerce prisoners for sex in exchange for food and phone privileges.[49]

Can theoretical alternatives about punishment reach such accounts? Conventional ideas about penology do not begin to answer this question, and it takes an outsider from another discipline to explain why. A theologian who writes about legal matters today, Oliver O'Donovan, reduces the ideas of punishment to three and decides that each misses the point of the suffering imposed. O'Donovan rejects the criminologists who compartmentalize the meaning of punishment: "those which find its purpose in retribution, those which find its purpose in reform, and those which find it in the protection it affords society." The "three-theory theory" is deeply flawed because it considers only the will of the punisher.[50]

O'Donovan knows that *"those affected"*—"victim, offender, and the rest of society"—cannot be defined by separating the categories of punishment into retribution, reform, and communal security, and he sees a more serious problem in the theoretical construct. "The three-theory theory encourages a style of argument like a race of hobbled horses," he says. "None of the beasts are capable of finishing the course, so the victory goes to the jockey who knocks his rivals over." O'Donovan also specifies the logical winner. The jockey who survives this struggle is going to be retribution, the default answer in a punitive system.[51]

We need only look to the punished to grasp O'Donovan's main point. How many prisoners, do you suppose, appreciate a claim of proportionality in retribution or pause to think of reform measures as anything but more punishment? Rehabilitation sounds great to the hopeful corrector; the person corrected hears more imposition of the system. Even the declared third theory of punishment, "the protection it affords society," will be meaningless to a prisoner. Protection is what every inmate sacrifices on entering the predatory zone of American prisons. The high recidivism rate in the country's prison systems suggests even more. Scholarly penchants for dividing punishment into intellectual categories have very little to do with solving crime.

Retributivism not only wins in O'Donovan's horse race, it leaves all other theories somewhere out on the track. Reprisal dominates American considerations of punishment on both philosophical and practical levels, and the predictable result has been more punishment. The facts are in. "The United States has become even more severe in its treatment of offenders in recent years."[52]

But if retribution is king, the winner of what is really a one-horse race, the reasons for it are complicated because the race itself, as O'Donovan admits, is an imperfect one. "None of the beasts," he has noted, "are capable of finishing the course." There is no real competition, and the theoretical inferences to be drawn are suddenly very different in a much messier intellectual situation than previously realized. Instead of retributivism vying with other theories, the issue is one of controlling retribution in the knowledge that there are few controls in place now. We need to know how this has happened. Why is retributivism so firmly in the American saddle of a race it can never really win?

Some superficial explanations must be dealt with first. Recidivism of inmates has justified reliance on retribution and confirmed most retributivists' interest in incapacitation. Both viewpoints prefer long, fully-served sentences as the definition of a penal obligation with massive overcrowding in American prisons the predictable consequence. Retribution says you are getting exactly what you deserve. A policy of incapacitation says you remain incorrigible until proved otherwise by serving all of your time without further incident.[53] The result is a vicious circle. Both positions forget that prisons now create more criminals than they reform.

If the logic is weak, the triumph of retribution is nonetheless complete and can be read very clearly in accelerating rates of incarceration. The completely incapacitated, the inmates serving life in prison in the United States, increased 83 percent from 69,845 in 1992 to 127, 677 in 2003. Lifers now represent 9.4 percent of all offenders in state and federal prisons. Over 33,000 of these lifers serve without the prospect of parole, a sentence banned in most other countries.[54]

Retribution also succeeds because it is simple to grasp. It relies on the oldest of ideas: the *lex talionis,* an eye for an eye. But lost in the equation, as even a leading retributivist points out, is a troubling question. "On what theory of *lex talionis* is it just to ignore repeated gang rapes inflicted on persons who have been convicted of drug possession or criminal fraud?"[55]

The question is a vital one because it bears in mind what convicts receive rather than what they are said to deserve. It looks to the reality of punishment as suffering in prison rather than an abstraction over the length of a sentence, and it points to a particular problem. Experts estimate that "nearly 200,000 inmates now incarcerated have been or will be the victims of prison rape," with the incalculable loss in dignity, identity, self-esteem, and safety that this means.[56]

For a retributivist to look this closely is to admit something else. The same questioner recognizes "a slippery slope of retributive thinking," and he concedes that it leads to harsher levels of punishment. He expresses it this way:

> The transitions from "because your act and your mental state at the time were blameworthy, you deserve punishment" to "you have a vicious character," to "you have a hardened, abandoned, and malignant heart," to "you are evil and rotten to the core," to "you are scum," to "you deserve whatever cruel indignity I choose to inflict on you" is, of course, not a logical transition. No single step logically follows from its predecessor. I fear, however, that the transition is *psychologically* a rather common and in some ways compelling one, one that ultimately may tempt us to endorse cruelty and inhumanity.[57]

Retributivism welcomes such angry dismissal, and that is what is happening in American punishment. In its ideological dominance, a dominance that fuels certitude, retributivism wants incarceration to be strict, and it presses against the flexibilities in prisoner release. To punish is always to administer pain, but retribution wants that pain to be in the name of the injured victim as much as for the more neutral state. It never forgets the impact of the actual crime or the lowering of penalties for it.

For the same reasons, retribution does not deal with proportionality in punishment as well as it might. Condemnation, accountability, standards, and righteousness control its modes of thought. "Retributive punishment for legal wrongdoing is justified in part because in treating the offender as a responsible moral agent it communicates to him a respect for his dignity as an autonomous moral agent."[58] So far so good, but *sentenced* criminals have abused that autonomy and so are expected to do without it.

An inexorable logic follows. Inmates have sacrificed the right to have their dignity respected at normal levels. The moral logic of retribution easily accepts the reflex in retaliation. It redefines the character of inmates through the attributes that have been lost to them, and that loss encourages the impulse to punish heavily.

More difficult to explain are the failures of other theories of punishment to reduce the impact of retributivism even though many experts argue vigorously for alternatives.[59] Most philosophers of punishment worry, in consequence, about excessive punishment in one way or another. Friedrich Nietzsche again leads the pack in condemnation, if not in constructive alternatives. "Thus do I counsel you, my friends, distrust all in whom the impulse to punish is powerful."[60] His point seems obvious enough if we accept that punishment, the imposition of suffering, has its pleasures. No one who likes to punish should be allowed to inflict it, and yet too much infliction remains prevalent in punishment regimes even when this restraint is honored and followed.

Excessive punishment is the problem talked about everywhere that will not go away no matter what is said about it. Why not? Is it only retributivism? Not exactly. How well a punishment fits a crime also defies philosophical solution, and the discrepancy remains especially vivid since the law always presumes to assign an exact fit with every sentence it delivers.

This paradox, philosophical confusion against an exact legal sentence delivered in court with professional certainty, recalls a famous assertion by Louis Hartz. "Law," he observes in *The Liberal Tradition in America,* "has flourished on the corpse of philosophy in America."[61] Many legal commentators give unwitting support to Hartz's claim by trying to treat punishment entirely through legal inquiry, but it cannot be done.

The sweeping philosophical investigations of the eighteenth century have shaped our modern theories of punishment and have given it whatever normative basis it has. They have established the terms that define ideas of punishment up to the present day, and they have provided the ideas, as well as the mechanistic principles, of the penitentiaries that have evolved into modern prisons. That their basic concerns are still our basic concerns may be an indication of how much we may still have to learn.

Not coincidentally, modern philosophies of punishment and the founding of the United States of America are parallel eighteenth-century achievements. Ideas about punishment are not just apparent in the national founding; they are fundamental to the creation of government and find their place in the Constitution of the United States. The figures that help define the modern polity—Niccolò Machiavelli, John Calvin, Cesare Beccaria, Thomas Hobbes, John Locke, Immanuel Kant, Montesquieu, and Jeremy Bentham, among others—make concepts of punishment central to government, and each has his influence on government and law in America. Hobbes speaks for all of them when in *Leviathan* he makes punishment "the nerves of the Artificiall Man, the Common-Wealth."[62]

Americans are not philosophically inclined, but some of their confusions over the nature of punishment can be traced to the philosophers they called on to help form a more perfect union. We can ignore these philosophers and usually do, but in a larger sense we cannot do without them. In the words of one persuasive American writer on the subject of punishment, not himself a philosopher, "The proper design of public policies requires a clear and sober understanding of the nature of man."[63] How you evaluate human nature, a central question in philosophy, controls what you will think about punishment.

Given the American propensity to punish severely, we can start a discussion of the philosophical implications behind it with two of the earliest guarantors of that propensity. Each also symbolizes a pillar in national formations. Niccolò Machiavelli, representing civic humanism, warns that "anyone who would act up to a perfect standard of goodness in everything must be ruined among so many who are not good."[64] The theologian John Calvin embodies the second pillar, the dissenting tradition in the Protestant Reformation, and he adds a warning of his own. Calvin assumed that the number of people punished eternally would be much larger than the number saved.[65]

The important thing to remember is that these very different warnings from very different directions of thought join on common ground. Machiavelli and Calvin were equally troubled by the thought of leniency. The goad of severity is a philosophical yardstick, and when other thinkers finally come to contest that stance, they discover they can never quite relinquish it either.

2

The Rachet Effect in Theory

We do not live in society in order to condemn, though we may condemn in order to live.

H. L. A. Hart, *Punishment and Responsibility: Essays in the Philosophy of Law*

The Logic of Severity

Serious thought about limiting punishment is relatively modern in the long history of ideas. It does not emerge in sustained philosophical inquiry until the Enlightenment, and like so many other conceptions from that explosion in thought, its formulations remain controversial.[1] Many of these controversies will concern us here, but they begin in a commonality worth noting. They all owe their existence to the same source, a breathtaking shift in human understanding at work in eighteenth-century exchange. The Enlightenment—with its calls on reason, intricacy of method, human value, mechanism, and a triumphant individuality—marks the distinction between modern life and all previous eras of civilization through higher regard for how people should be treated in society.

Punishment is an excellent source for appreciating this change. H. L. A. Hart's twentieth-century assertion—"We do not live in society in order to condemn, though we may condemn in order to live"—would have led to many more condemnations in earlier historical periods.[2] In the ancient world, you could be legitimately killed or enslaved (the two standard alternatives in punishment) for any reason at all. You could be dispatched for who you were, where you were found, whom you knew, when you were defeated, or even for what you had accomplished.

As often as not, punishment also came as painfully as possible with no questions asked or allowed. Brutality in punishment was the norm in antiquity. City after city, even whole civilizations, fell to the sword. Everywhere, in both war and domestic life, the guilty and the merely weak suffered appalling cruelty. Protest was futile. No one was safe from a sudden and violent end.[3]

Arbitrary punishment was so prevalent that gestures alone could convey meaning. Herodotus tells the story of Periander, who exceeded all rulers of Corinth in "bloody-mindedness and savagery" in the fifth century BCE. Periander learned how to manage his kingdom from Thrasybulus, the tyrant of Miletus, who responded to Periander's queries by silently walking into a wheat field and "cutting off all the tallest ears of wheat which he could see, and throwing them away, until the finest and best-grown part of the crop was ruined." Success is as dangerous as failure in the ancient world. "Thrasybulus has recommended the murder of all the people in the city who were outstanding in influence or ability," Periander realized, and he followed the same policy; "there was no crime against the Corinthians that he did not commit."[4]

Ruthlessness was so automatic that it did not need to be discussed. The rare instance when slaughter of a people is talked about at length involves none other than Athens, the exemplar of Greek civilization. In Thucydides's "Melian Dialogue," a story he tells against his own city, the Athenians kill all the men of Melos and sell their women and children into slavery with the explanation, "It is a general and necessary law of nature to rule whatever one can." The Melians have tried to remain neutral in the Peloponnesian Wars in defense of the liberty they have maintained for seven hundred years. Their protests mean nothing. Pleas of right and wrong, honor and shame, are summarily dismissed. The Athenians destroy Melos because they can: "We rule the sea, and you are islanders, and weaker islands too than the others."[5]

Biblical parallels are similarly brutal. The Israelites destroy what they conquer in their holy wars. God turns away from King Saul when Saul, victorious in battle over the Amalekites, saves the animals after being told to "slay both man and woman, infant and suckling, ox and sheep, camel and ass." The prophet Elijah's outright murder of the prophets who compete against him receives a similar justification. When "little children" make fun of Elijah's successor Elisha for his bald head, Elisha summons two she-bears from the forest who kill "forty and two" children on the spot. End of story.[6]

Texts from antiquity, the Bible included, are full of the blood of the fallen or merely careless and the destruction of everything they own. With no penal system to rely on, you destroyed your enemies or anyone in your way to keep them from seeking revenge or as part of the normal contemplation in things. So apparent and prominent were these tendencies in human behavior that they defined much of life. If they are not as common today, you can still find them anywhere in the world where they are not actively prevented.

Moderation works only in a world where moderation is enforced. Living in a sixteenth-century world without it, Niccolò Machiavelli advises his prince that "men are either to be kindly treated or utterly crushed." He dismisses all leniency between these extremes. Temperance, what we would call proportionality, is a policy dangerous to a punisher. Not morality, cold political calculation should control kindliness when dealing with those whom you can destroy.[7]

How much kindliness should be dispensed? A small measure of it in strict context. A conquered state that has lived under its own laws must be destroyed anyway. Why? It will never forget the liberty it once had. Like the Athenians, Machiavelli would have been ready to slaughter the Melians. Fear and cruelty control punishment because "men are such a sorry breed." Born, raised, imprisoned, personally tortured, and exiled from his city during the civil wars of sixteenth-century Florence, Machiavelli focuses on the vicious side in human nature. He lacks the means to construct an optimistic view of what punishment might accomplish, and it causes him to advise "there is no quality so self-destructive as liberality."[8]

Today it is almost impossible to comprehend how hard it was in earlier periods to think beyond the extremism in punishment. Religious theories on the verge of modernity help explain why. Fueled by a stark binary, either the salvation or the damnation of souls, orthodoxy inflicted suffering not just for crime or failure but in the name of deliverance and with no limits placed on it.

The logic used depended on the piety that all at least officially had to assume and declare. God was thought to punish eternally or save absolutely, so those who assumed divine sanction for their actions felt empowered to use pain in any way they could. Torture purified and saved those who could be made to agree, while those who continued to disagree received only what was already prefigured for them eternally in hell. No one was really safe from religious persecution anywhere in Europe until the eighteenth century.

The leading Protestant theorist on such matters is the astringent John Calvin, a trained lawyer as well as a leading theologian, and he is especially important for us because he has had a profound impact on American thought. His *Institutes of the Christian Religion,* first published in 1536 and expanded until 1559, quickly assumed a primary place in Reformation thought and exerted enormous influence on later movements in America, whether Congregationalist, Separatist, or Presbyterian in form.[9]

Collectively, all these movements bear the name of the author of the *Institutes.* Calvinism can even be called the dominant religious intellectual pressure on national formations, and it is relevant that Calvin maintained an informed and lifelong interest in theories of punishment. His first book, published in 1532 while still a lawyer, analyzes Seneca the Younger's *De Clementia.*

Was punishment a different matter for the theologian than for the lawyer? More likely, the lawyer galvanized the theologian's interest, but either way Calvin understood the universe through waves of punishment in the belief that "formless ruins are seen everywhere." Original sin had so distorted a lost perfection that everyone deserved damnation, and Calvin was certain that most were predestined to fall into a state of eternal pain.[10]

Punishment is Calvin's main teacher. God tests the virtuous with torments in order to discipline and humble them, and God attacks the wicked to condition them for "gnashing of teeth" and "unquenchable fire" (3.4.33; 3.3.9). No one on earth escapes these impositions: "Some are tried by one kind of cross, others by another." The human race struggles under a deserved curse. "God leaves no one free and untouched, because He knows that all, to a man, are diseased" (2.1.6; 3.8.5).

If anything, punishment provides relief for Calvin. It represents discipline for the beleaguered pious while assuring them that the wicked over them will soon suffer much more than the faithful if they are not suffering already (1.5.10; 2.11.3; 2.8.4). The fixation on punishment is so strong in Calvin that it sustains personal equanimity. "Unquenchable fire" for the wicked "is our sole comfort," he reports. "If it be taken away, either our minds must become despondent or, to our destruction, be captivated with the empty solace of this world" (3.9.6).

Why shouldn't extreme punishment be everywhere in such an understanding? Fear and trembling over the prospect define Calvin's ideal posture in a Christian (3.3.7). Even believers are "sheep destined for the slaughter" (3.9.6). There is no escape or even rest from this lawyer turned religious theorist: "That we may rightly examine ourselves," Calvin concludes, "our consciences must necessarily be called before God's judgment seat" (3.12.5).

The points to take away from Calvin should be clear. No thought of human leniency can enter his construct, and his celebration of the totality in divine punishment dictates how he must think about its earthly equivalents. The mentality involved is significant not just in its influence but in a characteristic stance. Calvin's total absorption is all his own, but for reasons that we are about to explore, his fascination with the extremes in punishment can be found in most theorists of the subject.

Near contemporaries in the sixteenth century, Machiavelli and Calvin preempt for their times all possibility of moderation in punishment by dominating the subject from the two directions of thought that shaped their world. As the first insisted on absolute punishment as a matter of good politics, so the second did so as a matter of religious conviction. Together, along with their many adherents, they explain why the logic of severity remained a preferred solution in punishment long after the Enlightenment introduced countervailing ideas in the middle of the eighteenth century.

We have already seen that strict retribution has formidable attractions in punishment theory, but to the extent that it could be justified as the best approach to prudent governance in Renaissance thought and simultaneously as the surest prospect of salvation in Christian dogma, there was no available answer to it that was safe from political assault or religious persecution. You could be burned at the stake in the name of either accusation, and the combination almost assured it.

When arguments for proportionality and limits in punishment begin to take hold in the eighteenth century, they required a radical shift in thought—a shift so radical and so frequently challenged that severity in punishment remained the accepted norm in social practice. Enlightenment thought sought changes through its interest in the individual, its faith in reason, its love of ideas, and its desire for measurement, but it accepted the status quo in its thirst for universal order and its related quest for perfectibility through that order.

It is then no accident, as sometimes claimed, that the philosopher who most powerfully insisted on the Enlightenment as a new way of thought also insisted on conventional severity in punishment. Immanuel Kant gives the rallying cry of Enlightenment in 1784: *sapere aude,* "Have the courage to use your own understanding." The source of Kant's belief in new thought is also plain. "For enlightenment of this kind, all that is needed is *freedom.*" There are, however, strict limits to this freedom. Kant's celebration of it does not extend to civic identity. Looming over his thought is Frederick the Great, absolute ruler of Prussia, who qualifies the impetus toward freedom with a message of his own: "*Argue as much as you like and about whatever you like, but obey!*"[11]

Emphasis on law and order foreshadows Kant's strict retributivism in punishment. So strict is the view of punishment in his major contribution, *The Metaphysical Elements of the Theory of Right* (1797), that critics have tried to dismiss it as an aberration by one who faltered late in life, but there is plenty of evidence that Kant knew what he was doing.[12] *The Metaphysical Elements* exhibits a range and power that every later scholar interested in retribution cites, and we are far better off accepting the implications of this late work than trying to challenge its validity.

If we recognize that Kant's stress on strict retribution belongs in Enlightenment thought as much as the new idea of proportionality, we are that much closer to larger truths. No matter how liberal in thought, the desire to punish exists somewhere in all serious considerations of the subject. In every theory, including those of the Enlightenment, there is some mechanism to justify further severity. The possibility of more punishment always exists, and its logical increase over time presages the deterioration in all punishment regimes.

Kant insists on the rigor in punishment. His search for pure justice and an immutable standard of right leaves no room for flexibility. This rigor drives him inexorably toward capital punishment and beyond to the *lex talionis,* an eye for an eye. The absolute morality that Kant assigns to human behavior demands that individual responsibility exist for every action taken, a stance that makes him a profound adversary of utilitarianism. His stance is exact: "Punishment . . . must always be imposed on the criminal simply *because he has committed a crime.*"[13]

Curiously in this man of reason, Kant couples an emotional appeal to the anger in punishment. "Woe betide anyone who winds his way through the labyrinth of the theory of happiness in search of some possible advantage to be gained by releasing the criminal from his punishment or any part of it." The gibe at utilitarian theorists is plain, but think of the price in it. Why should there be no possible advantage in any part of a release from punishment?

One may "dare to know," but older rigidities apply on punishment. "Only the *law of retribution (ius talionis)* can determine exactly what quality and quantity of punishment is required." Those who think otherwise indulge in "pure sophistry and distortion of the principles of right."[14] Kant, the philosopher who celebrates human initiative and progress, can find no room for humane variation when it comes to the punished, and the paradox reaches beyond Kant to all theories of punishment.

Take for a moment Kant's most notorious example. "If a people who inhabited an island decided to separate and to disperse . . . the last murderer in prison would first have to be executed in order that each should receive his deserts, and that the people should not bear the guilt of a capital crime through failing to insist on its punishment." Not to execute the criminal in this instance makes an entire people, even a people in the act of dissolving itself, "accomplices in the public violation of justice."[15]

Three things stand out in this logic. First, absolute conceptions encourage rigidity in punishment (flexibility is a major source of mercy). Second, acceptance of the logic of severity discounts the person of the punished in the name of an abstract map of humanity, the body politic. Third, the desire for certainty encourages rigor. Not for the first time or the last, the rationale of punishment turns on the punisher, not the punished.

Looking back, we can see that Machiavelli, Calvin, and Kant—admittedly thinkers with extremely different agendas—all recognize a special place for severity when the subject is punishment. Machiavelli needs it for political order; Calvin, for the parallels he draws between heaven and earth; Kant, for the consistency he establishes between reason and accountability. Severity is the intellectual norm, and all three thinkers use it to assume that suffering makes sense in legal punishment.

Several generalizations apply at this point. The grip of severity in both the theory and the practice of punishment is profound rather than superficial. The logic of severity is so strong because it simplifies the decision to punish, eliminates much of the uneasiness a punisher may feel in the act, legitimates the anger that accompanies infliction, and rationalizes the worst of crimes by agreeing on the extremes in punishment to be used. Moreover, any modern effort to reduce the extremes must cope with these comfort zones in the logic of severity and with the retributivism that justifies them.

The New Idea: Proportionality

Given the conventional forces against leniency, the first truly successful counterargument comes, appropriately enough, from well outside the mainstream in thought. In 1764 an obscure minor aristocrat from Milan, Cesare Beccaria, turned theories of punishment on their head in a short book of barely a hundred pages. *On Crimes and Punishments* was a sensation on both sides of the Atlantic. A pantheon of the most renowned thinkers of the age commended its views and praised its author: Jean d'Alembert, Denis Diderot, Claude-Adrien Helvétius, Voltaire, Georges-Louis de Buffon, David Hume, John Adams, and Thomas Jefferson.[16]

Form, as well as content, explains why *On Crimes and Punishments* gained such a quick and appreciative audience. Trained as a lawyer, Beccaria cast his thoughts in the mode of an eighteenth-century legal treatise. The works of such figures as Hugo Grotius, Samuel von Pufendorf, Emerich de Vattel, and Baron de Montesquieu were meant for general readers and were organized around very brief chapters with explanatory headings that supplied narrative trajectory.

Beccaria knew the genre well and reinforced it with a related style in writing. He couched all his arguments within the exuberance of Enlightenment thought. *On Crimes and Punishments* casts its ideas within the spread of knowledge, the erasure of ignorance and superstition, the availability of justice, the assumption of a benevolent order in all things, a love of system, and the belief that reason is a tool that will answer any problem in social relations when properly employed.

Sheltered within these rhetorical tropes, *On Crimes and Punishments* comes up with solutions that are new but suddenly fashionable. The importance of an optimistic stance on its positive reception cannot be overstated. Beccaria's generic acumen carries the willing reader along. Previous writers, most noticeably Montesquieu in *The Spirit of the Laws*

(1748), to whom Beccaria defers, had protested against atrocious practices in punishment, but Beccaria was the first to give systematic attention to the problem. The care he gave to his arrangements makes it hard to ignore him.

Beccaria makes five central claims. Commonplaces today, they struck at the core of punishment practices in their time: first, no excessive pain in punishment; second, proportionality in all punishment; third, public clarification and divided institutional responsibility in assigning punishment; fourth, equal application of the law to all; and fifth, unerring and swift punishment instead of harshness in it.

A slogan supports each of these arguments. It appears on the first page of the treatise in italics, and it will sweep through theoretical perceptions of punishment as a conceivable alternative to retribution: *"the greatest happiness shared among the greater number."*[17] If happiness is not just a possibility but something to be shared by as many as possible, can it also become a right, and if so, what does that say about normative considerations when there is an absence of happiness? Punishment in the lens of happiness becomes a different thing altogether.

Evidence suggests that this timid man hit much harder than even he realized. Beccaria was at first astonished by challenges to his book and then unnerved by the notoriety it gave him. Indeed, fear was a reasonable reaction.[18] He was attacked by legal officials and the Roman Catholic Church. His rejection of religious intolerance led to charges of impiety, threats of prosecution, and allegations that his book was really an attack on God. Official censure followed. *On Crimes and Punishments* was placed on the index of condemned books by early 1766, a restriction not lifted until the index itself was abolished in 1962.[19]

Beccaria succeeds as one of those intellectuals whose friends have made him, in Bacon's phrase, "wiser than himself."[20] Many of those friends came to resent his fame and broke with him, leaving Beccaria bereft and unable to write again at the same bold level. Still, in that brief amicable period of late 1763 and early 1764, he is every exemplary writer wielding a group's observations with more eloquence than they can manage themselves. It is a wonderful success story in the history of ideas: the power of shared influence in the creation of a new concept that many quickly accept.

On Crimes and Punishments came out of a short-lived intellectual association of young intellectuals known as the Accademia dei Pugni

(Academy of Fisticuffs). The group's combative approach to intellectual exchange in private meetings seems to have nourished an uncharacteristic bravado in the shy Beccaria. Forced to defend himself against spirited challenges in private debate, Beccaria pulls no public punches. He writes with the courage of others' convictions.

The two longest chapters in Beccaria's book, just six and seven pages each, condemn the use of torture and the death penalty, both in regular use everywhere at the time. He writes that such extremes achieve little. They fail to prevent crime and harden the sensibilities of a culture. Beccaria expresses these concerns through the punished as much as the punisher, and this too is a new idea, and suddenly an easier one for others to accept (69).

The sting in Beccaria's critique comes through ridicule. One hears the laughter of his group behind him. "How can a political body," he wonders, "which as the calm modifier of individual passions should not itself be swayed by passion, harbor this useless cruelty which is the instrument of rage, of fanaticism, or of weak tyrants? Can the wailings of a wretch, perhaps, undo what has been done and turn back the clock?" (31).

In words that enraged authority, Beccaria says the severity all around him is the mark of a primitive state of society, "a standing monument to the law of ancient and savage times" (41, 113). Ironic tones control. A "well-organized state" would have no need of such tactics, but where, Beccaria wants to know, is that more mature state? (66). Certainly not anywhere near. As for "the *judgements* of God" on earth, Beccaria pretends to search diligently for them. Not finding them, he discovers nonsense instead. How could anyone believe that "links which originate from the breast of the First Mover could be continually disrupted and uncoupled at the behest of frivolous human institutions"? (41).

Current punishments become the disgusting vestiges of an ignorant past, the work of ignorant and, by implication, disgusting people. "What are men to think when they see the wise magistrates and the solemn ministers of justice order a convict to be dragged to his death with slow ceremony, or when a judge, with cold equanimity and even with a secret complacency in his own authority, can pass by a wretch convulsed in his last agonies, awaiting the *coup de grâce*, to savour the comforts and pleasures of life?" Cruelty is not just a policy. It is "the uproar and the shouting of . . . blind habit" (70–71).

It means nothing to Beccaria "that almost all times and almost all places" engage in unlimited cruelty:

> What reader of history does not shudder with horror at the barbaric and useless tortures that so-called wise men have cold-bloodedly invented and put into operation? Who can fail to feel himself shaken to the core by the sight of thousands of wretches . . . accused of impossible crimes invented out of a cringing ignorance or found guilty of nothing but being faithful to their own principles, and who are then torn apart with premeditated pomp and slow tortures by men with the same faculties and emotions, becoming the entertainment of a fanatical mob? (64)

Beccaria's reliance on the rhetorical question for exposure of the punishment regime around him works because it is accompanied by insistence on the virtues of proportionality in punishment. The purpose of punishment is "to prevent the offender from doing fresh harm" and "to deter others from doing likewise" (31). Just punishments therefore require calibration. They "must be pitched at just that level of intensity which suffices to deter men from crime" (68). They should be "proportional among themselves to crimes, not only in their severity but also in the manner in which they are inflicted" (75). Above all, "a society cannot be called legitimate where it is not an unfailing principle that men should be subjected to the fewest possible ills" (48). Once again, happiness is the implied and available desideratum for all who are willing to embrace it.

Beccaria's positive arguments all strike at procedures that threaten existing officialdom. Legislators, not arbitrary magistrates, should define punishment (12). Defendants should be tried by their peers, know the charges against them, face those charges in a public forum, and suffer only the punishments that all classes suffer (29, 35, 51). Justice should not be delayed; it should be quick and unerring. "The certainty of even a mild punishment will make a bigger impression than the fear of a more awful one which is united to a hope of not being punished at all" (63).

Here, though, in ideas accepted everywhere today, we have the beginning of ambiguities. How much trust should we put in legislatures as opposed to magistrates? How do we measure the efficacy of laws that "ought to be inexorable" against belief in a benign lawgiver, who "ought to be gentle, lenient and humane" (112)? If there must be "fear of the worst punishment," what on a scale of measurement should qualify as worst (64)?

How much trust? How gentle? How lenient? How bad? Beccaria's problems with the measure in proportionality will soon be everyone's problems. The sliding scale in the gravity of crimes and answering punishments requires some severity, but what if they are enforced by people who want to punish? "If it were possible to measure all the infinite and untoward combinations of human actions geometrically," notes Beccaria, "then there should be a corresponding scale of punishments running from the harshest to the mildest" (20). This may be true in principle, but it is not possible to measure all the infinite and untoward combinations, and where on the scale should harshness begin and end?

Beccaria's response is ambiguous. "It is not the intensity, but the extent of a punishment which makes the greatest impression on the human soul," he argues. Perhaps this is again true, but the logic of the position encourages "the long-drawn-out example of a man deprived of freedom," a man turned into a "beast of burden," a man sentenced to hard labor for life (67). The danger in severity remains. As Beccaria admits in an aside, "All harms are magnified in the imagination," but if so, why not make them especially terrible to deter those who might be thinking of criminal action? (69)

The hope of moderation is significant but not yet a full plan in Beccaria. "If a punishment is to serve its purpose, it is enough that the harm of punishment should outweigh the good which the criminal can derive from the crime" (64). This makes perfect sense, but how do we ascertain and weigh "the good" in a crime such as murder? Beccaria, a child of the Enlightenment, cannot resist a cosmic answer. "If there were an exact and universal scale of crimes and punishments, we should have an approximate and common measure of the gradations of tyranny and liberty, and of the basic humanity and evil of the different nations" (20).

But there is no common or universal measure, and in almost the same breath, Beccaria admits "it is impossible to foresee all the mischiefs which arise from the universal struggle of the human emotions" (19). Beccaria's chapter "Lenience in Punishing" spends its two pages describing what harshness in punishment does to a people, its punishers, and those punished, but it gives no contrasting plan in leniency. The dangers in excess are clear; the path to moderation veiled (63–65).

If the principle of proportionality forces a different way of thinking, controls in answer to the excesses in punishment remain to be found. There are pleasures in punishing that lead inexorably to its increased use, and Beccaria is not without the beginnings of recognition. He demands gradations in punishments to fit each crime instead of a pervading severity, and he separates divine and human justice. Both ideas counter the arbitrary extensions of absolute punishment in his world.

The pleasure in punishment is also on Beccaria's mind. He knows what human nature can do to itself. "If [God] has laid down eternal punishments for those who disobey His Omnipotence," he insists, "what manner of insect will dare to add to divine justice, will seek to avenge the Being Who is sufficient unto Himself?" (22–23). Those who torture and maim in the name of religion have lost their own humanity; they are not even higher animals but insects impelled to sting and bite.

Beccaria's level of indignation is instructive for its ultimate source, a quantum shift in the conception of human nature. Theories of moderation depend on this shift. The writer of *On Crimes and Punishments* states what could not have been said a hundred years before. He has imbibed the Enlightenment ideal that happiness can apply to individuals, all of them, and this changes the meaning of punishment.[21] For if it is possible to find happiness in this life, its opposites, misery and pain, become logical subjects of protest.

There is courage as well as innovation in *On Crimes and Punishments.* Beccaria has no real mechanism to control the sliding scale in punishment, but he has taken rhetorical and substantive stands that demand more informed theories on the overall subject. He has forced a new discussion, and his influence extends to the thinker who believes even more conclusively in measurement and happiness. Jeremy Bentham is not slow to acknowledge his indebtedness. He names Beccaria "the father of *Censorial Jurisprudence,*" by which he means that he is the first thinker to critique punishment regimes beyond a description of them.[22]

The Utilitarian Answer

Despite their intellectual affinities, no two writers could have been more different in temperament and approach to their work on punishment. Beccaria's need for group support has no place in Bentham's aloof, solitary genius. John Stuart Mill, who knew Bentham well, gives us the best description. Bentham is worth reading because he is "the great questioner of things established." He has "the disposition to demand the *why* of everything" through "the method of detail; of treating wholes by separating them into their parts . . . and breaking every question into pieces before attempting to solve it."[23] This approach exposes the loose affirmations in a legal system, and Bentham used it to take an adversarial approach to the law of his day, though, it must be said, with limited effectiveness.

If Beccaria is rhetorically effective, Bentham, with more practical insight, is almost unreadable at a stretch. There is a metronomic quality to his prose, a steady beat of detail piled on detail. The effect is to reduce everything to a bland tonal level of comparable categories, and while there is merit in this approach, it ignores how much emotions have to do with punishment. Nonetheless, Bentham is responsible for the greatest innovation in punishment theory. He brings utilitarianism to a level of respectability that can challenge retributivism as an explanation of the subject.

The Rationale of Punishment, 1818 in French and 1830 in English, gives Bentham's most extensive treatment of the subject. He begins with the observation that punishment is an intrinsic evil. It is an evil because it features "the *direct* intention" to make another person suffer "on account of some act that appears to have been done or omitted," and it can be used only "so far as it promises to exclude some greater evil."[24] Despite the moral resonance in such language, Bentham's interest sticks to another plane. He wants a language and method that will objectively measure punishment on a grid of pleasure and pain.

The language chosen comes from economics but with Bentham's own vocabulary, "expense of punishment," a phrase he admits smacks of "pedantry." He chooses it anyway "as the only one which conveys the desired idea" of measurement "without conveying at the same time an anticipated judgment of approbation or disapprobation." In these terms, "the pain produced by punishments, is as it were a capital hazard in expectation of profit. . . . Everything ought to be taken into the calculation of profit and loss." How is this to work? "We should say then that a punishment is *economic,* when the desired effect is produced by the employment of the least possible suffering. We should say that it is too *expensive,* when it produces more evil than good" (66).

The curious conflation of moral and economic terminology accomplishes three purposes: it leaches the emotional problems out of punishment, it puts everything on the level of reason, and it introduces the prospect of certainty, something that every theorist of punishment desires but cannot locate. A compulsively rational machine himself, Bentham believes "in matters of importance every one calculates." He thinks "each individual calculates with more or less correctness, according to the degrees of his information, and the power of the motives which actuate him, but all calculate" (75). Put in this way, everyone can be held accountable for actions taken, but only through measurement of the need in punishment.

The holes in Bentham's way of thinking, particularly on the subjects of crime and punishment, are considerable. The possibilities of an irresistible compulsion or of uncontrollable malice or of simple willfulness in transgression never enter Bentham's lexicon. We are left once again with the observations of Mill. "Knowing so little of human feeling, [Bentham] knew still less of the influences by which those feelings are formed: all the more subtle workings both of the mind upon itself, and of external things upon the mind, escaped him."[25] These lacunae in the perception of human nature leave Bentham unaware of how easily harshness might creep into his economic grid of pleasure and pain through the more emotional interpretations of others.

Bentham does recognize the danger in "seeming harshness" in punishment, but what should we make of his statement, *"The greater the mischief of the offence, the greater is the expense, which it may be worthwhile to be at, in the way of punishment"*? What are the proposed limits on punishment here and the measure of mischief?[26] When emotional uncertainty enters Bentham's rote equations, so does the possibility of severity from a punisher. As he himself admits, "Wherever then the value of the punishment falls short, either in point of *certainty,* or of *proximity,* of that of the profit of the offence, it must receive a proportionable addition in point of *magnitude.*"[27]

How is proportionality to be measured here? The vagueness in the profit motive is its own trap. *"To enable the value of the punishment to outweigh that of the profit of the offence, it must be increased, in point of magnitude, in proportion as it falls short in point of certainty."* If, as Bentham argues, "the quantum of the punishment must rise with the profit of the offence," there might be no limit to the pleasure in profit that a person gains from a successful crime, particularly one of violence.

Be that as it may, no other writer of his era, and few of any other, scrutinize the details of punishment as closely as Bentham. One characteristic of this hard-driving, unemotional, penetrating mind is that it sees what there is to see clearly. It does not look away, as so many do, on punishment. Critics make a mistake when they give top priority to Bentham's creation of the panopticon, the all-seeing eye of the punisher, or to the restrictions in his utilitarian approach to penology.

Bentham is so much more valuable for detailing the actual harms in prison life. He does even more than that. He warns us against the conditions that we are still unable to face in the prisons we have built today. We need to realize why he is capable of showing these problems better than anyone else. We can learn from him far beyond the full credit he is given for theoretical advances.

The utilitarian goal of well-being—the happiness of the greatest number—is not just a philosophical abstraction in Bentham; it is a tool of inspection of great power. If you believe in the possibility of happiness, you not only notice its absence but its opposite, misery, and you have to regret and perhaps even challenge the presence of that misery. Bentham examines as no one else examines, and the payoff is impressive.

The chapters on imprisonment in *The Rationale of Punishment* can be read as a revelation of what has gone wrong and will always go wrong in prison systems. The duration of a penal sentence is the first problem addressed. Prison for any length of time, Bentham makes clear, destroys the prisoner. "In the course of a tedious confinement, his mental faculties are debilitated, his habits of industry are weakened, his business runs into other channels, and many of those casual opportunities which might have been a means of improving his fortune, had he been at liberty to embrace them, are irrecoverably gone" (119). These words apply just as well to prison life today.

There is much more. The long-term prisoner "will in a short time become a prey to various evils" because prison includes "every possible evil . . . rising from one degree of rigour to another, from one degree of atrocity to another . . . and this without being intended by the legislator" (119). The distance between the abstract assertion of punishment and its reality is palpable to Bentham and to anyone who reads him even though it remains a subject of debate now.

Chapter after chapter in *The Rationale of Punishment* details what the evils in imprisonment will always be and how they will increase over time in prison systems that are not designed to instill reform or penitence even if we call them penitentiaries (126). Bentham documents how prison conditions spread disease, how exclusion from external society increases alienation, how mixing with other prisoners promotes more crime and makes more criminals (120–122). All these ills apply today without much legal or public recognition of their ongoing significance.

Bentham is always specific. Solitary confinement for short stretches may respond to the problem of prison crime, but Bentham tells us that "if greatly prolonged," it leads inexorably to "madness, despair, or more commonly a stupid apathy" (129). "The effects of solitary confinement are not matters of mere conjecture," Bentham warns; "they have been ascertained by experience, and are reported upon by the best authorities" (130). We still resist what Bentham proved almost two hundred years ago.

Each of Bentham's careful realizations needs to be relearned. In American prisons, more than fifty thousand people languish in long-term solitary confinement, and most others live in overcrowded conditions with heightened levels of disease and the absence of minimal privacy. We have either forgotten or do not care to face what Bentham so lucidly already knows and explains. Bentham asks the world to realize there is no provision of punishment "that does not, in a more or less painful degree, wound the sensibility" (97). Humiliations of modesty, forced idleness, and meaningless labor are some of the other evils to be avoided if at all possible. Truth follows observed truth in these pages. "The labor obtained by the force of fear," Bentham explains, "is never equal to that which is obtained by the hope of reward" (96, 121, 153–160).

The humane aspects of these proposals sound routine rather than overstated in the linear tones of Bentham's explanations. Perhaps for the same reason, Bentham seems correspondingly oblivious when his own sense of proportion in punishment gives way even though he recognizes at one point, as so few do, that proportionality as a general concept "is more oracular than instructive" (69). As with other theorists of punishment, harshness retains a hidden place in the writer's schemes.

Bentham, like so many who oppose capital punishment, is ready to throw away the life that has been saved. The third and most severe stage of prison in his "General Scheme of Imprisonment" is reserved for such people. Since "the end of correction is precluded" in those presumed to be incorrigible, they "must never mix with society again," and the "stigma inflicted" on them will of necessity "be perpetual" (136).

Harsh, yes, but there is at least a touching twist in Bentham's view of a life sentence, and it too bespeaks his fervent belief that *everyone* has the right to whatever happiness utility can bring. "Here," he advises, "let the apparent condition of the delinquent be as miserable, and the real as comfortable, as may be." This is a brilliant sally. Deterrence can be maintained by keeping the outside world afraid of prison while a more secret reality leaves those in prison the option of being useful through the talents they retain (136). Only retribution stands in the way of such good sense.

As always, Bentham gives the details. Listen to his plan. "Let the gentleman occupy himself as he pleases. Let the yeoman who has an art, exercise his art, and let him be a sharer in the profits. Let the labour of the yeoman who knows no art be more moderate than in the temporary prison" (136). In Bentham's perfectly regulated and carefully graded world, even the worst behave according to plan. If aspects of the plan appear naive, they are refreshing in implication when one looks at the lost world of prison today.

So prescient is Bentham and so accurate are his observations that he, with Kant (for very different reasons), remains one of the two philosophical linchpins in all theories of punishment: retributivism (intuited through pure reason) versus utilitarianism (the primacy given to the sense perception of events).[28] Bentham knew the enemy well. In *The Rationale of Punishment,* he recognizes the strength of retributivism, but his full assault on the idea makes the mistake of expressing only contempt for it and for those who decide to hold that theory.

The battle of words opens with an admission that is more than one. "The great merit of the law of retaliation is its simplicity," Bentham begins. The other presumed merit is "its popularity," also "requiring little expense of thought." More directly, retributivism appeals to the simple-minded ("the multitude") or "those of a vindictive character" (93–94). Those who argue for retribution, he says, depend on "the ravings of enthusiasm, and the extravagances of superstition" (97–98).

Utilitarianism naturally emerges as the only answer for Bentham's mature intellect. "There will be no safe and steady guide for the understanding in its progress," he asserts, "till men shall have learnt to trust to this principle alone, to the exclusion of all others." All the alternative theories on punishment are "the mere babbling of children" (97–98). What Bentham fails to differentiate here is the legal source of strength in retribution. The individualistic focus of retribution trumps the collective orientation of utilitarianism when it comes to the working definitions of punishment in the legal process.

Debates over punishment always seem to produce more heat than light. As with Kant, the anger in punishment bleeds into a parallel anger in the person writing about it. Bentham's contempt misses the point, and the ensuing debates between retributivists and utilitarians have been shrill and unfortunately narrow ever since. The stereotypes for the two sides have been that retributivists look backward to assign a punishment for a crime, while utilitarians look forward to assay a punishment that will have the greatest benefit for society. Complicating debate have been ambiguous designations and crossing lines. Deterrence, proportionality, and rehabilitation as goals are now claimed by retributivists as readily as they are by utilitarians.

Bentham, of course, does not produce all this acrimony over punishment by himself. Less rhetorical causes are also at work. We have already seen that Hobbes in *Leviathan*—called "the greatest work of political philosophy in English"—puts punishment at the center of the body politic.[29] The right to punish is what gives authority its legitimacy, a position maintained not just by an absolutist like Hobbes but by the founder of classical liberalism and egalitarian principles, John Locke.[30] Debates over theories of punishment remain extreme today because they raise troubling issues about the meaning of the modern nation-state and the sometimes tenuous rule of law over it.

The Modern Debate

If anything, modern conditions have sharpened the controversies between retributivists and utilitarians. Totalitarianism, revolutionary responses to tyranny, widespread distrust of authority, and the technological means of expressing that distrust have played important roles in debate over theories of punishment. A stronger emphasis on individual rights has put more onus on government to protect its citizens even as the power of the state intrudes more and more on the people under its control.

The new shape given to these debates is also the result of a tighter theoretical perspective in legal thought. The rise of legal positivism has been a crucial determinant in how debates over punishment are now carried out. The first principle in positivism, sometimes termed "the separability thesis," posits that there is no necessary connection between law and morals.[31] Admittedly, some things are prohibited because everyone knows that they are wrong (*malum in se*), but even then punishment must depend on the meaning of a statute, and many more actions in modern life—for example, fishing without a license, violating a curfew, or a parking violation—are punished just because the law prohibits them (*malum prohibitum*).

Positivism circumscribes the normative considerations of punishment. It insists that we look to *jus positum*, the law actually in place, and not an ideal system of general reasoning or universal application to explain the meaning and legitimacy of legal action. Its proponents argue that law and its constitutive elements must be understood and measured with "an internal perspective." The integrity of the system as created becomes the assumed standard for proceeding.[32]

The strengths that hermeneutic control over law gives are considerable and make sense in the contemporary explosion of statutory law, but if everything must cohere internally, the possibilities of confusion within the system grow with any failure to agree, and the stakes in debate grow with them. Punishment has been one of these areas of disagreement, and since the emphasis on "an internal perspective" comes first from the greatest single interpreter of legal positivism, H. L. A. Hart, it is no accident that he also expresses the most dismay over ensuing disputes based on theories of punishment.[33]

Hart's *Punishment and Responsibility,* first published in 1967, gets quickly to the root of the problem. "General interest in the topic of punishment has never been greater than it is at present," Hart begins, "and I doubt if the public discussion of it has ever been more confused." Benthamite notions have been partially discredited by "realization that the part played by calculation of any sort in anti-social behavior has been exaggerated." At the same time, "a cloud of doubt has settled over deterrence as one of the keystones of 'retributive' theory." With more sophistication about how the mind works, can we still agree that transgressors have as much control over actions as previously believed?[34]

As a legal positivist, Hart writes to make the law holistic and in harmony with its presented forms. As he tells us, "The main object of this paper is to provide a framework for the mounting perplexities which now surround the institution of criminal punishment, and to show that any morally tolerable account of this institution must exhibit it as a compromise between distinct and partly conflicting principles."[35]

This language tells us even more when placed in Hart's own contribution to debates over punishment, which he expresses through the leading theoretical rivals Kant and Bentham (retributivism against utilitarianism).[36] Hart is essentially a Benthamite who regrets the excesses in Bentham's approach and who, unlike Bentham, is willing to give retribution its due as a theory of punishment.

There is, however, an even bigger problem for a legal positivist. Enmeshed in debates arising from what he has said in an earlier edition of *Punishment and Responsibility,* Hart identifies a "principal source of trouble" when he adds with some chagrin, "It is always necessary to bear in mind and fatally easy to forget, the number of different questions about punishment which theories of punishment ambitiously seek to answer."[37]

Confusion in law against its claim of holistic integrity is the legal positivist's responsibility, and in response *Punishment and Responsibility* takes seriously a basic reflex in legal thought best summarized more than 250 years ago by Lord Hardwicke, a founder of modern equity law. "Certainty is the Mother of repose," quoth Hardwicke, "therefore the Law aims at Certainty."[38] But how can certainty be achieved when the arguments between retributivists and utilitarians remain unresolved and continue without end?

Hart decides to restate the extent of the problem in search of a new level of agreement: "We have not settled from what we are to *deter* people or who are to be considered *criminals* from whom we are to exact *retribution* or on whom we are to wreak *vengeance,* or on whom we are to *reform.*" By leaving all possibilities on the table and everything "unsettled," Hart returns the combatants to a preargument stage in the debate, one in which procedural needs replace philosophical difference.[39]

A positivist's main recourse when challenged turns on elucidation within the system.[40] Everything one needs should already be there, and wisdom in analysis means learning how things properly fit together. Hart relies on a strategy of divide and conquer through reclassification. He tries to see retributivist and utilitarian aims as separate but mutually legitimate stages in punishment.

Neither retribution nor utilitarianism has all the answers, and this limitation provides the beginning of wisdom in *Punishment and Respon-*

sibility. Hart divides punishment between "a General Justifying Aim" and "principles of Distribution." The distinction allows him to brush away what upsets so many. "Much confusing shadow-fighting between utilitarians and their opponents may be avoided," Hart declares, "if it is recognized that it is perfectly consistent to assert *both* that the General Justifying Aim of the practice of punishment is its beneficial consequences *and* that the pursuit of this General Aim should be qualified or restricted out of deference to principles of Distribution which require that punishment should be only of an offender for an offence."[41]

Retribution can thus be satisfied generally while the particulars in punishment apply to individual cases under utilitarian conditions. Much of *Punishment and Responsibility* reworks the limitations in all theories of punishment while giving attention to the Benthamite ideas that Hart favors. Philosophically, the book is a tour de force of complexity recognized and problems handled through compromise. Practically speaking, the same problems remain despite Hart's attempt to finesse them as "shadow-fighting." For if most theorists after Hart have followed him with similar hybrid solutions, debates remain fierce, and they do not proceed in the way Hart would have liked them to go.

Late in Hart's treatment of punishment, he admits what Bentham knew but treated with contempt. Arranging himself in the interstices between retribution and utilitarianism, Hart accepts "signs of the vitality of the old ideas" in retribution; "we can find them easily enough." Still, he allows himself, much like Bentham, to predict a time "when retributive and denunciatory ideas of punishment are dead."[42]

A closer reality lives in Hart's fears. "To tell judges that the expression of the community's moral indignation is the ultimate justification of punishment," he writes, "is to tempt them from the task of acquiring knowledge of and thinking about the effects of what they are doing." These words imply that the people may be inherently retributive. Like so many others, including myself, Hart wonders whether the animus in punishment can be explained by "inadequate understanding or appreciation of facts."[43]

Hart's hopes—we just need more facts and better comprehension—are the palliatives that legal positivists love to hear. Just give us more time to work out the balances in the system. The request speaks to a punisher's comfort zone. Why shouldn't punishment regimes improve as theories of punishment are brought into ever greater coherence? Hart does his best here, but he has to whistle past a graveyard full of retributivists. Time, instead of being for him, has been against him.

Lost in Hart's manipulation of complexities are three uglier truths: the pleasures in punishing, the tendency of all punishment regimes to become more severe, and communal avoidance of the problems involved. One need only look at what has actually happened. Retributivists rule the day. The "old ideas" remain strong, and some would say they are newly charged.

Two theorists in particular help reverse Hart's sequential steps or stages toward leniency in punishment. Instead of moving from a general theory of retribution to the particulars of punishment in utilitarian distribution, the direction since the late 1970s has been toward ever stricter retribution through longer imprisonment terms imposed under more severe and sometimes mandatory sentencing guidelines.

As early as 1968, Herbert Morris made retributivism more philosophically respectable for modern reception by giving a sophisticated twist to a primitive doctrine.[44] Then, in 1975 James Q. Wilson called for a generally more punitive approach in his best-selling book *Thinking About Crime*. Wilson, even more than Morris, found a receptive audience by deploring the inefficiencies in a legal system that fails to deal with purse snatchers, looters, car thieves, and other offenders who deserve punishment.

Crime for both writers is a rational performance by calculating criminals who must be controlled more by authority. Wilson speaks for both of them when he defines his subject as "predatory crime for gain."[45] Gain is a vital concept here. Wilson's counter to Benthamite utilitarianism is so effective because it derives from Bentham's own insistence on an economic calculation of crime.

In "Persons and Punishments," Morris posits "a right to punish" offenders who willfully commit crime, which is fair enough, but he assumes that all crime basically fits that description. Choice defines personhood in his system, and it is therefore just to punish those who choose to use that personhood to violate the rules and create an "unfair distribution of benefits and burdens" for those who abide by the rules. It does not concern Morris that there might be other reasons for the unfair distribution of benefits and burdens.[46]

In Morris's scheme, criminals who renounce "the burden of self-restraint" have gained "an unfair advantage" over those who behave themselves, and so "the criminal 'has brought the punishment on himself.'" The words "has brought" remove all thought of external agency and demand an automatic response to crime. In a just world that can "maximize each individual's freedom of choice," Morris assumes, "the distribution of freedom throughout such a system is determined by the free choice of individuals." Criminals reduce that freedom in others when they violate the rules of choice. Punishment therefore answers an unacceptable loss of freedom in the law-abiding.[47]

Wilson makes the same assumptions with more inflammatory language in *Thinking About Crime*. He blames criminologists for foolishly concentrating on the causes of crime instead of dealing with the effects of them, dismisses the wrongheaded policies of police enforcement, and condemns judicial decisions that have become arbitrary and soft on crime. He is particularly scornful of liberal policies of reform. For a typically derisive comment, one of many, read the following: "By 1970, enough members of the liberal audience had had their typewriters stolen to make it difficult to write articles denying the existence of a crime wave."[48]

This enormously successful book carries the day by playing on the fears of potential victims, and those fears touch every reader. Wilson emphasizes punishment as a form of deterrence, wants long sentences for repeat offenders no matter what the crime, ridicules most efforts at rehabilitation, demands incapacitation for serious offenders, and urges the construction of more prisons for "a larger portion of the serious and repeat offenders."[49]

All these recommendations have come to pass in American punishment regimes, which also depend for their growth on a more general claim by Wilson. Rejecting the idea that most efforts at rehabilitation might have anything to do with reducing recidivism, Wilson derides that "mistaken notion" by playing again on the fears of law-abiding citizens. Releasing prisoners is wrong. "Instead we would view the correctional system as having a very different function—namely, to isolate and punish."[50]

Wilson's proposals rely on rhetorical strategies that breed distrust of authority in a culture of fear. Looking back on the first edition of his book with obvious satisfaction in a revised edition, Wilson tells us what the right pitch was then and always should be. "It is the duty of the statesman to link the confident instincts, immediate knowledge, and deeply held values of the citizen with the policy analyses of the specialist so as to produce by informed persuasion, reasonable programs."[51]

Why hasn't that happened? Where are the reasonable programs that should be in place? Wilson's statesmen have failed in their duties. America's leaders have not listened to the citizenry's commonsensical desire for protection. Foolish authority and misguided expertise are the problems that have allowed criminal activity to move beyond control.

Thinking About Crime focuses on the difficulty and drama of handling "an enemy within." The size of that enemy is unknown, but it appears everywhere in Wilson's book. There are large numbers of conniving criminals on the loose who routinely gauge "the costs and rewards of their activities." Against them, Americans are pictured as a generous and tolerant but basically naive people who have to realize they need more protection. "Our society has been, with individual exceptions, remarkably forbearing," he first comforts and praises his fellow Americans. "We have preserved and extended the most comprehensive array of civil liberties to be found in almost any nation."[52]

Wilson cleverly turns this presumed communal forbearance into fear by wondering whether such generous policies should continue in the face of "a rising crime rate and (during the 1960's) periods of massive social disorder." Security and common sense—the first term covers the need of a law-abiding people, and the second reveals their strongest asset—should dictate otherwise. After all, he warns, "arrests are far easier and trials less encumbered with evidentiary rules in most other nations." *Thinking About Crime* is about the need to change all that. Wilson demands "a larger investment in the resources and facilities needed to cope with those who violate the law."[53]

These recommendations come with vague threats. "Nor can a greater investment in criminal justice facilities be thought repressive if one compares what is with what might be." Sometimes the threats are not so vague. In the equally popular revised version of his book in 1983, Wilson adds, "A stable neighborhood of families who care for their homes, mind each other's children, and confidently frown on unwanted intruders can change in a few years, or even a few months, to an inhospitable and frightening jungle."[54] No one wants that. And it can happen so quickly. Urgent steps must be taken to prevent it. "We know that confining criminals prevents them from harming society," and the immediate goal should be to "confine a larger proportion of the serious and repeat offenders."[55]

Wilson's book holds that willful criminals are putting one over on the American people, and this must stop. The last words of *Thinking About Crime* hit the culture of fear hard. "We have trifled with the wicked, made sport of the innocent, and encouraged the calculators," Wilson concludes. "Justice suffers, and so do we all."[56] The theoretical source, if not the accuracy, of Wilson's rhetoric should be clear; he celebrates retribution over and against all other theories of punishment.

Together Wilson and Morris flatter the American people while condemning unnamed intruders (criminals full of calculation and malice) who have robbed the people of peace of mind when they have not robbed them physically.[57] Retributivism, as long as it assumes a rational criminal, can claim to punish hard enough to secure deterrence and prevent social harm with few if any restrictions on how hard that might have to be. The arguments are simple and easy to absorb.

The desire to catch criminals, the story Wilson wants to relate, is dramatic. Entertainment on television reinforces the plot every night of the week, and its basis in retribution works because the story is figuratively complete when a criminal at large is caught. Broader sociological attempts to target the causes of crime are less dramatic, and the story of actual punishment rarely achieves the same dramatic intensity or holds public interest in the same way. There is, however, a partial exception to this claim, one with a difference that confirms the tensions in existing theories.

Michel Foucault tells the story of actual punishment, the story of prison, as well as anyone. He has attracted a large intellectual elite, but his influence in academic circles does not reach many legal scholars, and he is ignored by those who control penal policy in the United States. Why his book *Discipline and Punish* (1979), one of the seminal modern counters to retributivism in punishment, has so little influence in legal circles reveals a great deal about current theories of punishment. Foucault resurrects the plight of the punished instead of contributing to conventional discussion of the role of the punisher. His challenges are not ones authorities want to hear.

Early in *Discipline and Punish*, Foucault launches a major criticism of current legal thought. He points to the separation between legal decision making and subsequent penal punishment. An independent penal operation does the actual punishing, and in that separation it "has taken on extra-juridical elements and personnel." The result is a major discrepancy in the concept of justice. "Criminal justice functions and justifies itself only by this perpetual reference to something other than itself."[58]

Prisons in Foucault's theory represent "that darkest region in the apparatus of justice." When punishment was a public spectacle, it had two purposes: first, to increase deterrence through fear in the watching populace, and second, to make the people themselves complicit as "the witnesses, the guarantors of the punishment." When punishment is hidden in prisons, the punished are invisible to the public eye, and that extra guarantee of lawfulness disappears. Without direct experience, the people forget all about the punished, and so do the decision makers who put them away.[59]

Left in place are "two possible but divergent lines of objectification of the criminal" in Foucault. Convicted prisoners are "'monsters,' moral or political," who have "fallen outside the social compact," or they are "the juridical subject rehabilitated by punishment."[60] If, like James Q. Wilson, you see little effectiveness in rehabilitation, you are left with the first alternative. Criminals become monsters who deserve severe punishment as deviants lost to social reintegration. The law can fall into reasoning of this kind in American punishment regimes today, but it does not like to be reminded of the fact.

Foucault teaches us that evasions in theories of punishment are the intellectual norm. One extraordinary example of the phenomenon can stand for all others. John Rawls, in *A Theory of Justice* (1971), has dominated American discussions of justice in the last third of the twentieth century and into the twenty-first, but he has little to say about punishment and avoids the subject when possible. Following Rawls's lead, most academic treatment of theories of justice have done the same.

In the Rawlsian "veil of ignorance," procedural fairness depends on the original position in social contract theory. The people who form the compact construct "a well-ordered society" because "they do not know how the various alternatives will affect their own particular case and they are obliged to evaluate principles solely on the basis of general considerations." But Rawls warns, "if a knowledge of particulars is allowed, then the outcome is biased by arbitrary contingencies." At this point, we enter a society of "partial compliance" in which society must deal with injustice, many more levels of inequality in its midst, and inevitably crime.[61]

Rawls hopes that "men's propensity to injustice is not a permanent aspect of community life." In "the well-ordered society," punishments will be mild. "These mechanisms will seldom be invoked and will comprise but a minor part of the social scheme." This optimism leaves Rawls reluctant to take up the subject of punishment even when he thinks it necessary in a society of partial compliance with justice. He holds to "the ideal scheme" where the major problem is an equal civil distribution of goods. At the very end of *A Theory of Justice,* he does pause to admit "I have said very little" about theories of punishment. His later and final "restatement" ignores the subject altogether.[62]

Legal scholars who try to take Rawls where he was reluctant to go quickly encounter theoretical problems of their own. They have to sacrifice Rawls's "ideal theory" even though Rawls implies otherwise. They must "dispense with Rawls's idealized picture of a well-ordered society" and treat societies where "partial compliance" means that punishment is needed. Clearly the idealism of Rawls does not work as well in these more practical realms. Nor does Rawls show creative interest in the subject of punishment beyond the Benthamite premises that he openly takes from H. L. A. Hart.[63]

There is a telling admission in the Rawlsian framework. Any attempt to grapple with bad actors leads to the same result found everywhere in punishment regimes: "disproportionately severe punishment of serious offenses."[64] Of those who must be dealt with severely, Rawls can only say fatalistically "their nature is their misfortune."[65] No one could be more optimistic in principle on punishment than Rawls when he claims "the precedence of liberty means that liberty can be restricted only for the sake of liberty itself," but it is only in his mythical well-ordered society that punishments remain perpetually mild.[66] In the climb from mild toward serious offenses, the logic of punishment retains a severity all its own.

Theories of punishment, in fighting with each other, cannot quite admit outright the dominant themes of this chapter, but the themes are there. The facts are these: a need to punish moves rather quickly into a desire to punish, habit reinforces that desire, severity has its own momentum in punishment regimes, and these regimes deteriorate over time through the imposition of greater levels of punishment than originally intended. No theory of punishment provides enough safeguards against these tendencies.

To understand why there are not enough safeguards, we must look elsewhere, not to a theorist but to a practitioner. One of the curious things about theories of punishment is that they rarely talk about actual punishers. The affirmations in theory avoid these ominous figures when they can—so much so that the gap between theorists and practitioners is figuratively the gap between heaven and earth. Everyone knows that the gap is there and that it is vast enough to be beyond full recognition. Perhaps the answer is to find a practitioner who will talk to a theorist who will listen.

The solution will take us far afield, but not without purpose. Fiction, in its concrete love of conflict, gives us punishers rather than assumptions about them, and it revels in the psychological vortices of explanation that law avoids in trying to judge through the surfaces in behavior. There is, in fact, no better example of a practitioner at work than the Grand Inquisitor in *The Brothers Karamazov,* and he engages intellectually with what we need. He reaches across the gap. Fyodor Dostoevsky's story gives us that rarest of situations, a punisher in full cry talking to heaven.[67]

Theory Lost in Practice

Two preliminaries: Dostoevsky is a strict retributivist in punishment, and critics forget that there are two stories of punishment in sequence, with the first story setting the stage for the one that follows.[68] We must consider the common thread in both accounts to get Dostoevsky's full meaning. In both stories, Dostoevsky has Ivan Karamazov, a disillusioned nihilist, toy with the religious faith of his younger brother, Alyosha, who at twenty is a novice in the local monastery. Ivan wants Alyosha to face the meaningless suffering in life. How could a merciful God allow such intense suffering to exist everywhere in the world?

Ivan, in the first story, claims to give a factual account, and there is historical evidence to support the claim.[69] A wealthy landowner who holds "the power of life and death" over the two thousand serfs who live on his estates has his hunting dogs hunt down and tear to pieces a boy of eight before the mother's eyes after the boy throws a stone that slightly injures the paw of one of his dogs. What should happen to this landowner? "What to do with him? Shoot him?" Ivan hectors Alyosha over the landowner. Alyosha, with a twisted smile, agrees. "Shoot him!" "'Bravo!' Ivan yelled in a sort of rapture, 'If even you say so, then . . . A fine monk you are! See what a little devil is sitting in your heart!'" (242–243).

The purpose of this first account is to put the gentle Alyosha on the side of the punisher so that the second story, "The Grand Inquisitor," can entrap him where Alyosha does not want to be. Ivan sets this second story, his own creation, in sixteenth-century Seville during "the most horrible time of the Inquisition, when fires blazed every day to the glory of God, and in the splendid auto-da-fé evil heretics were burnt," sometimes "a hundred heretics at once" (248).

The phrase "auto-da-fé" means "act of faith," and Jesus, the source of all Christian faith, chooses this moment to return "where the fires of the heretics had begun to crackle." Is it to stop them? No, this is just a temporary visit to "his tormented suffering people," and definitely not the promised Second Coming. Nonetheless, Christ is immediately recognized by all who see him, such is their yearning for him. Ivan feels this may be the best part of his "poem." Dostoevsky then has Christ again performing miracles, healing the blind, and raising the dead until the Grand Inquisitor, "an old man, almost ninety," finds him and has him seized by guards and imprisoned (246, 248–249).

Is it possible to have a colloquy when one speaks if the other only listens, "apparently not wishing to contradict anything"? The Inquisitor's long justification of his role as punisher to his always mute captive is more than a monologue or soliloquy. The end of the story comes when the figure of Jesus, after listening to the accusations and threats of the Inquisitor, "intently and calmly" but still silently kisses "the ninety-year-old man nearing death" on the lips. "That is the whole answer." The Inquisitor shudders. "The kiss burns in his heart, but the old man holds to his former idea." He opens the dungeon door and orders, "Go and do not come again . . . do not come at all . . . never never!" (250, 262).

This denouement holds every auditor, but the story for our purposes lies in the three things the Inquisitor states to the spiritual founder, really the original theorist of the system that this practitioner now rejects. He says to Jesus, first, your plan has worked only for the exceptional few and not the mass of mankind who need a different kind of help; second, don't interfere with the changes we have made in your name; and third, face rejection and a horrible second death at the stake if you try to interfere now.

The Inquisitor has twisted the spiritual message of the originator, the theorist, into the worldly and practical needs of an established institution of punishment. He represents the gap. Aspiration, the necessary spark in creating a legal framework, must give way to the maintaining power of an enforcer.[70] "We have finally finished this work," the Inquisitor, as the practitioner in the system and no longer really a follower, tells Jesus. "Why," he asks this originator more than once, "have you come to interfere with us?" (250–251).

There is a terrible admission in the question. "We have rejected you and followed *him*." Everything the Inquisitor does assumes and then embraces the physicality of a fallen world of punishment. He no longer believes in the power of the spirit. He knows and acknowledges that he now does the work of the devil. He accepts what he has become (250–251, 258).

There are many interpretations of this story, but the Inquisitor stands first and foremost for what he conceives to be the necessity of strict punishment to secure social order, and his punishment regime reflects the pattern we have already traced. The founding theorist's plan, while inspirational, cannot work in a dog-eat-dog world without adjustment. Theory devolves to practitioners, who alone know how to manage things and who increase punishment to manage the rebelliousness always found in human nature.

The doctrine of Christ, you will remember, includes punishment; it offers either hell or heaven in the hereafter. But the Inquisitor's own earthbound system of punishment and reward has foisted very different meanings on the world that Jesus meant to save. Any interference with those earthbound meanings will destroy the practitioner's established order and hence will be resisted ruthlessly.

The figure of Jesus is cast somewhat in the role of Kafka's outside observer of a punishment regime. He appears first as only a witness but then as someone who begins to act. The Inquisitor decides that witness or actor, it makes no difference, will be burned at the stake, but the question of Christ's agency is left up in the air. Has all attempt to act stopped at the prison cell door? That is the question that the story leaves open.

As readers, are we to follow Ivan, the calculating storyteller, or Alyosha, the protesting receiver of it, remembering that Dostoevsky has declared from the outset that Alyosha is the hero of his novel?[71] Either way, the Inquisitor has precedent to fall back on in his negative claims about human nature. Christ's own view of human nature has been negative enough at times. The Gospels of the Christian story present a punishment regime of lasting severity that the Inquisitor has recognized and accepts.

Jesus's comments in the Sermon on the Mount and elsewhere recognize a hell full of eternal punishment. They remind us that "strait is the gate, and narrow is the way, which leadeth unto life, and few there be that find it." For most of humankind there will be "outer darkness" and a more active "weeping and gnashing of teeth." The multitude of the cursed, many of them ignorant of the extent of their wickedness until the end, will find themselves in "everlasting fire," "everlasting punishment."[72] Dostoevsky's sixteenth-century punisher in Seville can and does claim to carry out what Christ has promised to do later.

The Inquisitor is undeniably an appalling figure, but we cannot dismiss him, and neither does the figure of Jesus. Among other things, this ruthless burner of heretics shows himself to be extremely well versed in biblical lore. There are twenty-two references to the Bible in his comments with seven of them in the Gospel of Matthew, from which the words of Jesus about damnation have just been taken.[73]

This level of expertise and the effort behind it are significant. The Inquisitor has tried to follow Jesus into the wilderness and failed, and in failing, he correctly tells the silent figure in front of him that all but a few will always fail in that effort. What can this strange auditor possibly reply? Here, at least, silence must be acquiescence. The ideals that the Christian story has set are beyond the practice of most.

Failure of the spirit has turned the Inquisitor into a consummate worldling, one who has made punishment in it his life. The result is a personal indictment of the human spirit. "You chose everything that was beyond men's strengths," he accuses Jesus. "I repeat, are there many like you? And, indeed, could you possibly have assumed, even for a moment, that mankind, too, would be strong enough?" (254–255). Tonally, the protests in these questions are also pleas. Why does the punisher always want the approval of the witness in his punishment regime, as we already saw with Kafka "In the Penal Colony"?

Punishment dehumanizes the knowing punisher who still wants exoneration for what he has done. Terribly, though, no need for understanding stops ruthless punishers from being everywhere in the world. "Who knows," Ivan warns, "maybe this accursed old man, who loves mankind so stubbornly in his own way, exists even now, in the form of a great host of such old men" (262). That is the message of Dostoevsky's story, except that the Inquisitor manifestly does not love humankind; he loves the failure in it. "Man is created weaker and baser than you thought him!" the Inquisitor challenges Jesus, and his negative appraisal of human nature from an assumed conventional position of institutional superiority and control tells us something about ourselves (256).

Punishment is the acknowledgment of human failure. The punisher's pleasure comes in isolating that failure in the punished in a claim of righteousness and in the assumed right to condemn. There is, horrible to say, a protective vitality in condemnation that is restorative in the ancient Inquisitor and that has kept him alive. Would Dostoevsky's story have been anywhere near as powerful if this speaker, instead of threatening, had bowed down before the presence of the figure of Jesus with a confession, an entreaty for forgiveness, and a promise to change everything?

Punishment, as an act performed and a story told, has an energy and even an animation that Dostoevsky insists that we see. The fight will always be to control that vitality in a way that theories of punishment do not discuss. Nor is that all. Until a theory does admit that vitality and tries to control it, until it takes into account the actual plight of the punished, infliction will remain in some cruel inquisitor's hands, and it will always be easy to overlook the suffering that is the punisher's stock-in-trade.

3

The Mixed Signs in Suffering

The Constitution does not mandate comfortable prisons.

Justice David Souter in *Farmer v. Brennan*

The Confusions in Pain and Punishment

Below the level of theory but directly involved in it and complicating it
are the simpler physicalities in punishment and the practical difficulties in talking about them. The mental and bodily pains in punishment
may be its most apparent characteristics, but both are poorly understood, difficult to translate, and hard to hold in place long enough to
make the precise decision that the law expects of itself. The pain for a
person may be immediate, even exact. The communicated intensity, the
impact, and the price of it plunge the subject into a wilderness of misunderstandings where the import of punishment becomes uncertain.
How much, after all, do we ever really know about the pain of another?

The linguistic conflation of pain and punishment is as ancient as it is
deliberate. Not only do the two words have the same Latin root in the
word *poena*, their first meanings today in the *Oxford English Dictionary*
are virtually identical except for the question of agency: "pain" denotes
"suffering or loss inflicted for a crime or offence," and "punish" means
"to cause (an offender) to suffer for an offence."[1] Yet, and despite the
conflation, the law stumbles over the distinction. Agency, in this case
a punisher, has no real idea of the suffering caused. Sometimes the law

recognizes this limitation in itself, sometimes it does not, and the difference tells us a great deal about how the law is willing to think about the penalties it imposes.

Certainly the law cannot establish the precision it wants on this subject. Every human being knows pain, but it is a difficult sensation to translate with accuracy in communication to someone else even in urgent complaint. The doctor's question "What is your pain level on a scale of one to ten?" depends as much on the threshold levels and personality of the person as it does on actual sensation.[2] Virginia Woolf's famous inability to convey the pain in her head is really everyone's. "The merest schoolgirl, when she falls in love, has Shakespeare or Keats to speak her mind for her; but let a sufferer try to describe a pain in his head to a doctor and language at once runs dry."[3] In any discussion, whether professional or personal, measuring pain presents difficulties in quantification, duration, and inconvenience.

Confusions exist at every level, and the law is not above using those confusions to hide from itself and those it punishes. The first confusion is historical. Attitudes toward the presence of pain have changed greatly over time. The discovery of anesthesia and the modern sale of analgesics have altered understandings dramatically. Scientific discoveries about the relation of physical to mental pain have added new levels of concern. The more we learn about the physicality of mental processes, the more difficult becomes the line drawn between kinds of pain even though the law is often asked to act on just such a distinction.

The life cycle also confuses matters. Aches and pains accumulate with age, but different people express very different attitudes toward these afflictions, and the changing definition of common ailments separates generational views on what pain means and how it should be dealt with. Where you are in the life cycle also makes a difference in law. The pain of a life sentence without parole for a nineteen-year-old offender presumably contains more suffering than that for an offender sentenced at sixty-five. Does that qualify the legal rubric "like punishments for like crimes"? Quite recently the Supreme Court of the United States has begun to suggest very gingerly that it might qualify things—gingerly because the rational impulse in law does not like to contend with mystery, and because measuring pain to decide the scope of punishment is a mystery.[4]

John Locke gives excellent instruction on the innate confusions in pain. He labels it an unknowable phenomenon. "Pain has the same efficacy and use to set us on work, that pleasure has," he writes in *An Essay Concerning Human Understanding* (1689), but concepts like "*pain* or *pleasure* . . . like other simple ideas, cannot be described, nor their names defined. The way of knowing them, is, as of the simple ideas of the senses, only by experience."[5]

Even so, and as unknowable as they are, these simple ideas control everything, including experience, and they have legal implications. "Good and evil," Locke concludes, "as hath been shown . . . are nothing but pleasure or pain," and he immediately draws a connection to punishment. "*Morally good and evil,* then, is only the conformity or disagreement of our voluntary actions to some law, whereby good or evil is drawn on us from the will and power of the law-maker, which good and evil, pleasure or pain, attending our observance, or breach of the law, by the decree of the law-maker, is that we call *reward* and *punishment.*"

Not so much by definition as by decree does the law make its connections between pain and punishment. If Locke decides that pain can destroy all happiness in a moment, an assumption anyone can verify, Edmund Wilson counters in *The Wound and the Bow* by tracing creativity to the goad that suffering forces on us.[6] Wilson's title plays off the myth of Philoctetes, who suffers from an excruciating wound but owns the one bow that always shoots straight and that must be procured for the Greeks to take Troy. Sophocles's use of the myth turns on the realization that only the suffering Philoctetes can bend the bow truly. Strength, wisdom, and accomplishment from pain are themes from its first appearances in the stories of Prometheus, Chiron the centaur, and Oedipus.[7]

Pain is a confusing problem for the law because it can be figured in so many different ways. It is a creative spur in Edmund Wilson's description, degradation in the screams of a sufferer, animalistic in its constancy, paralyzing in its intensity, and the sign of salvation in the Christian claim.

This last manifestation in particular, the sign of salvation, creates an important contrast at the law's expense. The exotic ability of the spiritual to manipulate pain and punishment can be shown in a single sentence: "For God so loved the world, that he gave his only begotten Son [to be crucified], that whosoever believeth in him should not perish, but have everlasting life."[8] The law, of course, has to live much closer to the ground in the more literal and seamier necessities of enforcement.

To appreciate the contrast, consider the legal alternative to the primal scene in the Passion, not in religious terms but through the secular lens of the Roman Empire. In the Gospel of John we learn that Roman soldiers break the legs of the thieves crucified with Jesus after Jesus has died. They do so to hasten the deaths of the thieves. The practice, known technically in Roman legal procedure as *crurifragium,* has a logic now forgotten. The Romans preferred crucifixion in punishment because it prolonged the public agony, humiliation, and exposure of death, but in this instance, the soldiers shorten the experience and the pain at the request of priests who want the approaching Sabbath left untainted.[9]

The punishment is as horrifying as it has been utterly subsumed in the transformations of religious explanation. The nails in crucifixion were not driven through the hands, as shown in religious paintings, where the sufferer might tear free, but securely between the bones of the wrist. The knees in crucifixion were similarly bent to prolong life and make the naked sufferer push up against the agony of the nails in the wrists and feet in order to breathe freely. You did not die suddenly from loss of blood or shock but slowly from asphyxiation when you were too exhausted to push yourself upward against the agony of being unable to exhale from the lower position. The process in a strong person could take two days.

Religion discards the sordid details in pain and punishment in a way that the law cannot. One remembers only the saints in martyrdom, not their punishers, and yet the sordid details do indicate how much of a shift in the legality of pain and punishment has occurred. The public spectacles of ghastly executions in history have given way to our post-modern qualms and arguments over whether or not a condemned person feels a single moment of undetected pain while sedated on the way to death.[10]

The magnitude of the shift in attitudes on pain and punishment and the confusions that result from it are the concerns of this chapter. Notably, pain is always a variable, in contrast to the announced precisions of punishment. Elaine Scarry, in her treatment of the subject, argues that pain must be understood through its "unsharability" and "resistance to language." It "resists objectification" through "an absolute split between one's sense of one's own reality and the reality of other persons." We know it in others only through the externalities of punishment or injury or disease, through the tools used to inflict it or through the physical damage done by it.[11]

Uncertainty over the meaning of pain turned especially bitter in the changing context of the nineteenth century. Before the introduction of anesthesia in 1840, pain was either God sent or nature's way of admonishing in order to correct or heal. It was inevitable in a thousand unstoppable varieties, and because it was, it was deemed a necessary part of life, to be endured with fortitude, character, and no complaints.

So strong were these presumptions that long after the introduction of anesthesia, many doctors refused to use it. The more a patient struggled with pain in an operation, the greater the chances of recovery, thought many a surgeon. Pain was a sign of life's vigor. Women in childbirth who wanted anesthesia were thought to be cheating nature and perhaps God himself. Why should they escape the divine injunction, "I will greatly multiply thy sorrow and thy conception; in sorrow thou shalt bring forth children"?[12] Pain was the price of lost innocence.

Accidental deaths from anesthesia also caused confusion, as did the absence of feeling that anesthesia produced, inasmuch as numbness in the limbs before the advent of anesthesia often meant gangrene setting in or approaching death. Not until the beginning of the twentieth century were these uncertainties drowned in the relief that so many could now enjoy. Only then did Abraham Jacobi, president of the American Medical Association and father of pediatrics in the United States, claim the polar opposite as truth: "The greatest gift America has given the world is not the realization of a republican government . . . it is anesthesia."[13]

How much does it mean today that people generally do not have to feel as much pain as they once did? The confusions in arguments over it—as in arguments over the meaning of punishment—turn in part on an emotionalism never absent from the subject. It is fair to say that anesthesia and other ways of reducing pain have only shifted the lines of debate.

Pain can now be conquered with drugs, but not without moral and legal objections to dependence and addiction. And what if painkillers prove insufficient? Normative stands in these situations are often volatile because they have as much to do with what people make of pain as they do with their assessments of character or behavior.

Nature vies with nurture over how pain should be treated. Relieving the unavoidable agony of the dying remains so controversial and legally problematic that doctors refer to "palliative sedation" rather than "terminal sedation," to counter the accusation of euthanasia. Medical rationales hide behind a Jesuitical equivocation known as "the rule of double effect." Here is how it works: "Even if there is a foreseeable bad out-come, like death, it is acceptable if it is unintended and outweighed by an intentional good outcome—the relief of unyielding suffering before death." Euphemisms abound in this situation. A faster death is said to outrun "a foreseeable bad outcome."[14]

One need only contrast the "last lesson" in *The Education of Henry Adams* as Adams watches his sister's drawn-out death from lockjaw to realize the difference. "Hour by hour the muscles grew rigid while the mind remained bright, until after ten days of fiendish torture she died in convulsions." Adams titled this chapter "Chaos," and "the terror of the blow stayed by him thenceforth for life." "Nature enjoyed it," he writes, "played with it, the horror added to her charm, she liked the torture, and smothered her victim with caresses."[15]

The ability to avoid such horror is one of the mercies of contempo-rary life, but more knowledge and expertise have brought their own quarrels. Contemporary debate has moved from physical to mental suf-fering and the relation between them. The more we learn about the body, the brain, and the mind, the more room there is for disagreement about torment. Freudian analysis with its discovery of unconscious motiva-tions, behaviorialism with its stress on conditioned responses, and neu-ral science with its separation of physical emotion from conscious feel-ing all have their claims on the definition of trauma, and the law is largely about dealing with one trauma or another.[16] Where is the law to take its stand?

The confusions have been worth documenting because they compli-cate the meaning of punishment and the ability of the law to assign it. Law naturally prefers to avoid those confusions, but it is called on to measure pain at times, and when the confusions cannot be avoided, they lead to legal evasions that find their way into decisions to punish because the pain cannot be measured in an accurate way.

There are, in fact, four areas where the law cannot avoid the vortices in discussions of pain in order to assign punishment, and these are also areas where it must cope with how other disciplines define the connec-tion of mental processes to physical behavior:

> *First,* in tort law, where "pain and suffering" is a term of art used to encompass physical distress and emotional trauma in determin-ing financial penalties for behavior that causes injury

Second, in criminal law, where the prohibition of "cruel and unusual punishments" in the Eighth Amendment of the Constitution of the United States raises the relation of pain to punishment

Third, in the new law of victims' rights, where levels of suffering in victims are used to help compute the level of punishment to be assessed on an offender

Fourth, in the law of torture, where the kind of infliction by authority decides whether behavior is cognizable as a crime or is merely convenient governmental policy in a crisis

In every one of these areas of law, indeterminacy in the relation of pain to punishment is a stumbling block in decisions. The stumbling block comes over the need for precision where none can be found.

Pain and Suffering as a Legal Term of Art

Tort law is a good place to begin because the law agrees to talk about pain in torts in a way that it tries to avoid elsewhere, and its difficulties here help explain why it tries to evade the subject elsewhere. The very word "tort," from the Latin *torquere,* "to twist," implies pain. The concept covers a loose amalgam of civil wrongs, mostly injuries of some sort, including bad faith in breach of contract, invasion of privacy, libel and slander, invasions of legal rights that are not criminal, and above all, the consequences of negligent behavior (the failure to use reasonable care in an act or omission to act in dealing with other people).[17]

Debates over "pain and suffering" as a term of art in tort law have been fierce since Louis Jaffe asked more than half a century ago, "Why should the law measure in monetary terms a loss which has no monetary dimensions?" All such awards, Jaffe argued, fall under "the arbitrary indeterminateness of the evaluation."[18] The debates have been fierce because all sides—plaintiff lawyers, defense lawyers, and judges—agree that pain and suffering awards turn out to be arbitrary and cannot really be measured. That said, and it is said often, they agree that such awards cannot be done away with either.[19]

Obviously, if awards for pain and suffering cannot be measured, they are going to vary widely for the same offense, and this element of arbitrariness distorts the system in a way that the other more adjustable components of relief (economic damages and punitive damages) do not. Nevertheless, these awards dominate the field of negligence. Pain and suffering damages have grown exponentially. They have reached the point where "fifty percent of all tort damages currently paid are for pain and suffering."[20]

Disputes over the impossibility of gauging pain and suffering take many directions. There are demands for the wholesale elimination of pain and suffering awards, or for statutory limitations on such awards, or for a standard grid of recovery for a particular kind of painful loss or physical distress, but each possibility runs aground over the right of an individual to receive judgment on the facts and the difficulty of quantifying human loss in objective terms. Financial suggestions all face the same philosophical difficulty: "The individual right to bodily integrity is simply not fungible with money."[21]

Every suggestion increases controversy by rehashing the problem. Not only are "the goals of nonpecuniary damages . . . ambiguous, incoherent, and contradictory," there are claims that all "general damages are incoherent, incalculable, incommensurable, and inegalitarian."[22] Even experts who agree resist change. The leading jurist and scholar Richard A. Posner covers both sides of the issue in a single court opinion. "No one likes pain and suffering," he notes, "and most people would pay a good deal of money to be free of them," but the price in effective governance would be high. "If [pain and suffering] were not recoverable in damages, the cost of negligence would be less to the tortfeasor and there would be more negligence, more accidents, more pain and suffering, and hence higher social costs."[23]

Plaintiff lawyers resist change for more venal reasons. In one of the unique features of American tort law, plaintiffs cover their legal expenses through contingency fees. "Attorney fees are generally set by contract as a percentage of the recovery, frequently thirty-three percent." Accordingly, because they often cover half of a fee, "pain and suffering damages are what drive our tort 'lottery.'"[24] Why would the personal-injury bar want to change the dimensions of such a lucrative arrangement?

The point to take away is that realization of the predicament in pain and suffering awards does not lead to a solution. Instead, the law constructs a comfort zone through fatalism and avoidance of the realities involved. The jury instruction in the state of California in such cases is worth quoting in full:

No definite standard is prescribed by law by which to fix reasonable compensation for pain and suffering. Nor is the opinion of any witness required as to the amount of such reasonable compensation. In making an award for pain and suffering you should exercise your authority with calm and reasonable judgment and the damages you fix must be just and reasonable in the light of the evidence.[25]

A more candid appraisal from the New York Court of Appeals comes with an angst that is instructive beyond itself:

An economic loss can be compensated in kind by an economic gain, but recovery for noneconomic losses such as pain and suffering and loss of enjoyment of life rests on the "legal fiction that money damages can compensate for a victim's injury." We accept this fiction, knowing that although money will neither ease the pain nor restore the victim's abilities, this device is as close as the law can come in its effort to right the wrong. We have no hope of evaluating what has been lost, but a monetary award may provide a measure of solace for the condition created.[26]

The legal system accepts an arbitrary standard in pain and suffering awards that come in either too low or way too high. It even recognizes that the second possibility, too much money, brings little satisfaction to an injured victim whose misery has been reduced to callow financial terms. The goal, in consequence, has been a pragmatic one based less on logic than on an end in mind. Something must be done, and it must be acknowledged to have been done and be allowed to pass out of legal cognizance with the loosest of calculations, namely, "a measure of solace for the condition created."

The psychological penchant to be done with it all in tort law is a key for us because the same proclivity extends to the treatment of prison populations. In the case of tort law, the suffering of a victim has been reduced to a finding of fact by a jury with a financial measurement meant to satisfy despite the knowledge that it cannot. Fair or unfair, the decision transforms a terrible situation of negligence into legal closure. But should a similar logic of dismissal apply when liberty and perhaps even life are at stake in a criminal case?

The Meaning of Pain in Cruel and Unusual Punishments

For an extreme case of hear-no-evil and see-no-evil on the relation of punishment to pain, listen to Associate Justice Clarence Thomas's concurring opinion in *Farmer v. Brennan* (1994). Dee Farmer, "a preoperative transsexual who projects feminine characteristics," had been sentenced to federal prison for credit-card fraud. He was raped and assaulted repeatedly by other prisoners after being transferred without safeguards from a lesser correctional institute to "a higher security facility with more troublesome prisoners." Farmer brought suit against prison officials for showing "deliberate indifference" to his plight and injuries.[27]

Justice Thomas's concurrence in rejection of the suit turns out to be "an easy one" by looking the other way. "Conditions of confinement are not punishment in any recognized sense of the term, unless imposed as part of a sentence," he tells us. Why? "Because the unfortunate attack that befell petitioner was not part of his sentence, it did not constitute 'punishment' under the Eighth Amendment."

The obliviousness of this comment to seriously inflicted pain is not sui generis. It belongs to an established tradition of avoidance first coined in 1981 by the Supreme Court in *Rhodes v. Chapman,* the bellwether case in a long line resisting application of the cruel and unusual punishments clause of the Eighth Amendment to clear cases of painful abuse of inmates either caused or allowed by prison authorities.

The court refused in *Rhodes* to address the pain in abuse unless it could be proved to be absolutely "wanton and unnecessary" and "grossly disproportionate to the severity of the crime warranting imprisonment." "To the extent that such conditions are restrictive and even harsh, they are part of the penalty that criminal offenders pay for their offense against society." Why should the crime committed be any gauge for determining the level of later physical pain inflicted in prison that will qualify as "grossly disproportionate" and therefore actionable? The decision in *Rhodes* essentially argues that yes, there is pain in punishment, but because punishment is pain, we will not recognize the subject.[28]

No one, the majority announced in *Rhodes,* should expect "an ideal environment for long-term confinement." In effect, the court ignored and declared that it would continue to ignore "the problems of prisons in America." Those problems "are not readily susceptible of resolution by decree," and "courts are ill-equipped to deal with the increasingly urgent problems of prison administration and reform."

Just how deep in the sand did the court bury its collective head in *Rhodes* on conditions in American prisons? This was an 8–1 decision, and the majority opinion begins by accepting that the common "day rooms" in the Southern Ohio Correctional Facility "are designed to furnish that type of recreation or occupation which an ordinary citizen would seek in his living room or den."[29] How accurate a description of the actual environment in a maximum-security prison is this likely to be?

The rationality of the legal mind prefers not to recognize what it cannot control or measure. The frustration found in tort law over the indeterminacy of pain becomes a convenience in the consideration of penal punishment and with vastly graver results. Horrible conditions prevail in most American prisons, and commentators have long argued "that prison conditions are part of the punishment of imprisonment and that any objectively inhuman conditions should lead to liability regardless of the presence of individual knowledge of these conditions."[30] Maybe so as a matter of simple humanity, but the law has done everything it can to counter the claim of a connection between prison conditions and serious pain caused by them.

Take another evasion in *Farmer v. Brennan,* this time from the majority opinion. Associate Justice David Souter, giving new force to a questionable observation from *Rhodes v. Chapman,* writes "the Constitution 'does not mandate comfortable prisons.' "[31] Think about this statement and the decision to reconfirm it as precedent thirteen years after the first egregious formulation of it. We have here a new version of the medical "rule of double effect" in dealing with pain. The court says that punishment may indeed mean suffering, not comfort, but it refuses to acknowledge the conditions that cause its existence.

Legal doctrine in cases like *Farmer v. Brennan* and *Rhodes v. Chapman* keep any harm that takes place in prison at a distance by requiring a heightened standard of official knowledge of abuse, a standard so hard to meet that it is virtually impossible to prove. The court resists recognizing all the major circumstances of common prison brutalities, and nowhere is this resistance more pronounced than where it should be heard, in questions over cruel and unusual punishments.

The Eighth Amendment of the United States reads, "Excessive bail shall not be required, nor excessive fines imposed, nor cruel and unusual punishments inflicted." When it was introduced into the Constitution of the United States in 1791, it was already a familiar concept, and it long remained one of the least controversial of the original amendments. Well before the federal Constitution, the same wording appeared in a number of state constitutions and then in the Northwest Ordinance of 1787. The concept would have been known broadly through Blackstone's *Commentaries on the Laws of England,* a profound source of American ideas in the formative era.[32]

What did the Eighth Amendment mean when it was passed? Early republicans worried about the horrendous punishments for treason that were still part of English common law. The last execution in England by drawing and quartering took place in 1814. Quartering and beheading were not officially abolished until 1870. "The burning of female felons [for treason] continued in England until the penalty was repealed in 1790."[33] Revolutionary Americans were nominally traitors and literally so if caught under English law. They logically decided to remove themselves from the worst punishments to the extent that they could. Debate over the language to be used proved unnecessary.

A few members of the First Congress did complain about vagueness of language in the Eighth Amendment, but these complaints became serious only when the prohibition of cruel and unusual punishments emerged as a vital concept in late twentieth-century jurisprudence.[34] The application of the Eighth Amendment to the states through the Fourteenth Amendment in 1962 marks the turning point.[35]

Doctrinally, though not consistently, the Supreme Court construes the meaning of "cruel and unusual punishments" through what it calls "the evolving standards of decency that mark the progress of a maturing society."[36] Insofar as words like "decency" and "a maturing society" carry a larger, if necessarily vague, meaning, they reflect changing attitudes in American culture toward pain. Any serious construction of the Eighth Amendment must take up the subject, one reason why the court's doctrinal evasions have had to be so elaborate.

Silently but unavoidably, the word "cruel" raises the corresponding idea of "pain." The crux for interpretation lies here and in such other modifying adjectives as "unusual" and "excessive," all of which unfortunately lack a comparative basis in the clause. Therefore, if the extent of pain remains known only to the sufferer, is effectively covered up by inflicters of it, or is understood by others only through indirection, the court easily finds room to equivocate in controversies over its meaning as punishment.

The abstract intensifiers in the Eighth Amendment carry away from a rule basis in decision making toward a standard basis. A rule is a requirement that must be followed, while a standard implies "a discretionary range of possible actions" that will vary according to the case, current sentiment, and the personal inclinations of the interpreter.[37] Rules prescribe a solution with little left to a decider except a finding of fact; standards provide more flexibility and more control, but with these qualities come the dangers of bias, arbitrary power, more argument, and confusing differentiation.[38] All these dangers apply to the standards that the courts have applied to Eighth Amendment challenges brought by abused prisoners.

Compounding the problem further are the number of ways in which the cruel and unusual punishments clause can be interpreted. Frank H. Easterbrook, currently chief judge of the United States Court of Appeals for the Seventh Circuit, gives no less than five ways in which interpretation might guide application of the Eighth Amendment, and he uses those ways to show that the Supreme Court has long been divided over which method to employ from case to case.

The five ways of interpreting the clause can be enumerated in shortened form. First, the Eighth Amendment might forbid judges from imposing punishments that are not authorized by law; second, it might be read to prevent legislatures from devising outlandish modes of punishment; third, it might apply to punishments once common but now viewed as cruel; fourth, without regard to history, it might apply to a punishment that modern penal theory does not support; fifth, it might forbid a punishment thought to be cruel by using a case-by-case review of proportionality between offense and punishment.[39]

How to choose among these possibilities depends on the interpreter's perception of the amount of pain that punishment should bring to bear on a convicted offender. There is, nonetheless, something more subtle at work in contemporary law. Another leading constitutional law scholar understands the overall purpose of the Eighth Amendment a different way. David Strauss argues that "the Cruel and Unusual Punishment Clause protects convicted offenders, a small and politically powerless group, against a vengeful society."[40] Strauss suggests a more specific need to protect those who have been rendered absolutely vulnerable through the exercise of state power.

The evolution of the Supreme Court's approach to cruel and unusual punishments, although uneven at best, has been toward sensitivity about pain inflicted, and the greater the sensitivity, the more likely the tendency has been to move slowly toward the more expansive views of interpretation, two through five in Judge Easterbrook's list. Less interest exists over the plight of a badly treated prison population in the way that David Strauss's interpretation of the amendment tries to encourage, and the reasons for that hesitation need to be explained.

Modern conceptions of the cruel and unusual punishments clause begin with *Weems v. United States* in 1910. Weems had been sentenced to fifteen years of incarceration on a chain gang, where the court indicated "it may be that even the cruelty of pain is not omitted. He must bear a chain night and day. He is condemned to painful as well as hard labor [with chains from wrist to ankle]." Weems's crime was falsification of an official document for the purpose of defrauding the government, an action that may have been mostly inadvertent. The Supreme Court ordered the judgment reversed and all charges dismissed.[41]

The physical pain of hard labor on a chain gang seems to have been decisive in leading the court in *Weems* to condemn the penalty as too severe for such a crime. But to address pain at all required an admission. The court had to confess it could discover "no exact measure" of "what painful labor may mean," and its uncertainty produced another stroke in logic that we have heard before; *Weems* introduced proportionality of punishment into interpretation of the Eighth Amendment.

Then again, the Supreme Court has not always been so generous. In *Harmelin v. Michigan* (1991), Ronald Harmelin, a first-time offender with no prior felony record, had been sentenced to a mandatory term of life in prison without parole after being found in possession of 650 grams of cocaine, surely a penalty lacking in proportionality. Associate Justice Antonin Scalia, writing for the court in a 5–4 decision with five separate opinions, concluded that "severe, mandatory penalties may be cruel, but they are not unusual in the constitutional sense." Scalia distinguished *Weems*, denied any "proportionality guarantee" in the Eighth Amendment, and restricted its meaning to "a check on the ability of the Legislature to authorize particular *modes* of punishment" unknown in the United States.[42]

A concurring opinion of three justices and three separate dissents in *Harmelin* argued against Scalia's restricted view of the Eighth Amendment by finding degrees of proportionality that could apply and by offering a more expansive interpretation that reached toward "irrational" punishments, as well as the death penalty. In other words, the question of what punishment essentially means is up for grabs in these differences.[43]

The difference between *Weems* and *Harmelin* comes down to the number of judicial interpreters willing to consider a broader approach to the Eighth Amendment under a standards-based method of decision making. At issue are visceral distinctions over the meaning of pain. Hard labor on a chain gang allowed the court to "see" pain in *Weems* in a way that an endless number of years in prison in *Harmelin* cannot actually be seen. For a majority of the court, imprisonment—no matter for how long or for what reason or where—does not raise the problem in suffering that punishment always contains.

Overshadowing all interpretations of the Eighth Amendment are conflicting attitudes, controversies, and growing difficulties about its applications to the vexed question of capital punishment.[44] The *Harmelin* opinion, which objects to an application of proportionality, admits that "proportionality review" would apply in capital cases, but it does so to restrict proportionality analysis of cruel and unusual punishments only to capital cases, a stand that a tangled majority of the court refused to accept even as it supported the admittedly severe punishment meted out to Ronald Harmelin.

Confusion reigns because there is no consensus on the court about what punishment means. Justice Scalia tried to use *Harmelin* to reiterate what the court had said before: "Death is different."[45] Yes, it is, but precisely how is death different on the vague scale of the cruel and unusual punishments clause? If the sensation of pain is always difficult to translate from a sufferer to an observer, death supplies the final act of inexplicable suffering in life. It comes as the ultimate pain that all must admit, no one can explain, and no one can quantify as punishment, so it is impossible to fathom. On the other hand, the amount of actual pain suffered in an execution hardly compares to that of a life sentence in a current American prison, or does it?

We get all this confusion at work in *Baze v. Rees*, a dispiriting Supreme Court decision from 2008 during which the nine members of the court struggle openly and angrily with one another over whether the potentially real but unseen pain of lethal injection during an execution should prevent it from taking place. The cocktail of drugs used by thirty-five states and the federal government in lethal injections begins with a sedative that renders the condemned person unconscious, followed by a paralyzing agent and then a drug that stops the heart. Pain will exist from the second two agents if the prior sedative does not first block consciousness, but how can we know whether pain exists if the condemned person is paralyzed and unable to cry out in pain?

We cannot know. But in 2008 this unanswerable question held up forty executions in a de facto moratorium that was welcomed by opponents of capital punishment and deplored by continuing proponents of it.[46] The real fight in *Baze v. Rees* is over whether capital punishment itself violates the cruel and unusual punishments clause of the Eighth Amendment, but the debate took place over the meaning and extent of the pain involved, subjects judges are ill qualified to handle.

Chief Justice John G. Roberts delivered the plurality opinion in *Baze v. Rees,* upholding the use of lethal injection in this and all *"substantially similar"* cases, but he wrote in some exasperation. He had been able to corral only one other justice in complete agreement with his opinion. Six of the justices who agreed with Roberts's decision insisted on writing their own opinions, an unusual slight of a chief justice.[47]

Getting to the nub of the issue, Chief Justice Roberts admits the difficulty that everyone faces in defining the range and meaning of the cruel and unusual punishments clause of the Eighth Amendment, and his exasperation deepens when he points out that there may always be pain "as an inescapable consequence of death." The definition of "humane methods of execution" is vague in this understanding, and it includes, for Roberts, the watching audience. The paralyzing agent that might mask the pain that a condemned person experiences is important for that audience, not the condemned. In Roberts's words, "It prevents involuntary physical movements during unconsciousness." Yes, and so? The state has an interest "in preserving the dignity of the procedure, especially where convulsions or seizures *could be misperceived as signs of consciousness or distress.*"[48]

There is, to be sure, no way of knowing whether an unconscious dying person's movements are misperceived as pain or reflect actual pain, and the uncertainty turns into a catfight between justices in *Baze v. Rees.* Justice John Paul Stevens, in a concurrence that is really a dissent because he has come to accept that "the death penalty itself" is cruel and unusual punishment, openly challenges Chief Justice Roberts's claim of a misperception over pain. "Because it masks any outward sign of distress," Stevens responds, "pancuronium bromide [the paralyzing agent] creates a risk that the inmate will suffer excruciating pain before death occurs." Veterinarians proscribe use of the drug in animals for that reason, he notes. Then he adds, "It is unseemly—to say the least—that Kentucky may well kill petitioners using a drug that it would not permit to be used on their pets."[49]

Adding further insult, Justice Stevens suggests that "current decisions . . . by this Court to retain the death penalty as a part of our law are the product of habit and inattention rather than an acceptable deliberative process." He makes it clear that the serious debate should be over the meaning of punishment as such. The court's approach rests instead "on a faulty assumption about the retributive force of the death penalty." These withering tones resemble Cesare Beccaria's eighteenth-century blast of primitive thinking by those who support a death penalty.

The anger in response from the chief justice, Justice Samuel Alito, and Justice Clarence Thomas is barely disguised, but it turns into open rage in Justice Antonin Scalia's vituperative reaction. Scalia blames Justice Stevens for the mess they are all in. Rejecting Stevens's points one by one in a direct attack, Scalia concludes that "of all Justice Stevens' criticisms of the death penalty, the hardest to take is his bemoaning of 'the enormous costs that death penalty litigation imposes on society,'" which "are in large measure the creation of Justice Stevens and other Justices opposed to the death penalty."[50]

Embarrassment, as well as anger, drives Justice Scalia's words. The court is trying to identify physical pain that it has condemned if present but that it can neither see nor verify as present. Scholars have been just as harsh over the confusion. In their descriptions, the court proves mostly that it has been unable "to tame the unruly Cruel and Unusual Punishments Clause" while wallowing in "doctrinal churning," "doctrinal incoherence," and "arbitrary, capricious, and discriminatory patterns of death verdicts." Right there on the legal surface of things as well is everyone's awareness of "the Justices' unhappiness with each other."[51]

How far have we come when even the slightest pain at the moment of execution provokes distress in onlookers, public sensibilities, and Supreme Court doctrine? Aesthetically, the distance between a momentary spasm of a sequestered and unconscious person strapped to a gurney is light-years away from the extended public executions in vogue a century ago or from the prolonged public displays of agony in earlier times. Psychologically, the distance might not be so great. The ugly presence of pain in punishment—and how much of it counts—continues to provoke the same feelings of conflict expressed across history.

We can observe as much in another recent legal controversy. Unable to agree on the presence and meaning of physical pain in the act of punishment, the American justice system has decided to privilege the presence of mental pain in criminal law, a phenomenon that it has absolutely no hope of ascertaining or measuring with accuracy. The new spectator sport in legal punishment—the current melodrama of pain reckoned—focuses on victims, the new field of victimology, and the creation of victim impact statements.

Victims and the Legal Right to Suffer

The rise of the victim as a central player in the legal process represents a major change in criminal law. Victims are now "important claimants in lawmaking and litigation, pressing for statutory provisions targeting certain crimes, greater victims' services in police departments and prosecutors' offices, and increased victim input into charging, bargaining, prosecution, and sentencing decisions." Recent decades have brought *"enhanced recognition at every stage of the crime response process of the rights and interests in crime victims."* It was not always thus, and the question again is why.[52]

The strength of this new legal impulse is unmistakable. In 1982 the President's Task Force on Victims of Crime proposed that the Sixth Amendment to the Constitution of the United States be amended by the addition of the following sentence: "Likewise, the victim in every criminal prosecution shall have the right to be present and to be heard at all critical stages of judicial proceedings."[53] Both presidential candidates in 1996, Bill Clinton and Robert Dole, supported such an amendment, and although no amendment on victim rights has been passed, forty-nine states and the federal government have passed provisions giving extensive new rights to victims.

The visibility of victims in court—the right to be heard—is now part of legal procedure. The Victims' Bill of Rights of 1990 requires that victims "be notified of court proceedings" and gives them the right "to be present at all public court proceedings related to the offense." Victims also have the added right "to confer with [the] attorney for the Government in the case." The same statute demands that courts and all legal officers "make their best efforts to see that victims of the crime are accorded the rights" so conferred.[54]

Specific events and saturation news coverage of them have had a special impact. Horrific crimes with innocent children as victims and the outpouring of grief from surviving family members during the trial of Timothy McVeigh in 1997 for the bombing of a federal government building in Oklahoma City in 1995 brought extensive media coverage to the rights of victims and changes in some laws, including the Congressional Victims' Rights Clarification Act of 1997.[55]

Victim impact statements had already become legal in death-penalty cases in 1991 through *Payne v. Tennessee,* in which Chief Justice William Rehnquist declared "a state may legitimately conclude that evidence about the victim and about the impact of the murder on the victim's family is relevant to the jury's decision as to whether or not the death penalty should be imposed." Concurring, Justice Antonin Scalia explained why the right would soon extend to all jurisdictions and other crimes. There is, he found, "a public sense of justice keen enough that it has found voice in a nationwide 'victims' rights' movement."[56]

Finding a voice is the key term of explanation here. Victims wish their pain and anger to be heard. Fear of crime, the cold objective wheels of justice, and what has been named "the melodramatic imagination" in media coverage all help explain the rise of the victim, but there is a more intrinsic psychological impulse at work that explains the sudden power of the victims' movement.[57]

The word "victim" automatically implies suffering, and it has two definitions that bridge the power in victim impact statements. The first meaning of "victim" applies directly to the crimes of assault and murder: "one who suffers severely in body or property through cruel or aggressive treatment." (Note again the use of the word "cruel" as relational to pain.) The second meaning defines "the collateral victim." As the term implies, such a victim is a survivor who suffers through the loss of another, "one who is reduced or destined to suffer under some oppressive or destructive agency."[58]

The bridge in meanings of the word "victim" is important to victim impact statements because it conflates "pain" (usually understood to be physical in nature) and "suffering" (a mental reaction). The collateral victim who stands up in court to recount the loss of "a loved one" bespeaks both the pain of the person killed and the continuing suffering of the speaker who has been "reduced" through the loss. Since the statement is freed of the objectivities and restraints that apply to testimony earlier in the legal process, it achieves an exaggerated effect in court and media coverage.

As a new institutional arrangement, the victim impact statement confirms Leslie Fiedler's sardonic comment that America has sacrificed intellectual discernment to a sentimental understanding of the world.[59] Justice John Paul Stevens says so clearly in his vigorous dissent to *Payne v. Tennessee.* The victim impact statement, he writes, "represents a dramatic departure" from established precedent, "serves no other purpose than to encourage jurors to decide in favor of death rather than life on the basis of their emotions rather than their reason," relies on "an argument that has strong political appeal but no proper place in a reasoned judicial opinion," "offends the Eighth Amendment because it permits the sentencer to rely on irrelevant evidence in an arbitrary and capricious manner," creates a new and wrong "mini-trial" based on the victim's character rather than the defendant's, and brings "the 'hydraulic pressure' of public opinion" to bear on decisions that belong in the legal process. "Today," Stevens concludes, "is a sad day for a great institution."[60]

The greatest problem in the right of a victim to deliver an impact statement lies in the misdirection or shift in focus to which Justice Stevens alludes. Articulation in court of the pain and suffering of the collateral victim, the mourning survivor, has a transferring purpose. Everything the victim records about the pain felt is meant to increase the pain to be inflicted on the convicted offender. The speaker, in shifting attention to the victim's pain, has the goal of increasing the pain of a defendant. The role of reason in conviction gives way to an emotional narrative in favor of punishment, and whatever the result or extent of juridical control, the courtroom devolves into an unquantifiable contest of feeling.

Even victims have worried about this phenomenon. "The solemn activity of mourning has become a raucous and public blood sport," explains one. "Family members leave the courtroom with high fives and fists in the air, as though sentencing someone to death were no more serious than a football game." Media sources naturally encourage these spasms of feeling and expressed suffering. "In the television age," explains a commentator, "anguish only seems real when broadcast over the airwaves."[61] In the sardonic slogan of the newsroom, *"If it bleeds, it leads."*[62]

If you read newspapers or watch television coverage of a murder trial, you might come away thinking that the victims have had their day in court instead of the defendant. They certainly appear more frequently and vocally on courthouse steps today.[63] Quantifying the pain in punishment no longer rests, as it once did, with the defendant. It belongs instead to the far more visible and recognized anguish of surviving victims. Public opinion then joins in shared rage with the victim, a rage that feeds on fear of crime through vicarious identification. The victim impact statement implicitly asks its audience, "How would you feel in my situation?"

The mixed signs in suffering encourage the mental transference. They can also make a great deal of pain disappear. Manipulation of the confusions in pain allows punishment regimes to protect themselves. No one should forget how successful obfuscations were in the debates over torture in the first decade of the twenty-first century; nor that they typically ran parallel to strategies used to hide unacceptable punishment in American prisons.

When Is Pain Torture?

The deliberate infliction of pain is a crime. What, then, does its clearly illegal manifestation teach us? Arguments over torture during "the war on terror" in Iraq and Afghanistan reached their zenith early in 2004 when photographs of the treatment of prisoners at Abu Ghraib became public.[64] The images of prisoners strung up, attached to wires, humiliated by the opposite sex, and dragged on a leash like a dog proved beyond question that the suffering inflicted by military personnel of the United States Army at the Baghdad Correctional Facility included torture.

Just as rhetorical evasion characterizes legal approaches to brutality in American prisons, so it controlled debates over atrocious behavior at Abu Ghraib and for three reasons. First, everyone agrees that torture is an odious practice, and no one wants to be publicly associated with it, so it is best not to locate it at all. Second, the law defining torture is comprehensive, clear, strict, and seemingly unavoidable; the price of getting caught is too high to be entertained. Third, the leading legal historian on torture, John Langbein, identifies a far more fundamental philosophical basis in the need for evasion: "History's most important lesson is that it has not been possible to make coercion compatible with truth."[65]

By federal statute, " 'Torture' means an act committed by a person acting under the color of law specifically intended to inflict severe physical or mental pain or suffering (other than pain or suffering incidental to lawful sanctions) upon another person within his custody or physical control." Other sections of the law prohibit "prolonged mental harm," "intentional infliction," the use of "mind-altering substances," and "the threat of imminent death; or the threat that another person will imminently be subjected to death, severe physical or mental suffering, or mind-altering substances or other procedures calculated to disrupt profoundly the senses of the personality."[66]

To avoid the sweeping scope of the federal statute, one must toy with the meaning of such words as "specifically," "prolonged," "severe," "imminently," "intentional," "incidental," "lawful," and "threat" or produce a category that keeps the statute itself, as well as the Fifth and Eighth Amendments to the Constitution, at bay. Government officials used both techniques to avoid accusations of torture during President George W. Bush's administrations.

Government officials began by claiming that what took place in largely hidden prisons abroad was not torture, For those who were not convinced, they added an exception using the presumption of presidential powers in a time of war to create a separate legal entity. To fight an unprecedented "war on terror," those captured could be officially designated "alien unlawful combatants." The new category meant that such combatants could be excluded from the normal protections of American law and the Geneva conventions relative to the treatment of prisoners of war.[67]

This first level of evasion (avoiding the meaning of the law) depends on psychological strategies. As in any punishment regime, the person punished must appear sufficiently different from and dangerous to the punisher to justify extraordinary measures. Captured Islamic Afghan and Iraqi insurgents designated as "alien unlawful combatants" could be treated as special threats endangering the common order much in the way that African Americans from poor ghetto backgrounds have been treated as sufficiently alienated from civil control to deserve harsher punishment in domestic prisons.[68]

Linguistic manipulations have been just as important in evading the law of torture. The nontransferability of pain and the inability to quantify it in someone else allowed government officials to use language in a way that would take torture off the table. Similar tactics have supplied justifications in domestic penal institutions. Insofar as suffering is an unknown variable in another, punishers will always make of it what they will when they are under pressure to justify what they do.

How did these ideas work on the question of torture? Policy makers redid documents "to take out language about what torture was or wasn't, to placate the sensibilities of those who didn't like seeing the law of torture and harsh interrogation even discussed." With new language, they argued that "the legal meaning of 'torture' is not as all inclusive as some people would like it to be." It followed that "breaking the 'will of prisoners' and making them 'wholly dependent on their interrogators,'" as well as other forms of "coercive interrogation," did not have to be classified as torture. The comprehensive statutory language of torture could be tailored to become "narrow, much narrower than popular understandings of the word," and in that narrowness, torture did not have to include "everyone who in any way might inflict severe mental or physical pain."[69]

If these strategies seem self-serving and insensitive to the actual infliction of pain, they were vital to their formulators as part of the second evasion in debates on torture. "Section 2340A of Title 18: Crimes and Criminal Procedures in Federal Law" states "whoever outside the United States commits or attempts to commit torture" can be "imprisoned not more than 20 years" or "punished by death or imprisoned for any term of years or for life" if a tortured person has died. The statute turns the punisher into the punished. It announces that "a person who conspires to commit an offense under this section shall be subject to the same penalties (other than the penalty of death)."[70]

Those active in setting new policies of punishment, especially at the highest level of responsibility, needed protection from a law that could put them in a jail cell. Some prisoners held in Abu Ghraib died under the torments they endured. So if one could not make the suffering less than torture through a preliminary rhetorical evasion—the photographs at Abu Ghraib made that hard to accomplish—then a second evasion had to separate anyone who could be accused from what happened there. Those even minimally engaged needed language that would protect them from prosecution. There were two methods: you could outsource to unknown figures who would extract information through torture, or you could build several administrative degrees of separation.

Any lawyer, though not necessarily every prison guard, had to see this problem. As a general rule in professional life, if you are unwilling to discuss the truth in a professional situation, you know you are already in trouble. Attorney General John Ashcroft, the nation's lawyer at the time, participated in the highest-ranking discussions of the Bush administration on the treatment of alien combatants, and in recognition of this problem, he asked after one such meeting, "Why are we talking about this in the White House? History will not judge this kindly."[71]

History has judged, and not kindly, in ways that have reached those White House discussions. In 2013 a review by a nonpartisan task force of the interrogation and detention practices after 9/11 concluded that it was "indisputable that the United States engaged in the practice of torture." The sweeping 577-page report also confirmed that "detailed discussions . . . occurred after 9/11 directly involving a president and his top advisers on the wisdom, propriety and legality of inflicting pain and torment on some detainees in our custody."[72]

As crucial as its findings were the task force's warnings. It blamed specious arguments by authority for concealing the infliction of unacceptable levels of pain and for creating a false debate about the limits of punishment allowed. "As long as the debate continues," it reported, "so too does the possibility that the United States could again engage in torture." The panel's answer, which applies as readily to abuse in American prisons, was also clear. "It's incredibly important," said former Republican congressman Asa Hutchinson, a leader of the task force, "to have an accurate account not just of what happened but of how decisions were made."

A torturer is a punisher who engages in excessive punishment, and there are several things to learn from that excess. First, Attorney General Ashcroft's discomfort shows that anyone who worries about harshness in legal punishment knows that something is wrong about it and should ask, "How wrong is it?" Second, any effort to evade an accurate accusation of wrongfulness in punishment will depend on secrecy.

Third, the knowledge of torture promotes indifference toward more ordinary levels of suffering.[73] Fourth, the infliction of deliberate pain will move from being thought exceptional to being treated as routine behavior in keeping with "gravitational laws that govern human behavior when one group is given complete control over another in prison. Every impulse tugs downward."[74]

All four lessons suggest that to prevent excess in a regular punisher, you had better have a very active plan to prevent the possibility. If you want punishment in any institutional forum to remain legal, you need multilevel controls in place at all times. For there is a fifth lesson to be learned. In the context of real or imagined defiance of a prisoner in the eyes of a punisher, the level of infliction will go up with no obvious end in sight. Think back to Justice David Souter's comment in *Farmer v. Brennan* from earlier in this chapter. Souter wrote "the Constitution 'does not mandate comfortable prisons.'" If you accept a continuum of discomfort for others, where does it end?[75]

Certainly not quickly or soon, given the hostility that always exists between punisher and punished. No possibility of sympathy exists within the relationship, and that unbridgeable psychological gulf is our next subject. One of the telling characteristics of prison punishment is an enforced intimacy without meaningful communication between open enemies. There is a closeness within a pervading coldness that breeds hatred and further complicates the mixed signs in suffering.

Reconnecting the Pain in Punishment

The plight of prison life is the subject of another chapter. The question for the moment is more limited but distinct and still complicated. Why is the pain of imprisonment so rarely a factor in legal discussions of punishment? One answer has already been given. It is impossible for an outsider to measure an insider's pain, and no one is more inside than a prisoner serving a sentence.

"Inside" in this case also has its own rules. One area of common ground in prison narratives is the compulsive need of speakers and writers to hide their suffering from others. Two examples out of many can serve that purpose here: "Norton #59900," a contemporary narrative by a woman prisoner, Judee Norton, known to officialdom only by her number, and *The Last Day of a Condemned Man,* an early novel by

Victor Hugo first published in 1829.[76] Similarities across almost two centuries suggest a timeless predicament. Pain felt in a prisoner is not always pain recognized nor pain meant for recognition.

Judee Norton's story is a deceptively simple one. As a prisoner, she was ordered into the captain's office of the Arizona State Prison Complex in Phoenix. There she was told that her visiting teenaged son had been disruptive on his last visit, against evidence and the truth, and when she questioned the evidence, she was told that her son's visits would be terminated for "an attitude adjustment period" because he "needs time away from you to learn to deal with the fact of your incarceration in a mature and sensible manner" (233). The cruelty in these words is palpable, but Norton did not bend until back out of the office, when she collapsed in tears, and only as long as she remained invisible to others.

The crux of the story comes in Norton's control of her pain and her practiced ability to hide her true feelings from everyone. When she is first ordered to report to the captain's office over a loudspeaker, she hides her shaking fear. "I feign indifference" with "the right degree of flippancy" and "arrogant disregard." "I can feel my face rearranging itself into a mask of haughty insolence," and it is vital for her to do so because the "scrutiny of a hundred watching eyes" informs her that "fellow inmates" are pleased that she is in trouble and wish her the worst (228–229).

During the office visit, where both the captain and his attending sergeant put Norton through minor humiliations of form, her attitude is one of masked defiance. She shows them nothing except a faint blush, for which she feels "mortified," and "a supplicating tone" against the captain's final decree, for which "I despise myself" (229, 233). Inner rebellion is held in check by outward courtesy until she is forced to speak for her son, "an intrepid lioness defending her cub." The conflict that marks this account comes through Norton's struggle between inner pain and outward composure. Her poise breaks only in a momentary dead space utterly separate from others. There she cries "in the broken-hearted way of a small child" and feels "naked and wounded, unmanned by grief and hopelessness" (234).

The denouement of the story comes in Judee Norton's controlled decision to hold her breakdown to this private moment; in public it would be "a sign of weakness and to be weak was to be a victim" (234). She immediately restores "the mantle of hard-ass prisoner on my soul" and turns "nonchalantly around the corner" to meet her inmate inquisitors. "This is my milieu, this is where I know exactly what is expected of me, precisely how to behave, what to do and say." A "disdainful grin" and dismissive profanity are her shield (235). No one is going to know how this person feels in a place that will be happier if she fails than if she succeeds. The point to remember is that there is no public outlet for the suffering she feels.

Victor Hugo's classic novel *The Last Day of a Condemned Man* conveys the same pervading sense of incommunicable suffering. It may be logically impossible to render the thoughts of a man who is about to be executed, but Fyodor Dostoevsky knew of what he wrote when he called the novel "absolutely the most real and truthful of everything that Hugo wrote." Dostoevsky and other socialists were arrested in Russia in April 1849 and sentenced to death. Three days before Christmas, they were lined up for execution at Semyonov Place in St. Petersburg. They received the czar's pardon and commutation to years of hard labor only after the rifles of the firing squad were pointing at them.[77]

Aware of the danger in misrepresentation, Hugo makes a virtue out of it. He prefaces the first edition of his fictional account by asking the reader to choose between reality, "the last thoughts of a poor wretch," and fantasy, "the work of a man, a dreamer who spends his time observing nature in the name of art" (3). Whether the book is to be regarded as a statement of fact or a work of fiction is left in the air. It opens with a simple assertion. The condemned man is "always alone" with his sentence; his mind imprisoned in the idea of it (37).

There may be no better example of the unseen pain in the punished. "Condemned to death," the sole speaker in Hugo's narrative finds "a wall between the world and myself" (41). He is "no longer the man I used to be" (56). On the day of execution, related in chapters 21 to 49, he is half himself, "a mind numb with pain" (66). How, he asks, can anyone believe that capital punishment does not bring hopeless suffering (86)?

The death penalty creates its own extreme form of solitary confinement. Some treat the condemned man better, many more treat him worse, but all treat him as a temporary object and differently than they would as a human being without a death sentence. More to the point, he cannot convey his suffering to anyone. In agony, he agrees "it would be wrong to complain," and he does not. He is prepared, and he is not prepared, as idle thoughts race through him of escape and the hope of a pardon that will not come. "There are times," he reveals, "when you think you can break a chain with a strand of hair" (81). So changed has he become that when his own child is brought to him near the end, she no longer recognizes him, wishes to be away from him, and speaks of her father as already dead (91–93).

Dehumanized, the condemned man observes the greater dehumanization all around him in those who are about to kill him. Objects take the place of people because they are at least indifferent to him. Hugo compounds all this agony by making his criminal a young, first-time offender, someone who can believably claim, "I was not a wicked man." He has had "many years of innocence and happiness," memories that he tries to fall back on as the only friends he has left (84).

All know they will die, but to know exactly when and for it to be part of public disgrace is a torture that Hugo reduces from weeks to days to hours. In perhaps the most graphic illustration of that torment, the condemned man is led away to be executed in an autumn rain. He murmurs, but only to himself in his terrible finitude, that the rain "will carry on for longer than me" (65).

The hermetically sealed perspective of this figure filled with pain is Victor Hugo's point, and it is a perspective and pain that no one else can perceive or recognize. The problem is not in a failure of sympathy, although often enough that is the case, but in the desensitized ceremony of death that all others engage in without facing the situation. In outward appearances, the condemned man dissolves into a cambric shirt from which the executioner has torn away the collar; it represents "all I had left of my former self" (95). No one should forget that everything done—the depersonalization of the condemned man with the shearing of his hair and removal of identifying clothing or, today for us, the unconscious figure prone on a gurney with anus plugged against loose bowels in death—protects the feelings of the punishers, not the punished.

Without losing the personal character of his protagonist, Hugo has managed the writer's trick of making the speaker an everyman. The doomed figure is one of us. *The Last Day of a Condemned Man* reaches beyond its moment in an "ongoing plea for every defendant now and in the future" (3). People no longer gather in crowds to watch executions, but the condemned man's final view of the crowd captures the turmoil that always applies in this situation. As he is led to the guillotine, he can "no longer tell cries of pity from shouts of delight, laughter from groans, voices from noise" (98).

Despite apparent confusion and controversy at the moment of an execution, 69 percent of Americans today support the death penalty, a figure that has remained remarkably consistent over time. Only a minority of about one in five thinks that the death penalty is imposed too often.[78] The difference from the past is that those in favor of the penalty prefer to avoid the event itself and would like it to eliminate physical pain when it is administered, preferably as quietly and solemnly as possible.

The modern citizen's ability to control much of pain works in ambivalent directions when the subject of punishment comes up. No one wants pain, but detachment from its influences separates the thought of penal degradation from the thought of serious pain. Inmates have been judged to have brought whatever discomfort they suffer on themselves, and there is little desire to measure their discomfort. Hundreds will gather for candlelight services at the location of an execution. Yet few blink an eye over a sentence of life without parole. Indeed, the percentage of those in favor of the death penalty drops to 48 percent if offered the still-draconian alternative of life without parole.

By keeping those in prison securely hidden from public view and by making sure that the criminals who perform serious crimes never reappear, society confirms that it does not want to think about whatever suffering takes place behind jailhouse walls even if it knows that humiliation, discomfort, crime, and physical abuse are prevalent there. Confusions in the relation of pain to punishment are masked by an indifference that controls communal attitudes toward the huge population in American prisons.

For the same reasons, conventional outrage against convicted criminals ignores the already-blurred distinctions between mental and physical pain. Life without parole says, "Let them rot in jail." More often than not, we do not realize what we mean when we think or say such things.[79] "Rot" is a passive construction that does not comprehend the active hopelessness in permanent incarceration.

Does a citizenry know what it is doing when it encourages massive incarceration through harsh laws and long-term sentences? How informed or uninformed are the American people on what happens in prison? Punishment comes in a wide variety of legal possibilities, and each level of officialdom brings different ideas to the punishment regimes that all sustain. It is time to look more closely at how punishment actually works in America.

The Legal Punishers

He do the Police in Different Voices.

The original title of T. S. Eliot's
The Waste Land[1]

The Privilege of Unknowing

Less visible than other parts of the law but vivid in implication, a punishment regime exists inside every legal process. From outside, a punishment regime is hidden from view; inside, it dominates the institutional momentum of its ostensible overlord, the law, even as it remains mostly unseen.[2] How can it both dominate and remain hidden? Defense counsel, procedural regularities, and basic legal rights provide safeguards, but punishment regimes operate across a legal system, not just within or at the end of it. Unless directly involved, we know the punishers in law through a vague euphemism: "law enforcement."

The limited public profile of institutional punishment veils its extraordinary dimensions, and the civic obscurity of something so large is hardly an accident. Officials do not like to talk about the nature and extent of the punishment regimes they manage. The figures are staggering. Annual spending by the states on corrections comes in at just under $52 billion a year, and the federal government spends an additional $6 billion with more local government expenditures totaling $26.5 billion for a grand total of over $80 billion a year on American prison systems.[3] Most officials deny the relevance of the phrase "punishment regime," but their disclaimers ignore the unprecedented numbers, the more than seven million people in America who either languish in prisons today, most without ever going to trial, or who live monitored through legal restrictions of probation or parole.[4]

An official reticence that borders on secrecy makes it hard to analyze punishment regimes or the mentalities that control them, and the sources for examining essentially closed systems are limited. Statistical evidence and formal institutional records fall short of what actually takes place in prisons. Unofficial sources give more active accounts, but limited access leaves most secondary sources stranded somewhere between the anecdotal and the analytical.

The range of these sources can be used to check and verify one another, but something more is needed if we want to grasp the atmosphere that characterizes punishment regimes—an atmosphere that is part animus, part evasion, part entrenched habit, part bureaucratic indifference, part an insensitivity that some would call stoicism, and every part surveillance at levels tolerated nowhere else in the course of social human behavior.

A third check on the ambience of the punisher can therefore be useful, and the choice here will be a literary text that combines imagination, pragmatic insight, compulsive realism, and tremendous balance on the subject. *The Just and The Unjust,* published in 1942 by James Gould Cozzens, is a classic courtroom novel. Its attention to professional detail serves present purposes, and so does Cozzens's unusual decision to make a prosecutor, normally the villain of such a story, the hero.

"Heroic," though, is too strong an implication to use here. Cozzens is after something more intricate and detailed but fascinating in its own right. After much study of the subject and time spent observing procedure in courtrooms, he appreciates the bland tonal realities in law-enforcement figures and their calculating manner in dealing with others. These traits are evident across all levels of the legal process, and they make his novel useful beyond itself. Time and again, Cozzens has something to add to the anatomy of punishers that form this chapter.

The Just and The Unjust succeeds by capturing the essence of a self-protective professionalism in the act of punishing. Cozzens signals his interest in the theme immediately. He dedicates the novel to a leading Philadelphia lawyer and judge, Edward G. Biester, with an epigraph from Sir Edward Coke's *First Part of the Institutes of the Laws of England,* better known in the profession as *Coke on Littleton*. The inscription reads, "Cuilibet in arte sua perito est credendum" (every skilled man is to be trusted in his own art).

Predictably, given the epigraph, Cozzens comes down on the side of the skilled professionals whom we ask to preserve law and order, but he notices what it does to them too. "The Just" in his novel are law-enforcement officers, and "The Unjust," who try to evade or misuse the law, are made to seek their approval in the end. But the epigraph raises a more subtle issue as well. It recognizes the separation of functions in punishment and the tenuous interactive trust this requires. Cozzens maintains a matter-of-fact distance and, with it, a nonintrusive acceptance of performance in other parts of the system for it to work well.

The protagonist in this novel, Abner Coates, is a young prosecutor learning his job and the mysteries in it. There are some things he can master only through sad experience on the equally sad subject of crime, and he makes some mistakes. A budding professional identity has left him emotionally withdrawn and a little too calculating in his social relations. "Never give anyone . . . any opening of any kind," he is told and accepts. It is his fiancée who asks with some bitterness after one particularly awkward moment, "Haven't you any sense?"[5] The teachers in this bildüngsroman of personal development are the highly valued, aloof judicial figures in the novel, a low-key older prosecutor, and laconic police officers.

Realism means that not everyone is admirable or even acceptable in law enforcement, so Cozzens adds a questionable politician, a glib defense counsel who plays fast and loose with the law, an even sleazier background lawyer on the defense side, questionable police interrogators, and defendants who plainly deserve punishment. Still, in making it clear that punishment is deserved, the novel raises a troubling concern for us generally. Some punishment is needed for defendants who are kidnappers and also gangsters, but Cozzens asks a sharper question that we will take up at various points in this chapter and the next. How much punishment is deserved?

Consider the momentum at work in contemporary American punishment regimes. If you are handed a citation by a police officer or arrested, you are already punished without being convicted. Your chances of beating the citation for double parking while momentarily unloading groceries in front of your house or letting your wife off in a crowded street are nil against bureaucratic impulsion and its systemic need for your money.

A more problematic arrest for the catchall category of loitering or being at the wrong party can generate an unpleasant time in a holding pen, as well as a permanent record for many to know about even if the arrest is not followed up. The computerized surveillance culture at work in the United States today means that you may have to explain your participation in a civil disobedience demonstration in a later encounter with the police, a future job application, or a credit check. If an arrest ends in a plea bargain or trial with conviction, your ability to procure later work, to vote, to enter a profession, to use subsidized housing, or to be eligible for food stamps or a driver's license could be impaired.[6] Punishment, in other words, can begin casually enough, and for some it never ends.

The impetus to penalize does not imply that protections or rights disappear. In a fundamental guarantee of fairness, no one plays more than one role in the legal process, and the assigned functions in a punishment regime are deliberately separate; hence Cozzens's insistence on a required element of trust between units. Separation also makes sense. Diverse skills apply at each stage of determination once the regime has its hold on a presumed transgressor.

Distinct but often sequential decisions—to stop, hold, cite, arrest, charge, indict, convict, sentence, incarcerate, or execute—demand different levels of understanding, expertise, and proof at each level of constituted authority. By design, these separate rungs of officialdom also connect. How they connect supplies fairness, but if they are misused, fail to connect, or connect in a mistaken fashion, they cause fairness to fade away.

In American culture, the separate functions in punishment belong to legislators, the police, prosecutors, juries, judges, and correctional officers, each of whom must coordinate with other levels to ensure a just system. Legislators create the laws on the basis of legal expertise in the system and rely on the system to enforce what they have passed. Police need the recognition and support of higher authority to put their lives on the line against criminal activity. Prosecutors, the definers of crime, depend on the integrity of police actions and findings. Grand juries generally do what prosecutors tell them to do, but they have to trust the accuracy of information from those prosecutors to accept the validity of proposed indictments.

In court, petty juries test the arguments offered to them by lawyers. They require credible evidence that has been properly submitted by those lawyers in order to convict. Presiding judges look to the adversarial process to check on plea bargains and to channel the flow of information at trial. They deliver sentences based on their acceptance of what takes place in front of them. Correctional officers rely on the judicial opinion tied to a sentence when they assign a convicted person to an appropriate level in the penal system.

But if a proper separation with cooperation secures the functional worthiness of a punishment regime, the priority given to separation creates some veiled concerns. In an overworked and rushed criminal justice system, passive acceptance easily replaces meaningful coordination. The checks on performance vanish in the shuffle of decisions that have to be made to keep things moving. Habit and the need to clear cases can replace serious deliberation. Without carefully acknowledged and maintained restraints across the system, a punishment regime moves toward severity in the exercise of its prerogatives.

Four general areas of concern deserve mention before examining the specific functions just listed. First, without effective coordination across a punishment regime, personnel in each part of the regime can shift responsibility for results onto other functions and ignore abuse elsewhere in the system. Second, although conviction, sentence, and confinement represent official punishment, each function possesses its own power to punish a presumed transgressor during its own stage of address. Third, those who use direct coercion in a punishment regime, police and correctional officers, possess the least education, training, and oversight in the system; controls of their ability to use physical force are minimal. Fourth, legislation and jurisprudence have increased the discretionary power of the first two active functions in a punishment regime. Police and prosecutors now exercise enormous control over what happens to anyone subject to punishment.

Bear in mind some implications that follow from these concerns, starting with the first, the potential lack of coordination among levels. One never fully knows a complicated system, and ignorance can be a defense mechanism. Philosophically inclined scholars refer to this strategy as "the privilege of unknowing." "Particular insights generate, are lined with, and at the same time are themselves structured by particular opacities."[7]

What will the members of a system *not* allow themselves to think? Every institutional structure has its forbidden or taboo subjects, and ignorance controls interpretive practices as much as knowledge. "Not knowing" reduces expression to a level that is convenient for a participant who remains passive rather than active in thinking about institutional practices.[8] How many in the legal process stop to think about the consequences of prison time? More than a decade ago, Justice Anthony Kennedy warned that we make a serious mistake when we allow lawyers and judges to have little knowledge or expressed interest in life behind bars.[9]

A second institutional concern, the ability to restrain at any level of the legal process, raises a misunderstood aspect of punishment regimes. Police can stop and frisk, let go or arrest, restrict movement or manhandle, and issue a summons or imprison. They can do so pretty much at will. Even an erroneous suspicion of a legal infraction is enough for them to act, and if the suspicion is correct—the lack of a buckled seatbelt in a car, jaywalking, a dog off its leash, failure to move on promptly in a park, feet on a subway seat—any minor transgression will suffice for arrest and possible imprisonment under current jurisprudence.[10]

Just above the police, prosecutors possess virtually unlimited powers over indictment and plea bargaining, the mechanisms that set the number of years to be served in prison. In the rare cases that enter a courtroom, juries decide to punish or not, depending on their intuitive sense of the defendant or their idiosyncratic conception of reasonable doubt. Judges set bail or not, monitor indictments, instruct juries, hold any court challenger in contempt, and control decisions by curbing the behavior of everyone in court.[11] Prison guards increase deprivations for inmates whenever they feel like it. Punishment, or the threat of it, oils the machinery of the system at every level.

The third concern raised about the separate functions of a punishment regime points to a more graphic source of exploitation. The potential for abuse is great (because unchecked) in the first and last levels of control, where frontline officers wield the ability to coerce physically. The right of police and prison guards to use force must be broad to protect them while they perform tasks that generate hostility. But how much force and under what circumstances?

Questions about the legitimacy of physical means during enforcement are rarely asked, and it would take a prodigy of intellectual self-control and emotional self-restraint not to be influenced under such conditions. Depraved criminal activity encourages police and prison guards to think of transgressors as "the worst of the worst" and to react sharply in response. Experienced police officers and prison guards act abruptly and strike first to avoid injury or to cut off any show of disrespect.[12] How much disrespect should a law-enforcement officer allow without a response? When a young man is arrested for giving the police the finger, is it "an obviously protected form of speech" under the First Amendment or a punishable offense that might land you in a holding cell with serious criminals?[13]

The added discretion given to the police and prosecutorial functions through recent jurisprudence and legislative enactment raises the fourth institutional concern.[14] Discretion gives more power to the two elements that already want to set punishment in motion. Police and prosecutors define the transgression to be penalized, and that determination turns in part on self-interest. Arrest quotas and conviction rates define success in the computerized age of law enforcement, and there is no outside control on either the numbers of arrests or the legal decisions that produce a conviction. Statistical standards for measuring performance now exist at the touch of a finger for anyone in the hierarchy of law enforcement. The availability and publicity of these statistics encourage more arrests and higher conviction rates.[15]

All four concerns—the lack of knowledge among levels, the ability to punish in some way at every level, unchecked coercion at the first and last levels, and greater discretion in the two initiating levels—have contributed to a punitive era in law enforcement, an era punctuated by overcrowding, inordinate expense, and strain on the nation's penal system. Must it be this way? It has not, after all, always been this way. One way to begin to answer this question is to test institutional vigilance across levels of engagement, where vigilance depends on the interactive professionalism raised in the epigraph of *The Just and The Unjust*. But to ask for that degree of professionalism—certainly to depend on it— exposes a paradox at work in punishment regimes.

The professional standards in law enforcement exist under unique pressures that differ from those in other trained walks of life. The unpleasantness and emotionalism in restraining another human being extract a price. Professionalism posits a number of characteristics: specialized training, certification, exclusive expertise, the authority to take discretionary action, a degree of occupational autonomy, the capacity to objectify through accepted standards, self-regulation through peer review, and dedication to public service beyond whatever personal rewards might apply.[16] The ugliness in punishment buttresses some of these characteristics while minimizing others, and the pressures on professionalism change at different levels in a system that is secretive, withholding, and hierarchical in its functions.

Can there be an effective professional identity shared throughout all aspects of a punishment regime with reciprocal connections between the highest and the lowest? That question is addressed in the following sections. Without mutual and supportive standards, the dangers, suspicions, risks, angers, and conflicts on the negative side of punishment dominate. History and laboratory experimentation teach that punishers will behave badly when they are left unchecked.[17] Standing in the way of too much severity is the presumed professionalism of the punisher. If that standard is not high, the elements in human nature that foster arbitrariness—concealment, cruelty, escalation, deprivation, indifference to suffering, and corruption—will control punishment.

Legislators: The Public Punishers

The most irresponsible punishers in America are state and federal legislators. That is a strong claim to make, but criminologists support it without making as much of it as they might. They have found that "criminal law, at least to the extent legislatures define it, adheres to no normative theory save that more is always better."[18] For the last four decades and counting, discussion of punishment has been more a political ploy than a reasoned discussion in criminal justice.

The levels of political capriciousness are so apparent, so persistent, and so habitual that one has the right to think the worst of one's lawmakers on this score. So many representatives in every legislative body in the country have called for unnecessarily punitive measures to enhance their own popularity that "inhumane" is a fair designation to apply to political debate and conduct when the subject of punishment comes up, as it does with regular frequency. Rare is the session in Congress or in a state legislature that does not put a new criminal law on the books. Congress may seem to do little, but it averages more than fifty-six new federal crimes a year.[19]

A primary fault in both state and federal legislative bodies has been overcriminalization. The creation of "strict liability crimes" (conduct without proof of a "guilty mind"), passage of multiple laws applicable to the same conduct, the prohibition of strictly moral offenses, and absolute discretion given to agencies of enforcement to decide when to manipulate these questionable categories have led to exponential increases in American arrest records.

Some of the examples are bizarre. You can face six months in prison in Delaware for selling perfume as a beverage. It is illegal in Massachusetts to frighten pigeons from their nest. Sending an indecent message in South Carolina can get you up to three years of imprisonment. The distinction between *malum in se* (a wrong in itself) and *malum prohibitum* (a thing that is wrong just because it is prohibited) is not only lost on American lawmakers trying to please specific constituencies, it is danced on by every legislative body in the country.[20]

Political leaders have a free hand to announce whatever they feel about crime without need of proof, relevance, or subsequent input. Anecdotal examples of dramatic criminal behavior rather than statistical evidence dominate political and then public understandings, and they are used to inflame the "volatile mix of fear, fury, and wishful thinking about simple solutions to violent crime" in communal perceptions.[21] Demagogic rhetoric reigns. The "politics of punishment" thrives in a "disciplinary no man's land." Politicians make it up on their own terms, and it is made easier for them because "criminologists avoid dealing with political issues, while political scientists have traditionally avoided crime and punishment as scholarly concerns."[22]

Lawmakers recommend draconian measures without bothering to share any responsibility for further interpretation or enforcement. All the sources of overcrowding in American prisons, where the population has increased four- to fivefold in recent decades, can be traced to such measures. They include strict drug laws for even minor offenders, misnamed truth-in-sentencing laws (where one must serve a high majority of a sentence given), high minimum sentences for many crimes, mandatory sentencing (taking discretion away from the judicial branch), three-strike laws, the removal of parole options, and the discouragement of pardoning powers.

The figures are astounding. In the last two decades of the twentieth century, "the number of drug arrests tripled from 581,000 to 1,476,000, while the proportion of drug offenders in state prison populations rose from 6.4 percent to 22.7 percent." By 1993 "nearly half the states and the federal government adopted some version of a 'Three Strikes and You're Out' law, requiring sentences of up to life imprisonment." Truth-in-sentencing provisions became popular when a 1994 federal crime bill added financial incentives for states that adopted such policies.[23]

Does all of this happen just because tough on crime sells at the polls? Since 1968 no national political party has been able to win the presidency without taking a hard stand on this issue. Successful politicians talk about "a simple rule": "Control of the crime issue is a necessary, though perhaps not sufficient, requirement for political victory in America."[24] Perhaps so, but does discussion of the crime issue have to be as simple as the rule?

Responsibility lies with legislatures because the answers lie there. Better rehabilitation programs and less recidivism may be goals, but "the iron law of prison populations" states that only legislative enactment of less time in prison will change massive overcrowding. Statistics tell the tale. "In the last thirty years, the average time served by people going to prison has almost doubled." "140,000 prisoners are serving life terms (twenty-eight percent without possibility of parole)." "One-fifth of prisoners serve sentences with a minimum term of twenty-five years or longer."[25]

Change, if it is to take place, must begin with your state representative, your congressional representative, and the two people who serve you in the United States Senate. "We got to this place as a consequence of a generation of policymaking. It will take a sustained effort of policymaking to get us out."[26] Who will those policy makers be? Will they belong to the current generation? Rare indeed is the current political figure with a proposal on prison reform. Of course, the ingenuity required for constructive change is even rarer, but one thing is certain. Real change will only come through new ways of thinking about punishment.

The State of the Police

"The state of the police" as a phrase does not mean to raise the prospect of "a police state" even if the second phrase taps a reflexive fear in modern society. Most police do their work as well as they can. If you want enthusiasm from a law-enforcement officer, listen to an account of a

good deed and, in listening, remember that police spend most of their time coping with victims, not catching criminals. We should understand the police better than we do, and to do that we need to recognize that the frustrations in their profession are great—great enough to make most officers proponents of a strict punishment regime.[27]

Even experts find it hard to define a police force that does so much multitasking.[28] The police maintain the law, search out crime, and keep the peace, but in only a partial listing, they also take care of the lost and vulnerable, counsel the lonely, answer cries for help, give first aid, direct traffic, monitor events, check civil demonstrations, deal with domestic disputes, encourage communal relations, carry out the ignored dead, listen to the mentally ill, try to calm angry people, and investigate questionable activity. Each of these duties brings mixed perceptions about them, depending on whether one wants "a police officer" or has been "stopped by a cop." "There is an enormous gulf between the image and the reality of policing."[29]

Still, we need a definition, and to the extent that the police initiate the active part of a punishment regime, it can be a relatively simple one. "The core of the police role" consists in the capacity to use legal force. Force has negative significance in a free republic, but it garners respect in a society full of violence.[30] So again there is ambivalence. The legal right to use force distinguishes the police from other officials who share some of the same functions, and that distinct power explains why commentary on the police can be pushed in either a negative or a positive direction.

Force is allowed to the police because it is the quickest way to secure obedience in a crisis. Punishment can come from them in an instant. So essential is the attribute that "it is exceedingly rare that police actions involving the use of force are reviewed and judged by anyone at all." When occasionally a use of police force goes awry, it alarms a community. That is why many indicate of the police "there is something of the dragon in the dragon-slayer."[31]

Most people know the police through the way they are helped and protected by them, but can we know them beyond our need of them? The question is harder to answer than might appear. Law-enforcement organizations are based on an inward-looking military model replete with captains, lieutenants, sergeants, and beat patrolmen. They work in strict hierarchy, governed by sharp lines of demarcation, guided by solidarity in the ranks, and self-controlled by a code of silence. The structure tends to keep police in a world all their own. Not without reason, they feel apprehensive about a public that turns on them easily. They stick with their own and learn to be closemouthed with others about what they do.[32]

A measure of cultural alienation in the vocation may be unavoidable. "The vast majority of policemen are eroded by their environment." The bad behavior they constantly encounter becomes a fatalistic norm. "It's not going to change," they say of crime on the street, and "You're certainly not going to change it." The opposite, in fact, happens: "The street rubs off on police." "They become reflections of the people they police." Police language comes to resemble the profane language and harsh treatment of the street.[33]

The price can be high. "The job runs against every good impulse you ever had," observes one thirty-eight-year-old detective. In dealing with crime they cannot stop, police develop a quiet bitterness. They resent the restrictions that prevent them from acting against people whom they know are guilty, and they lose respect for the parts of the legal process that make their jobs difficult and more dangerous.[34]

These tensions simmer and sometimes erupt into full-blown dispute. Starting in the long hot summer of 2012, to take a recent example, public debate has raged over aggressive "stop-and-frisk" policies used by the police in New York City and Philadelphia. New York tactics have been decidedly more aggressive and frequent but also seemingly more effective in reducing crime. Debates have centered on the quandary of stopping gun violence through frequent searches that simultaneously imperil the civil rights of citizens, and they feature the mayors, the police commissioners, the courts, communal leaders, and legal scholars of both cities.[35]

To what extent is police surveillance in a high-crime area racial profiling? The New York police made 684,330 stops in 2011, sometimes respectfully, sometimes not. Eighty percent of those stops inconvenienced people of color, but violent street crime was also skewed in that direction. There is no real answer to the competing interests at stake in such a question, nor to the acrimony they cause. Aggressive frisks of people who are frequently stopped lead a community to fear the police as much as crime.

But that balance of fear can quickly tip in either direction. When a court in the New York State Appellate Division throws out the conviction of a teenaged repeat offender for illegal possession of a firearm after a stop-and-frisk search and that offender has already committed a second gun crime between the stop and the court decision, an invasive search turns into "a hugs-for-thugs lottery," and it is said of the judges, "Are they nuts, none of whom presumably lives in a treacherous housing project?" New York mayor Michael Bloomberg called the court decision "the definition of insanity." New York police commissioner Raymond W. Kelly chimed in. "The decision by the Appellate Division to dismiss the case against a teenager in possession of a loaded semiautomatic gun may be as dangerous as the weapon itself."

Danger is the byword in police work. Risk and the sporadic but intimate knowledge of catastrophe set the job apart. Commissioner Kelly's newspaper defense of his officers put heaviest emphasis on the eight police officers already shot in the first five months of 2012. An entire uniformed police force turns out for the funeral of a fallen comrade. Many show their respect during these sad events, which almost always concern a young person with a grieving family, but no outsider knows how danger shapes the life of a police officer, and insiders do not talk about it.[36]

The cryptic stoicism with which police communicate with the outside world conveys a pungent toughness. The pithiest answers rule when a legal response is wanted. In *The Just and The Unjust,* the leading policeman in the novel condenses many pages of heated legal exchange into a single earthy sentence when a runaway jury rejects capital punishment for kidnappers who did not participate in the actual murder of their victim. "Are you people," he asks, "going to burn a man who maybe didn't actually take a gun and shoot anybody?" Police get to the root of a matter tersely or they remain silent. "An impersonal, disinterested manner saved trouble."[37]

Corruption exists, but not as much as believed. Police live in an environment of drugs, graft, illegal money, guns, and prostitution. They know these outlets through investigation of them, and on every police force some individuals, "hairbags," indulge in them. Broader scandals occur in departments if members of a department accept a " 'hear no evil, see no evil, speak no evil' approach" covered by the code of silence.[38] One officer describes the dangers this way:

> In any department, anywhere, you can take 5 percent of the cops and they will be honest under any circumstances and they'll never do anything wrong. They are the priests of the department. Five percent on the other end of the spectrum would have been criminals had they

not become policemen. They are, in fact, criminals who happen to be cops. The remaining 90 percent will go whichever way the peer pressure goes.[39]

All these defining characteristics together explain why police generally believe in strict punishment. The available use of force, the dangers and attractions of the street, cynicism over public reactions, an intimate and fatalistic knowledge of crime, frustration over legal restrictions, the risks of corruption, the need for internal cohesion, and guarded silence in dealing with an unsympathetic world—these are qualities that push in harsh directions.

The raw context of law enforcement forces officers toward simplistic moral judgments rather than objective stands. Situations quickly become black or white, for or against.[40] The evils that police face are also more starkly personal than in other professions. Doctors respond to disease. Ministers answer to a declaration of sinfulness that can be forgiven. Lawyers help the vulnerable. The police deal instead with the open malice of vicious individuals engaged in behavior that will continue and get worse if not stopped.

As one policeman in a high-crime area explains, "There are street criminals out there now who are irretrievable predators that just get off—it's a sexual experience—on people's pain and on people crying and begging and pleading. They get off on it. They love it." Why American society produces so many "irretrievable predators" will be a topic in a later chapter. Here it is enough to get why police can dehumanize criminals as "hemorrhoids" or "bottom feeders," and why they want them punished as heavily as possible.[41]

Do the police sometimes use excessive force when they catch such people? Unique pressures are at work at such moments, particularly if innocent people known to an officer have been hurt. Police rarely catch a serious criminal in the act, but they witness the human wreckage from perpetrators all the time. The name "bottom feeders" for criminals has a specific meaning. "We know about as much about crime and the streets as a fisherman knows about the bottom of the ocean," explains one officer. "We paddle around in the sea, but we are largely ignorant of what actually goes on down there."[42] When a serious predator surfaces, police want that person punished in retribution and to deter others roaming around in what they know to be a large ocean of crime.

Knowing the police requires accepting their view of punishment as distinctively based. As the first active stage in a punishment regime, they are also the front line against crime. They are the one aspect of the legal system that always sees the consequences of illegal behavior. The traumatized victim of rape, the battered wife, the mourning parent, the abused child, the maimed informer, the bitter widow, the terrorized shopkeeper, and the vandalized homeowner hardly ever make it into court in a legal system dominated by plea bargaining, but they have borne witness to a police officer who will have talked to them, probably more than once, and written out a full account of their pain.

Why, in the eyes of that reporting officer, should the person who caused so much pain not pay the maximum penalty that the law allows? It is unreasonable to expect any other way of thinking by those who fight crime on a daily basis. Punishment of an acknowledged offender is the goal, and it clears a case when so many others remain open.

Prosecutorial Discretion

"Prosecutors," as one of them explains, "are conviction machines," though the job description is much broader than that. They are "the people's lawyers."[43] Along with prosecuting criminals, they guard the constitutional rights of a community, articulate priorities in law enforcement, oversee the police, interpret statute law, and keep the public informed on security matters. They are supposed to ensure fairness in the legal process, a priority that should come before winning in court. Still, the self-portrait offered, "conviction machines," remains an accurate one.

Whether elected, as most state attorneys are, or appointed to a position in a federal office, prosecutors work under "the constant pressure to win cases, to keep the office statistics of 'guilty as charged' climbing from one political season to the next." Yes, they function as "the conscience of the community," but "when it comes right down to it they are more interested in winning," and that is how the public will evaluate their performance. A low conviction rate will drive a state and county attorney and their staffs from office and force turnover in a federal group. The natural inclination in response is to cherry-pick cases to maintain a high percentage of convictions. "Case selection," writes one very successful prosecutor, "is everything in creating records like that."[44]

The tensions in the position are in many ways the same as those for the police, but with less justification when those tensions take over. Prosecutors are supposed to win because they normally hold the trump cards in the adversarial process. They decide whether to prosecute or not and at what level with more resources than the other side. Lengthy sentences, which are often mandatory, give them leverage to intimidate a defendant into accepting a plea bargain for a lower sentence. It doesn't hurt that many judges are former prosecutors who will grant the state leeway in presenting a case.[45] Taking too much leeway rarely inconveniences the people's lawyers. They are basically immune to the penalties that other lawyers face for misconduct.[46]

The power given to prosecutors tops that given to any other figure in an American punishment regime. Through the charging function, which often connects to mandatory sentencing guidelines, "their decisions determine the course of the criminal process, and in making those decisions, they act with broad, generally unregulated discretion." This power has increased. "The scope of prosecutorial discretion has steadily expanded in recent decades."[47]

That is not all. "So long as there is probable cause to believe that the accused has committed an offense, the decision to prosecute rests within the prosecutor's discretion," and this kind of decision "is particularly ill-suited to judicial review."[48] The absence of oversight is understandable, but it is also one of many places in the system where acceptance and unchecked behavior replace real coordination in the workings of a punishment regime.

The main control on prosecutors comes through professional aspirations that they are asked to meet. *The American Bar Association's Model Rules of Professional Conduct* emphasizes that a "prosecutor has the responsibility of a minister of justice and not simply that of an advocate." There is a "special duty" to be fair.[49] The best-known account of prosecutorial professionalism, often reprinted, is that of then Attorney General of the United States Robert H. Jackson. Speaking in 1940, shortly before becoming an associate justice of the Supreme Court, Jackson told his assembled United States attorneys, "Your positions are of such independence and importance that while you are being diligent, strict, and vigorous in law enforcement you can also afford to be just. Although the government technically loses its case, it has really won if justice has been done."[50]

Lawyers become prosecutors with these standards in mind. But if the idea of public service attracts many to the job, the job itself quickly attaches less noble expectations that must be met. The government in losing a case may indeed have won "if justice has been done," but prosecutors who lose were supposed to win, and they are criticized for failing by both the public and the legal circles around them. A losing prosecutor must justify the failure to win twice. Why did you lose? Then, since you lost, should the case have been brought in the first place? Under these twin pressures, winning is more than a desire; it is a prosecutorial necessity.

What will a prosecutor do in order to win? In the same speech to assembled prosecutors, Jackson warns "the prosecutor has more control over life, liberty, and reputation than any other person in America." Can one expect a prosecutor not to use that control in an important case? The position grants name recognition, experience in preparation for a lucrative private practice, advancement in government or politics, and a possible later judicial appointment. If a prosecutor loses too many cases or fails in a high-profile trial, some of the options for career advancement will close.

Other tensions in a prosecutor's life increase the need to win, and the worst of these tensions is unavoidable. The inherently negative impact of punishment corrodes attitudes and performance in noteworthy ways. Prosecutors, just like the police, deal with "the worst of the worst," and in working with the police, they use the same pejorative terms in speaking of perpetrators. The job is not as dangerous as a police officer's, but there are still risks. Some prosecutors receive threats from those they indict and carry a gun for their own protection. If you feel the need to carry a gun for protection, it changes your outlook generally, as well as the nature of the job, not least in the language used to describe criminals and the desire to have punishment applied.[51]

Not used to crime, new prosecutors soon become inured to it or pretend to. Colleagues expect an exhibition of public toughness, especially against opposing counsel, and that toughness becomes a way of life. "You see all of this cop mentality, and all this violent mentality among the people you're dealing with day in and day out," reveals one prosecutor, "and you become that. You get jaded about life and death. It's stupid to say, but you go to an autopsy and make fun of certain parts of somebody's anatomy."[52]

The job can destroy normal sensibilities more rapidly than one would like to think. "The way you start looking at the world is less than human." "What a prosecutor sees every day is the homicide reports. Every day, you see the pictures that you never want to see." Coping with "really rotten-type people" creates a unique and at times lonely view of things. "The public does not have any perception of how bad some people can be."

With more professional training than the police and working one step removed from direct violence, prosecutors should handle these problems better than the police, but on the balance scale of punishment the outcome is the same. "You essentially become the wrong side of the public conscience," confesses one prosecutor. "At one point I didn't care who went to jail, because everybody was guilty of something." This attitude has its uses; it helps a prosecutor accept "it was just a matter of winning."[53]

The adversarial process takes a bizarre twist through prosecutorial thinking. "I don't know how in the hell you rehabilitate somebody who denies guilt," argues another prosecutor even though he accepts that a "not guilty" plea is standard procedure in court. The "us-against-them" mentality of the police thrives again here. In a prosecutorial view of punishment, winning when challenged requires a sentence with more time in prison, not less.[54]

The severity of American sentencing structures gives leverage to prosecutors who already control most of the legal process. The plea bargain, once thought to help defendants, now hurts many of them. Not for the first time, a good idea turns into a bad one in the evolving harshness of punishment regimes. The threat of a much longer sentence forces most defendants to settle out of court for a lesser one. Injustice enters when codefendants receive radically different sentences for the same offense.

The coercive features of plea bargaining involve "horse trading," to use the Supreme Court's own crude description of the practice.[55] Bargaining often means "an exploding offer," one that disappears if it is not accepted quickly, and it applies to separate defendants at different times in order to break down solidarity among codefendants. A prosecutor says, "Take the bargain now, or the offer is dead or goes to your codefendant." For strategic reasons, defendants are threatened with trials even when the prosecutor has no intention of seeking one.[56]

These maneuvers work through deliberately arranged severities in sentencing policies to get the result in question. "Legislatures have increased statutory sentences to enhance the bargaining power of the resource-constrained prosecutor." Ask yourself the following question: How can a peripheral defendant in a crime resist the bargain of a three-year sentence against the gamble of a twenty-year sentence at trial?

One reason to worry about the unchecked prosecutorial power in plea bargaining is precisely that the discrepancies in punishment can be so great. "[Defendants] who do take their case to trial and lose receive longer sentences than even Congress or the prosecutor might think appropriate, because the longer sentences exist on the books largely for bargaining purposes. This often ends in individuals who accept a plea bargain receiving shorter sentences than other individuals who are less morally culpable but take a chance and go to trial."[57]

The Supreme Court worries about these practices and has begun to level the table in bargaining sessions by insisting on more formality and publicity in currently cloaked bargaining exchanges. "The reality is that plea bargains have become so central to the administration of the criminal justice system that defense counsel have responsibilities in the plea bargain process, responsibilities that must be met to render the adequate assistance of counsel that the Sixth Amendment requires in the criminal process at critical stages." Here, in *Missouri v. Frye,* the court faces "the simple reality" that "ninety-seven percent of federal convictions and ninety-four percent of state convictions are the result of guilty pleas" in a process "with no clear standards or timelines and with no judicial supervision of the discussions between prosecution and defense."[58]

Unchecked power always increases. Although most prosecutors think they exercise self-restraint, there is always the question of what counts as restraint in an organizational context. The valued opinion of one's peers, the desire to put away someone who deserves punishment, and the general weakness of the adversarial process in criminal justice dictate choices as well as effects. Personal inclinations give way to ingrained habits when an institutional frame of reference undercuts personal reasoning with more general psychological and social influences.

Studies in social cognition and evolutionary biology claim that "moral judgment should be studied as an interpersonal process" through a "social intuitionist model." Judgments about good and bad actions "are made with respect to a set of virtues held to be obligatory by a culture or subculture." Tests show that "people are highly attuned to the emergence of group norms," and that "moral reasoning is usually done interpersonally rather than privately." Even important moral decisions come out of "a custom complex." A person making decisions looks for reasons to justify what are "already-made moral judgments."[59]

A prosecutorial arrangement easily fits this social intuitionist model through official policies to prosecute as vigorously as possible. All lawyers argue within a rhetorical stance of "already-made moral judgments": guilty or not guilty. Prosecutors proceed only if they hold a preconceived belief in the guilt of the accused, which in an office dealing with constant crime can create predisposed ideas about levels of punishment. Remember the words of the self-fulfilling prosecutor quoted earlier: "I didn't care who went to jail, because everybody was guilty of something."

The frequency with which prosecutors cite conviction rates in public as proof of performance attests to what happens. The need for a high conviction rate creates an assembly line of informally managed guilty pleas with levels of incarceration that are still significant. The assumption of guilt that lies behind every plea-bargaining process encourages fast, cost-saving, successful prosecutions without having to prove guilt under the higher public standard enforced at trial.[60]

For all the reasons presented, momentum grows across these first two active stages of a punishment regime, those of the police and the prosecution. Once you are held, the needs of the regime take over, and there is a certain ruthlessness because severity in charging is required for the system to work smoothly. Why should the police and prosecutors who thrive in the system question an arrangement that guarantees success?

The answers that *The Just and The Unjust* gives to these problems and questions are instructive. The novelist's method is one of an ideal but hardheaded realism in its treatment of the punitive sides of the law. The local district attorney, Martin Bunting, sets the theme. "There is always theory and there is always practice," he advises his assistant, Abner Coates. "If you think you're going to change that, you're wrong. Theory is where you want to go; practice is how you're going to get there." The context of this remark is instructive. Coates has complained about the harsh treatment of a prisoner, and Bunting overlooks the physical tactics of the police in the case. He can "trust" the police because "they know when a man is guilty" (281–282).

The novel covers the life of Abner Coates across three days in the town of Childerstown, which is run by an educated, self-disciplined, but comfortable legal elite contending with a lot of minor transgressors. The town itself has been shocked by a high-profile trial of gangsters, but the comfort zone remains intact. The gangsters are interlopers who come from outside of town. During those three days, Coates decides to get married, agrees to run for district attorney, and loses the trial of the gangsters to a runaway jury.

All kinds of minor events keep interrupting this young prosecutor in perhaps the best single fictional representation of a prosecutor's daily life. The overworked Coates needs to keep many balls aloft at once, and he drops a few of them along the way. He bungles a few things while learning to exhibit the self-discipline, poise, and stolid emotional control that regularly appear in the older colleagues around him.

The inference of the novel is that Abner Coates will prove to be an even better prosecutor than his boss, who is moving on to the attorney general's office, and that he will eventually become a leading judge in the town, like his father and grandfather before him. Retired from the bench, Coates's ailing father tells him that he should be glad to spend his life in the law. "There are disappointments; there are things that seem stupid, or not right. But they don't matter. It's the stronghold of what reason men ever get around to using. You ought to be proud to hold it. A man can defend himself there. It gives you a groundwork of good sense; you'll never be far wrong—" (109). You'll never be far wrong? Complacency in the punisher depends on the assumption that those who are punished get what they deserve.

Cozzens makes his prosecutors sympathetic by having them lose in court even though they uphold the right professional standards. They show the restraint, "the dry exactness," and "wisdom and foresight, patience and temperateness" that a prosecutor should in the adversarial process, while the jeering, sardonic defense counsel, Harry Wurtz (the name rhymes with "worst"), wins with theatrical effects; he is "cheap but good" (26–27, 350, 114).

The Just and The Unjust assumes that authority in the law will always know best even when it is thwarted. "Harry had the proper appeal, the appeal to vanity, sentimentality, and plain boneheadedness. The slick talker by his contemptible slickness had borne down Bunting's unadorned arguments." A "fast talker" overwhelms the prosecution, but only through the fallibility of "a foolish jury" (401). Juries, though, are a potential check on punishment regimes, and that detail, whether fact or myth, becomes clear in the last pages of the novel.

Trial by Jury

Citizens are asked to do three things for the common good: vote, pay taxes, and appear for jury duty. Only the first activity is an appeal rather than a demand. The state will punish you if you do not pay your taxes or if you ignore a summons for jury duty. But if the threat forces compliance in the paying of taxes, it is more about establishing a value in the right to serve on a jury. There is some evidence that jurors leave a courthouse "with a refreshed civic spirit and a greater willingness to engage with community and political life"; jury service "causes previously infrequent voters to become more likely to vote in future elections."[61]

But whatever the collateral benefits in jury service may be, the United States remains the exception among liberal democracies by making trial by jury a worthy constitutional issue. The Sixth Amendment to the Constitution of the United States attaches specific value to the idea: it guarantees the right to "a speedy and public trial, by an impartial jury of the State and district wherein the crime shall have been committed."

The premises behind the constitutional claim are important though not altogether obvious. Locality is insisted on, but the know-how in locality must not extend to prior knowledge of the situation at hand. So the kind of impartiality guaranteed—living in a community but uninformed on the crucial conflict—might not be easy to find.[62] Certain ideals support the arrangement. Jury duty assumes that ordinary citizens can decide a question of guilt in a tangled situation, that common sense will win out, that twelve random individuals will agree on the merits in a serious dispute, that jurors will see through special interests, and that jurors, when called on, will accurately gauge the meaning of loss of liberty.[63]

These ideals are confirmed, in turn, by deep-seated fears. Suspicion of the state as punisher comes first to mind. Antiauthoritarianism and questions about state power are fundamental impulses in a long history of opposition to government action, and these impulses are especially strong when it comes to punishment. "Society in every state is a blessing, but government, even in its best state, is but a necessary evil,"

Thomas Paine cried in galvanizing the American Revolution of 1776. "Government, like dress, is the badge of lost innocence." "That government is best that governs least," added the abolitionist Henry David Thoreau in 1849. Thoreau put his words in quotation marks as a public rallying cry. He wanted to make them "the motto" of America, and he succeeded beyond his wildest dreams.[64]

Versions of these oppositional cries are now heard in every election year, and the same spirit—"Let the people decide!"—makes its way into courtrooms through the jury system. The people randomly impaneled, whether on a grand jury vetting indictments or on a petty jury listening to the presentation of a case, are believed to stand in the way of oppression. Looked at through rose-tinted glasses, juries are thought to guard the Eighth Amendment to the Constitution, which prohibits excessive bail, excessive fines, and cruel and unusual punishments by the state.

The legitimacy of juries rests on their unprofessional status in a space dominated by professionals and expertise beyond them. The impaneled citizen is a safeguard on how the working system talks and thinks about itself, often with the complacency earlier noted. Technically, at least, the adversarial process accepts this qualification to its work even though it contends with jurors who fall asleep, do not understand, fight with one another, let guilty people go, punish the innocent, ignore directions, and fail to reach a conclusion that should be obvious.

Why, against every inefficiency and possible error, does the legal profession accept an arrangement that it will admit to avoiding whenever it can? In answer, it surrenders the ultimate right to decide to juries in order to protect its own vulnerability. Juries are a buffer. They insulate the legal profession from corrosive elements in the task of punishment. They maintain the fiction that it is the people who punish the people.

One of the most nuanced justifications of the jury system appears in the pages of *The Just and The Unjust*. When a runaway panel engages in jury nullification in the town of Childerstown, one judge threatens its members with jail for misbehavior, and another lectures them on failure to do their duty. But the oldest and wisest judge in Childerstown—a town run by an enlightened gerontocracy—thinks otherwise. Judge Coates gets to the essence of a jury's function. "It's like a cylinder head gasket," he informs his son, Abner. "Between two things that don't give any, you have to have something that does give a little, something to seal the law to the facts. There isn't any known way to legislate with an allowance for right feeling" (427).

The phrase "an allowance for right feeling" sounds a little fuzzy. "Justice," Judge Coates explains, "is an inexact science." In dealing with that uncertainty, no legal system can avoid "the ancient conflict between liberty and authority"—an inherent conflict so uncomfortable that "it's a question how long any system of courts could last in a free country if judges found the verdicts" so uncomfortable that "it doesn't matter how wise and experienced the judges may be." In the tangle of unavoidable problems, "a jury has its uses":

> Resentment would build up every time the findings didn't go with current notions or prejudices. Pretty soon half the community would want to lynch the judge. There's no focal point with a jury; a jury is the public itself. That's why a jury can say when a judge couldn't, "I don't care what the law is, that isn't right and I won't do it." It's the greatest prerogative of free men. They have to have a way of saying that and making it stand. They may be wrong, they may refuse to do the things they ought to do; but freedom just to be wise and good isn't any freedom. We pay a price for lay participation in the law; but it's a necessary expense. (427–428)

There are three prongs in this argument, moving from the practical toward the philosophical. First, juries are a safety valve protecting the system. Second, all legislators, most prosecutors, and many judges are elected and have strong incentives "to produce the range of outcomes the public desires." That range includes the distribution of prosecutions and convictions that the public wants.[65] A jury stands in for that public. Third, if "a jury is the public itself," at what level of remove does the public get to decide what punishment should be?

Juries, it turns out, agree with judges the majority of the time even though they convict more often than a judge running a bench trial.[66] But if conviction rates are higher with juries, studies also show that jurors would like to punish someone they have convicted less severely than the rest of the legal system.[67] Data suggest that degrees of distance from the sentencing mechanism make a difference. A citizenry, the public at large, will favor harsh sentencing in the abstract, as the frequent successes of tough-on-crime politicians demonstrate at election time, but the individuals who actually punish—those jurors with the liberty of a defendant in their hands—often feel differently and would punish less if they could.

Jurors, if they want to, can bring a distinctly normative level of concern to a case. They are then more than a safety valve. "The criminal justice system exists not only to protect society in a reasonably efficient and humane way, but also to defend, affirm, and, when necessary, to clarify the moral principles embodied in our laws."[68] One of those principles, securely anchored in the Sixth Amendment, is the right to "an impartial jury."

What, then, does it signify that less than 5 percent of the accused are now punished in a public trial and even fewer before a jury? Judge Coates argues that a legitimate legal system cannot last long in a free country if professionals decide punishment. He assumes the public nature of jury verdicts before an observing citizenry that watches other citizens decide. But that is no longer the case. Today prosecutors determine the result in well over 95 percent of cases through plea bargains that are kept from public view. How can the people grasp what is happening, much less verify a decision, when they cannot see the legal process at work?

With the loss of formal trials, "the privilege of not knowing" is less a matter of willed ignorance than a danger to worry about. Judge Coates's "cylinder head gasket," his analogy in describing the function of a jury, is worth pursuing. A cylinder head gasket in a motor prevents coolant or engine oil from leaking into the cylinder of an internal combustion engine. It maximizes the efficiency of the engine and keeps it from catching fire.

Today the engine of American criminal justice is misfiring without that gasket in place. Juries do not accomplish what they once did because they are not part of the legal process except in those rare cases where a defendant can afford to take the risk of a longer sentence and the expense that a jury trial requires.[69] Punishment regimes have donned a mask. They now function in the shadows where accountability goes untested.

If they ever did, the people no longer decide. Police and prosecutors control the legal process now, and no one should be surprised that the upshot has been a more punitive system. Yes, a judge must approve a plea bargain, but that informal negotiation in front of the bench or in chambers is not witnessed by the public, and much of the power to arbitrate such a finding has been stripped from the judicial function. Juries are not the only institution to control less of the legal process. Something comparable has happened to the figure on the bench, the person who oversees and guarantees the integrity of the criminal justice system.

The Presiding Judge

Judges remain the official punishers in law; they are the royalty, the princes and princesses of punishment regimes.[70] As such, they are honored but mistrusted, and the ambivalence stems from the tangle of gratification and revulsion in punishment itself. Called "your honor," judges are nonetheless the only officials regularly accused of "activism" in governments chock-full of action. They can be singled out in this fashion because to punish is to be active in a personally threatening way. More often than not, judges decided punishment throughout the first two centuries of the nation's history. That changed in the late 1970s when mistrust outran respect, and legislative restrictions curbed judicial discretion in sentencing.

Change, no matter how good the original idea, usually means more punishment in the momentum of a punishment regime, and this has happened here. Judicial discretion naturally produced discrepancies in sentencing in different courtrooms, depending on the nature of the judge, whether authoritarian or liberal minded, legalist or pragmatic in orientation.[71] In reaction, liberal legal experts joined conservative ones to ask for change, not worrying as much as they probably should have that judicial discretion provides flexibility for parsing variations in the circumstances of crime.[72]

Concern over judicial leniency led to restrictive statutory demands in punishing. Congress and state legislatures created mandatory sentencing guidelines with higher maximum sentences and reduced the spread in minimal sentences for many crimes. They also prescribed administrative commissions to enforce stricter sentencing. The result, as expected, was more uniformity in sentencing, but at the expense of the flexibility that discretion allowed. Further restrictions on judging came through statutes adding crimes and new penalties for the same kind of crime with more discretion in the hands of prosecutorial plea bargainers. Too often, judges, still the formal sentencers, have become rubber stamps in the act of punishing.[73]

Reinforced by the suspicion that always surrounds the judicial function has been the idea that judges have been "soft on crime" and have
thereby contributed to crime instead of stopping it. Between the mid-
1970s and 2000, attacks on the judiciary altered what it meant to be in
court. Condemnations of "idiosyncratic beliefs of the judges" challenged
the orthodoxies in their role. Judges, by law, believe "the function of
the courts is to determine the guilt or innocence of the accused." Champions of punishment in the 1970s and 1980s began to urge a different
purpose: "It is to decide what to do with persons whose guilt or innocence is not at issue."[74]

Those in favor of more retribution decided that "the important decision concerns the sentence, not conviction or acquittal"; they argued "a
good sentence . . . minimizes the chance of a given offender's repeating
his crime" and "deters others from committing a crime." Leniency was
assumed to be the system's biggest problem in attacks that reached deep
into the judicial function: "It is not too much to say that many sentences being administered are, in the strict sense, irrational."[75] The attacks worked because to the extent that rationalism defines decision
making, those who wanted more incarceration charged that flexibility
was unfounded in reason and had to be replaced with the presumed
rationality of obligatory sentencing.[76]

"A populist punitiveness" took over in the 1970s and remains in
place. "Crime became the fodder of political campaigns; 'lenient'
judges were parodied on the evening news and the bourgeoning 24/7
cable outlets." "Efforts to restrict or even eliminate judicial discretion
in sentencing paralleled efforts to strip judges of authority in a number of other areas." So effective have been these intimidating tactics
that when the Supreme Court in 2005 made federal mandatory sentencing guidelines advisory in *United States v. Booker,* most judges
continued to follow the guidelines rather than explain a deviation from
them.[77]

All of this said, the bench is still the place where punishment is heard.
No one arrested or incarcerated should forget that he or she is in a
judge's hands. Judges issue arrest and search warrants or deny them.
They allow or revoke bail, rule on crucial procedural motions, decide
on the evidence to be allowed, set the trial docket, control the behavior
of lawyers in court, and decide between minimum and maximum sentences in the statutory spread of punishment.[78]

Ceremonial control gives this official punisher communal visibility. Judges announce sentence to a public audience, as well as the convicted defendant. Speaking sometimes at length in this moment, judges shed their objective aura and chastise one who has been found guilty. The emotion in that declaration is then confirmed with a symbolic gesture of anger for all to see and hear. Judges conclude a sentence by pounding a gavel in punctuation of punishment. This unusual physical act informs a defendant, "I am the hammer, and you are the nail." It brings curt finality to the decision. All may now leave the courtroom: the public freely, the convicted criminal in another and much lonelier direction.

The most famous courtroom sentence in recent years conveys the stakes in such a moment. The example is useful because the judge in question felt compelled to explain his sentence in later commentary while confessing that "sentencing is the most difficult thing we do." On June 29, 2009, Denny Chin, then federal district judge in the Southern District of New York, sentenced Bernard Madoff to the unprecedented penalty for white-collar crime of 150 years in prison.

The case, if not the details, is well known. Madoff had pleaded guilty to eleven federal felonies: securities fraud, wire fraud, mail fraud, money laundering, making false statements, perjury, theft from an employee benefit plan, and false filings with the Securities and Exchange Commission in the largest Ponzi scheme in history. The scheme led to $18 billion in individual losses, took the life savings of smaller investors, upended solid institutions, and threatened a major-league baseball team, the New York Mets. Public outrage over Madoff's behavior and the devastation it caused so many was widespread and enduring.[79]

Judge Chin's sentence created its own controversy. None of the felonies that Madoff acknowledged carried a sentence of over 20 years, and any one of them was enough to keep a man of seventy-one in jail for the rest of his life. To reach 150 years, Judge Chin had to stack the maximum possibilties in each count on top of one another, an unusual step in an investment-fraud case.

Noting that step, the defendant himself complained from prison in tones hinting at the lack of remorse that Judge Chin noticed in punishing him. Madoff said that Judge Chin had turned him into "the human piñata of Wall Street." "I'm surprised Chin didn't suggest stoning in the public square." More objective experts had criticisms of their own. They accused Judge Chin of symbolic overkill and of "pandering to the crowd." But if so, the act was successful on those terms. The average citizen expressed satisfaction that Madoff would "rot" in prison many times over.

The mixed reactions show how many different things a sentence of punishment must accomplish for concentric audiences. Judge Chin—well known in legal circles for being a humble, courteous, gentle person—went out of his way to make Bernard Madoff comfortable in his courtroom during litigation phases and took steps to control outbursts from victims who testified during the sentencing hearing. But final sentencing represents a very different moment and forum; it transforms the punisher as well as the punished. The judge in this moment is a different personage. The sentencer turns into a public orator who renders a performance beyond the idea of self.

Judge Chin spoke in tones that he would not have used as a private person. He described Madoff's crimes as "extraordinarily evil." Their unparalleled scope justified a sentence three times longer than even the probation office suggested. Symbolic punishment was "important for at least three reasons": retribution, deterrence of others, and justice for the victims, and in so arguing Chin targeted and gratified three separate audiences.[80]

Playing on tradition in his sentence, Chin wrote "an offender should be punished in proportion to his blameworthiness," which meant that Madoff got proportionately "what he deserves." Arguably so, but the ideas of desert and proportion thrive on variables. Did one have to guarantee that Madoff would die in prison, something the prisoner expressed special regret over? Chin decided that the absence of letters in support of Madoff against hundreds wanting strict punishment was especially "telling." But should support be expected or merely possible?[81] Perhaps Chin found it "telling" in his desire to cap public rage with a communally acceptable answer. But what kind of balance should a judge strike between recommended punishment and the public's wish to punish severely, and how should the public's wish be measured in that balance?

Again, James Gould Cozzens offers a useful answer in *The Just and The Unjust*. Judge Thomas Vredenbergh presides over the major trial in the novel. He has an accurate mind for detail but also a temper. He lacks what guides his colleague on the bench, the president judge above him. He does not have "Horace Irwin's feeling for the law."

The difference is emphasized. Vredenbergh, just one rank below the older and longer-sitting Irwin, represents the average good judge. He is "full-blooded, the intelligent sensual man, irascible about what struck him as wrong or unfair, astute about the failings in human beings, dealing with facts and things as they were, with no special interest in why." His weaknesses—irascibility and not caring about why—limit him when he knows that the people charged before him are guilty. Cozzens, using a novelist's license, gives Vredenbergh a wayward daughter to cement this character sketch. By way of contrast, "Judge Irwin thought constantly of why," and his "reserved and aloof" demeanor supplies better control in the courtroom (106, 117, 263).

When sentence must be passed on an especially distasteful crime, Judge Irwin's approach to the situation gives us the balance for which every judge should strive. He seeks "to know why" by testing the meaning of normality, and this puts him in the place of the criminal. "I think we all recognize in ourselves occasional impulses or ideas which, if put into practice or disclosed to the world, would cast the gravest doubts on our own normality." Even though "it is right to penalize [the criminal] when he fails to conform," Irwin announces, "we should bear in mind that what is none to us, may be to him a great temptation" (262).

Cozzens uses the scene to convey how an ideal judge should punish. Judge Irwin's "air of virtue, instead of being hateful, had in it an austere sweetness," and so "he aroused, even in a heavily sentenced prisoner, no special resentment" (117). Acceptance in receiving punishment is an important goal in the closure that all want. Another goal is recognition of a return to normalcy that all can share. "When Irwin went into one of his monologues, sign always that he was greatly upset, he talked less to the person he addressed than to himself. With his great resources of knowledge and experience he assayed new explanations of the inexplicable; patiently, unwilling to despair, he argued the world around him back to some degree of reason" (262).

A wise judicial sentence explains the inexplicable so that the world can understand and proceed on its way. The punishment in the Madoff case can be seen in this light. An unprecedented crime must be encompassed in some way. Judge Chin had previously dealt with fraud in the hundreds of thousands of dollars. He now had to sentence for a crime incomprehensible in scope—as much as $65 billion lost, with the ruin of thousands of innocent people. Chin responded by describing one victim in detail. He told the story of a bewildered new widow who took her life savings to Bernard Madoff and lost everything. The anecdotal pain of this one victim is every victim's and turns a sentence that makes no sense in the life cycle, 150 years in prison, into a public realization of what Madoff's crime has meant.[82]

Punishing severely but fairly requires a delicate balance, and it obviously troubled Judge Chin. It should trouble anyone on the bench. The negative continuum in a punishment regime stipulates severe penalties, and some punishers will be undone by the regular exercise of it. Theorists have already explained in the abstract how this can happen, and we see as much in a cautionary tale that every judge should read.

The tale in question would qualify as a confession if it were not such an angry declaration. In *Guilty: The Collapse of Criminal Justice,* Judge Harold J. Rothwax begins his career as sympathetic counsel for the Legal Aid Society representing disadvantaged defendants in a system stacked against them. But by his own admission, he turns himself into the renowned "Prince of Darkness," the judge who punished more harshly than others while sitting on the New York State Supreme Court for more than twenty-five years.

Three basic influences convert the idealistic defender of the vulnerable into such an acerbic punisher of the guilty. In the first influence, the presumption of innocence disappears when Judge Rothwax concludes "about 90 percent of the people who go to trial in this country are guilty." In his reasoning, defense counsel "constantly represent guilty people" and lie to protect their clients, while prosecutors tell the truth. Like Judge Vredenbergh in *The Just and The Unjust,* Rothwax grows "irascible about what struck him as wrong," and he takes out his anger on defendants and the lying counsel who represent them. Rothwax admits to convicting the liars he faces more happily when he can catch them in a lie on top of their manifest crimes.[83]

A second influence occurs when anyone sits on the bench. Challenged in a television interview for being "a liberal who has been mugged by reality," Judge Rothwax agrees with the thought, if not the language, by giving an analysis of the different functions that he has performed, first as defense counsel and then as judge. "When you're a defense lawyer," he says, "you're focused on representing one person against the world. When you're a judge, you're concerned with the defendant, you're concerned with the victim, and you're concerned with a fair and efficient administration of criminal justice. So you have a much wider and a broader perspective."[84]

When considered for what they actually indicate, these words have a chilling impact. Judge Rothwax admits that wider perception of the punishment regime has turned him into a more severe punisher. Does the same transformation, if not the observation, apply to other trial judges who have sat as long as Rothwax has? His tendency to punish more may be unusual only in that Rothwax came to his judicial position through the role of defense counsel, a role that normally abides by the time-honored phrase "tender of the accused." Many more judges come through prosecutorial ranks, where punishment has been the road to success.

The third influence on Rothwax comes through his personal experience as a punisher, and it applies throughout a punishment regime. We have seen that the ugliness in punishment has its own price and can lead to more of it. "And so it goes," Rothwax writes as he smiles in the face of a defendant while delivering a sentence after listening to a specious argument. "One case followed by another. Often, the details are so similar we must fight not to make horror ordinary."[85] Punishment wears you down like almost nothing else in life if you are a decent human being. How does one cope with that? Horror can turn ordinary in a frequent punisher.

How much did Judge Rothwax think about the consequences of the punishments that he handed out? In the same television interview on *NewsHour,* Rothwax receives questions about his desire for a more efficient criminal justice system, given the unprecedented numbers already sent to prison. His answer borders on the tautological: "Saying that a lot of people are going to jail is not to me an argument; it's a way of saying that a lot of people are going to jail. The issue is: Should they be going to jail, or should they not be going to jail?"[86] Today we know that so many are going to jail that the system is choking on itself.

The odd separation of dimensions—the safe distance between Rothwax's decisions and a lot of people going to jail—is not unusual. It has an institutional basis. Judges have little control over what happens to prisoners. Judge Denny Chin can sentence Bernard Madoff to 150 years in prison, but he cannot select the prison in which that time will be served. The nature and momentum of punishment move on within a punishment regime. Judge Chin actually recommended that Madoff be sent to the Federal Correctional Institution in Otisville, New York, seventy miles from Manhattan, but the Federal Bureau of Prisons ignored the request and assigned Madoff to the Butner Federal Correctional Institution in North Carolina, forty-five miles from the city of Raleigh, far away from friends and family connections.[87]

The severity of the sentence, not the judge who delivers it, guides the assignment to a prison, where a separate discipline begins. Judges, like others in the system, are insulated from the practical implications of their decisions. Where a prisoner is assigned can mean either a barely tolerable life or a horrible existence, and here again we have a partition rather than a coordination of functions. Judges "say go to prison," but go where? New inmates yield themselves to another and separate "indispensable autonomy." They are received by that last symbol of "punitive sovereignty," the prison guard.[88]

The Prison Guard as Correctional Officer

Just as no one hopes to end up in prison, so nobody grows up wanting to become a prison guard. Employment generally comes by default.[89] The attractions of the job are a good salary and secure state benefits for a person with limited education and means. The downside is steeper. You deal on a daily basis with people who hate you. They are good haters, too, and you have to contend with their malice, cruelty, and violence every day under oppressive working conditions. Many other disadvantages follow from the essential task: your job is to enforce suffocating restrictions on people who were once free and know what freedom meant.

Unpleasantness in prison is a pervasive phenomenon, some would assert by design. As a prison guard, you deprive the objects of your employment of just about everything they want to do or have, including their physical dignity through frequent strip and body-cavity searches, and you always have the power to take away whatever little they do retain during unannounced cell searches. You must cope with horrifying criminal behavior among prisoners. Injury and disease are rampant around you. Above all, you must demonstrate the demeanor and physical strength to impose discipline when challenged, which happens with some frequency.

If you love the job, you are a sadist. If you do the job the right way, you rely on patience, courage, consistency, and fairness. But even if you possess and demonstrate all these qualities, still you are hated. Nowhere are the insidious dynamics of punishment more in evidence. Anyone who has complete control over another human being is likely to exploit it at some point, especially if the person in question refuses to cooperate, and cooperation in prison is rare. A prisoner who sides with a guard for even the best of reasons risks retribution from other inmates.

Levels of alienation and hostility between guards and prisoners fluctuate in intensity according to the situation. No one spends more time dealing with serious criminals ("the worst of the worst") than prison guards, and the daily contact between people who despise each other has a predictable outcome. Every prison narrative—there are no exceptions—describes humiliations, insults, cruelty, insensitivity, and physical mistreatment by guards. The slide in the continuum of punishment is greatest in the war between the watchers and the watched.

The prison scene of abuse is part of a vicious circle. A guard enjoys very low status in law-enforcement circles and the community at large. Correctional officers, their preferred term, feel derided by everyone. Even the term is suspect. Guards hardly ever "correct" if the term connotes a desire to reform. Morale is low, and guards tend to distrust the supervisors above them. When everyone works in an impossible organizational situation, managerial guidelines fray, and the line between theory and practice becomes problematic.[90]

Lacking any other avenue to vent vocational frustration, many guards take it out on the prison population under their control, which reciprocates by finding ways to hinder authority when it can. Guard logic runs this way: Prisoners deserve the punishment they receive, and if they create difficulties, they only prove their continuing recalcitrance and criminal status. Hence most inmates deserve more punishment or, if you will, more correction. If existing punishment has not brought a change in attitude, it should be increased.

Guard mentality dehumanizes the relationship between keeper and kept. Most prisoners are known by their identification number or their crime, and guards are not above belittling inmates or physically punishing them for the crime that led to incarceration.[91] Mistreatment completely alienates an already-hostile subject population, and as with the police, guards decide that a quick physical response is good policy when challenged. In the settled patterns of many prisons, groups of guards wearing protective body armor and tear-gas masks will join together to gas and beat an uncooperative or simply a complaining prisoner.[92]

Stress is another factor in abuse. Many people, particularly people trained in physical confrontation, react aggressively when under stress, and work-related stress in prison guards is high enough to be termed "an important concern."[93] Some guards react by trying to control everything in a setting where minor transgressions and deviance are norms. When even total surveillance and repression fail to maintain control, guards feel increased anxiety and enter a heightened cycle of abuse to exhibit and confirm control. The tensions between guards and inmates in most prisons are always close to the possibility of breakdown.

The anxieties from stress that trigger physical retaliation by guards are not imaginary ones. "Every year, correctional officers are injured in confrontations with inmates" in ways that cannot be dismissed. "Correctional officers have one of the highest rates of nonfatal on-the-job injuries."[94] Inmate overcrowding, the prevalence of gang activity, black markets in drugs, and more prisoners serving life sentences with nothing to lose when they misbehave—these burgeoning conditions have created major problems in prison security. All of them complicate the task of maintaining order and increase the risks that a prison guard must cope with.[95]

What training does the average state prison guard receive to handle such pressures? Most states require a high-school education and six weeks of training, maybe with added experience in military or related work, inasmuch as a number of guards have military backgrounds. At a prison complex in Monroe, Washington, a typical graduation ceremony in 2008 focused on "anxiety," "fear," and "stress" as touchstones to be met in the position with a posted caveat that read, "If you knew you'd be fighting for your life tomorrow, would you change the way you train today?" When a model trainee destined for one of the best jobs in his graduating class is told that he should be "a role model for inmates," he says that the idea makes no sense. "How can I be an example for these offenders?" he asks. "These are convicts."[96]

The distance claimed even before the experience is telling. Correctional-officer training emphasizes preparation to meet an enemy more than rehabilitation techniques. It is true that the United States Bureau of Labor Statistics includes "aid in rehabilitation and counseling of offenders" as one of six duties in the position, but even at the advanced level required for a position in a federal facility, the accent remains on the other five negative categories—enforcing rules, keeping order, maintaining surveillance, searching inmates, and reporting inmate violations.[97] Is it any wonder that when guards think about prisoners, they identify their situation as a war of us against them? Any sophistication in theories of punishment disappears in their images of combat.

Vast numbers now work in prisons with this essentially punitive orientation. The number of correctional officers has mushroomed to meet parallel increases in incarceration rates. Correctional officers filled 493,100 positions in the United States in 2010. Incredibly, one in nine state government employees now works in corrections.[98] And yet the numbers alone do not convey what their collective power entails. The major change in the role of correctional officers in recent decades has been in their ability to organize in unions that have political clout and growing control over penal policy throughout the United States.

Not just the plight of inmates but many legal and institutional policies increasingly belong in the hands of prison guards, the employees with the least education and the greatest animus in dealing with prisoners. Correctional-officer unions sponsor and successfully lobby for laws that increase prison terms. They fight reforms that would shrink state prison populations. They donate large sums of money to "law-and-order" candidates and fund opposition to legislators, judges, and prosecutors up for election who do not espouse their views. A pressure group with enormous leverage, guard unions have been known to block the appointments of prison officials who oppose their interests.[99]

Political figures admit to feeling the pressure that these unions can bring to bear on their reelection. Even wardens will shrink from giving unions the chance to accuse them of "hug-a-thug" policies. Any measure that reduces prison-guard control, increases the comfort zone of prisoners, or works toward an innovation that might improve penal relations, such as "honor-yard" programs with greater freedom for model prisoners, receives a direct challenge from prison-guard unions. On penal issues, these unions are now "the biggest ball on the pool table, 'beating the other balls all over the felt.' "[100]

The sad state of penal reform comes home in the realization that only a very high-ranking official not subject to election will comment about these problems on the record. In February 2010, looking at prison-guard-union sponsorship of harsher sentences, Supreme Court Justice Anthony

Kennedy concluded, "That is sick."[101] All the same, no chorus in support of Kennedy came from elected officials or professionals in penology.

Opposition to reform from prison-guard unions represents a serious and growing obstacle to a better system, and the strength of that opposition allows us to extrapolate from Justice Kennedy's observation where others have been silent. Legal punishment as we know it is sick and getting sicker, with a much greater because separate sickness left to explore.

Profiting from Punishment

Nothing illustrates the full wretchedness and twisted nature of punishment in America as graphically as the sudden and rapid growth of private institutions of incarceration. The Protestant ethic, with its belief in the virtuous pursuit of prosperity, is deeply ingrained in capitalism, but that ethic has been turned upside down in prisons for profit. Capitalism justifies high incomes for the few based on the effort of the many by glorifying all work.[102] The privatization of punishment breaks this logic by making money off the enforced idleness of a prison population utterly separate from the trickle down in prosperity. Inmates housed in this way are basically fodder for private gain.

These new kinds of prisons arose during the rapid increase of prison populations in the punitive surge of the 1980s. As with the increase in prison guards, mass incarceration meant more prisons, and prisons run by private enterprise were convenient ways for state governments to hide budget overload and overcrowding in their penal systems. "During the 1990's, the number of private prisons increased rapidly. In 1990 there were roughly 15,000 private prison beds in the United States." By 2006 "the number of state and federal prisoners housed in private facilities was nearly 112,000" and growing. Prisoners in private incarceration arrangements now represent "more than 7% of the U.S. prison population."[103]

Acceptance of these swelling numbers, an increase of over 700 percent, disguises the fact that private prisons should have no place in a republican form of government. Their existence proves that the very idea of punishment has changed in American understandings. Punishment among a free people makes sense through public justice enforced under governmental authority and control, the only unit with the right to punish legally.

The priorities and legitimacies in legal usage change drastically if instead you are a private company paid by the state for taking charge of prisoners and continuing to discipline them. Nothing even remotely good about punishment remains in place when there is a primary financial advantage to those who benefit from the arrangement of incarceration. Profit rather than recognition of a prisoner's plight drives the wheel. Such thinking becomes possible only when theories of punishment turn exclusively on the role of the punisher.

Look at how many of the standard policies in imprisonment change. The profit motive dictates that you keep as many people as long as possible instead of preparing them for a return to civil life. The state pays you by the prisoner, and a half-filled facility is not a money maker. Overcrowding becomes an aspiration instead of a problem. The marginal utility curve in making a profit goes up and the marginal cost curve goes down with each new prisoner pushed into an already-crowded facility.[104] Correction and rehabilitation mean nothing in private prisons. They are expenses instead of concepts, and their records in these commercial ventures are miserable ones.

For the same reasons, managers of private prisons seek longer and tougher sentences from their legislatures. Money replaces legal needs. Minimizing costs dictates the construction of cheaper facilities with less expensive security arrangements and fewer personnel with poorer training and lower salaries. The combination makes many private prisons more dangerous than state prisons because of poor surveillance and high escape rates. Cronyism between politicians and entrepreneurs hired to manage these prisons follows as surely as the night does the day. Legislatures who support private prisons are invariably somewhere on the dole. If they were not on the dole, they would make private prisons illegal.

Scandal after scandal in for-profit arrangements reveals rampant corruption when money calls the tune. In Harpersville, Alabama, county courts have used a private probation company to manufacture and stack new fines in order to force people guilty of misdemeanors into a twenty-first-century version of "debtors' prison," the phrase used by a judge who tried to stop this "judicially sanctioned extortion racket."[105] The snowballing of extra fines by budget-strapped courts can also be found in Cambria County, Pennsylvania. In many places "this revenue-oriented approach" proceeds through for-profit companies hired by courts to collect fees with the right to add their own "hefty fees" sanctioned by legal threats of arrest and imprisonment.[106]

Journalistic investigations of private prisons reveal much worse. Privatization has made Louisiana the punishment capital of the world. The state's incarceration rate "is nearly triple Iran's, seven times China's, and 10 times Germany's." "One in 86 Louisiana adults is doing time, nearly double the national average," and "a majority of Louisiana inmates are housed in for-profit facilities." There is a reason for such high figures. In Louisiana "most prison entrepreneurs are rural sheriffs" who head for-profit companies and barter with the central system for bodies to keep their prison beds full; these beds, with the financial impulse behind them, are named "honey holes." Reveals one manager of a private prison, "We realized that prisons are like nursing homes, you need occupancy to be high." Louisiana has an entire economy "designed to make profits off of prisoners."[107]

Much naturally ensues from Louisiana's prison market. The managers of private prisons fight in the state legislature for harsh sentences and more time served. A second car-burglary conviction will get you twenty-four years in prison without parole. Passing bad checks might mean a ten-year sentence. "Murderers automatically receive life without parole on the guilty votes of as few as 10 of 12 jurors." Three drug convictions will put you away for the rest of your life. Louisiana has more prisoners serving sentences of life without parole than any other state.[108]

The financial well-being of whole communities in Louisiana is linked to private prison companies, and the finances depend on high sentencing levels for "keeping the beds full." Reform efforts have no chance against that economic necessity. "The lobbying muscle of the sheriffs, buttressed by a tough-on-crime electorate, keeps these harsh sentencing schemes firmly in place." One expert examiner of Louisiana's penal system observes, "You have people who are so invested in maintaining the system—not just the sheriffs, but judges, prosecutors, other people who have links to it. They don't want to see the prison system get smaller or the number of people in custody reduced, even though the crime rate is down."[109]

The profit motive creates a punishment regime out of control. Lest one assume that privatization issues are a Southern dilemma, New Jersey has fashioned a system that is just as appalling in the way its profit motive fails to protect prisoners in institutions misnamed "halfway houses." These so-called houses are huge, poorly constructed facilities with as many as a thousand beds and no meaningful supervision. "Roughly 10,000 prison inmates and parolees a year—equivalent to about 40 percent of the state prison population—now pass through the system of halfway houses" in New Jersey.[110]

Recognition of prison problems always comes from outside of them. In a ten-month journalistic investigation of New Jersey's private prisons, the *New York Times* found that "with little oversight, the state's halfway houses have mutated into a shadow corrections network, where drugs, gang activity, and violence, including sexual assaults, often go unchecked." How poorly run are these places? The *New York Times* counts the many ways. "Since 2005, roughly 5,100 inmates have escaped from the state's privately run halfway houses."

The newspaper's investigation uncovered falsification of records, serious custodial abuse of prisoners, extensive unpunished crime among inmates, drunken supervisors, little or no state oversight, and a predator-controlled atmosphere in the largest of these institutions. Deteriorating conditions go hand in glove with contractual agreements that stress cost cutting. To keep these facilities filled and therefore profitable, "the percentage of New Jersey inmates convicted of violent crimes but lodged in halfway houses has been rising to 21 percent [in 2012] from 12 percent in 2006," with murder, rape, and drug racketeering as the direct result.[111]

The turnover of officialdom in halfway houses is extreme. A former regional vice president of one of the companies spoke openly to the *New York Times* about problems in a Newark facility during his tenure there in the 1990s. "About 200 offenders walked away, many of whom had serious criminal records," and authorities made no attempt to find or punish escapees, who often committed new crimes. "Employees were often inexperienced, incompetent, untrained, and underpaid, and lacked the requisite skills to supervise and provide services." "Staff members had distorted loyalties, the ability to exploit certain offenders, look the other way, or abuse their authority." Government oversight of halfway houses remains "minimal and inefficient." Knowing what he does about current arrangements, this former official of private prisons adds, "I see that little has changed."[112]

Why is such rampant abuse allowed to continue? Whenever large sums of money are to be made, you can expect institutional momentum and political cover-ups to control thought. The same kind of favoritism found in Louisiana's privatization movement dominates New Jersey's. Friends of the governor hold important positions in these companies, contribute heavily to the political campaigns of elected officials who support the movement, have their own contacts appointed to political positions, and socialize with top elected officials. They also move back and forth between government employment and their moneymaking operations.[113]

Corruption is inevitable in such arrangements, but the real problems in the privatization of punishment run deeper. Prisons for profit defy every normative frame of reference, one reason they breed corruption. An attuned citizenry should know that making money off the misery of the imprisoned is unacceptable. Many citizens, to be sure, ignore these institutions, but they are helped by the false propriety and repute that law gives to them.

We have seen how disconnected the parts of American punishment regimes can be from each other in the separate functions they perform and the harshness that can result from failures in coordination that turn into a lack of joint responsibility. When no function really restrains another, separate identities develop independent habits without real oversight, and the next step is a short one. Governments imbued with this kind of institutional thinking outsource punishment with very little compunction and no effective control over the private institutions they create. The results have been alarming in more ways than one.

When too much money and the law go hand in hand, there is always going to be a problem. The enormous inmate populations that punitive sentencing has produced have left state penal institutions strapped without the financial means to cope effectively. Something had to give, and the prolonged recession of the first decades of the twenty-first century have made private prisons and overcrowding in them one answer. These arrangements become attractive because they provide a government guaranteed profit for the politically connected as long as there are no expensive forms of rehabilitation and security to interfere with that profit.[114]

But is a political bargain an attractive financial option for government? No one can accurately claim that "the $2 billion private prison industry" eases state budgets. Officials agree to the new industry to avoid personal reckonings over governmental deficits. They do so by arguing that prisons for profit are cheaper than state prisons, a contested assumption, and by hiding private prison budgets. Only the budgets of state prisons must be released to public scrutiny.

How are for-profit institutions cheaper, if they are? The lack of meaningful security and professional surveillance in crowded unsecured rooms cuts costs in half by increasing the risks to the inmates in them. Private prisons thrive and continue to expand in America at the expense of those inmates whose vulnerability counts for little when the gauge of merit, the bottom line, is the financial calculation in punishment.[115]

Lost in such mechanical reasoning are the wretched people actually in prison. They become pecuniary ciphers geared to the profit motive. Confronted with abuses in privatization, a state assemblyman in New Jersey openly dismisses them with precisely this kind of casually dehumanizing reference. "It's a cheaper way of doing business," he shrugs, "so that's why it behooves us to use that option."[116] It makes no difference that the objectified "option" or "business" destroys the product instead of helping it.

We have let this happen as a people without thinking of the human cost. Here and elsewhere in American punishment, we have created suffering that makes no sense in normative terms. The validation given to prisons for profit is, after all, only the extreme manifestation of a general phenomenon. State and federal prisons also destroy people with little or no concern from the outside world, and we need to stop and realize why this is happening.

Sooner or later, punishers turn the punished into objects to be dealt with. It is a natural propensity. When punishers go to work, they do not like to think about the essential bond, the more fundamental equality in a living human being that links them inextricably to the punished. By ignoring that bond, the system loses sight of what it is doing to people and begins to forget what a person is irreducibly understood to be. We are moving closer and closer to a disturbing boundary line in American punishment.

Human beings now count as transferable cargo measured in dollars and cents. They turn into someone else's property in ways that are reminiscent of the history of slavery in this country.[117] What does "being the object of property" mean? It means the struggle to reclaim "that from which one has been disinherited." When one is reduced to the "market theory" of others without the ability to participate, it takes "attention away from the full range of human potential." It separates self-possession from self-knowledge. These words and the ideas behind them come from one of the great contemporary essays on the meaning of slavery.[118] To what extent do they apply to the debasement of the imprisoned as it is practiced in today's punishment regime?

There is, in fact, a whole constitutional category very close to the degradation of being officially owned. The Thirteenth Amendment abolished slavery in the United States, but it did more. It maintained an exception to the rule. Passed in 1865, near the end of the Civil War, it states, "Neither slavery nor involuntary servitude, *except as a punishment for a crime whereof the party shall have been duly convicted,* shall exist within the United States."[119] How far from slavery is an American prisoner when cast into an officially sanctioned realm of involuntary servitude? We are about to find out.

5

The Legally Punished

On the whole, the problem of imprisonment and in general of punishing those who violate the law is one of the most disheartening ones that face modern civilization. It represents the breakdown of human intelligence as well as good will. It shows perhaps the ugliest phase of our human nature.

Morris R. Cohen, "Moral Aspects of the Criminal Law,"
Yale Law Journal, April 1940

The Difficulty in Knowing the Punished

The hardest chapter for most readers will be this one. Prison punishment has no bottom, and although there is no end to ugliness in the descent, we must take it. Responsibility for massive incarceration and what might be done about it depend on awareness. We have to see the punishment ground for what it is to ask one of the important questions. Do we know what we are doing?

The easiest preliminary answer is also the most tragic, and it responds to the puzzle raised at the end of the last chapter. The relation of American slavery to contemporary imprisonment and mass incarceration should be clear to everyone. The connection is racial profiling. African Americans make up 13 percent of the population today, but males in that category are 40 percent of prison populations. If current projections continue, one in three black men will go to prison in their lifetime, as opposed to one in seventeen white men.[1]

The loss in larger possibilities is staggering. "The odds of an African American man going to prison today are higher than the odds he will go to college, get married, or go into the military."[2] Everything continues to point in two directions for minorities: more aggravation and less opportunity than deserved.[3] For example, after the Supreme Court made federal sentencing guidelines advisory instead of mandatory as it did in 2005, black men again began to receive longer prison sentences than their white counterparts.[4]

Of course, statistics and comparisons, however revealing, only point to the punishing ground; they do not show it. Actually knowing what inmates endure presents a serious complication with no simple solution. Is punishment at this level something that we can really comprehend? To take the discrimination patterns just described, we can document racial profiling, but can we know what it means as a physical force when applied against those in prison? Some subjects defy explanation to an outsider, and this is surely one of them.

In a parallel worth pursuing, Charles Dickens presents the epistemological nature of the problem well in *Bleak House,* probably his greatest novel, when he describes "an iron barrier" between the poor and everyone else. "What the poor are to the poor," he writes, "is little known, excepting to themselves and God." Dickens tries to solve the problem by surrounding it with points of view, and he comes closest when Mr. Bucket, a detective of ambiguous intent, guides Mr. Snagsby, the timid proprietor of a law-stationery shop, on a night trip into the worst slum of London to find Jo, the destitute orphaned child who sweeps the streets. Snagsby is every person who has not seen what there is to see.

Dickens proves the complexity of his point with a lighted oil lantern. The lantern, in the hands of a policeman, pans across the ghetto crowds that swarm around the visitors like insects. Unlike insects, because they are made up of human beings, these swarms fade away the moment "the angry bulls-eye glare" falls on them. They are "a dream of horrible faces" and "imprisoned demons," a nightmare vision that belongs to Snagsby but through him to every reader. Snagsby, "who has lived in London all his life, can scarce believe his senses," and when he is restored to his own part of London, he remains "confused" and "doubtful of the reality" all around him.[5]

The problem of describing the poor is ours in rendering prison punishment. No outsider can fully grasp it, and no inmate can avoid the frustration, limitation, and embellishment that mark inside accounts. We either become a Snagsby in this chapter or we learn what we can from a variety of points of view, as Dickens did, and our ambiguous guide will be the lifelong prisoner and murderer Jack Henry Abbott, who, whatever his many limitations, wrote the most powerful prison narrative in American literature, *In the Belly of the Beast,* in 1981.

Abbott is an unreliable narrator, but there are no fully reliable narrators on this subject, and in addition to an accurate description of prison horrors that he has experienced, he represents the problem in incarceration that defies solution. Abbott is the archetypal predator who mesmerizes American society. He takes us immediately to the heart of the problem. What is to be done with the dangerous criminals that punishment regimes of America have done so much to help create?

Is prison itself partially responsible for creating Jack Abbott? "No one has ever come out of prison a better man," he insists in self-defense, and he proves the point in singular fashion. He is the person you never want to meet on the street. Unfortunately, someone does. If you read *In the Belly of the Beast* with care, it will come as no surprise that Abbott, just weeks after gaining his freedom from prison on the celebrity of his book, killed again in a senseless minor quarrel.[6]

So yes, the decision to make this defective observer a guide is questionable, even upsetting, but consider the reasons for it. Fully trained "participant observers" who study prison life for years admit serious limits in comprehending a world fundamentally closed to them.[7] For his part, Abbott repeatedly dismisses all outside experts on the subject (5, 78, 114). How, he asks in smoldering rage, can outsiders know "the hidden dark side"? How can they hope to understand "the foul underbelly everyone hides from everyone else" in prison? (13). In the words of another long-term prisoner, "Doing all day behind bars in a hard-core prison is a lot like explaining sex to a virgin."[8]

The phrase "doing all day" is important in this last remark. No prison storyteller who wants to hold readers can afford the boredom that defines the enforced doing of nothing. "The reported stories fail to grab us because, for the most part, nothing *happens*," explains a journalist. "It isn't the horror of the time at hand, but the unimaginable sameness of the time ahead that makes prisons unendurable." Not "the lock and the key" but "the lock and clock" dominate inmate settings. "That's why no one who has been inside a prison, if only for a day, can ever forget the feeling. Time stops." Time rendered meaningless divides inside from outside. "What prisoners try to convey to the free is how the presence of time as something being done to you, instead of something you do things with, alters the mind at every moment."[9]

Context is always going to be a problem in describing prison. Recognition of public indifference leads to sensationalism in journalistic coverage to create interest. Inside, the oversight of officialdom produces a tortured language of evasion. Anger and shame, as well as fear over what authorities might do in response, distort what can be written. Between outside experts, officials, and inmates, we get a thrice-told tale with similarities but many discrepancies over what happens and the reasons for it.

This chapter attempts to peel the layers of the prison onion while realizing that the innermost layer will still be a sticky mess. Outside accounts offer a general picture of what society feels it is doing to the punished. Legal decisions give required glimpses of prison life, and they come next, although they are most revealing for what they will not contemplate. A third layer, that of prisoners' accounts, will then complicate these records.

Abbott, with *In the Belly of the Beast,* provides a floating perspective, mostly for verification, across these three levels, and he questions even as he confirms the larger problem under discussion in each section. Admitting his own obvious instability, Abbott argues "this instability is *caused* by a lifetime of incarceration" (11). He appears regularly in these pages because he represents an underlying truth. Cause and victim, he exemplifies the harshness that defines American punishment today and the reason for it.

More problems than solutions will emerge from the layers in these points of view, and the differences among them help explain why nothing is done. But if intractability gives no answers, one must start somewhere. The issues recognized in common across these separate accounts beg for solutions, and that degree of commonality can be preparation for thinking about when and how better answers might be forthcoming.

Society Looks at the Punished

Americans like to think of themselves as belonging to a society of opportunity in which exceptionalism gives identity. Success, no matter how achieved, is admired, and it has a corollary. Failure is your fault and close to a social sin. If you are also in jail through that failure, you have proved yourself to be unsocial as well as antisocial in a consensual culture. You have become a complete failure with no entitlement to standing in the world. You are a total loser in the common struggle for success, and you deserve to be where you are.

Over and over again, this is the point that Jack Henry Abbott refuses to acknowledge. *In the Belly of the Beast*, he will not accept that his life in prison has been "self-inflicted." Contrition is the furthest thing from his mind. The system has made him fail, and he has his own explanation of how prisoners occupy the lowest caste as untouchables in a democratic society (15–16, 78, 113, 118, 165). Prisoners, he contends, immediately become "public enemies" who deserve anything that happens to them when it comes to punishment: "This country has an excessive number of people who take *pride*—openly or secretly—in the fact that their government is so inhumane, so evil; take pride in the fact that their government so thoroughly crushes men they consider 'enemies'" (58).

The quotation is doubly significant. It helps establish Abbott's qualified appeal as our guide to prison life. An adult existence spent almost entirely in prison has kept Abbott in a confessed state of arrested adolescence where only angry extremes appeal to him (12–13). We glimpse this not so much in his claim that government can be "inhumane"—it can be—but in the unearned rhetorical add-on "so evil." Hyperbolic expression may be all we can expect from a writer who "experiences this world as a horrible nightmare," and yet the essential point he makes is true (3). Society does regard convicted criminals as public enemies subject to unlimited punishment as long as the term "enemy" is thought to apply.

A heartbreaking irony of communal dismissal lies in the way prisoners accept it as their own. "Something deep within me . . . turns over in its grave each time I notice that I look like my 'brothers,'" Abbott acknowledges. Many inmates accept their "outlander" status. Some, and Abbott is one, proudly embrace the further status of "*outlaw*." But Abbott sees something else in the looks around him. "It is the face of men both *declassed* and *decultured*" (85). A serious prison sentence puts you at the bottom without conceivable aspirations.

American prisons therefore contain but also create people who can never return successfully to civil life. Abbott agrees that "the most dangerous convicts in American prison history are behind bars today," and he knows he has become one of them (20). "The model we emulate is a fanatically defiant and alienated individual." At the summit of this hierarchy of total alienation are "dangerous killers who act alone and *without* emotion, who act with calculation and principles, to avenge themselves, establish and defend their principles with acts of murder that usually evade prosecution by law" (13).

Anxiety over this level of criminality is one reason society punishes all criminals more harshly than it needs to even though the level that Abbott describes is much smaller than society thinks. Pause, however, to consider how Abbott has come to his conclusion. His need for identity in the cage built for criminals has led him to create a status for himself at the top of it. He makes himself the symbol of what cannot be rehabilitated. He deliberately stands in the way of thoughts about what meaningful reform might mean.

One has to believe the angry writer, if not the thinker. Abbott readily concedes that he has only just begun to learn how to think in his thirties after a youth of blind reactions to the pressures around him (18). How difficult has that been? His struggle to become a writer has been "learning to swim on land" (21).[10] Just as his readers are disconnected from the experience of prison, so Abbott gives an account totally estranged from the society he addresses, but with the compulsive need to relate his expertise as a lifelong inmate. His value depends on revealing a world hidden from us, a world we do not want to recognize but know exists.

Society, Abbott teaches, does not care what happens to inmates in prison, and he proves it through his own experience. He receives regular beatings from prison guards (sometimes while shackled or even spread-eagled on a board). He is placed in blackout cells with no light for weeks on end, put in cold strip cells without clothing for much longer periods of time, left in solitary confinement in the tiniest of cells for months on end, starved, made to beg for water that is withheld, taunted over the death of his mother, threatened with death, and forcibly injected with harmful drugs (23–35).

The extremes are what count here because Abbott can prove "the law has never punished anyone for hurting me" (117). "If I were beaten to death tomorrow," he explains, "my record would go before the coroner's jury—before anyone who had the power to investigate—and my 'past record of violence' would vindicate my murderers" (16). Why hasn't the law punished anyone for what are obviously beatings beyond all need or reason?

We have already heard the answer from authority, but it means more coming from the knowledge of the punished. "It is held in this country that the punishment *ends* upon sentencing and commitment to prison," writes Abbott. "This means a prisoner is not punished further while he is in prison" (111). The explanation sounds extreme, even bizarre, until we remember that it is given officially by Associate Justice Clarence Thomas in *Farmer v. Brennan* and again and again in the judicial decisions of the next section.[11]

The law's general disregard of inmate abuse must be understood against the fact that the pain and forms of extreme deprivation regularly inflicted are considerable. *In the Belly of the Beast* was the first generally available popular narrative to inform the public that rape and other forms of violence are endemic in prison life. It was also the first to show that prison authorities are complicit in the phenomena at two levels: first, by leaving much of the social management of prisons to the inmates, and second, by using that arrangement as an instrument in their own desire to punish inmates (79–80).

If claims about terrible treatment throughout *In the Belly of the Beast* sound excessive, there is plenty of more recent corroboration from sources other than Abbott. You can be gang-raped without being convicted when put in a crowded holding cell after an arrest on civil disobedience charges, and the attacks can come with the active instigation of correctional officers.[12]

Abbott identifies stark alternatives in prison. You are either "a predator," one ready to use violence at the slightest provocation, or "a punk," one who succumbs to predators. "If you are a man," he explains, "you must either kill or turn the tables on anyone who propositions you with threats of force" (79). Confirmation of Abbott's claims comes in recent testimony before the National Prison Rape Elimination Act Commission: "[Prisoner rape] takes minor criminals and turns them into violent felons."[13] Those who go to prison face impossible choices. They enter "a violent whirlwind of moral, mental, and physical destruction" (111).[14]

No one in American life today should be surprised by these perils. As early as Clint Eastwood's movie *Escape from Alcatraz* in 1979, the atrocities of prison life, including rape, have been familiar cinematic fodder. Thirty years later and counting, television regularly depicts the unpleasantries in prison as entertainment. The popular television series *OZ*, a dark prison drama, ran for fifty-six episodes between 1997 and 2003 on the HBO cable network. It featured life in a prison named Emerald City, complete with gangs, murders, rapes, and prison-authority corruption.[15] *The Wire*, a police show set around a group of Baltimore detectives, aired in regular episodes from 2002 to 2008. Its entire second season concentrated on the evils of prison life. Wrote its creator, David Simon, "I'm not about pretty."[16]

Nothing about prison is pretty, but how ugly must it become? The levels of pernicious behavior are now so ingrained that attempts to reform them can end up doing more harm than good. Three aspects of penal policy help reveal how the best intentions go awry. Indeterminate sentencing, solitary confinement, and various forms of physical deprivation are all worth a closer look in this regard. They deserve special attention because they convey an underlying reality. The way in which strategies to improve prisons have failed suggests that nothing is going to change unless the nature of the system itself and how we regard the whole idea of punishment are changed.

Twentieth-century reform movements introduced indeterminate sentencing in the hope that the incentive to work for shorter sentences would relate to the objectives of rehabilitation. The original idea depends on a flexible schedule between a minimal and a longer number of years. The length of the sentence is not decided when judgment is imposed but later by an administrative penal unit while the sentence is being served, an arrangement understood to be "an instrument of enlightened reform and a boon to offenders."[17] The exact opposite rather quickly became true. "Although nothing in theory made indeterminate sentences longer than others, in practice indeterminate sentences substantially increased the time offenders spent in prison."[18]

Jack Abbott is steeped, as usual, in the practice rather than the theory: "When the judicial sentence is *indeterminate,* he [the prisoner] is sentenced to a longer term every time any pig [correctional officer] feels like it." When an inmate "is disciplined, punished for infractions of prison 'rules'—which are as arbitrary as the currents of the wind—he is in effect *resentenced* to prison before the parole board," and "there are no procedures before the parole board that guarantee him 'judicial due process'" (112–113). Indeterminate sentencing leaves an inmate at the mercy of the punishment regime and its wishes, not to the enlightened theorists who proposed the idea in the first place.

The original theory behind solitary confinement is just as benevolent but even more disastrous when put into practice. In the new United States of 1787, the idea took hold first in the Philadelphia Society for Ameliorating the Miseries of Public Prisons and became regular practice "as a morally progressive social experiment in the 1820s by Quakers, who wanted lawmakers to replace mutilations, amputation, and the death penalty with rehabilitation. The hope was that long periods of introspection would help criminals repent."[19] Quaker doctrine posits an inner light as the path toward revelation, but in the secular approach of the law, prolonged solitary confinement has become a disaster. "Human beings are social animals." "Whether in Walpole or Beirut or Hanoi, all human beings experience isolation as torture."[20]

The reality of torture in solitary confinement has been documented early and late, but it has not kept generations of American lawmakers from making it a standard punishment. As early as 1830, as we saw in Chapter 2, Jeremy Bentham could cite "the best authorities" for "ascertaining" that solitary confinement causes "madness, despair, or more commonly a stupid apathy."[21] Charles Dickens at a glance came to the same conclusion in 1842 on viewing the experiments at the Cherry Hill State Prison in Philadelphia.[22]

The Supreme Court of the United States, similarly appalled, came close to abolishing solitary confinement as early as 1890. Questioning the use of it in *In re Medley,* Justice Samuel Miller described the consequences with devastating accuracy: "A considerable number of the prisoners fell, after even short confinement, into a semi-fatuous condition, from which it was next to impossible to arouse them, and others became violently insane; others still, committed suicide; while those who survived the ordeal better are not generally reformed and in most cases did not recover sufficient mental activity to be of any subsequent service to the community."[23]

Detailed studies show that solitary confinement leads very quickly to psychological deterioration and toward aggressive rebellion as the main resource in sustaining an isolated person's dissolving identity.[24] In short, solitary encourages what it seeks to punish in the first place: impairment and insubordination. You are placed in solitary because you have been found to be mentally disturbed or physically aggressive, and solitary disturbs you more and makes you more aggressive. Experiments have verified both insights from a more positive direction. If you reduce the number of inmates in solitary confinement with more cooperative relations between guards and inmates and give more zones of liberty to inmates, you improve mental health and reduce levels of violence and resistance in prisons.[25]

Again, Jack Abbott supplies personal corroboration. *"The composition of the mind is altered,"* he tells us of his extensive experiences in solitary confinement. "When I was let out, I could not orient myself." Everything "bewildered me." "I was slow and slack-jawed and confused—but beneath the surface I raged" (50–51). Under these pressures, rebellion becomes Abbott's way of maintaining a self. "I have never gone a month in prison without incurring disciplinary action for violating 'rules,'" but he also notes, "A man's mind can be turned to steel in prison." "I know how to live through anything they could possibly dish up for me" (5, 14, 41).

Eerie confirmation of the torture in solitary confinement can be found in Edgar Allan Poe's tale of terror "The Pit and the Pendulum." Just as Poe's character in the darkened cell of the Spanish Inquisition counts stones, feels for cracks in the walls, diagnoses the exact dimensions of his cell, uses movement to gauge time, becomes fascinated by the insects and rats that share his isolation, assumes malevolence in every external source, and rails aloud against his unseen controllers, so Jack Abbott and other prisoners in solitary confinement follow each and every one of these patterns in trying to hold on to their sanity.[26]

Anyone who studies solitary confinement concludes that it is a form of torture, and international law has declared it to be so.[27] Nonetheless, more than 100,000 inmates in American prisons suffer in prolonged solitary confinement today, and those numbers have been reached through dramatic increases in recent years.[28] The figures are inexact, and the actual number is probably even higher because some states and the federal government do not release full counts. Since the terrorist attack of September 11, 2001, supermaximum-security prisons known as "supermaxes" have cut off virtually all media access for "security reasons."[29]

Why should excessive secrecy be necessary in dealing with totally incapacitated prisoners in solitary confinement with no contact with others? Jack Abbott asks the question that is also an explanation of all prison concealment. "The law *does* forbid the methodical use of torture and corporeal punishment," he reasons. But "how can anyone *prove* such practices exist when only *convicts* witness it?" (58).

Punishment takes two basic forms: infliction and deprivation. The third and last reform movement mentioned above, physical deprivation, was originally conceived to be a truly merciful form of correction, but the line between infliction and deprivation is hardly exact, and everything

depends on how much deprivation. The tendency of punishment regimes toward greater severity takes care of the rest. Limiting clothing
to almost nothing, reducing food to a bare minimum, shining bright
light twenty-four hours a day, plunging someone into continuous darkness, restricting movement sharply, withholding all forms of entertainment, and refusing meaningful outside contact are the most obvious
deprivations used in prisons today. Jack Abbott suffered all of them in
extreme form during his years in prison.

It is, however, the sudden rise of the supermaximum-security prison,
the supermax, that has turned "deprivation of sensory stimuli" into an
art form. In 1984 there was only one prison, the federal penitentiary at
Marion, Illinois, that could be termed a supermax. Today there are at least
fifty-seven supermax prisons in forty states, an increase that accurately
mirrors the punitive era in American concepts of punishment.[30]

Supermax prisons are shrouded in secrecy. Their "dynamics of domination, control, subordination, and submission are fundamentally different from those in regular maximum security prisons." The approxi-
mately 20,000 prisoners in current supermax prisons are held in
prolonged solitary confinement for at least a year and often much longer without contact with other prisoners or even prison staff. In a supermax, inmate movement and environmental stimuli are restricted to
cells of poured concrete roughly ten feet by twelve feet. The cells have a
built-in combination steel toilet and sink and a sliding device or small
trapdoor low down on a steel door that allows food to be passed imper-
sonally to a prisoner by an invisible hand.[31]

These kinds of prisons do not exist in Europe. With elaborate mechanisms that guarantee complete isolation coupled to continuous video
surveillance, they are a technologically driven American replica of Jeremy Bentham's all-seeing but unseen panopticon. Any movement outside a small individual cell takes place in shackles for a short exercise
period once a day or for a shower once a week, both alone.

Disobedience by an inmate in a supermax prison adds time to what
is usually an automatic one-year term in solitary. A show of aggression
is punished severely even though "the line between aggression precipitated by a sense of injustice, and aggression precipitated by mental illness is not clear." In one known example among the many unknown, "a
prisoner who threw water and spat on a guard was offered a plea bargain of eight years." Displeasing a guard in any way can reduce the food

that is shoved through the trapdoor to a "mealoaf," a tasteless bar with just enough nutrients to keep a prisoner alive.[32] Can anyone avoid the calculated cruelty in the deprivation that is mealoaf?

Little more in detail is known about supermax prisons, which are built in rural areas with sharp restrictions on outside contact. They are kept full and contain prisoners who have displeased authorities or have been violent in other prisons. Regular deprivation reaches punitive levels that are difficult to imagine unless you are on the receiving end for an enforced period of time.

Robert Hood, the former warden at the federal supermax prison in Florence, Colorado, gives perhaps the shortest accurate definition of this kind of institution. Interviewed about supermax prisons on the television program *60 Minutes*, he called them "a clean version of hell."[33] The phrase is telling. The Christian version of Hell is deliberately and very openly filthy. The demons are physically loathsome and some of the misery of the condemned comes from their inability to avoid the foulness and stench all around them. What, then, does it mean to call the American "version of hell" *clean?* The pain of the condemned sinner is hot and visible; that of the convicted inmate cool and hidden. The emphasis on cleanliness disguises the nature of punishment in a country that does not want it to be seen.

Official avoidance of inmate distress takes several forms. Courts looking at the pain that prisoners experience in a supermax or any other prison generally restrict their consideration to infliction rather than deprivation in punishment, and they use another distinction set in law by Congress and many states when they dismiss mental pain in the name of physical pain. Section 1997e(e) of the Prison Litigation Reform Act of 1995 provides that no prisoner can bring a civil action "for mental or emotional injury suffered while in custody without a prior showing of physical injury."[34]

What is the utility in this distinction? Mental pain belongs to the category of deprivation rather than infliction, a difference with little meaning in the extreme situations that actually apply in most prisons. When does deprivation, instead of an acceptable gradation, become an unacceptable physical degradation and hence an infliction? That is a question courts are reluctant to ask, and the law helps that reluctance.

The judiciary has repeatedly failed to respond to situations that would seem to have crossed the line into unacceptable degradation. Prisoners have been denied relief when "placed in cells with human waste and subjected to the screams of psychiatric patients; or forced to sleep for two months, despite repeated complaints, on a concrete floor in a cramped cell with a mentally ill HIV-positive prisoner who urinated on him; or had urine thrown at her by a guard which splashed on her face and shirt."[35]

Are there rules for when degradation becomes an infliction? Again, the courts are silent. Strip searches are part of prison life, but should a federal court of appeals have dismissed damage claims when prison officials "ordered prisoners to strip naked, and performed body cavity searches while members of the opposite sex were present; physically harassed some prisoners; . . . made harassing comments to an inmate because of his perceived sexual orientation; and ordered one prisoner to 'tap dance' while naked"?[36]

Unacceptable degradation defines prison life in most inside accounts of it. "You are indoctrinated to blindly accept *anything* done to you," writes Jack Abbott (16). Guards, he explains, are "the very symbol of injustice." *"Prisoners do not make guards to be what they are,"* he adds. "The *state* does. It gives them *arbitrary* power over prisoners," and "they embrace it *as a way of life*" (60–61). "We are not animals, but we are herded like animals" and therefore behave like animals. "It is the prison system in America that drives [inmates] to outrages on one another" (84).

Nothing attracts in this picture. Nor does deprivation as a form of degradation end with release from prison for those who have managed to regain their freedom through "good behavior." Laws continue to qualify the civil rights of individuals with criminal records. State and federal statutes limit "ability to obtain employment, eligibility for public housing, eligibility for public assistance and food stamps, eligibility for student loans, access to records for non–criminal justice purposes, voting rights, driver's license privileges, and rights to be foster and adoptive parents."[37]

These and other continuing deprivations are serious barriers for a released prisoner trying to reenter society, and this is especially true given the lengths of many sentences and the conditions in prisons today. If you happen to be one of the more than 140,000 inmates serving a life term in the United States—now an unprecedented 10 percent of the prison population—you gain your freedom only after decades in prison, if at all.[38]

Put yourself in the situation of an inmate released after many years of confinement. Your family, if there still is one, has moved on with new generations that absorb time, attention, and identity. You have no resources and have not had the chance to learn marketable skills in prison. If you have mastered anything, it is probably a more detailed knowledge of crime. There may be no one left close enough to you to help, and if there is someone, your reappearance may only remind that person and his family of the shame and fear you brought on them years ago.[39]

You have gotten out, but your situation and prospects for leading a straight life in society look bleak. Perhaps that is why the legal system has shown such limited interest in you while in prison, and why it puts restrictions and surveillance mechanisms in the path of your recovery now that you are free. Is it right for the law, which has the responsibility of preparing a return to civil life, to have the same level of suspicion that society does?

Law Looks at the Punished

Legal suspicion begins and often ends with the prisoner. Courts have been reluctant to question the practices of officials who are charged with abuse of prisoners. Time and again, the prisoner has no case. The clearest statement of "deference to the appropriate prison authorities" comes in *Turner v. Safley* (1987) when the Supreme Court confirms " 'courts are ill equipped to deal with the increasingly urgent problems of prison administration and reform' . . . all of which are peculiarly within the province of the legislative and executive branches of government." It follows that "separation of powers concerns counsel a policy of judicial restraint." *Turner* does not announce a hands-off policy regarding challenges to the treatment of prisoners, but it comes close.[40]

Two narrower doctrinal holdings make the Supreme Court's hesitation to address allegations of abuse a legal reality. In 1984 *Hudson v. Palmer* made it close to impossible for inmates to ask for most civil rights protections. Ten years later *Farmer v. Brennan* in 1994 set a very high bar, using "the deliberate indifference doctrine," for finding prison authorities guilty of abuse. These cases, along with others alleging abuse, deserve attention not just for the deference shown prison authorities but for the picture of prison life given in them. Since judicial decisions belong to a public record, they can also be said to inform a general citizenry.

Hudson v. Palmer makes it clear that Ted Hudson, a prison guard, maliciously destroyed inmate Russell Palmer's lawful personal effects during a random search of Palmer's prison cell "for no reason other than harassment." Hudson then instigated a related "false charge" of "destroying state property" against Palmer, which led to additional punishment. The trial court openly acknowledged the harassment, as well as the artificially instigated prison hearing over destroyed property that required Palmer to "reimburse the State for the cost of the material destroyed." It did so recognizing that the hearing brought an official reprimand with length-of-sentence implications. The property that Palmer supposedly destroyed? It turned out to have been a torn pillowcase found in a trash can near Palmer's cell bunk.[41]

Injustice is all over these facts, and an intermediate appellate decision agreed. It upheld Palmer's claim that "the 'shakedown' search was unreasonable." The appellate court granted Palmer "a 'limited privacy right' . . . against searches conducted solely to harass or to humiliate." Be that as it may, the Supreme Court did more than just reverse this court's decision. It adopted the prison authority's defense down the line. It accepted the prison authority's contention that "the Court of Appeals erred in holding that Respondent had even a limited privacy right in his cell," and it further accepted the authority's request that the court "adopt the 'bright line' rule that prisoners have no legitimate expectation of privacy in their individual cells that would entitle them to Fourth Amendment protection [against unreasonable searches and seizures]."[42]

The facts, fully acknowledged in the lower court, disappeared in the Supreme Court's decision. In its own interpretation of *Hudson v. Palmer,* the court decided "society is not prepared to recognize as legitimate *any* subjective expectation of privacy that a prisoner might have in his prison cell."[43] It ignored the issue of harassment behind the original dispute, and the rhetorical means it used to defend its decision are as significant as the decision itself.

Chief Justice Warren Burger began his majority opinion in *Hudson v. Palmer* with the seemingly irrelevant fact that Palmer, the complaining prisoner, was serving sentences for forgery, grand larceny, and bank robbery. Why are these extraneous facts more relevant than the ones in actual dispute? In court, as well as in prison, an inmate is understood

first through suspicion and the stereotype of his criminal offense. Burger then digressed for several pages on prisoners "who have a demonstrated proclivity for antisocial criminal, and often violent, conduct." So dangerous is prison life that correctional officers deserve a free hand in monitoring it.[44]

Nowhere in the record of *Hudson v. Palmer* is there any indication except the trumped-up charge of ripping a pillowcase that inmate Palmer had been violent or antisocial in prison, but that counted for nothing in the court's abstract balancing act: "the interest of society in the security of its penal institutions and the interest of the prisoner in privacy within his cell." With this balance of projected interests in mind, the court decided "imprisonment carries with it the circumscription or loss of many significant rights," and it gave prison management absolute priority to conduct random searches as an "effective weapon" against the criminals it guards. The language used reveals everything. Talk of an "effective weapon" assumes a state of war between guards and their prisoners.[45]

After *Hudson v. Palmer,* and with the addition of *Farmer v. Brennan* in 1994, the constitutional route left to prisoners against abuse comes down to the rarely used Eighth Amendment prohibition of cruel and unusual punishments, and the amendment applies only when prison officials can be proved to have shown a " 'deliberate indifference' to substantial risk of serious harm."[46] The three qualifying adjectives— "deliberate," "substantial," and "serious"—make the standard of reaching the Eighth Amendment difficult for an inmate to meet, especially since only obvious physical violence or the prospect of it defines "serious harm." Even prison rape does not always meet that test, presumably because it occurs so frequently.[47] The courts are inclined to look the other way because "prisons are dangerous places" that house "violent people in close quarters, where some level of brutality and sexual aggression among them is inevitable no matter what the guards do."[48]

Rape, of course, is a crime that should be punished, and it was generally known to be widespread in prison for decades before 1994, the year the Supreme Court first reached the issue in *Farmer v. Brennan,* a case we looked at briefly for other reasons in Chapter 3.[49] Dee Farmer, who had altered his body and dress to appear entirely female, was serving time for credit-card fraud in a protected unit of a relatively mild correctional facility because of his sexual vulnerability. When he was transferred without explanation into the general and more violent male population of the United States Penitentiary in Terre Haute, Indiana, he was repeatedly beaten and raped by other inmates and became HIV positive through their assaults. Farmer, in bringing suit, alleged "deliberate indifference" by prison authorities for failing to take precautions "despite knowledge that the penitentiary had a violent environment and a history of inmate assaults, and despite knowledge that [Farmer], as a transsexual, who 'projects feminine characteristics,' would be particularly vulnerable to sexual attack."[50]

This time, in an apparent breakthrough for prisoners, the Supreme Court reversed an earlier summary judgment in favor of prison officials, but one must look to the remand of the case back to the trial court to determine the likelihood of serious redress. A prison official can be held liable under the Eighth Amendment "for denying humane conditions of confinement . . . only if he knows that inmates face a substantial risk of serious harm and disregards that risk by failing to take reasonable measures to abate it" (1972–1973). Upping the ante, the court then defined "substantial risk" to mean "excessive risk" (1979).

Justice David Souter's tortured logic is worth examining as a living text. In writing for the court, he indicates that the harm alleged "must be objectively, 'sufficiently serious'" because "'only the unnecessary and wanton infliction of pain implicates the Eighth Amendment.'" "To violate the Cruel and Unusual Punishments Clause, a prison official must have a 'sufficiently culpable mind,'" a "state of mind" so clear that it exhibits "'deliberate indifference to inmate health or safety'" (1976–1977). Souter takes these remarks from earlier case law to confirm the "deliberate indifference" doctrine, but he also has to admit that the court in previous cases "never paused to explain the meaning of the term 'deliberate indifference'" (1977–1978). Nor does Souter supply his own meaning here. "We reject petitioner's invitation to adopt an objective test for deliberate indifference" (1979).

Instead of a definition, *Farmer v. Brennan* surrounds the doctrine of deliberate indifference with qualifying language. The standard must be "more blameworthy than negligence" and requires "more than ordinary lack of due care for the prisoner's interests or safety." "An Eighth Amendment claimant must show more than 'indifference,' deliberate or otherwise." "An official's failure to alleviate a significant risk that he should have perceived but did not, while no cause for commendation, cannot under our cases be condemned as the infliction of punishment." Why not? "The Eighth Amendment," Souter explains in the court's clincher, "does not outlaw cruel and unusual 'conditions'; it outlaws cruel and unusual 'punishments'" (1978–1979).

Very little legal purchase is left to inmates if one studies the qualifications in *Farmer v. Brennan*. The court turns back every inmate plea for clarification. It resists the argument that the absence of an objective definition of "deliberate indifference" leaves prison officials "free to ignore obvious dangers to inmates," and it refuses to allow an inmate to parse the doctrine through judicial opinions in the way that the court has just done. "Deliberate indifference" must be read loosely and apparently only by judges. It might not even be a doctrine. The phrase may be nothing more than "a judicial gloss, appearing neither in the Constitution nor in a statute" (1980–1981).

The restrictions and qualifications in *Turner v. Safley, Hudson v. Palmer*, and *Farmer v. Brennan* tell us two things of importance about cases on the abuse of prisoners. First, only an egregious set of facts and circumstances will get a complaining inmate successfully into court. If Dee Farmer had not become HIV positive through repeated sexual assaults, how much attention would his complaint have received? The mere abuse of prisoners will not reach the high bar of judicial cognizance. Second, the grimmest realities of prison life remain the way Jack Abbott described them in 1981. Things have, in fact, become demonstrably worse in some areas of abuse because of greater overcrowding everywhere. A federal appeals court in 1991 indicated as much in one explanation for denying a rape victim recovery.[51]

Abbott describes Russell Palmer's predicament and that of every other prisoner *In the Belly of the Beast* when he says that nothing of personal value is safe in a prison cell. There can be no identity through personal possessions: "Any little odd-or-end you happen to have, anything that is neither issued to all inmates nor explicitly allowed in a pathetic list of half a dozen items, is confiscated" (83). Abbott also sees Dee Farmer's plight. "Every single prisoner every day must exist with the *imminent* threat of assault at *the very least*—and from any quarter" (112). The arbitrary power left to prison guards is not challenged in the cases just discussed nor in the ones to follow. "Always, *always* every guard in prison is a tyrant," Abbott argues, "and prisoners are his subjects" (56).

A terrible irony rules the legal rhetoric of prisoner-abuse cases. Usually implicit but always there, court rhetoric runs something like this in its address to a complaining inmate: you have helped make this prison a dangerous place and so have no right to complain when prison authorities contribute to those dangers or your personal lack of safety. A more comfortable logic covers the irony. You are here not by your choice but by our choice and cannot now hope to make choices about an environment we have created for you. Remember that you are the punished. Your antisocial behavior forced us to bring you here, and you now have no right to claim social amenities or social protections that your crimes so manifestly denied to others.

Irony and logic work together through stereotypical inversions in these cases. The fact that prisoners have collectively made prison dangerous trumps their individual rights to better protection, while only individuals receive standing in a court of law. Simultaneously, the collective irresponsibility of the punished, as convicted criminals, covers the individual unfairness shown by a correctional officer. A prison guard's malice can be made to disappear in the "monumental tasks" that prison authorities have been asked to perform.[52] As Justice Harry Blackmun recognizes in his concurrence, searching for a stronger holding in *Farmer v. Brennan,* "The Court's unduly narrow definition of punishment blinds it to the reality of prison life."[53]

Overcrowding naturally contributes to many cases of questioned abuse, but where does that leave the responsibility of prison authorities? In *Whitnack v. Douglas County* (1994), the United States Court of Appeals for the Eighth Circuit held that holding convicted prisoners awaiting sentence and pretrial detainees in a filthy cell did not constitute cruel and unusual punishment because there was no proof of "deprivation of a single, identifiable human need." The court did admit that the conditions presented were "deplorable."[54]

How deplorable were the prison conditions in the Douglas County jail? "Cell C-18's toilet was covered with dried feces on both the inside and outside, the sink was covered with hair and vomit, the floor was covered with garbage and rotting food, and the walls were covered with dried human mucus"; there may also have been "a skin problem allegedly caused by insects in Cell C-18." Can we assume there were no other available cells to contain these prisoners? Perhaps so, but there is some evidence of malice in play. The holding–prison guard not only refused to move the complainants, he refused to give them cleaning supplies to improve where they were.[55]

It may be harder to blame overcrowding in *Wilson v. Wright* (1998). The eighteen-year-old plaintiff, "a 5'8" tall, 136 pound white male" with "a low-security classification," was soon assaulted and raped when assigned to share a double cell with "a thirty-eight-year-old, six-foot one-inch, 290 pound African-American male" rapist and child molester with "a high-security classification" and a previous record of abusing prisoners. Even so, the United States District Court for the Eastern District of Virginia deferred to prison authorities and granted summary judgment for the defense. The assigning correctional officer might have known of "a general risk to the prison population," but plaintiff had not proved that the officer "was deliberately indifferent to a specific risk" even though the plaintiff had "urgently requested a cell change" and been refused.[56]

Can one avoid the conclusion that the legal system protected one of its own in *Wilson v. Wright*? The defendant, the assigning correctional officer, denied that the rape took place despite medical evidence to the contrary, denied any memory of personally reviewing the files of both prisoners at the time of assignment despite the fact that "prison policies" mandated it, and further denied any mistakes made in the performance of "all . . . assigned duties in a responsible manner." The three denials compete with each other, but together they overwhelm the charge of "deliberate indifference." The answering court condemned prison rape, but "this does not mean that restrictive or even harsh prison conditions must be avoided." The law has to assume "a sentence of imprisonment appropriately requires that an inmate endure many hardships."[57]

What is the vision of the punished in these statements? Why shouldn't "harsh prison conditions" be avoided whenever possible? The notion that imprisonment "appropriately requires . . . many hardships" admits that time served is not enough of a penalty for someone convicted of a crime, any crime. The statements reek of complicity. They convey that prison authorities do not have to concern themselves with anything other than the bare minimal circumstances of life in prison. "Restrictive" conditions can "appropriately" be "harsh" conditions.

Consciously or not, the law has moved the line where it will show concern, and even then, seemingly unacceptable conditions will require a level of proof almost impossible to meet. An easy claim of ignorance protected the prison guard in *Wilson v. Wright*. What possible meaning can the distinction between "a general risk" and "a specific risk" have for a vulnerable and weak inmate housed with a powerful serial rapist?

Three more recent cases all involve direct abuse of prisoners by guards and reach more deeply into the state's responsibility for injustice in prison life. In *Hall v. Terrell* (2009), the United States District Court for the District of Colorado granted a female inmate a punitive award of $1 million after she was repeatedly sexually assaulted by a guard over many months and then, on her refusal to accept further advances, was raped so severely that she required surgery. "Almost inconceivably," the court noted, the Colorado Department of Corrections permitted the guard to plead down to a class 1 misdemeanor leading to just sixty days of imprisonment. The size of the civil award had an obvious but curiously tepid purpose. The prison guards, the court declared, need a message "to cure them of their disrespect for the law."[58]

In *Green v. Floyd County, Ky.* (2011), the United States District Court for the Eastern District of Kentucky heard that a new inmate who had abused a minor had been improperly classified by prison guards who placed him in a communal cell and informed his cellmates why the inmate was there. The guards then turned "a blind eye" while cellmates "brutally tortured" and beat the victim until he suffered "a number of broken bones and was in a near-vegetative state" that required a guardian to plead "the tort of outrage" on the victim's behalf.[59]

Guards later watched as prisoners led the wounded man around on a leash and made him bark like a dog. "Whether the defendants," observed the court of the prison guards' surveillance, "really intended to cause extreme emotional distress or simply physical pain is a close question." It was apparently such a close question that "the Court cannot rule out the possibility that some of the guards stood by, aware *only* of this humiliating, but painless, conduct." The strained parsing of mental and physical pain allows a complete evasion. "If so," the court announced, "there is no question those particular guards acted only with an intent to cause emotional distress."[60] No question?

In *DeLee v. White*, again from 2011, guards were alleged to have beaten and sexually tormented an inmate in the Attica Correctional Facility of New York after he complained of a false charge of $75.15 for commissary goods that he never requested or received. His complaint almost certainly exposed a system of prison graft. There is also evidence that prison authorities filed false inmate misbehavior reports and used physical intimidation to try to cover their own actions. The inmate suffered serious injuries to his back and testicles from the alleged assaults, but the court dismissed his claims anyway; there was no proven pattern of *regular* beatings.

Intimidation aside, how many attacks would it take for a successful suit? No one knows. The court in *DeLee* observed that "plaintiff points to no policy or custom, or the equivalent, suggesting that any Defendant regularly subjects prison inmates to physical or sexual assault against any inmate who avails himself of DOCS [New York State Department of Corrections] inmate grievance procedure, including Plaintiff." There existed, in sum, not enough evidence to prove "plaintiff was subjected to any violence, was injured or suffered any harm, much less any injury or harm *sufficiently serious* to constitute an Eighth Amendment violation."[61]

Cases of dismissed brutality, like the ones just discussed, reinforce Jack Abbott's claims and suggest that little has changed. In the pages of *In the Belly of the Beast,* Abbott notes that any show of individuality— even a look, or a question asked, or a way of walking, much less a complaint—will lead a prison guard to punish an inmate physically. Extenuating circumstances will always be found to justify a guard's attack. Explains Abbott, "This is the doctrine of the American judiciary when it insists prisoners are to blame for whatever harm is inflicted upon them." Not unreasonably, he adds an overriding question: "Is that the right of government founded by free men?" (56–57).

The courts in the three cases just examined all expressed concern over alleged injuries to inmates, and most courts will find a moment to voice regret over what has so clearly and awfully happened to an inmate. But these regrets come with a pro forma answer that is not one. Judges typically urge administrative routes of inquiry that prisoners might seek when they are denied court relief, but these suggestions ignore how bureaucratic obfuscation, self-protection, and outright intimidation work in prison hierarchies to prevent lower-level solutions from taking effect. Courts are naive when they invite prisoners to pursue internal remedies. Even so, they regularly offer the administrative remedy when it is an empty ploy. No alternative, it falls under the category of one more device for avoiding inmate distress.[62]

How much deference should courts give to prison authorities when there is evidence of abuse? Recall that *Turner v. Safley* insists on deference because "courts are ill equipped to deal with the increasingly urgent problems of prison administration and reform."[63] But what if those urgent problems become urgent in a different way and on so many levels through overcrowding and inadequate staffing that they raise unavoidable questions about prison officials themselves? What if everyone concerned turns out to be "ill equipped"?

These are the questions the Supreme Court had to face in *Brown v. Plata*, a decision in 2011 so contentious among the justices that it carried the crisis of the American prison system into public discourse and open debate. In this narrow 5–4 decision, the court ordered the California prison system to reduce its prison population by more than 30,000 inmates. It acted after proving that massive incarceration had overcome existing prison facilities and the authorities who ran them.[64]

Divisions in the court over *Brown v. Plata* raise a question that will become larger and larger as we proceed. Whose crisis is it when a prison system is in crisis? Justice Antonin Scalia vehemently rejected the decision as "the most radical injunction issued by a court in our nation's history." The majority, he complained, had foisted "a judicial travesty" on the nation and taken "federal courts wildly beyond their institutional capacity."[65]

The bitter conflicts in *Brown v. Plata* inform discussion of the punished in important ways. The majority, defending itself against the attacks of four dissenters, gives the most detailed description of prison life that we are likely to get from the Supreme Court, and the differences among the justices reveal the ideological fault lines that have made massive incarceration an intractable problem. All the same, these exchanges begin to show what might be done in a penal system that is beginning to topple under its own punitive weight.

Justice Anthony Kennedy, writing for the slimmest of majorities in a case that he has to admit is de novo (unprecedented), openly recognizes the difficulty of his task in clarifying the issues that have forced the court to forgo its traditional stance of deference on penal issues. How does one convey the degree of crisis needed to act in a world so hidden from our own? In an unusual step, the most vivid aspect of his answer, Kennedy submits photographs in appendixes to go with his written account. Two of the photographs depict terrible overcrowding with little or no surveillance by prison guards of underdressed inmates cheek by jowl in open dormitories. Tightly confining "dry cages" without room for a person to sit down appear in a third photograph.

This third photograph dominates Justice Kennedy's presentation for a reason. "Because of a shortage of treatment beds," he explains, "suicidal inmates may be held for prolonged periods in telephone-booth sized cages without toilets." "A psychiatric expert," he points out, "reported observing an inmate who had been held in such a cage for nearly 24 hours, standing in a pool of his own urine, unresponsive and nearly catatonic." The image is arresting, but there is more. "Prison officials explained they had 'no place to put him.'"[66]

The admission in the anecdotal account is crucial to Justice Kennedy's opinion. Prison authorities have acknowledged a serious problem they cannot solve under present conditions. Their expertise, to the extent that it should be deferred to, has been found wanting. Kennedy's description also gives new meaning to one of Jack Abbott's more dramatic complaints. "If I were an animal housed in a zoo in quarters of these dimensions, the Humane Society would have the zookeeper arrested for cruelty" (46).

Kennedy establishes the fact of a system out of control. "Prisoners in California with serious mental illness do not receive minimal, adequate care." Those "suffering from physical illness also receive severely deficient care." Pages of examples, including deaths from neglect, follow these claims. A medical expert has testified "that extreme departures from the standard of care were 'widespread' . . . and that the proportion of 'possibly preventable or preventable' deaths was 'extremely high.'" Another summoned expert evaluates "living quarters in converted gymnasiums or dayrooms, where large numbers of prisoners may share just a few toilets and showers." These quarters have become "'breeding grounds for disease'" (1924–1925, 1933).

The majority opinion is careful to objectify blame. "Cramped conditions promote unrest and violence, making it difficult for prison officials to monitor and control the prison population." Nevertheless, descriptions of the difficulties reach beyond the expertise available. "After one prisoner was assaulted in a crowded gymnasium," Kennedy writes, "prison staff did not even learn of the injury until the prisoner had been dead for several hours" (1933–1934).

The vast numbers in prison have staggered everything and everyone. They have overwhelmed even the difference between life and death. How does one comprehend the size of an issue that has become its own problem? Comparisons can help here. "California now has the biggest prison system in the Western industrialized world." It houses "more inmates in its jails and prisons than do France, Great Britain, Germany, Japan, Singapore and the Netherlands combined."[67]

Use of a stock qualification cloaks Kennedy's standard for deciding on court intervention while providing cover for his shaky majority. "As a consequence of their own actions, prisoners may be deprived of rights that are fundamental to liberty," Kennedy admits. "Yet the law and the Constitution demand recognition of certain other rights. Prisoners retain the essence of human dignity inherent in all persons. Respect for that dignity animates the Eighth Amendment prohibition against cruel and unusual punishment" (1928).

Kennedy, more than any other sitting justice, has fought publicly for a more humane penal system, and he seizes this opportunity. "A prison that deprives prisoners of basic sustenance, including adequate medical care, is incompatible with the concept of human dignity and has no place in civilized society." A foregone conclusion follows hard on this statement. "If government fails to fulfill this obligation [sustaining human dignity], the courts have a responsibility to remedy the resulting Eighth Amendment violation" (1928). By implication, the court has overruled that part of its Eighth Amendment jurisprudence that distinguishes between cruel and unusual punishments and cruel and unusual conditions.[68]

The failures of prison administrators figure another way in this decision. Responsible authority has not responded for years to more than seventy court orders seeking remedies. Kennedy lays out that record. Whether these failures have come through inability or obstructionism, the Supreme Court affirms a previous order given by a special three-judge federal court to provide early release to those prisoners posing the least risk to society as the only logical way left for the court to eliminate excessive overcrowding in California's prisons. Kennedy limits the deference the courts will now give to prison officials. "Courts may not allow constitutional violations to continue simply because a remedy would involve intrusion into the realm of prison administration" (1928–1929).

Brown v. Plata should be read as a philosophical benchmark. It contains the full spectrum of American views regarding the punished. The contrast in attitudes expressed by the majority opinion and the attitudes expressed in angry dissents by Justices Scalia and Samuel Alito could not be greater.

Justice Kennedy's language joins the imprisoned to the rest of humanity through "the essence of human dignity inherent in all persons" (1928). Justice Scalia counters by distinguishing inmates from ordinary citizens. He warns of "the inevitable murders, robberies, and rapes to be committed by the released inmates" and of "the terrible things sure to happen as a consequence of this outrageous order." His comments include a sneer over "our judge-empowering 'evolving standards of decency' jurisprudence (with which, by the way, I heartily disagree)." Oral dissents are rare at the moment of an announced decision of the Supreme Court, but Justice Scalia uses one here to offer a sarcastic stereotype of the prisoners to be released by the court: "Many will undoubtedly be fine physical specimens who have developed intimidating muscles pumping iron in the prison gym."[69]

More temperate but just as irate, Justice Alito limits himself to abstract forebodings about the "grim roster of victims" that will result from the court's planned prisoner release. "I hope that I am wrong. In a few years, we will see."[70] Two years and counting, the results of "realignment" in California (putting more nonviolent prisoners in local rather than state facilities, instituting better parole arrangements, and reducing crowding in state prisons) are uncertain, but California crime rates, especially those of violent crime, have dropped.[71]

Where does this leave California and the rest of the country on prison conditions? In May 2012 Matthew Cate, secretary of the California Department of Corrections and Rehabilitation, expressed hope and optimism for a change in attitudes. In recent decades, he said, "America has seen prison as a place to throw people away," but, drawing on the title of his position, he hopes that Californians may now be reconsidering the whole meaning of "corrections and rehabilitation." Is there cause for optimism or at least less cause for pessimism in these remarks? Maybe, but time may tell in another way. Matthew Cate resigned his position as head of California prisons just five months after making these statements.[72]

Must suffering make sense? The dissenters in *Brown v. Plata* have a recognizable but limited response to that question. They inform inmates that you have been bad, deserve the punishment assigned to you, and cannot receive the right to minimally normal conditions, or our respect and trust, until you have suffered in full as we have directed, and we will not in the meantime look at the real nature of your suffering. Those justices who accept the majority opinion respond with more of a question than a declaration in a more qualified view of what punishment should be. Shouldn't everyone, they implicitly ask, be entitled to a minimally decent life under the circumstances required?

Retributivism, the punishment that assumes that prisoners have been placed where they deserve to be placed, is the key to the first position. A more tentative and less fixed idea animates the second position; it depends more on a standard we rather helplessly refer to as the dignity in human nature to which all are entitled. This second position, definitely less distinct, is inaccurately dismissed as a rehabilitative impulse, but that is not its essence. It says instead that the difficulties in life should be manageable enough for people to have the chance to order themselves wherever they are.

The ideas forced in this court conflict over *Brown v. Plata* will be important again in concluding sections of the book when we grapple more directly with the philosophical meanings in punishment. For unmistakably, if only implicitly, the two positions taken divide over the meaning of punishment. What exactly must be done to those serving time in prisons? The punished currently live in a zone between these two understandings, with the retributive aspect dominant but viewed increasingly as part of a larger problem. Strict retributivism as policy is the main source of overcrowding in prisons. But the alternatives sound hazier and are not without risk; they assume that more inmates will manage their lives productively in a prison environment that encourages them to do so.

The final questions that then arise are not always asked, but they are crucial ones. What is the time in prison for? What is it supposed to accomplish? What does it accomplish now? What are its most useful limits? Even for those suffering under these questions, the answers will vary, but it should surprise no one that they have some ideas of their own.

The Punished Look at Themselves

No matter what the crime and no matter how deserved the sentence, prison means oppression to those confined within its walls. Jack Abbott gives the focus of all prison narratives when he notifies his readers "you'd be surprised to learn what a little old-fashioned oppression can do to anyone" (61). In one of the many ironies across the divide, the punished naturally agree with the severest of their punishers that retribution is the key to their status.

Prison writings are captivity narratives. The oppressive atmosphere of prison is always present in them, and their authors move along a continuum that opens in anxiety, turns into exasperation, and ends in despair. Themes begin with deprivation: the loss of the natural world and outside contact, the lack of privacy, and the yearning for silence amid the endless noise of angry people in a refracting metal world. Common physical annoyances come next: the bad smell and proximity of bodies not clean enough, the boredom, and the nuisance of unwanted companions (the dysfunctional, the mentally ill, the sexually aggressive, the foolish, and the predatory).

Most accounts that make it into print arise out of more subtle problems not of the writer's own making, and they include the indifference or worse of authority, the presence of activated hatreds, the absence of meaningful protection, the constant threat of violence, and over all, a pervading fear of the unexpected. At this level, the prison narrative turns on how to control a helpless situation or how to hold on to identity when one cannot control it.

A spirit of resistance controls what are also protest narratives. That spirit can be creative or destructive, but it declares, "I'm still trying to be myself while you insist on dehumanizing me." Resistance of some kind is necessary for identity in a world saturated with shame and degradation. The conflicts that make prison narratives interesting focus on the attempt to overcome debilitating intrusions, on managing or failing to manage discordant situations, on mastering an environment that defines but does not limit the writing persona.

There is great poignancy in a resistance that must live without hope or expectations. "The majority [of inmates] truly feel regret and shame for who they've become." After all, "No one starts out wanting to be a criminal or claims 'I want to be removed from society and made to live in a six-by-ten cinderblock bathroom.'" Yet this is the prisoner's world. "Many can't conceive of ever being different; either because they've never known otherwise, or have become so habituated their minds don't know where to begin."[73] The inmate who takes up a pen begins by finding a voice, and that voice says to the outside, "You need to know who I really am instead of just thinking you know."

Resistance finds its institutional level in the "prison rules" generated by inmates themselves. The proximity of the lawful and powerful to the unlawful and subjugated breeds an entrenched hostility toward authority, and much of any thought of prison reform depends on whether this hostility can be diffused or rechanneled in a useful way. If it cannot be diffused or at least curtailed, the subjugated create rules of their own to hold on to themselves, and those rules tend to be ruthless, in keeping with the criminality of those who make them.

Inmate rules originate in the impulse to avoid institutional cooperation. They exist on the divide between power and the powerless in order to move some control to the subjugated. By definition, they also give sway to the worst aspects of prison life by making it tough for authority to function or correct. "War is war and us is us and them is them . . . never trust a screw [the guard on duty]." A less obvious rule demands "jailface": "You freeze your face so nothin' moves." No one is ever to know how you feel. Still another main rule stipulates that you do not show weakness to anyone; always be tough, never apologize. "If you go around telling people you're sorry you ain't gonna survive two days in this place."[74]

All inmate rules are essentially negations, but not without creativity, given a truly oppressive world and the need for resistance to it; they provide an inmate population some identity. The worst rule for institutional well-being is an ironclad prohibition: never inform on another prisoner, whatever the behavior involved. ("Be loyal to cons." "Never snitch.")[75] Punishment from within the inmate population for breaking silence is certain and occasionally absolute.

Common sense in the twisted world of prison life supports these rules. Inmates learn that what should be true is not true. It is not true, for example, that "if I can just tell somebody decent, they'll see that a stop is put to it."[76] A further consequence is the creation of a linguistic world with its own language and manners. The quality of that separate world is another matter. Its rules reduce behavior in prison to the lowest common denominator. Given free rein are gang violence, petty acts of revenge, and every other leveling tendency.

The demand of a fast learning curve among generally uneducated and poorly adjusted individuals is especially striking. When a new prisoner, "a fish," tries to spend too much time in his bunk and creates "a home" in his cell with books, writing materials, and artwork, he receives good advice from "a cellie," an older hand: "A man who spends too much time in bed sends the same signal as that of a bleeding fish in shark-infested waters." You might be burned alive for appearing better than other prisoners. The wise inmate stays off his cot and sticks to minimal belongings. This particular fish survives long enough to become a cellie and to give his story, but the reality behind the story eventually becomes too much to take. The futility of a permanent sentence leads the writer to hang himself in a cell that he leaves absolutely bare.[77]

The drama in prison narratives comes through fictional exposure of the code of silence. By definition, an inmate's account breaks all the rules so the outside world can benefit from hearing it. It passes on the injustices that make prison life an absorbing story of conflict. Left in its wake is the ticking away of meaningless time. "How does a prisoner count the time when it has no end?" Jack Abbott asks at one point (112). Most prison stories feature an incident that gives meaning to time by disrupting the monotony of doing nothing.

The occurrence in a prison narrative that breaks the meaningless routine can be trivial, or comic, or serious. It can be as incidental as the sudden appearance of a strange white owl in "the battleground of the main yard," a moment that unifies the racially divided prisoners and allows them an instant of freedom from the orders of the tower guards.[78] Or it can entail ludicrous behavior by a prisoner that stupefies authority.[79] Or it can be as grave as a prisoner wrongly punished for an event not of her own making that leads her to tell the truth in a racially twisted situation. "Lee" is put in "the hole" for it, but she is "all right with it." She has kept her own integrity intact. "Most of the time it's all twisted and sick, but sometimes there is a right and a wrong, even here."[80]

Many other stories concentrate on the barrier between prisoners and guards. These stories turn on the brutality that absolute power doles out whenever it feels like it. "Please and thank-yous pass between cops and inmates like bricks through a keyhole," but civility applies when a particularly hated prison guard shows awkward courtesy while escorting a prisoner to a family funeral. In his rough way, the guard acts better than the prisoner's own family members, all of whom are distressed to discover their disgraced member at the public event. In a parallel story, a guard admits an injustice and makes it up to the prisoner another way.[81]

It is, of course, possible to deconstruct the meaning of these stories. The canniest prison narratives do in some way. One prisoner warns, "Don't think that I will allow myself to be used as consolation for a civilian audience," but that same writer wants you to hear the common protest that always marks the genre. "Self-defense is without justification," he warns of prison violence. "If you're hurt," the guards shrug, "you shouldn't have been there." Aggressor and prey become the same things. "Prison managers are unwilling to recognize assault because of the lawsuits. So they do their damnedest to make everyone look guilty or well-deserving."[82]

Can describing such things change anything? This particularly cynical voice thinks not. He calls prison writing "dead wood" but goes on because he knows he is telling the truth and wants it to be known.[83] "Because of their fear of being assaulted where no one could see them," explains another prisoner in confirmation, "many block guards never patrolled the inner perimeter and spent most of their time avoiding conflicts at all cost, even turning the other way." The consequences of such indifference for the weak and unprotected are terrible, but no one cares. "In the struggle to survive, it was easier to distrust everyone," but here as well is the corrosion of a world. "Turning the other way" from unchecked injustice introduces total arbitrariness, the opposite of the order that justice can provide. Isn't everyone diminished when injustice is so obviously overlooked?[84]

Can we know what it means to distrust *everyone*? Jean-Paul Sartre in *No Exit* famously announces "Hell is—other people!"[85] But what if hell is more than that? What if it is *every* other person? The unique loneliness, fear, suffocation, anger, danger, hopelessness, and mean-spiritedness when your hand must rise against every other is what turns American prisons into the infernos of the twenty-first century.

The proof, if there can be proof, comes in our misguided guide, Jack Henry Abbott, who claims in *In the Belly of the Beast* that the lack of oversight in prison turns him into the killer he becomes. In the free-for-all that is prison, with prisoners making their own violent rules to live by, "never come into bodily contact with another human being . . . except in combat; in acts of struggle, of violence" (54). The rules state "it is an insult to grapple hand-to-hand with anyone. If someone ever strikes him with his hand (another prisoner), he has to kill him with a knife." Abbott admits to acting on this principle. It is "the only thing you could do." This is "Moral self-defense": *"All the violence in prison is geared for murder"* (75–76).

Despair in a world out of control fuels much of this violence. "Writing bridged my divided life of prisoner and free man," writes one prisoner.[86] But what if the bridge is to nowhere? The quick snatches at prison life in the writings of inmates always come up against the unbearable nature and length of the reality. One out of ten prisoners in the United States is serving a life term. Six prison systems—Illinois, Louisiana, Maine, Pennsylvania, South Dakota, and the federal penitentiary system—do not offer parole for prisoners with life terms, and many other states resist parole for inmates who have committed violent crimes even if those crimes were committed long ago.[87]

Our penitentiaries and houses of correction are holding pens. They do not lead, as stated, to penitence or correction. Prisons today are about more crime, whether detected or not, and it does not matter whether the incarcerated person manages to make a successful adjustment to life there or not. No one, it seems, can do that in an intolerable situation forever. Even Jack Abbott, the self-styled independent "state-raised convict," could handle it for only so long. At fifty-eight, on February 10, 2002, he hanged himself in his cell using bedsheets and his shoelaces. There is, in effect, no answer to him or for him, but there should be more of one about him.

6

The Punitive Impulse in American Society

A great number of apparently insoluble problems disappear at once if we decide to give up the notion that the motives by which people *believe* themselves to be motivated are necessarily the ones which drive them to act, feel and think as they do.

Erich Fromm, Escape from Freedom

The Question Asked Again

We have seen enough to know the problem in most of its dimensions. Punishment is a volatile subject for what it does to people, and it is not easily understood or appreciated. Theoretically in conception and institutionally in practice, it also moves toward extremes, and that has happened with unusual force in the legal punishment regimes of the United States. Moreover, the law has encouraged these tendencies, the judicial function has been insensitive to its excesses, and the entrenched oppositions in prison life stand in the way of reform even though changes are desperately needed in a dysfunctional system geared to pernicious incentives that now control everything. The angers in punishment have taken over in a criminal justice system close to breakdown.

Against these negative lines of force, the ultimate question takes on new urgency and should be addressed more directly than it has been. Is the criminal justice system of the United States so harsh because Americans welcome a strong punitive impulse, or have circumstances created a problem beyond everyone's expectations? Does the country want the system to be this way, or is massive incarceration the result of contingencies that have come together and need to be disentangled?

A great deal turns on the answer. A decade ago, in a seminal study titled *Harsh Justice,* James Q. Whitman proved the severity of American punishment regimes by comparing them with European regimes, and he thought that the entrenched nature of that severity left little hope of reform. His study ended not with a response to the question but with a statement of the two possibilities. Either communal intent or unfolding circumstance could explain the situation.[1]

Complicating the question and any answer to it are the dozen or more studies since *Harsh Justice* that have documented an overly punitive impulse at work in American culture, and yet these studies have had little appreciable effect on a carceral system that grows worse year by year. Can we expect more or less attention to problems in the criminal justice system as those problems become more obvious? Either way, answers to the overriding question remain important for two reasons.

If the punitive era turns out to be a temporary manifestation of late modernity—an assumption questioned by some criminologists—it exists subject to meaningful reform.[2] If instead current punishment regimes reflect permanent and perhaps growing communal desires, the answer becomes strategic in a very different sense. Recognition of an innate harshness would go far to define the United States of America.

Legal theorists of all periods agree that how a country punishes says something important about its nature. Montesquieu, a philosophical touchstone in the formation of the United States, leads a parade of political philosophers who claim that severity in punishment marks despotic tendencies in government. Moderate governments are characterized instead by "a softer way of correcting." They manage better because "slight penalties" serve as well as heavier ones in countries "known for the lenity of their law."[3]

Leniency hardly describes criminal justice in America today despite the fact that few think of government in the United States as despotic in tone or practice. Why, then, do the American people, proud of their free society, respond so positively to tough law-and-order politics whether or not they reflect the social reality in which they live? Why do they clap so many people into the largest prisons in the world with heavy sentences that ruin literally millions of lives?

It is simply a fact that voters promote to high office those politicians who want tougher penalties. They just as frequently approve of the legislative enactment of harsher sentences for criminal offenses.[4] So strong are these inclinations that leaders who do not think in these terms have learned to remain silent about the problems involved in order to stay in office.

The patterns leading to severity are too clear to ignore. Public opinion polls reveal that harsher sentencing "consistently garners the support of at least 80 percent of the public." More tangible evidence supports those polls. Law-and-order candidates have a better record of winning national office.[5] The legislative outcome across the country has been higher mandatory minimum sentences, three-strike provisions that lead to life in prison for minor offenses, extension of the death penalty to cover more crimes, "truth-in-sentencing" provisions that require at least 85 percent of a sentence to be served, and significant increases everywhere in prison time served.

A punitive impulse has controlled criminal justice in America for almost half a century, and its tenacity continues even though crime rates have dropped in recent decades. Can we measure that impulse, and in measuring it, how do we judge the gap between communal affect and reality? Everything brings us back to the original question with new emphasis. Does harsh punishment represent a permanent element in American ideological thought, or is it more of a historical contingency subject to the possibility of change?

Answers must begin with the intractability of the problem. Gridlock over mass incarceration exists against much ignored professional expertise in favor of reform, an expertise based on recognition of a system in trouble.[6] The level of communal obduracy in response raises its own question. How much of popular and institutional intransigence can be traced to the number of variables in play?[7]

An intractable problem is one that a community recognizes but cannot solve despite realization of the need. It cannot solve the problem because too many conflicting lines of force reinforce each other in a variety of ways. The lines of force compete, but they join in a mutual assessment: they will let nothing happen if the price is an adjustment in ideological priorities currently held. All sides in dispute then accept a fatalism that prefers no action to uncertain change, and things get worse.

Stalled between realization and meaningful action, those seeking a solution must look outside of the conflict in an intractable problem. The hope has to be that sooner or later the growing size of the problem will drive new assessments. Either catastrophe (in this case, the approaching state of breakdown in American prisons today) or an alternative frame of reference (realizing that imprisonment as currently understood does not solve crime) must change enough views. To come to a fresh understanding of an intractable problem, some of the people in dispute must change their view of the nature of the problem they face.[8]

Even then, there may be another obstacle to overcome. For some period of time, the need for change falters over an inchoate desire to return to the past, to a time when the problem was not perceived to be as serious as it has now become. This proclivity thrives on a nostalgia always present in the changing American scene.

America is a nation that loves to think about the way we never were. Sooner or later, though, the combatants in an intractable problem must accept that the past is irretrievably lost to the present because of the accelerating pace of change all around them. They must then either come up with a new idea or find a new way of phrasing an old idea that will lead in a new direction.[9]

Deconstructing the Intractability in American Punishment

The variables that solidify the punitive impulse in America are hard to grasp in their relative importance. There are so many variables with little consensus over which ones actually control or should control the situation. Experts in penology put primary emphasis on factors that other experts dismiss. Disagreements proliferate over the elements as well as the solutions. No one knows quite where to begin, and yet everyone agrees that the answer lies somewhere in the relation of law and society. Whether society or law should take primacy in change remains to be seen.

If we start with society, it is because the disciplines that study it work more closely than law does with how constituted habits form thought. The linguistic philosopher John Searle, in *The Construction of Social Reality*, believes in "a thesis of the background" to comprehend "a peculiar kind of self-referentiality" in the underlying concepts that name social facts. The search for meaning must begin with "a set of background capacities that do not themselves consist of intentional phenomena."[10]

The sociologist Pierre Bourdieu agrees, though with different terminology. Bourdieu probes "collectivities of social practices" in people, "their socially constituted nature," what he calls "the habitus" or *generative capacities of dispositions,*" the elements that prefigure "the express, explicit norm or the rational calculation."[11] If you want to explain the wider scope of behavior, you have to recognize that "all the oppositions constituting the system are linked to all the others," and "every opposition can be linked to several others in different respects by relationships of varying intensity and meaning."[12]

We must, in consequence, delve deeper than what people say to ascertain why they hold the positions they do. Again in Bourdieu's terms, it is "necessary to take back . . . the 'active side' of practical knowledge," the thing that allows people to "assert their difference" at primary levels of understanding, where "they merely need to be what they are in order to be what they have to be."[13]

The goal for the moment is therefore to appreciate the intrinsic social variables that shape American attitudes toward punishment within the lines of force that give them power, and to do it in the knowledge that much of that power comes through preconceived dispositions not fully articulated. Many attitudes on punishment derive from positive underlying cultural norms in American identity. Even so, and this is the point, they apply inversely when turned to the subject of punishment.

Given the contentions in this area, no list of variables will ever satisfy everyone as complete, and others who study punishment might come up with different names for the ones listed here. In any case, the interactive or collective power in these variables is what counts in the chart that follows. The fourteen factors arranged in the chart between abstract norms and concrete impulses engage vertically as well as horizontally, though specific reactions in cause and effect apply horizontally, as the numbering used implies.

The chart relies on a major supposition identified by Steven Pinker in *The Stuff of Thought:* "Even our most abstract concepts are understood in terms of concrete scenarios."[14] The animus in punishment naturally leans toward the concrete. That said, the arrows in the chart aim in both directions, toward abstract concept and concrete scenario, to indicate that opinion always emerges in crosscurrents. The items on the list are indeed variables. They are presented not with the idea that the concrete scenarios of punishment will always be held. They will, however, be entertained. They will come up as opinions to be accepted or refuted when the abstract concept is in play.

The Punitive Impulse

ABSTRACT CONCEPT		CONCRETE SCENARIO
1a. Proportionality	⟷	1b. It must go up with the scale of crime.
2a. Judicial Independence	⟷	2b. Means leniency in sentencing.
3a. Mercy	⟷	3b. Criminals take advantage of it.
4a. Crime Prevention	⟷	4b. Has no effect on committed criminals.
5a. Distrust of Authority	⟷	5b. Crime is not controlled by it.
6a. Exceptionalism	⟷	6b. No one should try to tell us what to do.
7a. National Security	⟷	7b. Enemies are everywhere.
8a. Military Prowess	⟷	8b. Force is one answer.
9a. Bearing Arms	⟷	9b. They can be used when threatened.
10a. Forgiveness	⟷	10b. Not until sin is paid for.
11a. Equality	⟷	11b. No exceptions.
12a. Toleration	⟷	12b. Not if convicted.
13a. Individualism	⟷	13b. Strict accountability.
14a. Freedom	⟷	14b. A shame when taken away.

Energizing the crosscurrents between abstract conceptions and concrete scenarios are the equally embedded anxieties in "a culture of fear."[15] These anxieties can best be seen through open-ended questions that have no real answers. Everyone asks one or more of them at given moments, but it is how frequently they are asked that signifies the levels of fear in a community.

1. Where will criminals strike next?
2. Who has information that can be used against me?
3. Why is there so much violence?
4. How do I protect myself from intrusion?
5. What does crime have to do with race?
6. Whose help can I depend on?
7. When does a community handle crime?

The spread in interrogative pronouns—Where? Who? Why? How? What? Whose? When?—tries to mark the confusion and uncertainty in a culture of fear. For if there are no real answers, there is comfort and a degree of certainty at a more tactical level when a criminal is found and punished.

How do all these elements work together and achieve such cohesive force in punishment? Theorists of ideology outline "the way in which meaning (or signification) serves to sustain relations of domination" with subliminal anger against those who need to be dominated and hence controlled.[16] The sociologist Georg Simmel adds another dimension. The "collectivist minimum" in communal conflict, the bond that is most fundamental in group formations, is "the drive for self-preservation." People who disagree about almost everything will act together against an offender who threatens them.[17]

Our chart of the elements in the punitive impulse and the list of fear-ridden questions that drive that impulse are admittedly inadequate devices for conveying the actual synergy and integration of forces at work in legal punishment. But observing the main components of the impulse together in one place suggests a dialectic at work in them. The chart expresses how the components might dictate as well as reinforce severity in punishment. At the same time, the configuration actually consists of relatively amorphous associative elements.

Thus, despite their collective strength, the looseness of affiliations in the desire to punish might contain opportunities for rearticulating the problem. Sometimes a serious quarrel—and punishment in the United States certainly qualifies as serious—will change the quarrelers as well as the conflict. In 2013 some experts have even begun to talk about "a 'sea change' in America's approach to punishment" on these grounds.[18]

Of course, the strengths in the desire to punish remain, and we must first document how they come together. Fear of crime predisposes a community to prefer extremes in incarceration through laddered proportionality. Thoughts about the kind of community that will answer crime puts judges who show mercy on the spot. Uncertainty over where new crime will occur causes all legal enforcement actors to want to maximize incarceration. A repeat offender is a problem for every actor involved. When those who were held responsible for recidivism were slapped down in the 1970s, they learned to hew to the higher end of sentencing guidelines.[19]

Harder to document are the ways in which fear works on the imagination to control reality. American society is obsessed with crime through its media and entertainment outlets. Belief in the prevalence of vicious criminals dominates communal perception because serious predators appear more frequently on television screens in American living rooms than fact in the world warrants. Writes one criminologist, "Such offenders do exist, but there are nowhere near as many of them as society imagines, and they constitute a tiny fraction of the actual population of offenders prosecuted." "Why are we so eager to believe in monsters?" Answer: "Monstrous crimes and monstrous criminals provide appetizing fare."[20]

Why is the fare so appetizing? A "melodramatic imagination" in reportage and entertainment bifurcates the world into stock modes of good and evil.[21] Video sources do their best to imprint outsize criminals on communal conceptions. Supervillains get dispatched only after they have provided the last twist in dramatic possibilities, and we get to watch it all in every detail on the screen.[22]

One often admired example should suffice. The favorite and longest-running prime-time crime television series in recent decades, *Law and Order,* "an ode to all the terrifying things that can happen in New York City," used the same formula forever: criminal shown and then finally exposed. The police typically get their man or woman, but the ensuing courtroom drama in the second half of the show does not always produce a conviction.[23] The effect of that occasional discrepancy on an appreciative audience should not be underestimated.

Crime shows used to be known through the sanitized designation "cops and robbers." Now they plunge a viewer into terrifying domestic crime scenes with unhinged sociopaths who deserve the worst. Just as we expect longer sentences for serious crimes, so the movement in cinematic versions has been from abstract violence to a more visceral "ultraviolence" with greater compensatory punishment in response.[24]

Experts who deplore the trends in imaginary depictions of violence believe "viewers form affinities for screen characters based on how such people would be viewed were their behavior occurring in the real world."[25] Measuring the impact of imagined violence is impossible, but the fear quotient it creates in cultural attitudes is considerable, and so is the prospect of imitators adopting some of the transgressive behavior depicted there.[26]

The more proactive nature of entertainment today brings everything closer to imitation. There are now video games where players get to be gangsters or street thugs. The marketing demo for one of the latest versions of the video-game series Grand Theft Auto—a previous version sold 25 million copies—features a character who "pours a ring of gasoline around a truck and lights it on fire."[27]

All, to be sure, is not film or games. Cinematic predators gain their credence from news reportage of the real thing.[28] High homicide rates and equally high unsolved crime rates—higher than in other modernized countries—prove their presence. Central to concern about crime is the realization that more crimes are committed than are reported with untold victims left in their wake. Knowing that criminals "are out there" is frightening, especially when we learn that violent criminals not caught are statistically more likely to assault, rape, and kill again. Even reform-minded criminologists admit to futility in coping with some criminals by any other means than permanent incarceration.[29]

But how many criminals fall into this terrible category? A violent offender who has completed the criminal conditioning process from brutalization to belligerency, to violent acts, and on to a more steady and destructive virulence in behavior patterns may require "selective incapacitation." But little work has been done on the relation of objective risk to communal concern in dealing with dangerous offenders. Should selective incapacitation apply to the many who are enduring long-term imprisonment or only to a "selective few"?[30] Right now most citizens do not want to take that risk. They worry more about potential violence than about who should not be in jail.[31]

Think again about how the fourteen inclinations in the punitive impulse reinforce one another. No single abstract concept might control, but together they foster punitive inclinations in concrete scenarios, and several of those inclinations bring patriotic identification to the censure of criminals. Number six on the list, pride in the claim of American exceptionalism, means that none of the moderate punishment regimes that exist in Europe apply in principle here.[32] Items seven through nine (the threat to national security, the strength of the military-industrial defense complex, and the right of every citizen to bear arms) all support a qualified right to search and destroy enemies of the United States, and this extends to a citizen's right to protect the home and to punish a domestic enemy vigorously.

An independent citizenry of individuals has long emphasized preparedness. The need to protect that independence by responding quickly to threats has shaped political discourse in the country since at least 1941, and the impact of this discourse on military preparedness and the right to bear arms has been profound on the expression of all other areas of national concern and domestic policy.[33]

Central here, and part of the culture of fear, is the desire to crush anyone who appears to threaten even indirectly the national fabric. Never mind that the United States, by any measure one can reasonably make, has long been the safest civilization that history has ever seen.[34] Reason lies not in the need but in the vulnerability that so many Americans feel about the lives they lead, a vulnerability that ties national security to a punishing mentality.

The high regard that Americans reserve for their armed forces, abstract concept eight in the chart, reinforces items six, seven, and nine—all within an acceptable patriotic bent. Most citizens take pride in the nation as a superpower, and that pride registers in ceremonial displays of it. The nation's armed forces represent the most respected institutions in the land. No other governmental operation comes even close. Seventy-eight percent of Americans express great confidence in the military, while just 3 percent lack confidence; the comparable figures for Congress are 12 percent in favor and 48 percent having a very low opinion.[35]

Ideas that are not disputed in a culture control thought, and the political price of controverting them is very high. Civic belief in an armed state nationally and domestically is one of those ideas. Calls for more spending on bloated defense budgets go unchallenged, and down the scale of involvement, the individual citizen's desire for weaponry in order to use force to defend the home goes uncontested. The newly imposed terminology of "Homeland Security" bridges the distance between foreign and domestic threats, and the rhetorical effects for the punitive impulse are direct.[36]

Just as national leaders never admit to anything less than the most intense search-and-destroy policies when it comes to locating the country's enemies, so they dare not object to the widespread availability of guns for punishing a potential invader of the home. Nor, in a jump in everything but the logic of politics, do they target the side issue in domestic security, the possession of firearms in the wrong hands.[37] New concealed-gun-carry laws in many states, together with equally new stand-your-ground laws that expand the right of self-defense, intersect to give anyone with a gun who feels seriously threatened the right to use it. Tragic misunderstandings are a frequent result.[38]

The analogy of national defense to the private ownership of firearms may be imperfect, but it is emotionally entrenched in American abstract conceptions of identity. More to the point, it confirms that fear of violence does not reach the source of that violence. People mistakenly think their own gun will help more than it will hurt them, just as a powerful military will defend them from external attack. The truth is that guns placed in the home for self-protection are forty-three times more likely to kill a family member, a friend, or a familiar acquaintance than the much-feared intruder.[39]

Should we encourage the powerfully held right to self-protection at any cost in order to sustain the right to punish a criminal on one's own terms? The question is complicated. *McDonald v. Chicago* (2010), in which the Supreme Court prevented state bans on the ownership of guns, was decided in favor of Otis McDonald's right to have a handgun plus two shotguns to protect himself. McDonald, it should be noted, was a community activist supporting alternative policing strategies in a high-crime neighborhood, and he had received threats from drug dealers because of his activities.[40]

Even so, widespread gun possession defies the logic of protection. Guns kill more than they protect. Estimates in 2012 put 270 million guns in private hands in the United States, more than one for every adult in the country.[41] Close to 30,000 Americans die annually from firearms, mostly by accident, with twice that number wounded. The major causes of uninsured hospital stays are gunshot injuries, and they cost hospitals $800 million a year.[42]

The mayhem from guns is not limited to the spectacular. The totally innocent suffer most. Nearly 3,000 children die from firearms in the United States every year.[43] The unregulated possession of firearms also explains why fatalities from crime greatly exceed those in other countries. It makes no difference. Americans focus on the aftereffect of violence, not the mundane but more effective prevention of it.[44]

Time and again the nation's favorite narratives depict individuals who step in with guns where the law has failed to do so. All of them disguise that firearms are the cause of violence, not the solution to it. A country born in revolution, distorted by civil war, steeped in frontier lore, and long engaged in military combat puts its hope in the false security of personal readiness: a gun in the house and now under a coat.[45]

The corollary to such thinking on the subject of punishment should be lost on no one. When violence disturbs the body politic, its answer is more punishment. Americans and their legislatures do not think about control of guns; they ask for longer sentences in response to gun crimes that might not have happened without guns. In explanation, theorists of ideology show how values dictate cohesive national understandings beyond the facts of a situation. "The central imaginary significations of a society . . . are the laces which tie a society together and the forms which define what, for a given society, is 'real.'"[46]

Left on our chart of positive abstract concepts are vague but powerful virtues (items ten through fourteen) that citizens definitely think of as "real" in the makeup of the United States. As a reminder, they are (10) forgiveness; (11) egalitarianism; (12) toleration; (13) individualism; and (14) freedom. The thrust that moves these concepts from aspiration toward punishment comes in the exclusion of inmates from all of them. Benjamin Franklin, a canny observer of the American scene, may have said it best in the nation's most famous autobiography: "All Crime will be punished and Virtue rewarded, either here or hereafter."[47]

With the nature of the hereafter more in question than previously, the idea of punishment means punishment now for twenty-first-century Americans, with nothing left to chance in futurity. Prison sentences, much like divine punishment, are not just about accountability; they are about removal, the loss of all rights, and the absolute dismissal of protective communal status. The sentence denies equality, freedom, and individualism, as well as all the claims to dignity and forgiveness that might go with them. Implicitly or explicitly, law-abiding citizens think of prison as a secular version of hell, an analogy often used in contemporary descriptions of prison life.

Penal theory and empirical evidence also demonstrate that it is easier to relegate someone to such a secular hell when that person appears to be different from you. A majority of prisoners in America come from impoverished ethnic minorities, whose members are arrested more frequently and punished more heavily than other citizens for the same crime.[48] Toleration may be an acknowledged national virtue, but it disappears in the desire to censure those who accentuate their difference by breaking the law. Strict accountability leaves plenty of room for bias to reenter the picture of punishment.[49]

We have tried to show in this section how the shared inclinations to punish pile up and reinforce each other. The severities they allow in dealing with criminals turn into "habits of the heart"—Robert Bellah's phrase, taken from Alexis de Tocqueville, for communal understandings so intrinsic that they fill the interstices between "how we live and what our culture allows us to say."[50] The result is broadly consensual thinking that thrives on the exclusion of others, and no one is more easily excluded than a convicted criminal.

Still, there is a soft underbelly in the nation's muscular desire to punish. American exceptionalism carries only so far.[51] Other countries embrace the same virtues—forgiveness, egalitarianism, toleration, freedom, and individualism—and they just as surely turn them into pivotal sources of national cohesion, but these virtues do not translate into harsher punishment there. Why, again, do Americans punish more heavily than their counterparts in other countries?

The vulnerabilities already mentioned give part of an answer, and this is true whether they are real or imagined. Dread about where crime will occur, horror in the face of so much apparent violence, fear of intruders, dismay in the face of electronic theft, and alarm over racial differences are widely held apprehensions and lead people to strike out blindly against the forces that complicate modern life.

The desire to guard against so many ills comes to rest on the most logical symbol of them, the criminal who is ready to take from you in one way or another. If you have things of value, and most people who fear crime in America do have things of value, the world is full of people who lack them, know you have them, and want them. Today that person can be someone far away, someone you will never see, identify, or find.

Many of the new trepidations are painfully real. "At some point you will get hacked," observes a leading security officer in technological systems. "It's only a matter of time."[52] Why would you not want to punish this unknown person or any other person who in deliberate malice takes from you?

Shame and Fear as Variables

One part of the answer to the punitive impulse is especially disturbing because it reflects an offshoot of the pleasure in imposing it. The levels of shame that Americans heap on the fallen in their midst may be the culture's most unattractive trait. To return for a moment to Robert Bellah's use of Alexis de Tocqueville, Tocqueville identified a "restless quest for material betterment" in the United States and coined the term "individualism" to describe it. He saw more. He decided that this peculiar brand of American individualism was "strangely compatible with conformism."[53]

Conformity as betterment, the conventional story of success, drives cultural concern in America, and its use by the well-off against those who have failed supplies meaning in a country that now registers the greatest disparity between wealth and poverty among major Western democracies.[54] Cultural critics label the condescending nature of this focus "the rise of selfishness in America" and the "zero-tolerance" of an increasingly affluent "exclusive society." The viewpoint of those financially and culturally above is clear: it says if you are on the bottom, get out of the way.[55]

Something more enduring in class terms has also long been at work. A people without an identifiable aristocracy, Americans have drawn on "a philosophy of individual success" to obscure class distinctions while obliquely maintaining them.[56] Why, for example, do Americans ride on airplanes that seat you in designations that begin with first class but devolve quickly into such disparate classifications as business class and tourist or economy class? One does not have to look hard for an answer. To designate a specifically downward structure in class terms would raise accusations of elitism. Everyone would like to be number 1. No one in the United States raises two fingers to cry out, "I'm number 2."

Success, in order to disguise its invidious distinctions, turns to what sociologists designate "the institutionalization of categorical pairs." The pairing, for instance, of riding in first class against tourist or economy class depends on the assumed objective fact of more money against the relative absence of it. Nonetheless, how does a professedly democratic culture legitimize "durable inequality" in an increasingly plutocratic United States?[57]

The use of shame for those without the fungible commodities that money provides is part of the answer. The transformation of money into desirable things or a preferred place (that first-class seat) can define morality in a consumer culture defined by material possession. But if the affluent are to maintain their hegemony on anything like normative grounds, wealth must establish the worthy side of the pairing, while exploitation and opportunity hoarding silently reinforce the negative side.

Categorical pairings only work if the distinction keeps all parties willingly in place, and this is where shame operates as a social control. "The very notion of *shameful* differences assumes a similarity with regard to crucial beliefs, those regarding identity." If people who have not succeeded are to agree, at least conditionally, to the stigma in failure, they must share "a language of relationships" about identity. They must in some way incorporate "the same mental make-up."[58] Those expected to feel shame must accept their negative category in the pairing.[59]

By implication and soon enough by direct inference, the failures who do not accept their assigned category and who have no other means out of it are headed for crime. Crime occurs when those who have no other means of joining consumer culture decide to take what they need. The poverty-stricken and the criminally minded thereby hold relative places in a "criminalization of marginality." They fill "dispossessed categories" in policies of containment—the first through economic forces, the second through prospective penalization.[60]

Criminals who get caught carry categorical pairing and the criminalization of marginality to an absolute standard that is useful for others. As inmates, they represent a double failure: they are beyond mere poverty while providing a cautionary tale for any of the impoverished above them who might be tempted to commit crime. They allow everyone in an egalitarian society that is in truth very hierarchical to feel above the imprisoned.

The ideological common ground that makes the shame in the pairing of success and failure possible is the myth of universal opportunity. All classes in America continue to believe in the myth despite growing social inequality, obvious unfairness in the distribution of resources, and a now-permanent "poverty trap." A public opinion poll by the Pew Foundation from 2011 reports that "nearly 7 in 10 Americans had already achieved or expected to achieve the American Dream at some point in their lives."[61]

Failure, if it comes, is one's own fault, a cause of personal shame, and an object of external shaming. Never mind that the negative side of the categorical pairing is vast. Data from the Census Bureau show that "104 million people—a third of the population—have annual incomes below twice the poverty line."[62] Nor does it seem to matter that the wealthiest 1 percent of American households have 34.5 percent of the country's wealth, while the bottom 50 percent of all households hold just 1 percent of that wealth.[63]

The myth of opportunity works because even the law-abiding poor have someone to blame and shame. Those who live in prison exist without all materiality or opportunity and invite universal contempt. All others exist above those deprived of freedom. To enter prison is to be dispensed with and to be remembered only as a category. The average American crime show proves that orientation by ending at just this moment: televised closure comes in the cultural satisfaction of punishment announced and received just before the criminal disappears from view.[64]

Convenience in the connection of shame to punishment lies here, and it pursues those who try to rise by illegal means. The criminal as punished inmate becomes a byword of shame. The once-feared transgressor devolves into a "jailbird," and the term has its exactness. A dehumanizing stigma, "jailbird" describes a prisoner, but it labels ex-cons as well.[65] In the metaphor of capture, it indicates what inmates can never do: they can never fly away or escape the category they have assumed.

Helplessness codes the prisoner's shame. Anthropological distinctions between shame cultures and guilt cultures may no longer pertain with the same analytic force today, but prisons are shame cultures. Guilt is assumed, and shame is a daily practice inflicted on the vulnerable there because of it. Guilt manifests itself as an inward phenomenon, while shame involves exposure before a group. Yet even this theoretical distinction is more difficult to sustain in American culture, where one cannot divest the term "shame" from its "common meaning in English— 'consciousness of guilt.'" "The one is a surfacing of the other, the other a concealment of the one."[66]

The context of punishment proves the connection in America. Mere legal accusation, much less formal guilt, exposes a person to an elaborate cultural ceremony of shame in the first stage of the country's punishment regimes. The country's image culture allows a vast electronic audience to view those who fall afoul of the law when they are paraded before cameras in handcuffs and sometimes in garish jumpsuits.[67] "Perp walks," practiced only in the United States, are a relatively new phenomenon and represent a unique form of penal shame before the fact.

Perp walks shape the public's pejorative response to crime. The physical restraints worn during these ceremonies can sometimes be justified on security grounds, but nothing justifies the exposure to media outlets except the desire to shame. When Dominique Strauss-Kahn, managing director of the International Monetary Fund and a leading political figure in France, was arrested for attempted rape of a hotel maid in New York's Sofitel Hotel on May 14, 2011, the images of him paraded in handcuffs on the way to prison exploded into international fare. Americans were amused; the French, outraged. Airing images of a suspect in handcuffs is illegal in France before conviction.[68]

Excess is the norm in perp walks. Was it necessary to parade the physically harmless, seventy-four-year-old New York state senator Shirley Huntley in handcuffs before cameras in August 2012 for allegedly conspiring to redirect state grants? The reasons for her perp walk had nothing to do with security and could be found in the picture and headline on the front page of the *New York Post:* "CUFF LINKS! All the rage . . . the hot new fashion accessory for New York Politicians."[69]

The practice turns shaming into a video art form. When the frail and troubled young starlet Lindsay Lohan failed to meet her community service obligations on time, what were the dangers that worried officialdom when she was handcuffed and led out of a Los Angeles courthouse by stout police officers? The purpose of the exercise was to expose "a train wreck" to media audiences. "Lindsay gets a set of shiny new bracelets," screamed the front-page lead and picture in the *New York Post.* Did it serve any legal need when convicted former New York Police Department commissioner Bernard Kerik was displayed in shackles and a jumpsuit under a similar headline, "THE FALLEN MIGHTY"?[70]

A seeming coincidence that is not one marks all these events. Interest in shame as a vehicle of correction has grown exponentially in the punitive era of criminal justice. It has become a cultural norm, a means of informing the public that law and order have been successful and are on the job. The police, like everyone else, enjoy having their pictures in the newspaper, and that enjoyment expands into communal schadenfreude, the pleasure people derive from the misfortune of others.

Just as perp walks humiliate defendants in public, so do new forms of sentencing in their appeal to an image culture. In recent judicial decisions, convicted offenders have had to wear signs and be photographed in public identifying their crime; other signs have been affixed to automobiles and homes of offenders. A slumlord receives a sentence of house arrest in one of his own slums; a brick thrower who blinds a person in one eye must wear an eye patch in public; a burglar has to watch his victim rob the burglar's own house. Other offenders find themselves making "shaming speeches" on courthouse steps. A swindler of horse trainers has the task of cleaning out stalls in a horse stable.[71]

Officials who demand public degradations lose sight of the dignity that an offender has the right to keep in the name of all of us. Shaming within the punitive impulse pushes that offender beyond the minimal norms that hold us together as a people, the norms that tell us who we are. It maintains that those subject to public mortification don't count. All the same, reformers in search of answers have begun to think of humiliation as a legal tool of punishment. There may be no clearer sign of a punishment regime losing its way. Current speculation extends to thoughts of reintroducing corporal punishment.[72]

Criminologists began to track and sometimes support judicial practices in shaming during the mid-1990s, and their exchanges about its use continue in the twenty-first century. Common ground in these debates comes with a grim admission. Judges, scholars, and litigators all know that imprisonment does not work well if correction is the goal, and some have begun to support shaming as an alternative sanction. Shaming, the argument runs, is less expensive than imprisonment, satisfies a communal need to see punishment, and uses a very effective element of control in human behavior.[73]

It took a leading scholar steeped in the history of punishment to recognize the real problem in shaming. James Q. Whitman grants that "shame sanctions are fully compatible with standard punishment theory," and he acknowledges the desire for alternatives to "the generally acknowledged failure of imprisonment." But feasibility, another abstraction of the distant punisher, hardly justifies implementation. Whitman's controlling insight reaches beyond the creepiness in humiliating another human, and he quickly dismisses the rationalization that humiliation also comes in prison.[74]

Whitman puts the major difficulty elsewhere. It is what shaming does to the audience who witnesses it. "Once the state stirs up public opprobrium against an offender, it cannot really control the way the public treats that offender." It awakens "a dangerous willingness, on the part of the government, to delegate part of its enforcement power to a fickle and uncontrolled general populace." Shaming stirs political demons. It allows people "to punish in an undisciplined and unthinking way."

These observations are surely correct, especially at a time when the United States already punishes more heavily than other countries. The last word on shame goes to a sociologist who comes closest to explaining the phenomenon while summarizing the sketchy nature of commentary on the issue. Thomas J. Scheff describes shame as a powerful but covert enforcer of conformities that take "a malign form" through chain reactions of anger. Can we afford to stoke the punitive impulse in this way? The result of shaming can be lasting hatred and on rising levels. It can control behavior "not only between individuals, but also between groups, or even nations."[75]

The uncontrolled spread of shame as a device may be its most perilous trait. There is always a hidden price to pay. One is asked to conform up, not down, and shaming works by looking down on others. You would expect a fair-minded culture with democratic sensibilities to avoid that tendency even when the object of scorn is the illegal bottom rung in society. That does not happen, and we need more of an explanation why it doesn't.

The second variable to be considered in this section sheds some light on the problem. Communal fears undercut the impulse to be fair insofar as they apply to those in prison. When people are afraid, they want to diminish that which they cannot eliminate, and this move is especially significant if they can think of the feared element as somehow beneath them. Shaming does that. Ridicule is a strategy that intimidation and aggression have difficulty handling. Even the nastiest criminal seems less when accurately belittled in public, and the affect eases fear in the beholder of it.

Of the major emotions, fear is the one that most insidiously cuts across class categories. Everyone can be afraid at once, and that commonality can be used—and frequently has been used—to unify otherwise stratified social systems. Fear is a powerful, if haphazard and misguided, teacher. One fear raises a host of others, and together they lead communal understanding astray.[76]

Four centuries ago, Francis Bacon knew whereof he spoke as an Elizabethan living in dangerous times. He joined fear to suspicion and named such thoughts "bats." "Among birds, they ever fly by twilight." Fear and suspicion breed uncertainty and unhinge thought. They "cloud the mind."[77] Montaigne, in his essay on the same subject, believes that fear "exceeds all other disorders in intensity." It "engenders terrible bewilderment." When he writes, "The thing I fear most is fear," he has been indicating how fear causes punishers to be that much crueler when they make their victims suffer.[78]

Modern scientific investigation reduces the same philosophical insights to elemental levels. An animal, including the thinking animal *Homo sapiens,* exhibits three innate reactions, the three Fs, when frightened: "freezing (keeping absolutely still and silent), flight, or fight."[79] The first two responses are defensive reactions to a superior threat. If instead the person assumes a superior capacity to the threatening object, the response may well be to strike first on the theory that "the best defense is a good offense." Some relatively neutral examples: one might flee from a mob, freeze in the path of flying hornets, but fight, by destroying, a colony of ants found marching across the kitchen floor.

Coupled together, the philosophical and scientific insights about fear allow us to appreciate distortions in the punitive impulse. Bacon and Montaigne show that fear creates its own reality and produces an overly reactive reply that is otherwise difficult to comprehend. Science explains how those distortions apply in different circumstances, and the circumstance of crime is particularly instructive.

An early empirical study about fear of crime is one of the best. Arthur Stinchcombe, in *Crime and Punishment—Changing Attitudes in America,* possesses a rare capacity to explain tabulated data in commonsensical terms. He and his study team came slowly but profoundly to the statistical conclusion that black communities experience higher levels of crime and have greater fear of it than other communities but, curiously, do not seek higher punishments for criminals. The aggressive response, the demand for greater punishment, comes instead from surrounding white communities.[80]

The reasons for these responses can be traced to the risk calculations in elemental levels of fear. Just as black communities need strategies of avoidance from immediate threats ("freezing") and control their apprehension through more direct knowledge and less racial emphasis, so white communities, with less reason to feel threatened, less knowledge of crime, greater willingness to think in racial terms, and more power over mostly white state legislatures, respond aggressively. It is the surrounding communities that want tougher punishment through law-and-order candidates who are also white suburbanites with much more to gain than they have to lose by appearing tough on crime.

Imbalances in the strategies that deal with fear translate into policy. Overcriminalization from "law-and-order movements" falls heaviest on minority neighborhoods, a foreseeable outcome. "Police officers are quick to treat black men as suspects in settings where white men would not be so treated."[81] "Yes, police stops take place most frequently in crime areas, but the result is just as often a pretext for an arrest."[82] The cynicism in racial profiling even uses code terms. "D.W.B." (driving while black) is shorthand in police argot for zeroing in on minority drivers.[83]

The long-term consequences of intense police surveillance in minority neighborhoods have been devastating. Symbolic political interventions, "the war on crime" and "the war on drugs," have given added leverage to racial profiling, with predictable results. "Crime and drug control policies since 1980 have greatly increased the numbers of young minority citizens, especially males, entangled in the justice system's tentacles," and this process is "undermining social policies aimed at fuller integration of disadvantaged people into the fabric of American life."[84]

How is it that the punitive impulse can overlook the harshness in this situation? We have discovered that there are many reasons why, but two stand out. First, the induced fear of crime allows a law-abiding citizenry to disregard the frequency with which minorities are imprisoned, often at a very young age; second, most Americans hold to the conventional individual emphasis of the criminal justice system, which says, never mind the circumstances, "You do the crime, you do the time."[85]

But shouldn't it be more difficult to avoid the social demographics, the number of lives from one sector of the population that are being thrown away in repetitive cycles from father to son and now in drug convictions from mother to daughter? Or is it difficult? The problem—but perhaps also a long-range answer in response—is that the punitive impulse sees only what it wants to see in order to perform its tasks. We may have to look around the punitive impulse in order to change it.

Seeing Injustice

Injustice is easy to find; far more difficult to address. It comes down to what a culture is willing or unwilling to overlook. Take an obvious example. Because the nation's prisons are filled with young inmates from ghetto neighborhoods where gangs are rife, the prisons themselves are gang ridden. Most Americans know this much, but few bother to consider the effect beyond the fact.

What will it take to recognize the extent of gang violence in prisons and the need to do something about it? In October 2008 it took the death of an eighteen-year-old boy, temporarily imprisoned for a parole violation, in the Robert N. Davoren Center on Rikers Island in New York City, a facility holding 600 juveniles between the ages of sixteen and nineteen. Christopher Robinson, in his part of the facility, was beaten to death in his cell by other organized juvenile inmates for not cooperating in a gang-related extortion racket.[86]

A clear pattern of prisoner-run intimidation, extortion, and violence had existed in the Davoren Center since 2007 and undoubtedly long before that. Prison authorities admitted they had known about the problem beforehand. "We were both proactive and aware of bullying and extortionate behaviors among the adolescents at R.N.D.C. and in other jails," the New York City correction commissioner later reported. "That is why, long prior to the Robinson homicide, we took steps to prevent such behavior." To be aware of the problem but not of its dimensions is where injustice often lives.

Many of those dimensions were visible on the face of the problem. The gang-run operation in the Davoren Center determined who could sit on a chair, who could use the telephone, who could go to the bathroom and when, who would be forced to give up his allotted commissary-account money, and who would be allowed to enter the public day room. There were twenty-four-hour surveillance cameras. Without any difficulty, a guard on duty could watch the leaders of this extortion racket visibly at work. Leaders of "The Program" or "Team" could be found sitting on top of a number of stacked chairs while other inmates had to sit on the floor.

Any minimal check of commissary accounts or monitoring of telephone use, any active surveillance of inmate movement in the facility, any research into the condition of prisoners who had been injured would have revealed more about the horrors taking place in the Rikers juvenile center. An inmate who did not cooperate was "chicken winged" (arms held back) while beaten by foot soldiers in "The Program" called "pop-off dummies." Christopher Robinson was the one beaten too severely to survive. Others before him had suffered collapsed lungs, broken eye sockets, and other serious injuries. Why, with such evidence, wasn't the extortion ring stopped before a much-publicized death?

Only media coverage of the homicide made a difference, and while coverage extended well beyond the event of October 18, 2008, it did so for peripheral reasons beyond the homicide. Christopher Robinson's death publicized a pattern of successful lawsuits for beatings that had to acknowledge prison-guard neglect. But the investigation of this homicide discovered something else: prison guards had taken an active part in the intimidation ring of the Davoren Center. The guilty guards would receive short sentences for their role in the tragedy, and this would be the side of the case that dictated media coverage.

The crucial distinction at work in the Rikers tragedy came out of the mouth of the assistant district attorney who prosecuted the prison guards. "They didn't simply turn a blind eye to violence," he charged. "They authorized and directed it." A mere blind eye might have meant a successful lawsuit against the city but not prison terms for guards, and that lawsuit would have been settled quietly, like others, for money out of court. Only when authorities are complicit is there a chance of really changing the plight of prisoners through legal action. Charnel Robinson, Christopher Robinson's mother, deserves the last word in this terrible case. She received $2 million from the city in a civil suit, but who would disagree with her assessment? "It's not justice; it's unfair."

Addressing an arena of injustice is not the same thing as punishing the unjust, and we need to appreciate why that is particularly true where the punitive impulse is concerned. Both popular and legal attitudes toward prison life lack *"a principle of equivalence,"* a balancing mechanism of crime against punishment that will place a victimized inmate in a strong-enough light to reach a victimizer, whether a prison guard or another inmate. Equivalency in "the metaphysics of justice" requires that denunciation become action.[87] Without that equilibrium, victimized inmates must fend for themselves, and we are left with a metaphysics of injustice.

When will a just society recognize injustice and act on it? The question contains a philosophical uncertainty (what counts as actionable injustice?) within a psychological puzzle (what persons fall *"outside the boundary in which moral values, rules, and considerations of fairness apply"*?).[88] To grasp intractability in the impulse to punish, we have to grapple with connections not made and exclusions maintained. At issue is what the historian Lewis Namier famously termed "the crowning attainment of historical study": "an intuitive understanding of how things do *not* happen."[89]

All too often, injustice remains philosophically hidden from view. John Rawls published the seminal modern American study of justice, *A Theory of Justice,* in 1971. No later study can avoid it, and most do not get beyond it in any significant way. The index of *A Theory of Justice* contains eleven subcategories under the word "justice" with eighty-seven entries assigned to many pages in the volume; they fill a full page in the index. There is, however, no entry for "injustice." The closest parallel, a single entry for a single page, "unjust man," does not help us nearly as much as it should.[90]

On that one page Rawls distinguishes "the unjust man," who "seeks dominion for the sake of aims such as wealth and security which when appropriately limited are legitimate," from the merely "bad man," who "desires arbitrary power because he enjoys the sense of mastery." Here Rawls offers an interesting safety valve for dealing with the unjust man. An "inordinate desire" can be "duly circumscribed." The more serious contrast comes in a third figure, in "the evil man," who "aspires to unjust rule precisely because it violates what independent persons would consent to in an original position of equality."[91]

The measure of injustice incorporates all three: the unjust man, the bad man, and the evil man. But in the ways of the world, there is an interesting difference in the ability to perceive each of these figures at work. "What moves the evil man is the love of injustice: he delights in the impotence and humiliation of those subject to him, and he relishes being recognized by them as the willful author of their degradation." The evil man wants to be recognized, and this makes it easier to see him than "the unjust man," who may be guilty only of a miscalculation not shared by others, or "the bad man," who enjoys arbitrary power. Media and video sources focus on visibility. It follows that they are more interested in covering this evil man than the merely unjust or bad one.[92] Mere injustice takes second place.

Personification of the problem ("man") also simplifies the philosophical uncertainty as well as the underlying psychological puzzle in injustice. Rawls assumes a visible agency, which is where the problem of institutionalized injustice, the kind one finds in punishment regimes, only begins. To be fair, justice, not injustice, is Rawls's interest, but it is striking that injustice as such receives such minimal attention, and the difficulty runs deeper than the writer's lack of interest. Justice does not automatically invoke the concept of injustice, and when it does, an easy polarity can be misleading.[93]

There are countless articles on justice; relatively few on injustice. The most significant book on the subject, Judith Shklar's *The Faces of Injustice,* was published in 1990, nearly a quarter of a century ago. Shklar begins with a simple but ignored truth: injustice transcends the absence of justice. She underlines the fact by clarifying the continuum from misfortune to active injustice. She proves not only that injustice exists as an independent phenomenon but that people want to avoid that conclusion. "It will always be easier to see misfortune rather than injustice." "The difference between misfortune and injustice involves our willingness and our capacity to act or not to act on behalf of the victims, to blame or to absolve, to help, mitigate, and compensate or to just turn away."[94]

Fatalism becomes a major problem when injustice is read as misfortune. People are inclined to accept the status quo, however unjust, by shrugging, "That is just the way things are." Shklar counters this kind of easy resignation, the kind that led President John F. Kennedy to dismiss the subject in a press conference. Questioned about the injustice in troop call-ups of reservists during the Cold War, Kennedy famously answered, "Life is unfair." Life can be, but how unfair must it be before injustice requires an answer? Those who "say life's unfair," Shklar counters, take "the favorite evasion of passively unjust citizens."[95]

Passive injustice, one of the most powerful insights in Cicero's *De Officiis,* lets Shklar realize that justice, iconographically blindfolded in representations of the figure, can itself be blind to the injustice beyond its immediate purview. "Normal justice," she argues in noting its limits, provides "a way of living less dangerously" and grants "a feeling of enhanced security," but "it can do nothing to improve the law-abiding citizen." Nor does it encourage citizens to face "the endurance of iniquity" around them.[96]

Justice, in this normal sense, takes care of those who are entitled to its protection and excludes those who are not. The punitive impulse is about those exclusions in the name of protection and the extent of the segregation allowed. For example, can the theft of a $23 bottle of vitamins from a supermarket justly land a drug addict with eight prior convictions in jail? Yes, it can, but is it justice to give that person a sentence of twenty-five years to life for the crime? That is what happened to Michael Wayne Riggs in 1999 when the Supreme Court allowed California's "three strikes and you're out" law to stand in his case.[97]

Under a positivist understanding—control through statutory law— the Supreme Court refused to review *Riggs v. California.* "If injustice consists of voluntary acts," Shklar reasons in her definition of injustice, "there must be at least two persons, an agent and a passive victim, and often a third one to decide their conflicting claims."[98] In *Riggs* there were three ascending levels of court action and many lawyers acting as "third ones" to decide the conflicting claims. Court reasoning held that Riggs was a guilty agent, not a passive victim. Normal justice delivered a life sentence; it kept to Riggs's unjust act.

What kind of justice can reach beyond these limitations? Perhaps Riggs is only a guilty agent until he lands in jail forever. A defendant's permanent communal invisibility in serving a life sentence for a minor crime surely deserves more of a response. How concerned should we be that no one is left to care about the extraordinary length of sentences delivered to Riggs and so many others in American prisons today?

Compounding the question is the fact that a reasoned application of normal justice has produced this seeming injustice, and although injustice can be an independent phenomenon, it is readily perceived only where there is a conscious framework of other expectations—a higher justice?—somewhere in place.[99]

Nothing demonstrates the intractability of the punitive impulse more directly than the tangled relationship between justice and injustice, where justice allows injustice to exist and simultaneously enables a just society to obscure the very knowledge of that injustice. Those in charge of punishing criminals respond to this paradox by restraining "the worst of the worst," which normal justice requires, and often enough that is the case. More often, though, American punishment regimes are making "the temporarily bad" worse and turning those who are "worse" into "the worst." We must see it for what it is if we are to handle it in a different way.

7

The Law against Itself

The future will not be ruled; it can only possibly be persuaded.

Alexander Bickel, *The Least Dangerous Branch*

The Rule of Law and Punishment

The punitive impulse has been so difficult to analyze, much less control, because it has two masters. It is independently the creature of society and of law, and the puzzle is in how the two pieces come together. You can, for example, trace how every state's incarceration rate more than doubled between 1977 and 2000 by delineating the social and demographic shifts behind that increase.[1] Nevertheless, the law punishes and far more exclusively than in the past. As a recent study proves, "The machinery of criminal justice . . . has taken on a life of its own far removed from what many people expect or want."[2]

Society or Law? Confusion of cause and hence of effect reigns wherever one turns on this subject. The length of an imprisonment may be a social effect, but the actual suffering comes from the arm of the law. Disentangling causation extends to the simplest specifics. When we decide punishment is deserved for a certain number of years in prison, how much of the assertion is based on a social gauge of the dignity and autonomy that should be taken away, and how much is based on the gravity of the crime? Surely, both are at issue, and any plan to change punishment in the United States must take both into account.

196

The law takes precedence here because it manages the anatomy of punishment, but if we turn in that direction, it must be with the insight that only a different communal perception will improve its management. The values that attach to a person's rightful autonomy and the measure of that autonomy in an actor under legal investigation are as significant in the right to punish as the nature of the crime.[3] A balance must be drawn, and arguably it is the loss of such balance that has created an era of massive incarceration and misguided penal policies.

Where should the balance be drawn? The institutional, political, social, and theoretical foundations of the punitive impulse have been explored in previous chapters, but there is a last and more fundamental control to consider that bridges the interface between society and law. Left for attention is the rule of law that rationalizes the system for social belief, a system that is currently so brutal that anyone who looks must see that it does not work well for anyone who is not making money off it. Admittedly, the law has never claimed to be efficient; it only claims to be just. To grasp fully the fallen nature of punishment in America, we need to approach the law on its own terms and ask how its claims of justice apply to the penal system.

As such, the question reaches beyond the practices already noted, practices that keep in prison a number equivalent to the populations of Rhode Island and New Hampshire put together.[4] Philosophically speaking, what is it in the American rule of law that allows harsh sentencing and mass incarceration to remain such intractable issues? To ask the question in this way plunges us back into the tangled mix of law and society for an answer.

The rule of law in a democracy receives its meaning from "transactional associations" that flow back and forth between official and public perception. Individuals in society agree to be socially bound by law as citizens, but the people retain their right to express competing views about law from outside its stipulations even as they consent to the formulation that they are given.[5]

The transactional associations that form the rule of law will differ in time and place, but the increasingly one-sided aspect of them in modern times has opened a troubling debate among legal theorists over the law's intellectual detachment from society at large. What has happened to the balance needed?

Led by Lon Fuller, legal philosophers in the middle of the twentieth century began to deplore a stance that was taking some of the transactional out of the associations that make up the rule of law. They accused legal positivists, so named, of looking only to the complexity of existing law for their guidance. "While one may significantly describe the law *that is*," the positivists assumed, "nothing that transcends personal predilection can be said about the law *that ought to be*."[6]

Fuller saw legal thought reaching for an "exclusive hegemony of its own." More and more in law were trying to free themselves from "the complications of ethics and philosophy." Why did so many urge such a move, and how did it come to dominate legal thought? An exclusive purview simplified matters at a time of growing complexity. It distinguished "between those ideas or meanings which are only trying to become law and those which have succeeded." For the legal positivist, only those laws that crossed "a kind of finishing line" were worth talking about.[7] The law, such thinking went, should concentrate on what it did best, the interpretation and enforcement of the laws that were on the books.

Fuller complained about "the essentially sterile nature of any form of legal positivism which purports to divorce itself from a definite ethical or practical goal." It has no way to reform itself through the priority it gives to "assumed 'pure fact of law.' "[8] More recently, the leading philosopher of legal rights, Ronald Dworkin, has attacked the same weakness on more specific grounds. Dworkin argues that the narrow focus of legal positivism keeps it from identifying the larger reckonings in decisions and shields it from problems the law needs to face.

Dworkin is direct about these problems. Anyone who insists on a set of valid rules as "exhaustive of 'the law' " fails to distinguish a different basis for difficult and bigger decisions that have to be based on looser standards. "Standards," Dworkin explains, "do not function as rules"; they "operate differently as principles." "Rules are applicable in an all-or-nothing fashion." A standard or principle works in another way. It "sets out a goal to be reached, generally an improvement in some economic, political, or social feature of the community." It pursues "a requirement of justice, or fairness or some other dimension of morality."[9]

Law privileging itself *as it is* cannot see law as *it should be*, and the implications for thinking about problems in punishment are vast. Some rightly believe "the distinction between *is* and *ought* is the most important one we ever draw" if we are to achieve the goal of "moral clarity" on a given issue.[10]

Previous chapters have argued that intractable problems yield to outside influence or internal catastrophe. Legal positivism resists outside influence through the inner integrity it claims for itself, and it therefore frequently lacks the temperament to discover a catastrophe on its own doorstep. We are on the cusp of larger explanations, on the very edge of knowing why the conservative nature of legal thought does not openly or regularly challenge the severity of punishment that its systems have created.

Pause for a moment over the implications. One can hardly expect the affirmative spirit that dominates public declarations of the rule of law to announce its own failings, particularly on what takes place behind the closed doors of the country's punishment regimes. Punishment is the end game in legal determination, what is famously known today as "closure." It is, however, the axis of concern in most literary treatments of the subject. Rare is the courtroom novel that does not portray either too much or too little punishment in an unfolding plot with an added criticism of law somewhere in mind.[11]

American literature offers many examples. In perhaps the most notable case, literary protest helped end flogging in the sailing ships of the nineteenth century. Sea fiction figured the Republic as "a ship of state" and turned the tyrannical control of harsh punishment by sea captains into a synecdoche for unjust power in democratic understandings.[12] Herman Melville wrote as the undisputed master of this genre, and in a final tour de force unpublished at his death in 1891, he left the country an account of the intellectual trap that would lead legal positivism toward intractability in punishment.

The novella *Billy Budd, Sailor (An Inside Narrative)* does what the law is reluctant to admit, and it vexes every approach today for a reason. Whenever readers refuse to accept the story's deepest implications, they, in effect, misconstrue the nature of the American punishment regime they live with today.

The Positivist's Dilemma

Melville recognized that an emergent legal positivism—strict construction of the law as written out for consistent enforcement—had displaced broader philosophical beliefs based on combinations of divine, natural, and human law.[13] By the 1890s the explosion in statutory and case law had brought greater precision and professionalism to legal inquiry, but it also encouraged a narrower perspective on human endeavor. *Billy Budd* depicts the loss of primal connections and the costs involved.

Distance often clarifies. Melville sets his story in the summer of 1797, "the time before steamships," but in a significant gesture to the history of ideas, this is also the time when the forming and still-disparate United States struggles with combinations of divine, natural, and human law in its search for a collective identity.[14] Melville chooses the earlier period without forgetting his own.[15] Into an eighteenth-century world dominated by Enlightenment thought, he inserts a rigid form of legal agreement remarkably similar to the statute-driven orientations of modernity. The result is a punishment that outrages modern readers, and that effect is deliberate. Melville uses it to wonder whether or not those same readers will remain oblivious to parallels in their own legal world.[16]

Readers of *Billy Budd* invariably look for someone to blame. They fasten on the unsettling story line with its built-in need to disturb but fail to grasp how it reaches beyond all thought of individual blame.[17] Melville has broader interests in mind. He focuses on the systemic nature of punishment and the philosophical construct that supports its purposes and directions. If he makes us protest the result, it is to make us look at punishment and the reasons for it more closely than we want to.

The plot of the novella is simple, almost a fable, with all of the figures given stereotypical traits and programmatic roles. John Claggart, the malicious master-at-arms aboard the English warship *Bellipotent,* ensnares and accuses nature's child, the innocent foretop sailor Billy Budd, of mutiny before the always-perceptive captain of the vessel, Edward Fairfax Vere. Captain Vere makes Claggart confront Budd in his cabin in the accurate belief that Claggart is lying, but the sailor, who stutters, cannot respond orally to the charge and in exasperation strikes out at Claggart, killing him with a single blow. The blow, without the reason for it or the result of it, is already a capital offense under the Mutiny Act of British maritime law, and Vere, understanding everything, orchestrates a drumhead court of inquiry that leads to the execution of Billy Budd, who is hanged the very next morning.

The story could easily be adjusted so as not to disturb. Billy Budd could receive a sentence of some years in prison for involuntary manslaughter; he has, after all, killed a man. Would that result be about right?[18] Yes, it would, but it would also destroy the reader's interest as well as the story itself. Fiction is only interested in law when something

goes wrong. Invariably its plots turn on either too much punishment or too little.

Excessive punishment is what drives Melville's tale, and it is crucial to his purposes. He means to unsettle and complicate every reaction through acknowledged harsh punishment, and it is in this sense that he proclaims the story "a narration essentially having less to do with fable than with fact" (128). Melville knows that the world punishes heavily, frequently, and cruelly more often than it shows mercy, and he presents it that way.

To make the account as painful as possible, Melville gives each main character sterling qualities that do not help him. Billy Budd, the archetypal "Handsome Sailor" loved and admired by all, becomes a murderer condemned for it through his one flaw (44, 53). Claggart's extraordinary intelligence exists only to mask what he cannot control: "an antipathy spontaneous and profound such as is evoked in certain exceptional mortals" (74). Captain Vere misses nothing. "Something exceptional in the moral quality of Captain Vere made him, in earnest encounter with a fellow man, a veritable touchstone of that man's essential nature," but his profound intuitions do not help him (96).

To predetermined machinations Melville adds a psychological dimension that qualifies everything that occurs: no one aboard ship thinks in a way and with a capacity that might change things. No apparent knowledge can prevent what happens aboard the *Bellipotent*. Nor is that all. Confirming every seemingly predestined act is a narrative voice not Melville's own, as so many critics try to claim.[19]

This austere voice relates the story from high above the action. It is fatalistic in theme but elegiac in tone. Somewhere further above its quiescent tones, we also have what many have described as the writer's "last will and testament."[20] *Billy Budd* presents Melville's final word as a writer, and it is crafted fitfully, even painfully, across the last five years of the author's life after many more years of failure and silence in fiction. Typical of a testament, Melville leaves the manuscript unpublished at his death in 1891, a death prefigured by the death of several others, the passing of a beloved sister who greatly helped his work and the deaths of two sons, one a suicide that he discovers himself.

The long silence in fiction, across more than thirty years, has to have been a willed act. *Billy Budd* reveals a craftsman at the height of his power. Why does Melville leave this last masterpiece in a drawer where it is nearly lost?[21] He would have realized what he had accomplished, so the decision is a significant one. The writer knows that his contemporaries have no use for his fiction or for the ideas he presents. America would not identify its greatest novelist until well into the twentieth century. It would not accept Melville because it could not yet fully grasp what he already knew.

Billy Budd, first published in 1924, gives Melville's ultimate view of the human condition—the same condition that perturbed a troubled life—and it drives the characters of his story inexorably down. Authors are murderers by trade in the process of moving their plots along. This time, however, the slaughter is complete. Every main character dies: Claggart at Billy's hand, Billy orchestrated by Vere, and Vere shortly after in combat with a French ship significantly called the *Athée* (atheist). Even so, the story is not so much a tragedy as a reflection, a monody of regret.

Regret is, in fact, everywhere, but muted through misunderstandings that rob the story of the final clarity that goes with tragedy. Ruthlessly, even diabolically, after having all his characters mistake each other, Melville ends his novella with two utterly false stories that will be the only ones the world will ever know. The first is a newspaper account in which Billy Budd is the villain and Claggart a valued patriot sadly lost. The second, a sailor's poem, turns the inarticulate Billy into the soul of eloquence. The point Melville makes is not sardonic or acrid so much as wistful. "The truth uncompromisingly told," the narrator says, "will always have its ragged edges" (128).

Three strategies can help us cope with the frustrations built into *Billy Budd*. Above all, we must read for tone. The aloof narrator orchestrates each frustration without joining in any of them. We must also accept the meaning of the author's title at face value. His "Inside Narrative" carries us philosophically inward. Finally, we must accept the hints the story gives about the nature of the world it presents. We must formally separate the three constructed points of view offered: that of the narrator, that of the author above the narrator, and that of the worldview that the story claims to represent.[22]

The narrator plies the reader with unanswered queries. "What was the matter with the master-at-arms?" (72). This incessant question is worried across three whole chapters, with the only real answer becoming "the mania of an evil nature . . . in short, 'a depravity according to nature'" (78). Knowing the answer to be unsatisfactory, the always quiet voice in control of the account gives up with an evasive shrug: "the re-sumed narrative must be left to vindicate, as it may, its own credibility" (76–77). As the ostensible owner of this story, the narrator says you must trust me only so far as you can and apply your own thought for meaning.

Much the same kind of directive applies to the central character, Cap-tain Vere, the one person who sees everything immediately and whose penetration and erudition befuddle the slower minds all around him. "Whether Captain Vere, as the surgeon professionally and privately sur-mised, was really the sudden victim of any degree of aberration, every-one must determine for himself by such light as this narrative may af-ford" (102). At every turn we are moved along by this voice with its detached ironies and indirections, but we are carried only so far before we have to think for ourselves.

The ultimate question, delivered by Vere, is just as compulsively left to the reader's resources. "How can we adjudge to summary and shame-ful death a fellow creature innocent before God, and whom we feel to be so?" Vere asks this of the officers he selects for his drumhead court, and to assure that no reader dodges the pain in this question, it is immedi-ately reinforced: "Does that state it aright?" (110).

Well, does it? The mystifying interrogative mode forces readers in-ward where Melville wants his "inside narrative" faced more than an-swered. The story has many layers, and when we get to the innermost, the narrator once again leaves the reader alone for an answer. In this, the most intimate moment of the story, Captain Vere's final private meet-ing with the condemned Billy, the sources of explanation offered be-come precisely the ones rejected in the drumhead court: divine law and natural law against human law.

In this scene the three separate spheres present themselves without explaining or cohering. "Beyond the communication of the sentence, what took place at this interview was never known," the narrator in-tones. Still, "some conjectures may be ventured." What are they? "There is no telling the sacrament seldom if in any case revealed to the gadding world, wherever under circumstances at all akin to those here attempted to be set forth two of great Nature's nobler order embrace." Arch, some-what tangled syntax perfects the narrator's escape route, but not before ignorance is made a permanent stipulation: "Holy oblivion, the sequel to each diviner magnanimity, providentially covers all at last" (115).

By merging into the mystery of things, the narrator cuts off every escape for the reader. Those who would blame Captain Vere find no comparable intellect aboard the *Bellipotent* capable of maintaining an alternative. Those who reject the sudden drumhead court and want Billy Budd sent to the fleet for trial misunderstand the consequences. A sailor who has been accused of mutiny and who then strikes and kills a superior officer would have met a horrible fate: he would have been either flogged or keelhauled through the fleet until dead and probably after as an example to deter others.[23] Over everything hovers the fear of mutiny as a present danger aboard the warship *Bellipotent*, one that requires quick judgment. Melville has made this fear palpable through extensive references to "The Nore" or "Great Mutiny" just months before the events in question (54).

Narrative insistence on so much mystery and so much entrapment forces us to interpret the world that the story conveys as much as the incidents in play, and here the clues are at once obvious and subtle. By making his victim an impressed sailor on his man-of-war, one forced into military service, Melville separates the ideas at stake. Billy is impressed from the *Rights of Man*, a ship governed by intuitional belief in the natural man, to the *Bellipotent*, where the strict letter of military law governs.

This movement from natural law to positive law is more subtle at the generic level. The narrator gives us the apparently gratuitous claim that the story "is no romance" of the kind rendered in the 1850s by the novelist Melville most admired, Nathaniel Hawthorne (53). The reference is no idle one. Melville thought so highly of Hawthorne in 1851 that he dedicated the most renowned American novel of all, *Moby-Dick; or, The Whale*, to him.

What exactly is a romance? Hawthorne wrote in 1850 that "in writing a romance, a man is always—or always ought to be—careering on the verge of a precipitous absurdity, and the skill lies in coming as close as possible, without actually tumbling over."[24] Melville showed his own earlier commitment by writing a novel about a sea captain who searches the Pacific Ocean for a white whale and actually finds it.

A nineteenth-century romance conflates levels of reality, the spiritual and the material, "where the actual and the Imaginary may meet, and each imbue itself with the nature of the other."[25] Hence in Hawthorne's second novel, *The House of the Seven Gables*, an angry character tells the villain of the novel, "God will not let you do the thing you meditate." God doesn't. Providence kills off the evildoer with a miraculously timed intervention in the very next scene, turning him into "nothing better than a defunct nightmare, which had perished in the midst of its wickedness."[26] In Hawthorne's novel, God listens and then acts to save the situation. Yes, it is a close thing, but different worlds cohere.

Melville contests that very scene in *Billy Budd* through words of realization ascribed to Captain Vere moments after Billy kills Claggart. "Struck dead by an angel of God!" Vere cries. "Yet the angel must hang!" To the "prudent surgeon" who overhears Vere's "interjections," the words are "mere incoherences," but not to the reader. The words signify that divine law and human law now belong to separate realms, and they prepare us for the primal scene of full recognition, Melville's courtroom (76).

Unlike the charismatic leader to whom he is compared, Lord Horatio Nelson, Captain Vere cannot rule by the force of a romanticized personality. He commands as the most thoughtful and intelligent regular captain one can hope for. Vere must lead through the directives available to him rather than with spiritual ascendancy. " 'With Mankind,' he would say, 'forms, measured forms are everything,' " and the clearest measures in any institution are the stipulated laws that govern it (128).

Vere therefore insists on the written law, first as witness, then as defense counsel, then as prosecutor, and finally as "coadjutor" of the drumhead court that condemns Billy Budd. His manipulation of procedure is reprehensible, but Vere, as the absolute holder of law aboard ship, takes the measure of what positive law demands of him and acts to separate its relevance from "natural justice." He constantly reminds his officers, "We proceed under the law of the Mutiny Act" (107–111).

Melville pulls no punches in the story's courtroom scene. Notably, Captain Vere prepares the speech that controls his junior officers and ends it from exactly the same point of view: "gazing out from a sashed porthole to windward upon the monotonous blank of the twilight sea" (109, 113). Nature will not interfere, nor will divine law. Religiosity aboard the *Bellipotent* "is as incongruous as a musket would be on the altar of Christmas" (122). Neither possibility is now part of legal determination.

The absence of these previous connections allows Vere to dismiss the puzzle in Claggart's death as "a matter for psychologic theologians to discuss." "But what has a military court to do with it?" he asks (108). "At the Last Assizes it shall acquit. But how here?" "Private conscience should not yield to that imperial one formulated in the code under which alone we officially proceed." Vere insists on "military necessity," "a lawful rigor singularly demanded at this juncture" (111, 113). Flexibility in a comparative frame has become the enemy here.

The drumhead court must not be "casuists or moralists" and certainly not "a jury of casuists" (110). Relativism does not apply. Any answer outside the Mutiny Act will be "pusillanimous" and a public source of "shame" (113). Vere wields the written law to reduce the qualms of his officers and to challenge their manhood. When they hesitate to decide, it is as if they are "waylaid by some tender kinswoman," not realizing that "the feminine in man, is as that piteous woman, and hard though it be, she must here be ruled out." Everything but the simplicity of the law must be ruled out. "Do these buttons that we wear attest that our allegiance is to Nature? No, to the King," and through the king's buttons "war looks but to the frontage, the appearance." Anything else will "enervate decision." Reason lies with what others have written down: "Let not warm hearts betray heads that should be cool" (110–112).

It is revealing in this speech that the closed world of written law stands for a decisive simplicity while everything beyond it conjures up complexity, soft thinking, hesitation, and avoidance. "Your scruples," Vere hectors his officers, "do they move as in a dusk? Challenge them. Make them advance and declare themselves." Challenge them with what? Vere answers with the narrowing law on the page, and it addresses "nothing but the prisoner's overt act" (110). What positive law so obviously has going for it is a certainty based on "the frontage, the appearance" in things.

Billy Budd reveals how much American legal attitudes had changed by the end of the nineteenth century.[27] In an 1830 summation, "the greatest ever delivered to an American jury," Daniel Webster, an earlier prosecutor, could convince his auditors that there are no secrets, no crimes safe from heaven's exposure. "Providence hath so ordained and doth so govern things, that those who break the great law of Heaven by shedding man's blood seldom succeed in avoiding discovery."[28]

Divinity presides over human understanding and action in Webster's world. Anyone who tries to cloak lawful duty in darkness forgets the divine light that will expose the truth and "pain us wherever it has been violated." Webster's God, also Abraham Lincoln's as late as 1865, is immanent in human affairs. Half a century later, Melville's God has no place in the earthly judgments of those "by whom offenses come."[29]

The shift in legal conception by the 1890s puts the legitimacy of law entirely on human ingenuity, with an ensuing difficulty. How can mere artifice invest law with the authenticity it requires? Legal positivism handles this problem through procedural visibility. It takes as its guide what has been written out, declared as law by appropriate institutions, and followed to the letter, but the letter of the law instills a rigidity of temperament. Captain Vere personifies that rigidity when he tells his drumhead court, "One of two things must we do—condemn or let go" (112).

Since antiquity, the philosophical underpinnings of the legal alternatives proposed by Vere have referred to different frames of reference: "Necessitas publica major est quam privata" (Communal necessity trumps private necessity) versus "Fiat justitia ruat coelum" (Let justice be done though the sky or heavens fall). Taken together, these assertions distinguish positive law in its calculation of social interests from the natural and divine frameworks of doing justice no matter what.

As the first orientation depends on human ingenuity, so the second reaches for a solution above the problem by locating controlling and presumably universal normative values within nature. Vere, the legal positivist, can reject the second alternative in the name of the first because legal positivism "at the very heart of its case, affirms the reality of legal obligation, based on nothing more than the actual law in effect."[30] The last chapters of *Billy Budd* then question this emphasis without ever challenging it directly. Nature and Providence reappear in miraculous interventions to dignify Billy Budd's execution and funeral.

With the court decision behind us and "to the wonder of all," Billy suffers none of the natural spasms in death by hanging. The sun simultaneously bursts on the horizon: "The vapory fleece hanging low in the East was shot through with a soft glory as of the fleece of the Lamb of God." Then at Billy's burial, "certain larger seafowl" circle the sinking corpse with "the croaked requiem of their cries." Billy in death signifies natural man ("rare personal beauty") and God's servant ("the young sailor, spiritualized now"). With his last words he cries out a benediction for all, one that the crew instinctively repeats: "God bless Captain Vere!" (123–124, 127). All three frameworks—divine law, natural law, and human law—still exist in *Billy Budd,* but they do not connect in human enterprise.

A last qualification hangs over all others in Melville's story, and it further complicates the problems of legal positivism. In the argument that ultimately persuades the drumhead court to condemn Billy Budd, Captain Vere observes that the ship's crew have "native sense"—the instincts that natural law and a divinely instilled moral sense have given them—but "not that kind of intelligent responsiveness that might qualify them to comprehend and discriminate" when any disruption of positive law occurs (112–113).

Vere convinces his officers that the people will not understand leniency. "Your clement sentence they would count as pusillanimous. They would think that we flinch, that we are afraid of them—afraid of practicing a lawful rigor" (113). That is always a question in divergences from the applications of positive law. Will the people understand? Will they accept anything but punishment duly prescribed?

The Limits of Fundamental Law

The peremptory punishments aboard Melville's eighteenth-century warship no longer apply, but the challenge of too much severity may be even greater in an era of legal positivism practiced on a massive scale. Judges preside in American courtrooms today much as Captain Vere did over his drumhead court. They sentence more harshly than they would like to as individuals and declare, once again, that the people will not understand anything else. Everywhere the letter of legislated law requires judges to give punishments that they themselves feel do not fit the crime but do fit the people's officially declared agreement in statute law.

Life behind bars includes a large number of essentially minor offenders in American prisons who have violated harsh drug laws. Stephanie George, twenty-seven and with three small children at the time of her sentence, is now fifteen years into a life sentence without parole. Her offense? She played a subsidiary role in a drug ring run by an ex-boyfriend who had hidden a stash of cocaine in her apartment without her knowledge. Said her judge at sentencing, "Your role has basically been as a girlfriend and bag holder . . . so certainly in my judgment it does not warrant a life sentence." Unfortunately, federal law required such a sentence without the possibility of ever achieving release. Of the law that he had to enforce, the judge observed, "The punishment is supposed to fit the crime, but when a legislative body says this is going to be the sentence no matter what other factors there are, that's draconian in every sense of the word. Mandatory sentences breed injustice."[31]

Examples exist in every federal jurisdiction. Putting a first offender away for life without parole, a federal judge in the United States District Court of the Southern District of Illinois admitted to a twenty-six-year-old defendant that the sentence was "excessive and disproportionate." "Maybe somewhere down the line Congress will relieve the people in your situation." Well down that line, the defendant is now forty-one and still in prison. In the Northern District of Illinois, a defendant at nineteen who is now thirty-eight was told, "This is your first conviction, and here you face life imprisonment. I think it gives me pause that this was the intent of the Congress." "It's an unfair sentence," declared another federal judge, this time in the Southern District of Iowa, while delivering a life sentence without parole to a man who distributed LSD dissolved in blotting paper. "There is no authority that I know of that would permit a different sentence by me," added a federal judge in a similar situation in the Western District of Missouri.

You do not have to be a violent person to receive a life sentence without parole in the United States. It is enough if you are a repeat offender, have been caught with a large amount of drugs, or have been convicted as a dealer when more serious offenders testified against you to receive a lighter sentence. Many drug offenders are among the 41,000 inmates serving life sentences without parole, a sentence that does not exist elsewhere or is limited to heinous crimes in which innocent people are hurt. More than half the people behind bars today are there for nonviolent offenses.[32]

As in *Billy Budd*, the problem is systemic rather than personal. One cannot blame judges for following the law. When judges in the 1970s exercised discretion to reach fairer results, they were publicly attacked, and the attacks led to the severe legislated sentences that we have today. Blame, if there is to be blame, must be assigned to the American people who listen to demagogic claims of "law and order" from ambitious politicians who know that such language will get them elected.

When will people learn to resist the false appeal in such language? It may help to realize that the law-and-order slogans that now dominate the rule of law first resonated in the body politic to protect the institution of slavery and to stop the extension of suffrage.[33] Of course, the need to resist political sloganeering is easily said, but how do you change a people's attitudes? Other things stand in the way.

Americans like to think of themselves as a righteous community fighting crime. In the most legitimate modern claim on that designation, President Franklin D. Roosevelt, speaking on the day after the Japanese attack on Pearl Harbor, predicted "no matter how long it may take us to overcome this premeditated invasion, the American people, in their righteous might, will win through to absolute victory."[34] They did win through in the four-year struggle that still defines them, World War II.

In biblical terms, righteousness creates might. In a more secular state, a collective people can believe quite the opposite: that might makes them righteous. Many contemporary Americans identify and cherish the affinities between power, the ability to dictate a just solution anywhere in the world, and the right to punish the unjust on those terms, but there is always a price to pay in might realized.[35]

Worldly success in a righteous punisher can rob it of empathy for those who fail in the midst of so much success or who fall short of lofty communal expectations. George Kateb writes "the passion for excessive punishment" grows out of the desire to avenge lèse-majesté (an offense against the honor of the state). The righteous punisher enjoys "a hypertrophied sense of his own dignity, his stature," and responds "even more savagely to what is perceived as a savage assault" not just on people but on the moral fiber of the state. In the vernacular of *Billy Budd*, "the king's buttons" control. The righteous punisher can forget that punishment is a necessary evil and should remain as limited as possible.[36]

What might be done about the exalted demeanor of the punisher in a people full of anger at the transgressors in their midst? A shift away from excessive punishment sounds hopeless until one recalls the confused forms of justice at play in national discourse and the need to separate them in declarations of the rule of law for new thought to become possible. A more intrinsic slogan than "law and order" can help us, this time from the Pledge of Allegiance, "justice for all."

Justice in the pledge has three related significations in American declarations. It can point toward the greatest happiness for the greatest number ("to the Republic for which it stands"); it can mean the citizen's freedom of choice (the full phrase in the pledge reads "with liberty and justice for all"); and it can mean the common good through right communal thought and action ("one nation . . . indivisible").[37]

A leading political philosopher, Michael Sandel, nicely separates these three elements while pointing to defects in the first two. Utilitarianism appeals to a consumer culture, but it turns justice into a calculation rather than a principle and flattens rights into that calculation. The second variation, freedom of choice as justice, comes much closer to a rights conceptions in American law, but it dignifies only certain rights, and it does not question the large number of choices that dictate imbalances in social life.

Sandel supports the third and vaguer goal of a generally conceived good life. "Justice is not only about the right way to distribute things. It is also about the right way to value things." Seeking the good life through the right way to value things implies more than getting or taking or choosing. It requires a return to the very last words in the Pledge of Allegiance, the good life "for all."

There are, to be sure, problems here as well. Disagreement over what constitutes the good life presents a serious obstacle in this third conception of justice, and the stubborn nature of the impasse returns us, at least initially, to the limited agreements enforced by law in the second idea of justice: namely, freedom of choice guaranteed by fundamental rights under the protection of law. The return is not without merit. Fundamental rights should be a concern in any thought for a better plan in prison life.

Again, though, we discover the law against itself. If we assume for the moment, an assumption borne out by polls, that a majority of Americans actually support harsh levels of punishment, prisoner rights face a major difficulty within the rule of law. The Supreme Court has been willing to front a majority of Americans only when an acknowledged fundamental right has been at stake, and the price of such interference has been careful limitation of it.[38] Almost every court articulation of fundamental rights has been supported by a more essential encompassing fundamental right, the right to liberty, and that is precisely what has been taken away from the millions who reside in American prisons.

There are more formal difficulties. The Supreme Court has restricted fundamental rights to a special category. In *Washington v. Glucksberg* (1997), the court held that assisted suicide is not a fundamental right protected by the due process clause of the Fourteenth Amendment, and in making that decision it articulated the stringent nature of restrictions that will always apply in any decision dealing with fundamental rights.

Out of respect for the democratic process and to prevent judges from overreaching through their own "policy preferences" when it comes to rights, Chief Justice William Rehnquist in *Washington v. Glucksberg* spoke for a unanimous court: "We have regularly observed that the Due Process Clause specially protects [only] those fundamental rights and liberties which are, objectively, 'deeply rooted in this Nation's history and tradition' ('so deeply rooted in the traditions and conscience of our people as to be ranked as fundamental')."[39] Fundamental rights must be found first in the people's understanding, and that understanding must be deeply and long rooted.

No one can argue that better care for the nation's inmates has been deeply rooted in national traditions. The opposite comes closer to the truth.[40] The long history of vacating rights of prisoners has become a new concern because the punitive impulse in state and national policies has created a crisis through serious overcrowding. Prisoners who previously would not have been thought of as a threat worthy of serious detention are now held alongside dangerous offenders in conditions that are not secure. Massive incarceration and failures in correction have changed the nature of imprisonment.

Established law tells us that the barriers blocking constitutional remedies for the plight of inmates in American prisons are serious ones, but that should not stop legal interest in problems that demand attention. Consider again Michael Sandel's preferred conception of justice in the question that controls his study: "What is the right thing to do?"[41] "Doing the right thing" reaches toward a more universal comprehension of conduct, and the doing of it implies that constitutional barriers need not preclude a problem-oriented approach to prisoner needs. Nor do those barriers prevent the viability of rights that might still pertain, given the terrible conditions in prisons today.

Franklin D. Roosevelt's still-moving articulation of the four freedoms might be a place to begin. Two of the four freedoms lack constitutional authority, but Roosevelt meant for all four to apply everywhere in the world in his State of the Union address to Congress on January 6, 1941. Roosevelt called for freedom of speech, freedom of worship, freedom from want, and freedom from fear.[42] The four together symbolize a modern view of natural or abstract law. Together they encompass what every human being deserves: the need and the chance to develop. The urge to develop beyond oneself is a trait that can be appreciated in the behavior of any small child in any civilization. Conversely, an enforced lack of development twists human nature and distorts behavior.

In whatever limits incarceration might mandate, all four of Roosevelt's proclaimed freedoms would seem to apply to people held under ostensibly benevolent government control. Freedom of speech might be curtailed but not eliminated. Freedom of worship should be a given as long as it poses no threat to institutional discipline. Freedom from want includes at least the right of an inmate and the obligation of the state to avoid hunger through minimal standards of nourishment.[43]

Freedom from fear presents the biggest challenge. The first three freedoms may exist even in terrible prisons, but no prisoner in an overcrowded prison today lives without daily fear of harm, humiliation, brutality, and failed regard for needed attention. The horrors in American prisons cannot be avoided. They are a blight on national integrity and shame every citizen who knows about them and then ignores them.

No one currently living in the United States should want to ignore conditions that turn nonviolent first offenders into experienced criminals. Many inmates handle prison by adapting to their transgressive environment, and they reemerge in public life more dangerous than when they entered. High recidivism rates are the product of prison life in twenty-first-century America. If a system is broken—and this one is—everyone should want to fix it. But how?

Where Is the Line between "Less Just" and "Unjust"?

As clear as the problems are, they need to be made clearer in legal terms. Incarceration is where the surfaces of the law currently leave the prison system. The mantra "Put them away" takes its meaning from the judicial sentence that assigns a numbers of years in prison. As long as numbers provide the gauge of punishment, especially when the years assigned are many, inmates will be left in mental and physical states where time loses all meaning in the unavoidable counting of it.

What will it take to make "years served" meaningful for all concerned? No easy task, the possibility becomes that much harder as massive incarceration, with its dire logistical and retributive attributes, overwhelms rehabilitation programs that were not very good in the first place. Legal punishment must give intrinsic human value more of a place if its equations in defining punishment are to change. Remember Michael Sandel's insistence on "the right way to value things." Left to themselves as currently constituted, the legitimating surfaces of legal positivism justify a status quo based on habit, professional inclination, the path known, and the prosperity of its managers.[44]

Regimes, including punishment regimes, have as their first goal the very unphilosophical need to perpetuate themselves, and the greater their resources, the more they extend themselves through the conventional behavior that the status quo indulges. The United States spends well over $80 billion annually on prison costs.[45] The economic interests within this enormous outlay naturally work to sustain themselves, and severity in punishment promotes their existence. More prisoners with longer sentences nourish the system; it never seems to matter that each new inmate adds to the burden on already-overcrowded institutions. The machinery of the law grinds on.

The burgeoning punishment regime is thus a paradoxical entity. It may be the only industry in the United States that thrives on poorer and poorer performance. Much of this inefficiency, an inefficiency that trades in human cargo, is hidden from view and kept hidden by groups that prosper in the waste of other people's lives. Even so, the system itself would falter without the coherence that legal positivism supplies when it declares that it is proper to proceed as we have been proceeding.

Change to existing legal thought and practice to be possible must come from a different level of legal perception. It requires a perspective from outside current frameworks, but not too far outside and still available within that framework. What can challenge the law in legal terms if not another law? The most exalted vehicle is the check on legal enterprise that a higher sense of justice (beyond normal or day-to-day justice) can sometimes provide. "Sometimes" is the right qualifier here because a higher sense of justice cannot answer a "less just" situation; that is the province of law. Higher justice applies only when the situation in question is manifestly unjust.

There are situations, nonetheless, where a universal idea of justice can challenge the narrower dimensions that legal positivism brings to law enforcement. Modern philosophies of justice assume as much. They argue that justice is not exhausted "in the historical or positive fact"; nor limited to "the forms of the empiric world." Continuing respect for the law is a given, but the idea of justice retains "moral consciousness as an absolute requirement, even in opposition to its empirical or relative realizations."[46]

The standards are never clear, but when they are raised appropriately, "justice may proclaim itself as valid and effective even *against* a legal system actually in force, when the organism of the latter, through 'arrested development,' degeneration, or other pathological causes, is no longer in a condition to fulfill its functions or physiologically to renew its structure." Serious opposition becomes necessary when "the rules of the system in force are in irreconcilable conflict with those elementary requirements of justice that . . . are the primary reasons of its validity."[47]

When does possibility become obligation under the rule of law? To the extent that the American punishment regime is legally coherent within its own conception but defective in broader normative considerations, it should be subject to critique from outside itself through the idea of justice. To the further extent that a regime is degenerating and no longer in a condition to perform its role fairly, it should welcome ideas that will safeguard its proper functions. This, in fact, is roughly the message of the majority of the Supreme Court in 2011 when it insists on changes in the California prison system in *Brown v. Plata*.[48]

We have seen that without carefully maintained safeguards, a prison system will become less just, if not unjust. When does the greater severity that characterizes punishment regimes over time make it difficult to draw a distinction in the trajectory from "less just" to "unjust"? If "less just" is more legally acceptable than "unjust" in the management of prisons, where does one draw the line?

Five tenets in a study from 2010 explain the conditions that make a bad situation unbearable. The move toward injustice accelerates when "elitism is efficient, exclusion is necessary, prejudice is natural, greed is good, and despair is inevitable." Still, insofar as all five tenets, or some of them, are present, can one draw the line? Maybe so, but maybe not. So intrinsic to human conduct are these tenets that "the great injustices of our times are, for many, simply part of the landscape of normality."[49]

We do not have to search far to find all five tenets of injustice at work with brutal force in many American penal systems. An efficient elite excludes the undesirables in its midst through the sentences it delivers. Prejudice is natural enough against convicted criminals, especially when ethnic identifications dominate, as they frequently do when so many minorities end up in prison. Greed turns out to be very good for "the prison-industrial complex."[50] Despair in long-term imprisonment is indeed inevitable, and American society expects it in criminals who have been asked "to pay" for their crimes.

Prison systems elsewhere may have similar problems, but the intensity, entrenched economics, political power, and size of the American punishment regime bring many of its conditions to the line between "less just" and "unjust." Today the United States imprisons more people than any other country in the world, and the tally continues to spiral upward. America has less than 5 percent of the world's population but nearly 25 percent of its prisoners.[51] These numbers have their own importance in the context of injustice. Among other things, they have forced a whole new concept of imprisonment known as "warehousing."

The accelerating rate of incarceration in American prisons—state prison populations increased more than 700 percent between 1972 and 2011—has turned imprisonment into a "strictly custodial function." There is a "new penology" and it "seeks not to deter or rehabilitate individual offenders but merely to warehouse the riskiest segment of the so-called urban underclass."[52] A report conducted by Amnesty International captures how overcrowding has reduced American prisoners to a body count under conditions too primitive to secure minimal standards of behavior:

> Every day in prisons and jails across the USA, the human rights of prisoners are violated. In many facilities, violence is endemic. In some cases, guards fail to stop inmates assaulting each other. In others, the guards are themselves the abusers, subjecting their victims to beatings and sexual abuse. Prisons and jails use mechanical, chemical, and electroshock methods of restraint that are cruel, degrading, and sometimes life-threatening.[53]

What are the causes of warehousing and its dehumanizing aspects? The laws of the land. Harsh sentencing begins with a judge's gavel, but it ends in the unruliness of prison populations held cheek by jowl, without hope, with nothing to do, under conditions worse than those given to most domestic animals.[54]

The breakdown of the American punishment regime also has its questionable economic side. Lack of prisoner care does not mean lower costs. Financial obligations have skyrocketed with the numbers in prison, and so has recidivism through policies that warehouse inmates in deplorable conditions. The annual cost per inmate in state prisons now averages $31,286, more than a year at most colleges, and those costs are rising because of the special care needed for a burgeoning elderly population serving life sentences.[55] "A state will spend upwards of $1 million to incarcerate a life-sentenced person for forty years," and the vast majority of these prisoners will not be dangerous for most of their end-game sentences.[56]

How long ago in the march of prison reports and statistics did we cross the line from "less just" to "unjust"? More than anything, the idea of justice is about how to make the best and fairest use of human conduct. Every human being must develop in some way, if not on its own terms, then as part of a plan that other participants have made. Absence of development means a lack of health and the assurance of disruptive behavior. Circumstances that stifle development, that repress a natural urge to grow, that enforce idleness, and that restrain avenues of interest inevitably increase transgressive behavior, the very thing prisons are supposed to prevent.[57]

That is the situation in American prisons today as overcrowding and attempts to cut costs by eliminating restorative programs become widespread. To pay for a crime, any crime, with a substantial prison sentence condemns a majority of current inmates to a life of transgression, whether in or out of prison, while the law looks the other way until a new crime makes it time to punish again.

Are there answers to this ugly spiral? Criminologists disagree over theories of punishment, but the problems are so elemental that most theorists come together on the issues that need to be addressed. Common ground includes easing American drug laws, shorter sentences, better educational opportunities, more reentry programs, restorative justice initiatives, acceptance in prison of more basic rights, better physical conditions, elimination of overcrowding, diffusing the impact of prison gangs, elimination of prison violence, more interactive communication about the nature of criminal behavior, curbs on arbitrary behavior by prison officials, and an end to long-term isolation and idleness as punishments in inmate populations.[58]

Against these commendable, if stock, recommendations, we have passive legal interest in reform coupled to the knowledge that the American people favor imprisonment for crime, prefer stiff penalties, and want life sentences for serious offenses. "Virtually everyone agrees that the public of the United States harbours punitive views toward offenders." That, however, is no longer the whole story. Americans, it turns out, also believe in restorative programs. America may still be a land of second chances. "Research conducted over the past two decades reveals consistent support for rehabilitation as a correctional goal."[59]

Confusions in the interface of society and law over punishment obviously go both ways; when examined more closely, they may present fresh opportunities. The dysfunctional nature of the American punishment regime is a greater concern than in the past. Journalists and leading newspapers, as well as academics and even popular television programs, raise the deplorable, even disgusting conditions in American prisons for all to see. Citizens also have learned to worry more about the exorbitant costs of incarceration during the current recession than in periods of prosperity. The problems are intractable but not unsolvable, and they lead to the next question.

What Might Be Done?

Change in institutions never happens easily when more than minimal reform is required, and even minimal reform is hard to accomplish in the institutional setting of incarceration. On the other hand, recognition of rampant levels of prisoner abuse now extends from the highest legal officers in the country to the average citizen—really to anyone who happens to watch television in America today.

Long ago, in 1980, Associate Justice Harry Blackmun reported the horrors of prison rape in terms meant to outrage. Those terms are now commonplace acceptances in communal attitudes. "The atrocities and inhuman conditions of prison life in America are almost unbelievable; surely they are nothing less than shocking," Blackmun wrote then. "A youthful inmate can expect to be subjected to homosexual gang rape his first night in jail, or, it has been said, even in the van on the way to jail. Weaker inmates become the property of stronger prisoners or gangs, who sell the sexual services of the victim."[60]

These awful details now belong to mundane plot formations on long-running television series, such as *OZ* and *The Wire*. More professional, if bloodless, estimates indicate that 70,000 sexual abuse cases a year take place behind bars. One in twenty prisoners reports being raped, and the actual percentage, given fear and shame over reporting, has to be much higher.[61] Terrible criminal acts against helpless people are now understood to be the habit and custom of prison life. Inmate abuse has become a norm fatalistically accepted by law and a mechanism of entertainment in social vehicles. Can a rule of law with integrity ignore what everyone knows?

We have to accept at some level that we are responsible for these crimes because they take place under the control of the governments we elect. Ten long years before Harry Blackmun's comment, Chief Justice Warren Burger had already used the same physical setting to define why we are responsible: "When a sheriff or a marshal takes a man from the courthouse in a prison van and transports him to confinement for two or three or ten years, this is our act. We have tolled the bell for him. And whether we like it or not, we have made him our collective responsibility. We are free to do something about him; he is not."[62]

Chief Justice Burger delivered these thoughts to the American Bar Association, and in keeping with the bell that tolls, he gave them a title, "No Man Is an Island." The words come from John Donne's classic meditation "No man is an island, entire of itself; every man is a piece of the continent, a part of the main," but Donne's words are not true in Burger's application of them.[63] We put our prisoners on a separate island that we do not know, or seek to know, or want to associate with in any way. Inmates in America are not "part of the main."

Much of this book has been about why we do not care about the people we put away enough to treat them with a modicum of decency. The answer proposed here is a devastating one. We do not believe that the current carceral system is broken because we do not want to think about how much it violates the basic principles that supposedly define us as a culture. To render the system more compatible with those principles, we must acknowledge the hidden problem in what we have created: namely, our pleasure, our need, our urgency, our anger, our enthusiasm, all within a very strong will to punish.

Of course, some people do think about how much current prison systems seem to violate the basic principles that define us as a culture. Current efforts at reform involve mostly private groups and educational institutions that try to work with officialdom on improved reentry programs into society, better educational opportunities for inmates, and more attention to vocational skills that might prevent recidivism.[64] These reformers divide between optimists and skeptics. Both groups know what should be done, hence the optimism. The skeptics see all the barriers to larger implementation beyond voluntary pilot programs.[65]

Arguments begin over how to change directions in a largely unreceptive penal system. Suggestions extend from modest initiatives within current prison settings to insistence on a very different kind of "therapeutic prison" as "no longer a utopian dream." The ideal carceral institution would be characterized by "a documented code of ethics," "a history of adopting new initiatives," "organizational harmony," and "professionally trained [directors] with at least a graduate degree in one of the helping professions." It would be maintained by personnel who exhibit "enthusiasm, warmth, respectfulness, flexibility, nonblaming, genuineness, humor, self-confidence, empathy, engaging reflectiveness, maturity, and intelligence" along with all the "skills related to service delivery."[66]

One is caught here between a prudent incrementalism that does not begin to reach the staggering size of the problem and overarching solutions that resist the practical mechanics of prison conditions today. The first alternative lives with a problem it cannot solve. The second fails to take into account what must change for a better prison system to exist. Neither quite grasps how recalcitrant the law is to change on punishment or how objections to what it thinks must begin with the elemental.

Chapter 1 in this book opened with the seven conventional features that define legal punishment:

1. Punishment is the infliction of something unwelcome to the recipient.
2. The infliction must be intentional and done for a reason.
3. The inflicter has the right to do so.
4. The infliction responds to an infringement of law.
5. The recipient's infringement has been voluntary.
6. The inflicter must justify the act.
7. The intent of the inflicter, not of the recipient, defines the act.[67]

Only two of these features refer directly to the view of the person treated in the act. The infliction has to be unwelcome to the recipient, and it has to target a voluntary breach of law, but the determinations in even these subsidiary features are made by the punisher, not the punished. All seven features contribute to fairness, but are they enough?

None of them control the impulse to punish more heavily. None of them begin to reach an articulated theory of human nature that might give meaning to punishment. None establish limits beyond the all-too-easy request that the punisher justify what is done.

Lost is the person who suffers and the amount of suffering to be inflicted. Lost as well is a concept of human understanding, the key to all theories of punishment and a meaningful rule of law. What Justices Blackmun and Burger may be missing most in their hand-wringing over prison rape is a handle on human value in the definition of punishment, something that might reach directly to the minimal concerns of inmates through the cruel and unusual punishments clause of the Eighth Amendment.

But if the definition of punishment is incomplete, we must be careful about correcting it. Talk in terms of rights regularly defeats the purpose in this situation. Theoretically, the punished possess nominal rights; practically speaking, people in prison retain no rights of importance when conflict with authority gets them before a court. Time and again, as we have seen, official rights talk privileges the punisher over the punished and locks the law into conventionally narrow ways of thought. More is required for meaningful change, or perhaps less, but either way a different way of thinking is in order.[68]

The thing to remember is that punishment is a necessary evil; so when it is inflicted excessively, it diminishes the punisher as much as the punished. Unnecessary punishment alters the behavior of all who are even remotely concerned in the enterprise. It strips punishers and anyone who supports or even knows about their actions of dignity, and it corrodes the punished in their hatred of the unjust act and actor.

It follows that the limits placed on punishment depend on two meanings of the word "dignity": that of the rightful privilege or enabling status in the punisher and that of the most elemental level of decorum reserved to the punished out of respect for what every human being deserves to receive. Without both meanings, all claims on dignity disappear when punishment becomes excessive.[69]

How might a conception of human nature—an eighth feature in the definition of legal punishment—begin to change basic thought? The current definition, while efficient, privileges the punisher and targets the punished. The objective should be to correct that imbalance as effectively, efficiently, and comprehensively as possible. But what relatively objective expression might accomplish that task without compromising the legitimate objective of penal correction, the removal of major rights that defines all incarceration? Think of the appended language as part of a conceivable answer:

> 8. The life of the recipient of punishment must continue to be worth living.

This proposed eighth stipulation is mostly a reminder. It stipulates the avoidance of unnecessary pain and degradation in the name of human understanding. It tells everyone that what is held in prison is *a person*. Normative registers have been added without the panoply of procedural rights. The addition asks for a more basic level of recognition: that of a human bond beyond the inherently destructive and hostile one-sided vigilance of guards guarding the guarded. It restores a basic awareness of what it means to be consciously alive and responsive to the mortal limits that all must struggle to absorb against a common fate.

What exactly might a life of continuing worth mean in prison? Three conditions apply to this level of concern, and each could be made possible even in prison: first, the need to retain some idea of self, and from it some small but defined area of self-control; second, the desire for productivity in some form; and third, the prospect of continuing growth. The most abominable phrase in the popular language of punishment is "Let 'em rot!" This phrase insists on total inactivity in prison, an intolerable stasis. It tells an inmate your job is to wait, and for many this means until you die. The idea behind the phrase takes away the very nature of existence as intelligence has allowed anyone to define it and want it.

What would be the payoff for a prison system? Life must be worth living at some level, and it will use transgressive ways to accomplish that purpose if there are no positive outlets. Unless the aim of imprisonment is to further criminalize the criminal, the three elemental needs just mentioned should be met. But how is this to be done within such a generally dysfunctional population and situation?

There must be an incentive system with rewards that encourage productive endeavor. Meaning lies in possibilities separate from despair, and one of the fundamental human desires is the wish to be useful in some way through a goal achieved and for it to be valued by a cohort ready to grant some respect for that achievement. Gangs currently provide the negative common denominator of this desire in prison. A system that wants to improve must find positive ways to fulfill that basic search for identity.

What is an incentive? It offers something of worth that might alter a person's course of action where "both parties stand to gain from the resulting choice." The word itself has two meanings: it can arouse passionate feeling (incentivize), or it can appeal to the rational calculation of one's own interests (an incentive program). Both meanings will apply here. Incentives "move people to do what they would otherwise *not* want to do." They are top-down or power-oriented external prompts asking for a given response, and they are "intentionally designed to change the status quo."[70]

Injecting affirmative incentives into the power structure of a prison can be part of the answer, but only if those decisions incorporate the two-way gain required; they must help authority as well as those under authority. The right incentives could do this by creating opportunities and direction that would relieve the dreary scope of mere punishment—a problem for both sides.

The numbing boredom of prison life is a danger to everyone. One of the insidious problems in incarceration is the way sadistic behavior is used to relieve boredom. An incentive structure could supply a missing sense of the dramatic. As the leading psychotherapist and founder of the school of individual psychology Alfred Adler noted long ago in outlining the source of all positive behavior, "We cannot think, feel, will, or act without the perception of some goal."[71]

Prisoners, especially long-term prisoners, need something beyond the eventual hope of freedom from confinement, a hope that might never be realized, if they are to function mentally and physically with a degree of health. Incentives cannot substitute for hope, but they can limit a descent into hopelessness. We are not built to do nothing, and the word "hope" figures in the English language as both a noun and a verb. If hope cannot be "a desire accompanied with expectation of obtaining what is desired" (the noun), it can still function as a means "to cherish a desire" (the verb).[72]

How much hope and, consequently, a measure of well-being can there be without freedom or the prospect of it? American ideological beliefs make this a difficult question, but they do not eliminate the kind of hope that an incentive structure might work with. There can be a better future available even in prison, particularly if one realizes that aspirations must often settle for less than the ideal that gives them first breath.

Such pragmatism, the act of settling, can appear a shallow philosophy. Bertrand Russell once gibed that the idea could come only from an immature country like America, but it works in a situation of diminishing returns. "Growth," John Dewey said in defense of the reductionism in pragmatism, "is the only moral end."[73] Every soul thirsts for the ability to develop in some way. Growth over stasis: no one can find meaning and direction without a goal beyond the years to be served.

The suggestions for an incentive structure advanced here will be processive rather than declarative, with one exception, but every suggestion made asks for a new conversation about punishment in America, and taken together, they assume there must be other ways of speaking about the problems of incarceration if we are to make any headway at all. Imprisonment as we now know it is not just broken; it is wrongheaded. The proof of that? Its all-too-logical projection into massive incarceration has become the problem in punishment rather than the solution.

The one fixed rather than processive exception in these recommendations for moving forward should be clear at the outset. It stipulates the absolute necessity of physical separation from actual punishment of forms of rehabilitation. So polluted is the term "rehabilitation" from failures in its current iterations that the whole idea of institutional separation probably deserves a new term. So call the possibilities in reform-oriented programs "restorations," where that word connotes both more and less than reentry into civil life.

"To restore" signifies a more elemental goal than rehabilitation. It favors and urges the reconstruction of a positive self within the imprisoned self. A person in prison needs to think not only of what went wrong but of what might make it right again. Even permanent prisoners do not remain what they were. Everyone changes; the question always is whether that change will be for better or for worse. Doesn't each and every life deserve the chance to be better than it was in some way?

All other suggestions for new penal policies are necessarily tentative. Reform measures within the scene of punishment have to account for the historical truth that every suggested positive direction in penology seems to have led sooner or later down a new path of abuse. There is no getting away from the pleasure principle in punishment, nor from the intrinsic hostility that dominates interaction in all aspects of a prison environment.

Punishers will twist any mechanism to their own advantage. People in prison, just like people in normal life, react negatively when imposed on. Absolute physical control over other people creates an untenable situation in human behavior. Anything attempted or done, anything recommended, must therefore take the negative dynamics in incarceration as a given.

Legal solutions generally depend on an incremental process, but nothing will change without new dimensions in play, as the need for an added feature in the definition of legal punishment implies. A shift in understandings must challenge the ingrained habits that allow American punishment to proceed so ruthlessly and yet comfortably by claiming a normalcy based on necessity, fatalism, and habit.

Suggestions about what might work better can at least take heart in the knowledge that nothing works well now. For the same reasons, new initiatives will require a plan flexible enough to adjust to circumstances in midstream. Pilot programs could provide such a testing ground, but there is a world of sorrow in the selectivity that choice in pilot programs will require.[74] Do you pick only the best to work with and what will that tell you? The answers to these questions must be faced. Officially instituted pilot programs have to work if they are to lead to more general application.

Where to begin? Everyone agrees that mass incarceration requires attention, but should it be solved with more prisons or fewer prisoners? The easy answer, one that has failed, asks for more prisons, all of which are soon overrun through the workings of the punitive impulse. The harder prospect, fewer prisoners, must meet public skepticism and the nation's irrational fears about crime. It must convince a hesitant, disengaged, and critical citizenry that better use can be made of the billions of dollars allotted to prison systems that currently create more problems than they solve, always need more money, and ruin more lives than they help.

New parameters within a functional though cautious incrementalism are the methodology offered here. Four preliminary shifts in penal policy might begin to reduce overcrowding in prisons. First, and often suggested, mere drug possession should be depenalized. Second, anyone who maintains good behavior during a long-term prison sentence deserves a hearing by professional experts who would sit above prison guards and politicized parole boards and make adjustments in time served by prisoners and in prison conditions for continuing inmates. Third, as noted, rehabilitation/restoration must be held distinct from punishment as we now know it. Fourth, a different level of training and education must apply to all correctional officers used in a restoration program.[75]

Qualifications are immediately in order. Depenalization of drug use does not imply legalization, but it might mean amnesty for drug offenders who conquer their addiction in prison. Adjustment hearings for long-term prisoners might lead to better conditions and some privileges in confinement rather than release; change of any kind would require serious evidence, possibly with support from the original sentencing court, which might be asked to continue following the cases it decides. The many courts that have been forced to penalize more heavily than they wished might be given a second look at a problem. More professional training for prison guards will naturally face stiff opposition from correctional-officer unions, but that opposition might be overcome if guards are granted free educational programs while on paid leave. Once again, incentives must work both ways.

Separating rehabilitation from punishment as a form of restoration has difficult ramifications until one remembers that officialdom once defined prisons as "houses of correction." No one can honestly make that claim today, and the failure points to a philosophical discrepancy. Punishment is pain; correction is a healing process. Attempts to reconcile them confuse both issues and vex all theories of punishment.[76]

Improvement in prison life, no matter where one stands on the issue, must separate rehabilitation from retribution. Punishment assumes the ability to inflict suffering of some kind, either mental or physical, and that is what retribution, the dominant theory of punishment, entails. "Rehabbing," as it is termed in symbolic notice of its diminutive status in penal policy and inmate cynicism about it, is currently a pause in torment. Existing programs are gaps in the pain that is punishment. If incarceration wants to restore, it must alter the form that incarceration now takes.

Rehabilitation/restoration, to be meaningful, must work through a combination: it must develop a different outlook, and it must lead to new capabilities with the ultimate purpose of turning inmates into out-mates. It must be separate in order to be financially protected from prison budgetary pressures, and it must involve consequential work, whether or not reentry into civil life is a particular goal. Studies suggest that "correctional industry programs" and later "employment training and assistance" aid successful reentry, particularly if they relate to work skills and address the previous criminal behavior of an inmate.[77]

Right now the priority given to retribution in all American prisons prevents any form of restoration from having the steady emphasis it requires to succeed. It also explains the high recidivism rate in inmates. Prison solidifies the status of an unemployable underclass. It guarantees that release from prison will lead to a return for the many who cannot locate a law-abiding way to make a living in a rapidly changing and increasingly specialized workplace.

The repercussions in separating restoration from punishment do not end there. Given current prison populations, a separate institutional arrangement that can make a difference will require a three-tiered system beyond the stage of punishment as we now know it. Choices will have to be made, and they have alarming implications until we realize that we already have a tiered system based on security needs.

Nonetheless, the problem of choice remains. Who should decide between the restored and those left behind in pilot programs? Who will be found worthy of help in a better environment, and who will be deemed too unreliable for now? How many must be left in the current infernos of incarceration? Can one identify such a thing as an irretrievable predator, or is that the idle talk of law enforcement?[78]

The distinctions drawn will never be easy, but peer pressure and intimidation prevent many in the prisons of the United States from benefiting from help programs. The difficulties in change deserve to be measured against current problems. Sentencing already parcels the convicted into categories with more punishment for some and less for others, better prisons for some and definitely worse for others. The decision to segregate inmates by projected opportunity for correction must be understood against the fact that we now segregate by offense and do it badly.

Should the emotional element in distinguishing an opportunity from the lack of an opportunity stop the idea of separate institutional restoration programs? Juries, judges, and penal commissions currently make sentencing decisions based on facts from a single event, the crime and its repercussions. Evaluating the ongoing conduct and receptivity of inmates in prison will be harder to do, and there is no point in leaving those decisions to prison guards. Evaluation will require outside expertise across the fields of behavioral psychology, group therapy, education, criminology, medicine, social relations, and vocational aptitude. Why experts? The objectivity that professionalism is supposed to supply should at least temper the anger in punishment that will always exist.

Programs might begin with first-time offenders who demonstrate a willingness to participate and develop within an educational system, although one might have to be more selective. Young offenders are the most prone to violence. Mistakes in judgment both ways will occur and should be subject to provisional reevaluation with strict discipline coupled to oversight. Boards of experts will have to be chosen for compassion and emotional balance as well as professional knowledge. Frequent rotation and review of their standards and performance will also be needed.

Everything will depend on proving that much can be accomplished if a constructive and secure atmosphere for learning is provided for individuals who are willing to work within several levels of an educational framework. Better living conditions with more freedom and the potential for vocational training will be the major incentives. Those who are unable to cope or who prove recalcitrant when given the opportunity will be returned to basic incarceration. Screening for drugs, gang membership (it cannot be stopped, but it can be prevented from controlling an environment), weapons, and aggressive behavior will have to be absolute.

Prescription to work must have the threat of proscription behind it. The cruelty in leaving prisoners behind, some permanently, is a painful element in this plan and can be justified only on the basis of a crueler reality. Mass incarceration without meaningful education currently denies those without vocational skills the chance of a law-abiding life on release. Even those with relevant skills find it impossible to make a living through legal employment when the touch of a finger on a computer will bring up a prison record. What employer will risk hiring "a jailbird" when so many other law-abiding applicants are available in a time of such high unemployment?[79]

Work programs do exist in most prisons, but they mostly consist of demeaning tasks in prison maintenance and are limited to unskilled labor that will not be useful or remunerative outside. They are part of punishment. The general opinion is that prisoners work to pay back for their crimes rather than receive training. Even workers who receive some instruction lose continuity because of interference from prison management. "The goal of the system [management of the population] trumps the goal of the program."[80] Current prison work programs belong to the problem, not the solution. Nothing will change until systems of restoration are separated from direct punishment.

Separate pilot programs can begin to answer these problems, at least for some. The youthful, newly convicted of nonviolent crimes or peripherally engaged in violent crime, could be divided into unskilled groups and the better-educated. Literacy levels are low in prison. The unskilled would receive remedial education with vocational import. The skilled groups would be put on a training track with higher implications. Meaningful vocation succeeds only if it is geared to a larger opportunity. Those who already have lawful vocational skills should be allowed to employ them—not the case in prisons today.

How might these levels cohere? Second-tier training facilities could feed a third tier of small but cohesive business ventures where private capital might help fund enterprise. Employers who would never hire an ex-con might contribute to a separate business through charitable tax incentives. The distinction to be drawn in these businesses would be between hard labor, a form of punishment, and worthwhile employment, a form of preparation for an economy of production. Of course, the renewed use of prison chain gangs in the twenty-first century is hardly an encouraging sign. The return of cruel and completely exploitive physical work programs underlines the urgent need for new directions and better approaches to prison labor.[81]

Nothing is perfect in an imperfect situation, but the ideas behind these recommendations have the value of direction and development for those who are willing to try. Some successful trainees, given their sentences, might never emerge from third-tier ventures, but all would learn practical vocational skills, and many would acquire a craft. An unknown percentage in third-tier ventures could achieve a skill level and work record worthy of employment in private outside companies.

Success, when it comes, should lead more and more prisoners to want to participate constructively in programs. Those who advance might also be used in managerial capacities to help those who later enter programs.

Those who reenter society might be asked or required to engage in training ventures within the programs as part of probationary status or be released with the stipulation of joining permanent restorative justice initiatives in their communities. Internally, the goal would be for viable separate vocational communities with the promise of transitional possibilities toward regular civil life.

The care with which enterprises for third-tier involvement are chosen will be everything. Their economic viability will be essential if pilot programs are going to expand into broader operations. Emphasis might be placed on repair of the crumbling American infrastructure, environmental cleansing programs, various communication needs, support for health services, and transportation services. These opportunities would have the benefit of needing skilled workers (e.g., electricians, architects, landscapers, computer programmers, and managerial figures) but also manual laborers (construction teams, road crews, cleaning crews, and assembly-line employees).

A false pragmatism will argue that we cannot afford such programs or the institutional separations recommended. Indeed, the money is there. Some of it can come from rearranging existing expenditures in an unjust system that wastes its resources. The real problem, though, will be one of resolve. We now live in a plutocracy driven by moneyed interests more than public concern. In 2013, eight single managers of hedge funds in the United States made a combined annual salary of $9 billion.[82] By themselves, these financial overlords were paid 13 percent of the budget spent on prisons in the United States in the same year. Believe it. The money is out there.

Objections will also come from labor unions, unemployed workers, some governmental offices, politicians, and even social justice advocates. But only the advocates will be able to claim no personal self-interest, and their arguments will be the strongest. Why, they will ask, should we help the predators in the community when we fail to provide assistance to the impoverished communities that they torment? Why should we "coddle criminals" when we don't help law-abiding citizens who have few or none of the advantages or possibilities of success that we hold dear in this society? We should, the protest will run, change the communities, not the offenders in it.[83]

The only honest answer to these questions is as old as Aristotle. The law has always distinguished between rectifying justice and distributive justice. Only rectifying justice comes under direct legal purview.[84] Crime arrives in court and is subject to punishment and correction; general problems of social justice do not and are not.

Elsewhere, though, Aristotle adds an important qualification: "Evils bring men together when the same thing is harmful to both sides."[85] The ultimate task in this book has been to identify a prison system that has become an evil for all concerned. The question that remains is plain. Can those evils, when fully recognized, bring us together with answers to them?

How Might It Be Done?

More than seventy years ago, the leading legal philosopher of his day, Morris Cohen, explained why one should be hesitant to suggest reform in criminal law. "Those who are convinced of the existence of injustice in the established law and who struggle for their abolition are more often defeated by general inertia and unreasoning fear of change than by any rational counter argument."[86] The law does not change easily. Must suffering make sense? Apparently it does in punishment even if it does not when the law looks at its own practices, and the onus will always be that it does.

H. L. A. Hart puts the problem differently but he raises the same difficulty. In the face of "modern skeptical doubt about the whole institution of punishment," he sees the current arrangement as an unpleasant but hard-won compromise where "the disgrace attached to conviction for crime" is as important a deterrent as "the severity of the punishment."[87] All unpleasantness put to one side, Hart, the legal positivist, can still claim that a compromise has been struck. If so, who has the right to be difficult over negotiations already made? The barrier of established arrangements always resists reform even though, as we see once again, disgrace and shaming remain a part of the package in punishment, with no limits set on either.

Both warnings about the strength of the punitive impulse are important, but Cohen's is more comprehensive than Hart's. Cohen makes "general inertia" rather than an internal argument the problem. Much more than law is involved. The whole complicated interface of law and society is responsible. Moralists may respond, "If the alternative is inertia, outrage against injustice may keep you alive," but can that kind of answer be enough against the passiveness that characterizes civilization itself?[88] Probably not unless concrete acceptance and philosophical avenues of address somehow join in response to injustice.

Concretely, we are already there. The problem is very much before us. In the summer of 2013, 29,000 inmates in California state prisons went on a hunger strike to protest deplorable prison conditions.[89] Their protest on an unprecedented scale included two-thirds of the thirty-three prisons across the state and all four private out-of-state facilities where California sends inmates. The complaints? Overcrowding remains perilous everywhere, and 10,000 inmates in California live in long-term solitary confinement, a practice that most liberal democracies and human rights organizations identify as torture.

Ponder for a moment these concrete facts. Imagine how hard it is for prisoners to organize within one prison, much less across an entire system. "There aren't many protests in prison," explains one veteran inmate. How can there be? "Authorities exercise absolute power and demand abject obedience." Anyone who protests "has little to gain and too much to lose: his job, his visits, his recreation time, his phone privileges, his right to buy . . . in the commissary." There are no limits on what prison guards can do. "The ways even a bystander to the most peaceful protest can be punished are limited only by the imagination of the authorities." These words indicate what has to be true.[90] For a protest of any size to work, prison conditions have to be intolerable for everyone in them.

The long hunger strike of 2013 was the largest in the history of the state, and yet the California Department of Corrections and Rehabilitation—already facing a threat of contempt of court for failing to honor the Supreme Court's directive that 10,000 more prisoners be released from overcrowded facilities—began by refusing to recognize the fact of the strike "until inmates have refused nine consecutive meals." Says a lawyer who represented inmates during a much smaller strike in 2011, "Officials have this bunker mentality, but now it's like a house of cards is falling down."[91]

Matters really have reached a breaking point in American prisons. The many elements—theoretical, practical, economic, and psychological—that have caused punishment in the United States to increase by leaps and bounds have been in force for a long time and dominate institutional thinking. How dominant are these elements? None of the modest stock reform measures, much less the more intricate reforms mentioned in the last section, have a chance of being passed in prison complexes today. The genie of punishment is at large. How can we coax him back into the bottle where he belongs?

Concreteness by itself is clearly not going to be enough to effect prison reform amid a host of other ills in American life. As long ago as 1992, Pulitzer Prize–winning reporters identified a series of national dilemmas in a best-selling book titled *America: What Went Wrong?* Individual chapters covered the downward mobility of the middle class, difficulties south of the border, tax incentives favoring the wealthy, the collapse of vital businesses, malfeasance in global opportunities, the dangers of deregulation, the health insurance crisis, unscrupulous insider speculation, lost pensions, and political corruption in Washington.[92]

Sound familiar? All these difficulties remain unsolved and are worse today, and to them we can add widespread electronic fraud, war, the bankruptcy of a major city (Detroit), a long recession, and demeaning political deadlock over immigration, environmental issues, unemployment woes, food stamps, the budget, and general governmental policy.

The very way Americans think about themselves has changed in dealing with these problems. A once-rugged American individualism has devolved into "a deeply divided self " coping with equally fragmented external divisions. Theorists talk of "an imitative self " where "the call of personhood" might not be heard, "the disconnected self" consumed with self-love and therapeutic needs, "the embodied self " deep in "empathetic intersubjectivity," "consumer selves" with "inadequate resources to achieve the selves desired," and technologically driven selves controlled by the machines around them. Each of these selves recognizes the others in a common fear: "loss of self-coherence in the postmodern world."[93]

No thinking citizen can avoid contemplating these external and internal problems in one of two ways. Some feel that the country may be losing its way. Others respond that many of these concerns have to be balanced against advances in democratic understanding. Yes, society is "beset by unsolved problems," but "for women, wage laborers, racial, ethnic, sexual preference, or religious minorities, the poor, and the elderly, progress toward genuine inclusion in the past half century has been extraordinary."[94]

Frustration and conflict on issue after issue flow from this primal division in communal assessments, and with them comes a certain fatalism. Why start with the nation's penal system with so many other intractable problems on the table? Not coincidentally, whenever prison reform comes up in a group of lawyers, this question of priorities is the first one raised. The legal profession prefers individual predicaments to larger matters of social justice, and even on a social scale prison reform has low status; perhaps it comes too close to home.

Is there an answer to such fatalism? Rapid change and permanent difficulties can also be catalysts. They have a way of forcing new thought. A number of contemporary thinkers answer the postmodern condition with suggestions about how to cope with injustice now. They write to instill belief in philosophical avenues of address for dealing with the communal problems of today.

Some examples are more valuable than others. Daniel Kahneman in *Thinking, Fast and Slow* proves, contrary to much conventional wisdom, that "concerns for fairness" are often as important as self-interest in the way people make their decisions.[95] Thomas Nagel in *Equality and Partiality* posits the need for an "assumption of negative responsibility" in our relations to one another. "We are responsible, through the institutions which require our support, for the things they could have prevented as well as for the things they actively cause."[96]

The list of conceivable initiatives is long and involves our most original thinkers. Jürgen Habermas in *Moral Consciousness and Communicative Action* uses a concept of the philosopher Richard Rorty to reduce the frictions in conflict. "Commensurable discourses" (ones with "reliable criteria of consensus building") need to be distinguished from those that "are incommensurable" with the added proviso that incommensurable discourses can still be edifying if understood for how they claim to be *"sufficient unto themselves."* How we accept conflict is half of the answer to it.[97]

Postmodern angst and public malaise exist, but they do not disturb what Amartya Sen in *The Idea of Justice* defines as "the intellectual basis for moving from a general sense of injustice to particular reasoned diagnoses of injustice."[98] Nor do they prevent Charles Taylor in *The Ethics of Authenticity* from deriding a "culture of self-fulfillment" that causes "many people to lose sight of concerns that transcend them."[99]

Taylor goes further. He traces many of the separating forces in modern life to misguided "forms of individualism." "It does indeed appear that the more self-centered forms of fulfillment have been gaining ground in recent decades," accompanied by "a fall-off in citizen participation."

Taylor, like the other thinkers just mentioned, is not picking fights so much as minimizing the conflicts in difference. He identifies "self-centered practices as the site of an ineradicable tension." To establish new possibilities in community "requires a horizon of significance . . . a shared one" and better forms of "responsibilization."[100]

These writers concentrate not so much on a projected self or citizen, the lodestone in American identity in previous eras, as on something greater and more cohesive in response to the crush of an increasingly crowded, intrusive, contentious, and heterogeneous world that must find new ways to get along with itself. They grapple with the idea of what might be named "*a democratic persona*" in search of communal answers. Such a persona, a form of "general will" or collective identity, would give more priority to communal justice rather than individual success or prosperity or power as its concern.

It is, of course, a favorite academic sport of theorists to invent new terms for old concepts, but the novelty here lies in the notion of a mindful togetherness across differences in a way that might solve problems otherwise thought to be intractable. The search is for mutual ground that is not only possible but creative in the name of what Taylor labels "the equal value of different identities," a goal only possible in the fullest grasp of an inclusive democracy. Only then can we appreciate "how developing and nursing the commonalities of value between us become important."[101]

The most widely known current comment on civic indifference, on the lack of a working democratic persona, comes from Robert Putnam in his study *Bowling Alone* from the millennial year 2000. Noting the ebb in communal spirit, Putnam delivers a challenge of sorts: "We Americans need to reconnect with one another."[102] He can mount this challenge across many pages with enthusiasm because he thinks the problem can be the solution through a reversal of implications.

Putnam's thesis begins with the corrosive force of difference in contemporary society, and he agrees that it is everywhere and growing. In the short term, ethnic divisions will increase tensions and challenge social solidarity. However, in the long term, they will become a new positive force in the creation of "more encompassing identities." Social interaction, a form of "social capital," will develop better "norms of reciprocity" and "new levels of similarity" in a healthier community. "Social capital" happens to be fragile in contemporary America, and Putnam

has to admit "we do not yet see evidence of a general resurgence of social connection or involvement in the public life of the community." He
then counters the admission with a series of bridging functions that
will make a difference.[103]

There are practical reasons for all these abstract emphases in modern
American philosophy. Most of the problems that the United States faces
today are solvable, but they are not solved because its citizens do not
care enough about the collectivity to act, and the greatest negative symbol of that indifference is the forgotten inmate who is treated worse than
anyone else and certainly worse than anyone should tolerate. We need to
remember that it is how a culture treats the worst in its midst that defines it. Helping the helpless is the ultimate sign of cohesion in a modern
community, and not helping the helpless has larger consequences.

If a community simply dismisses its worst problems by putting people permanently away, where does it stop identifying problems that belong in that category? There is no obvious stopping point, and that has
been an element in the growth of the nation's punitive impulse. Soon
enough, the same logic allows a community to dismiss people at large
who have problems that defy easy solution, and the collectivity begins
to divide between those who feel on top of things and those who, however regrettably, must be left behind. It becomes easier and easier to
dismiss all problems and to accept misfortune as the natural state of
the unfortunate. We already see this tendency in prolonged communal controversy over a safety net for those who are too poor to afford
health care.

What happens to a community that does not care for its worst-off and,
portentously, seems to need the category of the fallen as part of its identity? Some scholars have started to identify the nature of the injustice
involved.[104] But the most graphic recognition comes from the American
fiction writer Ursula K. Le Guin in her most famous short story, "The
Ones Who Walk away from Omelas." This prize-winning account is frequently anthologized for its allegorical references and for Le Guin's direct claim that the story addresses discrimination in America.[105]

The idea for the story originates in a comment by the philosopher
William James, and Le Guin says of it, "The dilemma of the American
conscience can hardly be better stated." James, in "The Moral Philosopher and the Moral Life" (1891), wondered whether a people could accept a perfectly happy society "on the one simple condition that a cer-

tain lost soul on the far-off edge of things should lead a life of lonely torment." Would that society "clutch at the happiness so offered," or would it come undone knowing "how hideous a thing would be its enjoyment when deliberately accepted as the fruit of such a bargain" (275)? Le Guin makes unfair imprisonment the topos of that lonely torment.

"The Ones Who Walk away from Omelas" gives the story through its title. Le Guin posits a utopian society that depends for its happiness on one innocent desperate child imprisoned in horribly cramped, filthy conditions at the center of its city: "All understand that their happiness, the beauty of their city, the tenderness of their friendships . . . depend wholly on this child's abominable misery." Those who go see the child "are always shocked and sickened at the sight" when they are told "there is nothing they can do." They in fact do nothing, but some (no exact number is given) do act by walking away from the city of happiness, and they never return (282–284).

The innocent imprisoned child in Le Guin's allegory cannot be taken as the average inmate in an American prison, but the bargain struck exists on similar terms. Le Guin uses her "psychomyth" to draw attention to discrimination in America. How much of an ethnically inflected underclass forced to live in a crime-ridden and openly transgressive environment should be imprisoned in horrible conditions to assure the maximum security and happiness of the rest of society?[106]

The difference is that no one in the United States is made to go and look at the imprisoned, but what would happen if Americans did? What if a goodly number did tour a supermaximum-security prison instead of being prohibited access, as happens now? The keepers of the American punishment regime know the need for secrecy about much of what goes on in the nation's prisons. No one has to walk away from what is not seen, although some do in Omelas. Not everyone who leaves has gone to see. The knowledge of what is happening has been enough for some of them.

What should knowledge do to one who knows? Should one walk away or walk toward the problem? How bad must the situation be for something to be done? A playwright, Tennessee Williams, offers one standard for acting in *A Streetcar Named Desire*. Blanche DuBois, a character who lives a lie and offers up lie after lie, delivers an ultimate truth when pushed to the wall. Challenged there, she answers "Deliberate cruelty is not forgivable."[107] That is what we have found over and over again in the American punishment regime: not just incarceration but unforgivable cruelty.

Inferno: An Anatomy of American Punishment has tried to tell that story from all the angles that together have made unconscious cruelty so terribly overt and deliberate. Prisoners in this country have been put away, silenced, beaten, sadistically tormented, and most of all forgotten—frequently enough for their entire lives. They have been relegated to conditions and circumstances and physical degradation that shame us as well as them and that no one wants to recognize even though the failure in recognition defines a part of us.

No human being deserves that much punishment. The dignity of every life has to mean more than someone else's indifferent, much less vindictive, control over it. Anything less is a deprivation for all concerned. The American justice system claims that incarceration and loss of freedom are enough of a punishment. It needs to turn that claim into the truth instead of the lie that lives and breathes in every prison in the country.

The Psychology of Punishment

Ill-guiding is the cause that has made the world wicked.

Dante Alighieri, *Purgatorio*, 16:104–105

The distinction between condemnation and correction dramatically changes the psychology of punishment. The most powerful representation of the difference, also the greatest psychological study of punishment that we have, is a religious poem set in the last year of the thirteenth century. The *Divine Comedy*, or *Commedia*, as it was known to its author, presents a Christian pilgrim who witnesses the divine punishment of the dead in hell and purgatory on his way to heaven. The happy ending turns the poem into a comedy, so named, but its 14,223 lines also make it the most extended monody on the theme of punishment ever written.

For present purposes, the importance of the poem lies in a secular realism that reaches beyond its theological implications. The poet confirms this aspect himself when he steps back long enough to observe that his work is "no enterprise to undertake in sport or for a tongue that cries *mamma* and *babbo*. . . . The telling may not be diverse from the fact."[1] The two colloquial terms reveal something else. In keeping with the claim of realism, the dialogues in hell and purgatory are couched in vernacular Italian rather than the approved Latin then used in formal literary production.[2]

The lost souls in hell and the hopeful ones in purgatory explain how the mistakes made in life must now be paid for in the spheres of the afterlife. As such, they exhibit the struggle in all human existence. The punishment that each soul endures and describes gives their exchanges an "earthy character," "a concentration" on the turmoil in being.[3] Hell and purgatory, taken together, also convey the plight of their creator, who has himself been severely punished, with all the bitterness and hatred that condemnation means against the larger hope that correction might provide.

Dante Alighieri composed his great poem in the first years of the fourteenth century, between 1306 and 1320, while exiled for life on pain of death from Florence. Legal banishment brought disgrace, danger, loss of definition, and total defeat. It struck deeper than anything that can be imagined in the mobile world of today. Dante writes knowing he faces a horrible death at the stake if he is captured by Florentine leaders or if he ever tries to return to the beloved city he helped rule in 1300, the year he poignantly chooses to celebrate as the setting of his poem.[4] The *Commedia* must therefore be understood in the light of Dante's own struggle with punishment.

The poem opens in an implied parallel. Cast out of Florence, Dante wanders, he knows not why or how, "in a dark wood where the straight way has been lost." The exile stumbles from one danger to another in bitterness and flight with only "the pass which never yet let any go alive" as a way out (*Inferno* 1:1–28). Punished himself, this wanderer decides that the world has behaved so badly that its inhabitants deserve the punishments they receive, and as long as he holds to this state of condemnation, he will insist on a calibrated relation of permanent pain to punishment as the measure of desert.

The *Commedia* paints the human condition through the concept of punishment. Three elements in particular turn the first two parts of the poem, *Inferno* and *Purgatorio*, into a profound study of it. The concept finds its philosophical expressions in the exchanges of the two travelers, Dante (the living Christian pilgrim) and Virgil (the pagan shade or spirit who acts as his guide) as they move through hell, the realm of condemnation, into purgatory, one of correction. At stake in modern understandings are the differences between retribution and rehabilitation and what those differences do to both punisher and punished.

The first explanatory element of punishment consists in the journey motif that controls the *Commedia*. By encountering and questioning the souls of the dead in their anguish, Dante is more than a witness. He is the equivalent of a correctional officer approving infliction all around him. Often in fear but always with curiosity, he accepts justice at work in hell with some pity and sympathy, to be sure, but more often we get contempt, horror, and, yes, hatred. The essential posture is of the punisher, if we accept, as we must, that Dante aligns with God as the just distributor of pain and the righteous inflicter of it.[5]

A second element turns on the pecking order that Dante brings to punishment. Much of his creativity consists in the kinds of pain identified with each sin, the confinement associated with each particular form of pain, and the specific placement of each punished figure in prison arrangements of intricate variety and hierarchical import. In every case the punished know and accept their punishment through the poet's concept of *contrapasso:* each punishment fits a particular crime.[6] Here, too, is something quite terrible in the psychology of punishment. The interest of readers grows through Dante's arrangement of ever-increasing forms of pain more wretchedly inflicted.

The third element is the scene of punishment. *Inferno* metes out everlasting punishment; it can never be fully satisfied no matter what the doomed do or say. The absence of all hope—the signification that God has put on the entrance to his eternal prison[7]—breeds woeful candor in those who have nothing further to lose or to gain except the need to explain their misery. The comparable scene in *Purgatorio*—the word means "to purify"—gives a very different picture. Hope in correction instead of condemnation changes everything. The sufferers in purgatory are buoyed by the prospect of deliverance: "Do not dwell on the torment, think of what follows, think that at worst it cannot go beyond the great Judgement" (*Pur.* 10:109–111).

These lines make purgatory the puzzle of *The Divine Comedy* much more than anything we learn about hell or heaven. What are we to make of the anomaly that it is easier to grasp the darkness of hell than the light of purgatory? The uncertainty over what punishment in correction might mean turns *Purgatorio* into the most original part of the *Commedia*. As Virgil informs Dante, "Then thou shalt see those who are contented in the fire" (*Inf.* 1:118–119). But how can anyone be contented in the fire? Can fire purify enough to remove the agony? How can the pain of correction be a contented state?

First, however, we must deal with the negative trajectory in condemnation. The attitudes of the travelers change significantly when they move from *Inferno* to *Purgatorio,* and the change, more than anything we hear from the punished, tells us why rehabilitation should be kept separate from retribution in a punishment regime. No system should forget a hardening process in regular contact with punishment. Habit easily replaces other reactions. Somewhere in the descent through hell the screams of the tormented turn into background music. Dante actually becomes matter-of-fact in describing these horrors. Suffering becomes a norm, a self-evident truth, not something to protest.

As we descend into hell, pilgrim and reader alike know that another, more dire, and perhaps more interesting kind of punishment will be expressed in ever more ingenious uses of pain. Adaptation to this part of the poem comes through the psychology of the punisher. The torments inflicted by demons in hell and the corrections by angels in purgatory mirror the conceivable patterns of behavior of human beings in the world. Dante's spirits are contrasting projections of malice and beneficence in normal society. Between them, they provide the full continuum in punishment.

Punishment, after all, is a learning process. Dante first experiences it in canto 3, just inside the gates of hell, where he witnesses "those who lived without disgrace and without praise" alongside the fallen angels who refused to choose in the battle between God and Satan. All run and scream under a nameless banner while being stung by hornets and wasps, which cause streams of blood to gather for loathsome worms at their feet. Virgil so despises these figures that he looks away, refusing to talk of them, but Dante weeps openly. He is overcome with horror and swoons when he sees how many dead souls stand on the edge of Acheron to be ferried into hell. The beginning of punishment worries everyone.

Only the beginning. The gradual descent into "the abysmal valley of pain" turns the viewing of agony into a routine (*Inf.* 4:9–10). Yes, Dante weeps afresh in grief and pity in the second circle of hell when he meets the lovely Francesca of Rimini, punished for her lust in adultery with Paolo (*Inf.* 5:120–122), but by the fifth circle of hell in canto 8, where the wrathful are encased in the foul boiling mud of the Marsh of Styx, Dante uses his penny's worth of power over the helpless to increase the misery of Filippo Argenti, an arrogant Florentine whom he hated in life.

Later in the descent, in canto 11, where we are given the plan of hell, the *Commedia* explains how sensitivities can and must be deadened in a punishment regime. "We must delay our descent," Virgil explains, "that the sense may first get used a little to the vile breath, and then we shall not heed it" (*Inf.* 11:10–12). By canto 13, Dante will actively add to the pain of some of the damned simply to satisfy his curiosity.[8]

The greater the sin or crime, the more Dante shows his anger and the more he contributes to the suffering around him. In this he mimics the demons who control the damned in the lower circles of hell. As we go deeper, Dante, the exile, jeers at the damned from Florence. In the eighth circle for false counselors, he cries, "Rejoice, Florence. . . . Through Hell thy name is spread abroad!" (*Inf.* 26:1–3). Corruption clearly corrupts any witness who tries to be more than that. We know this when Dante pauses to enjoy the ridiculous bickering of Florentine frauds who are covered in disease and filth.[9] "A little more and I quarrel with thee," Virgil protests. Dante, stopping to enjoy the unfortunate predicament of the fraudulent in their idle gossip, exhibits the "base desire" in all punishment (*Inf.* 30:131–333, 149–150).

Dante's curiosity begins to make him part of punishment. The pilgrim has been case hardened by more than righteousness. He behaves at times like a tough cop who has seen too many people in jail. The unseemliness of the last cantos is not just in the damned. By canto 32, in the ninth circle for treachery to country, Dante does not mind stepping on the heads of sufferers encased to their eyes in ice, and he hurts them further if they do not do his bidding. So extremely does he torment one screaming traitor by pulling out his hair that another traitor asks, "What devil is at thee?" (*Inf.* 32:98–110).

Dante in hell can break the simplest promise of mercy. Asked to help another sufferer to open his frozen eyes in exchange for information, Dante reneges on the bargain. "It was courtesy to be a churl to him" (*Inf.* 33:150–151). So natural is it for a punisher to add unnecessarily to the assigned affliction of a person helpless in prison through hate for what that person has done or, for an even shoddier reason, through mere advantage over another being. Of "the worst of the worst" in hell, Dante sneers, "Better had you here been sheep or goats!" (*Inf.* 32:113–116). Objectifying human beings as less than human is a frequent defense mechanism for treating prisoners badly.

The pleasure in severity depends on the humanity of the punisher forgetting itself. No matter how much has been done, more can be inflicted on the condemned. The demon Scarmiglione, in the eighth circle, symbolizes the mentality of a bad prison guard in his desire to increase the level assigned (*Inf.* 21:105). Reflect, as well, on heaven's decision to redouble the pain of the damned when their more sentient bodies will join their souls on Judgment Day (*Inf.* 6:91–111). Even that is not enough. The souls of the most despicable sinners on earth receive punishment in hell before they have died (*Inf.* 33:118–135).[10]

Punishment as a corrective changes all that, and we learn early in *Purgatorio* that it cannot be understood by reason alone in the way retributive punishment can. Here is both the problem and the solution in any agenda of correction. As an indication of the difference, Virgil, Dante's guide and the symbol of reason and human artifice, no longer knows the way in purgatory (*Pur.* 2:61–65; 4:37–38). "Fair words" and "reason," Virgil's great strengths, no longer suffice (*Pur.* 1:92–96; 3:34–36).[11] Something more evanescent applies to the punishment that cleanses in purgatory. But if so, what is it that the shift to rehabilitation requires beyond the use of reason and skill?

Punishment through pain remains Dante's teacher, but it works differently in purgatory. It prevents sin, or unlawfulness, from taking place by breaking the habit of it.[12] The goal is correction; pain is the by-product that makes it possible. With correction as the aim, relationships in purgatory take on a different meaning. Dante is no longer just an observer here. He joins the penitents, and they exchange information to help each other in the climb from terrace to terrace through the seven deadly sins. In the journey through hell, he watched events as a witness to satisfy explanation; now he must use explanations to improve himself.

Why is this so important? Dante, it should be remembered, makes this part of his pilgrimage with the seven deadly sins cut into his forehead (*Pur.* 9:112–114). He knows he is like the others. There is a new reciprocity between the witnesses and the punished around them. Equality, the recognition of an intrinsic connection to anyone who suffers, changes the tenor as well as the scene of punishment. Friendships are not only possible but necessary in the purifying process of purgatory.

The damned struggle alone in hell except when they are fighting or hurting one another. Nothing like that ever occurs in purgatory. Instead of screams of pain, we now have welcoming embraces.[13] The setting is noticeably like regular society in its casual conviviality. Dante naturally expresses regret and pity when he finds a friend in hell; in purgatory the same discovery means delight and fellowship. "Noble Judge Nino, what joy it was to me when I saw thee not to be among the guilty!" (*Pur.* 8:53–54). There is no shame here, only a desire to get better than we are.

The souls in purgatory have sinned through misdirected love, basically selfishness. The antidote, correct love, manifests itself through kindness and mutuality.[14] Virgil drives the point home in canto 22 when he indicates "love kindled by virtue always kindles another" (*Pur.* 22:10–11). Relation joins the punished souls in the enterprise of improving themselves, and it reaches to the living (those outside prison) to help them. Here is the difference between mere prison and a house of correction.

Dante is clear on the importance of these external connections and the absence of them among the eternally punished, who deserve to be remembered, if at all, only pejoratively and as isolated figures. The doomed mourn the world they have lost but know only separation from it and all in it.[15] In purgatory the calls on the living by those being purified are direct, and they have everything to do with a new theory of punishment.

Correction, unlike condemnation, invokes transitional powers. Purgatory is by definition a connecting realm. It reaches both below, to the living, and above in the promise of heaven to come. It is the one transitory state in the *Commedia;* hence it comes closest to the struggle in human life, or what Dante movingly terms "those who live the life that is a race to death" (*Pur.* 33:54). Everyone's ability to move has unique value in purgatory. No one is stuck, and there is larger meaning in the relative freedom that this connotes.

The first flush of imagination that led to such an original conception remains shrouded in mystery, but it came out of a crisis in both situation and thought, and it demanded a new realm to be realized. To reach back to the chart of the punitive impulse in Chapter 6, abstract innovation seeks a concrete scenario to be properly and fully born. Ideas of punishment, with their visceral projections of restraint, may always require the correlation.

No precise historical moment can be named when purgatory achieved a viable place in the afterlife.[16] It was only relatively late, at the Second Council of Lyons in 1274, that a papal council gave formal definition, but the basic idea had been accepted as early as the eighth century, more out of communal urgency than doctrinal need. The stark separation of the damned in perpetual hellfire from a much tinier portion of the human race given eternal bliss was too devastating for a world consumed by its own sense of hopeless sin.

What was the uncertain believer who had made mistakes to do? Anxiety over eternal pain had to be relieved in some way. Part of the intolerable mystery in punishment had to be taken away from the inscrutability of God's final judgment. Purgatory supplied those answers. It arranged for a place where one had time to reform and gain salvation through a healing form of only temporary punishment. Just as important, it returned a measure of control to the living.

The quick, as opposed to the dead, could help by praying for the souls in purgatory. The living had the power to reduce suffering there, a power that the church would appropriate for political use. Human endeavor could also speed a soul's progress toward heaven. Everything in punishment changes when correction is understood to be possible, and it is easier to make that possibility work in a special place.

The need for external help in the rehabilitation of souls fuels the emotional trajectory of *Purgatorio*. It occurs often, but most immediately in canto 3, where Manfred, a famous worldling who sought God's pardon only in the last moments of a bad life, asks Dante to advise his daughter, Constance, that he is safely in line for admittance to purgatory. Prayers will help him advance though "horrible were my sins!" Dante must convey the difference when he returns. If Constance thinks Manfred is in hell, as she has every right to believe, prayers would be pointless, and she will not give them (*Pur.* 3:118–121).[17]

The role of the living in helping the worthy dead through prayer has great importance everywhere in purgatory. The phenomenon even allows a joke. When Dante detects a friend high on the sixth of the seven terraces of purgatory, he remembers a rascal in life and can only express his astonishment. "I thought to find thee down below," he blurts to Forese Donati, but not so! Forese, a regular if tepid sinner, has advanced rapidly through the offices (*condotto*) of his wife Nella: "By her flood of tears, by her devout prayers, and sighs, she has . . . set me free from the other circles" (*Pur.* 23:80–90).[18]

We should not be surprised by how much difference a corrective mode of punishment makes to one's understanding of the world or how much it depends on a different theory of human nature. Belief in the possibility of goodness counts. It is the basis of all reform. Throughout the *Commedia*, Dante expresses his sorrow and anger over the fallen state of Italy, but those expressions take on new purpose and direction in *Purgatorio*, and it is important to know why that happens (*Pur.* 6:78–80, 124–126).[19]

The pilgrim in *Purgatorio* wonders why such corruption should have been allowed to occur in the world when he notices so many good souls striving toward heaven all around him. Why haven't they made more of a difference in life? With a more optimistic worldview in the house of correction, he dares to send a challenge of colossal scope. Worrying quite legitimately, "if it be lawful to me," Dante interrogates God! "O Jove supreme . . . are Thy just eyes turned elsewhere, or is it preparation Thou makest in the abyss of Thy counsel for some good quite cut off from our perception?" (*Pur.* 6:120–123).

The question only makes sense within the power of friendship and cooperation of *Purgatorio*. The nature of punishment determines not only what a society can think of itself but what it thinks might be possible. Condemnation depends on an entrenched distrust of human nature, and that distrust breeds a corresponding pessimism about society. Punishment that corrects believes in something better.

Dante, of course, has the advantage of reducing the mystery in rehabilitative punishment through a divine plan and with an early fourteenth-century mind bent on salvation. A more secular recognition of punishment, of the kind we have traced here, depends on whether or not the *Commedia* can be "detheologized" in a useful way.[20] Dante is at once difficult and intriguing when we follow him into these registers. There are, in fact, no easy answers, but there are answers.

At a glance, the case for secular reform appears difficult. The demons and mythological judges of the dead and prison guards in the circles of hell—monstrous figures like Charon, Minos, Cerberus, Phlegyas, the Erinyes, the Minotaur, the Centaurs, lesser demons, and Geryon—are full of restless activity and hard to keep in check, but these very traits make them entertaining for a reader. By way of contrast, the dutiful but placid angels of purgatory quietly shuttle the penitents from one level to another when the move is deemed worthy by an all-seeing but unseen higher authority. Their relative passiveness runs against all punishment theory: correction will always require more effort and mindful interaction than condemnation.

Divine will turns the effort of angelic underlings into a mechanical enterprise. How can a comparable secular plan, with all the effort it requires, bring rehabilitation down to earth? We have already noticed that reason and artifice will not be sufficient. Something more is needed to match the optimism that heaven allows, but what? This is the burning question in any rehabilitation program.

The answer lies not in angels but in us. Human discipline, but with a purpose and direction, is the real inspiration of *Purgatorio*. On first entering, Dante learns "he that looks back returns outside," which is to say all is then lost (*Pur.* 9:131–132). When Dante hears the door of purgatory close behind him, he must resist the temptation to define himself through the transgressive life that he has left. "If I had turned my eyes to it what excuse would have served for the fault?" (*Pur.* 10:4–6).

Rehabilitation demands a progressive concentration with the help of others who are similarly minded. "Along this way," Virgil warns on even the highest terrace of purgatory, "the rein must be kept tight on the eyes, for it would be easy to err" (*Pur.* 25:118–120). Discipline is a matter of seeing correctly, as far as one is allowed to see. It translates outward forms to inward acceptance, which must then be demonstrated in external behavior while moving forward. Restoration requires a realized personal transformation that must then identify a way to exhibit itself to the surrounding community.

Two basic elements of the *Commedia* encourage the possibility of rehabilitation. First, Dante must move beyond the hatred he fed on when saturated in the condemnations of *Inferno*. It has warped him emotionally. Separation from it must happen for rehabilitation to make any sense at all. In the psychology of punishment, the nature of imprisonment controls the possibility of redress. Reform requires not just belief but a place for it. Second, the idea of a law-abiding desire depends on faith in a law-abiding society. Purgatory, like any other form of incarceration, is made meaningful by people on the outside who want to help.

As in the *Commedia*, a prisoner must want to be better, but no one who has fallen improves without serious assistance or encouragement, and the unrelieved downward thrust in contemporary punishment regimes lends little if any help in prison or on reentry. Dante is surely right that improvement cannot be done by reason alone, and the most troubling barrier in this regard can be found in the *Commedia* itself.

Those who take up Dante's poem generally save their fascination for *Inferno*. They follow *Purgatorio* out of a sense of duty. *Inferno* has greater appeal even though *Purgatorio* is the more imaginative conception. Dante's hell demonstrates the poet's ingenuity, but established conceptions define the shape of it and that part of the *Commedia*. Purgatory required far more independent levels of creativity.[21]

The poet is even proud enough of the difference to declare it. Pointing to the special inventiveness needed in his rendition of purgatory, Dante makes a rare call on his audience. "Thou seest well, reader, that I rise to a higher theme; do not wonder, therefore, if I sustain it with greater art" (*Pur.* 9:70–72). Why should such originality, such "greater art," satisfy less? Why should the act of punishing outweigh the "higher theme" of lending a helping hand? The answer is unpleasant. The frantic dynamism and malice of the devils in hell are more absorbing than the passive serenity of the angels in purgatory.

Punishment is a reflexive response to misbehavior, and punishers in their anger are always spontaneously at the ready. Rehabilitation requires thought, a plan, work, and the willingness to probe slow changes in more mundane objects of attrition. It will always be easier to ask for punishment than to institute a treatment program in a prison system where punishment comes first. The answer, to the extent that we can give one, lies in something separate, something either beyond or after punishment.

The Divine Comedy is a limited guide, but it does reveal the pernicious parameters in the psychology of punishment and gives a response to them. It teaches what is worst in ourselves, as well as a hope for the best. The self-confidence and sophistication of thought with which Dante Alighieri could spell out an elaborate plan of recovery in the midst of vulnerability, despair, and unmitigated violence in the late Middle Ages of Italy can be instructive in this regard even today.

It took faith, ability, vision, talent, courage, and a certain amount of faith in human nature for Dante to reach beyond the fear of his moment. Whether twenty-first-century American society can begin to match these qualities is an open question that a culture less justified in its fear should ask of itself. Criminal justice has gone astray, lost in a dark wood of its own making. It is time, more than time, to find a way out.

Notes

Introduction

1. I take these figures from Anthony M. Kennedy, "Speech at the American Bar Association Annual Meeting, August 9, 2003: An Address by Anthony M. Kennedy, Associate Justice, Supreme Court of the United States," 3, http://www.supremecourt.gov/publicinfo/speeches/viewspeeches.aspx ?Filename=sp_08-09-03.html.

2. The most important studies include James Q. Whitman, *Harsh Justice: Criminal Punishment and the Widening Divide between America and Europe* (New York: Oxford University Press, 2003); William J. Stuntz, *The Collapse of American Criminal Justice* (Cambridge, Mass.: Harvard University Press, 2011); Henry Ruth and Kevin R. Reitz, *The Challenge of Crime: Rethinking Our Response* (Cambridge, Mass.: Harvard University Press, 2003); Marie Gottschalk, *The Prison and the Gallows: The Politics of Mass Incarceration in America* (Cambridge: Cambridge University Press, 2006); Keally McBride, *Punishment and Political Order* (Ann Arbor: University of Michigan Press, 2007); Michael Tonry, *Crime, Punishment, and Politics in Comparative Perspective* (Chicago: University of Chicago Press, 2007); Bruce Western, *Punishment and Inequality in America* (New York: Russell Sage Foundation, 2006); Terance D. Miethe and Hong Lu, *Punishment: A Comparative Historical Perspective* (Cambridge: Cambridge University Press, 2005); Nichola Lacey, *The Prisoner's Dilemma: Political Economy and Punishment in Contemporary Democracies* (Cambridge: Cambridge University Press, 2008). The quotation is from Whitman, *Harsh Justice*, 207.

3. For the comment on Bentham's method ascribed to John Stuart Mill and for a good account of Bentham's radical rejection of common law in the name of a jurisprudence based on utilitarianism, see Gerald J. Postema, "Utilitarian Justice and the Tasks of Law" and "Plucking Off the Mask of Mystery," in *Bentham and the Common Law Tradition* (Oxford: Clarendon Press, 1986), 147–149, 263–301.

4. See, in particular, Pierre Bourdieu, *The Logic of Practice*, trans. Richard Nice (Stanford, Calif.: Stanford University Press, 1990), 56, 68, 86, 269.

5. The phrase comes from Abraham Lincoln's "First Inaugural Address— Final Text" (March 4, 1861). See Roy P. Basler, ed., *The Collected Works of*

251

Abraham Lincoln, 8 vols. (New Brunswick, N.J.: Rutgers University Press, 1953), 4:271.

1. Punishment Misunderstood

1. Nigel Walker, *Why Punish?* (Oxford: Oxford University Press, 1991), 1–3.
2. See Peter M. Tiersma, *Legal Language* (Chicago: University of Chicago Press, 1999), 243–244.
3. Michel de Montaigne, "Of Cruelty," in *The Complete Essays of Montaigne,* trans. Donald M. Frame (Stanford, Calif.: Stanford University Press, 1948), 311–313, 316. For an essay that details Montaigne's understanding of the struggle to overcome cruelty, see David Quint, "Cruelty and Noblesse," in *Montaigne and the Quality of Mercy: Ethical and Political Themes in the "Essais"* (Princeton, N.J.: Princeton University Press, 1998), 42–74.
4. Friedrich Nietzsche, *On the Genealogy of Morals* and *Ecce Homo,* trans. Walter Kaufmann (New York: Vintage Books, 1989), 65–66, 69, 76–77, 80.
5. Friedrich Nietzsche, "Genealogy of Morals: A Polemic," in *Ecce Homo,* in Nietzsche, *On the Genealogy of Morals* and *Ecce Homo,* 312.
6. Friedrich Nietzsche, "Aphorism 146," in *Beyond Good and Evil,* trans. Marianne Cowan (Chicago: Henry Regnery, 1955), 85.
7. William Shakespeare, *Measure for Measure* (New York: Signet Classic, 1998), 2.2.171–172.
8. Plea bargaining, crowded dockets, prosecutorial initiatives, and mandatory sentencing guidelines all limit the range and impact of judicial power. For these limits, as well as the high regard reserved for the judicial figure, see Robert A. Ferguson, "Inside the Courtroom," in *The Trial in American Life* (Chicago: University of Chicago Press, 2007), 29–43.
9. The legal scholar Ronald Dworkin uses the device of an ideal judicial figure, Judge Hercules, throughout *Law's Empire* (Cambridge, Mass.: Belknap Press, 1986). For a book-length study of the problems in the judicial administration of punishment, see Malcolm M. Feeley and Edward L. Rubin, *Judicial Policy Making and the Modern State* (New York: Cambridge University Press, 1999).
10. See, for example, H. L. A. Hart, *Punishment and Responsibility: Essays in the Philosophy of Law,* 2nd ed. (Oxford: Oxford University Press, 2008), 172. Hart, in describing "the claim of justice," writes for everyone when he indicates that the expression "'like cases should be treated alike' should always be heard."
11. Consistency is the "formal virtue" in proportionality. See Walker, *Why Punish?,* 102–103.
12. See, for example, Nigel Walker, *Punishment, Danger and Stigma* (Oxford: Basil Blackwell, 1980), 25.

13. Mosi Secret, "Big Sentencing Disparity Seen for Judges," *New York Times,* March 6, 2012, A25. Data from hundreds of thousands of cases acquired through the Freedom of Information Act and studied by the Transactional Records Access Clearinghouse indicate "vast disparities in the prison sentences handed down by judges presiding over similar cases." Ibid.

14. Anthony M. Kennedy, "Speech at the American Bar Association Annual Meeting, August 9, 2003: An Address by Anthony M. Kennedy, Associate Justice, Supreme Court of the United States," 3, http://www.supremecourt .gov/publicinfo/speeches/viewspeeches.aspx?Filename=sp_08-09-03 .html.

15. Norman Mailer, *The Executioner's Song* (Boston: Little, Brown, 1979), 91.

16. Adam Gopnik, "The Caging of America," *New Yorker,* January 30, 2012, 72.

17. Gerard E. Lynch, "Sentencing Eddie," *Journal of Criminal Law and Criminology,* 91 (Spring 2001): 565.

18. For one of the most recent accounts detailing the routine horrors in today's prisons, see Gopnik, "Caging of America," 72–77.

19. David Garland, *The Culture of Control: Crime and Social Order in Contemporary Society* (Chicago: University of Chicago Press, 2001), 14.

20. U.S. Bureau of Justice Statistics, "Correctional Populations in the United States, 2010," (December 15, 2011), http://bjs.ojp.usdoj.gov/index.cfm ?ty=pbdetail&iid=2237. I also use the sources and the language of Marie Gottschalk, *The Prison and the Gallows: The Politics of Mass Incarceration in America* (Cambridge: Cambridge University Press, 2006), 1.

21. See International Cenre for Prison Studies, "World Prison Brief: Entire World—Prison Population Rates per 100,000 of the National Population" (December 31, 2011), http://www.prisonstudies.org/info/worldbrief/wpb _states.php?area-all&category=wb_poprate; also quoted in Gottschalk, *Prison and the Gallows,* 1.

22. Figures quoted by Kennedy, "Speech at the American Bar Association Annual Meeting," 3.

23. See Vesla M. Weaver, "Frontlash: Race and the Development of Punitive Crime Policy," *Studies in American Political Development* 21 (Fall 2007): 230–265; and, more generally, Michelle Alexander, *The New Jim Crow: Mass Incarceration in the Age of Colorblindness,* rev. ed. (New York: New Press, 2012).

24. U.S. Bureau of Justice Statistics, "Reentry Trends in the U.S.: Recidivism," (September 17, 2013), http://bjs.ojp.usdoj.gov/content/reentry/recidivism .cfm.

25. Michelle S. Phelps, "Rehabilitation in the Punitive Era: The Gap between Rhetoric and Reality in U.S. Prison Programs," *Law and Society Review* 45 (2011): 33–63. Phelps traces a shift from educational programs in prison

to supervised reentry programs in keeping with "the management of classes of ex-felons for public safety identified in the new penology" (63).

26. For state corrections expenditures, which totaled $48.5 billion in 2010, see Tracey Kyckelhahn, "State Corrections Expenditures, FY 1982-2010," *U.S. Bureau of Justice Statistics* (December 10, 2012), http//www.bjs.gov /index.cfm?ty-pbdetail&iid=4556; for federal corrections expenditures, which totaled $8.5 billion in 2010 and local government corrections expenditures, which totaled $26.5 billion in 2010, see Tracey Kyckelhahn and Tara Martin, "Justice Expenditure and Employment Extracts, 2010—Preliminary," *U.S. Bureau of Justice Statistics* (July 1, 2013), http:// www.bjs/index.cfm?ty=pbdetail&iid=4679.

27. See, for example, Ruth Wilson Gilmore, *Golden Gulag: Prisons, Surplus, Crisis, and Opposition in Globalizing California* (Berkeley: University of California Press, 2007).

28. Kennedy, "Speech at the American Bar Association Annual Meeting," 1–11, 2, 8. The quotations from Justice Kennedy's address in the next paragraphs are from this source and will be noted by page number in parenthetical references in the text.

29. Alexis de Tocqueville, *Democracy in America,* 2 vols., ed. Phillips Bradley (New York: Vintage Classics, 1990), 1:280.

30. Ronald Gray, for example, calls it "the most terrible of all Kafka's stories." See Gray, *Franz Kafka* (Cambridge: Cambridge University Press, 1973), 20.

31. For the record of the unprecedented level, scale, and horror of torture and punishment in modernity, see Jonathan Glover, *Humanity: A Moral History of the Twentieth Century* (New Haven, Conn.: Yale University Press, 1999).

32. Hannah Arendt, "Franz Kafka: A Revaluation," *Partisan Review,* Fall 1944, 416.

33. For a quick run-through of the interpretive lenses applied to Kafka, see Ruth V. Gross, introduction to *Critical Essays on Franz Kafka,* ed. Ruth V. Gross (Boston: G. K. Hall, 1990), 1–17. The analysis that comes closest to my own interpretation is that of Keally McBride, *Punishment and Political Order* (Ann Arbor: University of Michigan Press, 2007), 27–36, although McBride, a political scientist, concentrates more on the political aspects of Kafka's tale.

34. Franz Kafka, "In the Penal Colony," in *Franz Kafka: The Complete Stories,* ed. Nahum N. Glatzer, trans. Will Muir and Edwin Muir (New York: Schocken Books, 1983), 140–167. All quotations from the story in the following paragraphs are from this edition; page numbers are indicated parenthetically in the text.

35. All these distancing elements in punishment can be found, for example, in Adolf Eichmann's explanation of his role in the deportation and mur-

der of millions of Jews in World War II. See Hannah Arendt, *Eichmann in Jerusalem: A Report on the Banality of Evil* (New York: Penguin Books, 1965), 42–44, 242–248, 287–289.

36. Gray, *Franz Kafka*, 99.

37. See ibid., 93. The other stories in the collection would have been "The Metamorphosis" and "The Judgment."

38. In the last two sentences, I paraphrase and borrow from the terminology of Paul Ricoeur, *The Symbolism of Evil*, trans. Emerson Buchanan (Boston: Beacon Press, 1967), 42–43.

39. You can see aspects of this interaction, the invested insider against the wary outsider, in every current court case that deals with prisoner abuse.

40. Jeremy Bentham, "Popularity," in *The Rationale of Punishment*, ed. James T. McHugh (Amherst, N.Y.: Prometheus Books, 2009), 97. (Originally published in French in 1818 and in English in 1830.)

41. See, for example, Marc O. DeGirolami, "The Choice of Evils and the Collisions of Theory," in *Retributivism: Essays on Theory and Policy*, ed. Mark D. White (Oxford: Oxford University Press, 2011), 193–194. DeGirolami argues that "scholarship too often sought—and still seeks—to identify something conceptually pure about each of the 'theories of punishment' and to argue that one of them ought to predominate." These attempts, he adds, "may not be well served by categorically denying the irreconcilability and inevitable collision of the values of the criminal law."

42. For a good quick explanation of these philosophies and how they stack up against one another, see Terance D. Miethe and Hong Lu, *Punishment: A Comparative Historical Perspective* (Cambridge: Cambridge University Press, 2005), 15–24.

43. Nietzsche, *On the Genealogy of Morals* and *Ecce Homo*, 76–77.

44. Jason DeParle, "The American Prison Nightmare," *New York Review of Books* 54 (April 12, 2007): 34. The accuracy of DeParle's summary is clear from John J. Gibbons and Nicholas de B. Katzenbach, "Preface" and "Summary of Findings," in *Confronting Confinement: A Report of the Commission on Safety and Abuse in America's Prisons* (New York: Vera Institute of Justice, 2006), 6-8, 11-17, http://www.vera.org/pubs/confronting-confinement.

45. The information and quotations in this paragraph have been taken from the currently pending official amended complaint of a sixth class-action suit charging prison-guard abuse in the United States District Court for the Southern District of New York, in which eleven plaintiffs, all inmates actively tortured and injured by prison guards at Rikers, detail the illegal events that led to their extremely serious injuries. Only serious injuries that have been thoroughly documented have a chance of being heard in such cases. The court record also shows that guards try to avoid video

cameras in their attacks on prisoners. See *Nunez v. City of New York*, No. 11-CV-5845(LTS)(THK) (S.D.N.Y. May 24, 2012), the following enumerated complaints: 1, 2, 5, 6, 28c, 30–34 (pages 1–2, 4–5, 19, and 21–22 of "Amended Complaint").

46. Joseph Goldstein and Randy Leonard, "Charges That Chief Ordered Rikers Beating," *New York Times,* June 27, 2013, A25.

47. "North Carolina: Warden and Guard Suspended," *New York Times,* December 5, 2012, A20.

48. Annys Shin and Aaron C. Davis, "Grappling to Control Prisons in Maryland," *Washington Post,* May 28, 2013, A1, A5.

49. "Horrendous Abuse in Mississippi Prisons," *New York Times,* June 10, 2013, A22.

50. Oliver O'Donovan, *The Ways of Judgment* (Grand Rapids, Mich.: William B. Eerdmans, 2005), 102.

51. Ibid.

52. For the most thorough account of the theoretical victory of retribution over other policies in punishment, see the book-length debate between Jeffrie G. Murphy and Jean Hampton, which concludes, "There is a legitimate retributive sentiment" that controls discussions of punishment. Murphy and Hampton, *Forgiveness and Mercy* (Cambridge: Cambridge University Press, 1988), 164. For the increase in punishment rates, see Victor E. Kappeler and Gary W. Potter, "The Trend to Greater Punitiveness in the United States," in *The Mythology of Crime and Criminal Justice,* 4th ed. (Long Grove, Ill.: Waveland Press, 2005), 317–327, 317.

53. Nigel Walker, a strong retributivist, makes all these points in *Why Punish?*, 49, 67–68, 126, 183.

54. I take these numbers and the paraphrase from Kappeler and Potter, *Mythology of Crime and Criminal Justice,* 320–321.

55. Jeffrie G. Murphy, "Some Second Thoughts on Retributivism," in White, *Retributivism,* 102.

56. See Michael Singer, *Prison Rape: An American Institution?* (Santa Barbara, Calif.: Praeger, 2013), 18. Singer also shows how prison rape targets and diminishes its victims, increases their general vulnerability, destroys self-respect, and threatens their lives. See 11–14.

57. Murphy, "Some Second Thoughts on Retributivism," 103 (emphasis in the original).

58. Dan Markel, "What Might Retributive Justice Be? An Argument for the Confrontational Conception of Retributivism," in White, *Retributivism,* 51.

59. Retributivism dominates even though "limiting retributivism has been widely endorsed by scholars, model code drafters, legislators, sentencing commissions, judges, and practitioners." See Richard S. Frase, "Punishment Purposes," *Stanford Law Review* 58 (2005–2006): 78.

60. Nietzsche, "The Tarantulas," in *Thus Spake Zarathustra*, trans. Thomas Common (New York: Boni and Liveright, 1917), 112. (Written between 1883 and 1885.)

61. Louis Hartz, *The Liberal Tradition in America: An Interpretation of American Political Thought since the Revolution* (New York: Harcourt, Brace and World, 1955), 10.

62. Thomas Hobbes, *Leviathan,* ed. Richard Tuck (Cambridge: Cambridge University Press, 1996), 9; McBride, *Punishment and Political Order,* 52–55. McBride has brilliantly traced the centrality of punishment to government in the theorists noted.

63. James Q. Wilson, *Thinking About Crime,* rev. ed. (New York: Vintage Books, 1985), 3. Wilson turns briefly to Beccaria and Bentham to flesh out his own theory of human nature. See the first edition of *Thinking About Crime* (New York: Basic Books, 1975), 46, 56.

64. See Niccolò Machiavelli, "Of the Qualities in Respect of Which Men, and Most of All Princes, Are Praised or Blamed," in *The Prince,* trans. N. H. Thomson (East Bridgewater, Mass.: Signature Press, 2008), 97–98; and J. G. A. Pocock, *The Machiavellian Moment: Florentine Political Thought and the Atlantic Republican Tradition* (Princeton, N.J.: Princeton University Press, 1975).

65. See Susan Neiman's account of Calvin in Neiman, *Evil in Modern Thought: An Alternative History of Philosophy* (Princeton, N.J.: Princeton University Press, 2002), 19, 124–125; and John Calvin, *Institutes of the Christian Religion,* ed. John T. McNeill, 2 vols. (Louisville, Ky.: Westminster John Knox Press, 1960), 1:724–25, 3:10:6.

2. The Rachet Effect in Theory

1. Donald Clark Hedges is one of many to prove "there is considerable disagreement among philosophers concerning the meaning and just function of punishment." See Hedges, "Punishment," *Philosophy and Phenomenological Research* 18 (December 1957): 209.

2. H. L. A. Hart, *Punishment and Responsibility: Essays in the Philosophy of Law,* 2nd ed. (Oxford: Oxford University Press, 2008), 172.

3. See Melissa Barden Dowling, *Clemency and Cruelty in the Roman World* (Ann Arbor: University of Michigan Press, 2006).

4. Herodotus, *The Histories,* trans. Aubrey de Sélincourt, rev. John Marincola (New York: Penguin Books, 1996), 313 (5:91). The general significance of this story of Periander and Thrasybulus is clear from the way it is repeated in other sources throughout the classical period.

5. Thucydides, *The Peloponnesian Wars,* trans. Rex Warner (New York: Penguin Books, 1972), 400–408 (5:84–116).

6. James L. Crenshaw, "Murder," in *The Oxford Companion to the Bible,* ed. Bruce M. Metzger and Michael D. Coogan (Oxford: Oxford University Press, 1993), 532–533; 1 Samuel 15:3–35; 1 Kings 18:40; 2 Kings 2:23–24.

7. Niccolò Machiavelli, *The Prince,* trans. N. H. Thomson (East Bridgewater, Mass.: Signature Press, 2008), 26. *The Prince* was known in some version in Italy as early as 1513 but was first published in 1532, five years after Machiavelli's death. The text spread very quickly to the rest of Europe and then to America. See J. G. A. Pocock, *The Machiavellian Moment: Florentine Political Thought and the Atlantic Republican Tradition* (Princeton, N.J.: Princeton University Press, 1975).

8. Machiavelli, *Prince,* 39, 56, 103, 105–106.

9. See John Baillie, John T. McNeill, and Henry P. Van Dusen, Introduction to John Calvin, *Institutes of the Christian Religion,* ed. John T. McNeill, 2 vols. (Louisville, Ky.: Westminster John Knox's Press, 1960), 1:xxix–xxxiii. The writers place *The Institutes* on "the short list of books that have notably affected the course of history, molding the beliefs and behavior of generations of mankind." The original extended title of the work in Latin, given here in English, did not suffer from false modesty: *The Institutes of the Christian Religion, Containing Almost the Whole Sum of Piety and Whatever It Is Necessary to Know in the Doctrine of Salvation: A Work Very Well Worth Reading by All Persons Zealous for Piety, and Lately Published.*

10. Calvin, *Institutes of the Christian Religion,* 1:203, 999 (1.16.5 and 3.25.2). All further quotations will be identified in the text by book, chapter, and section number of the passage.

11. Immanuel Kant, "An Answer to the Question: What Is Enlightenment?," in *Kant: Political Writings,* 2nd enlarged ed., trans. N. B. Nisbet (Cambridge: Cambridge University Press, 1991), 54–55, 58–59. In "Conjectures on the Beginning of Human History," Kant goes so far as to suggest that before civil society, "the history of *freedom* begins with evil, for it is the *work of man.*" *Kant: Political Writings,* 227.

12. See, for example, B. Sharon Byrd, "Kant's Theory of Punishment: Deterrence in Its Threat, Retribution in Its Execution," *Law and Philosophy* 8 (1989): 151–200 ff.

13. For the quotations in this paragraph and the next, see Kant, "The Right of Punishment and the Right of Pardon," in *The Metaphysics of Morals,* in *Kant: Political Writings,* 154–155. See also Hans Reiss, introduction to *Kant: Political Writings,* 8–10.

14. *Kant: Political Writings,* 155, 158–159.

15. Ibid., 156.

16. For the facts of Beccaria's life and the immediate success of his book, see Marcello Maestro, *Cesare Beccaria and the Origins of Penal Reform* (Phila-

delphia: Temple University Press, 1973), 3–19, 34–45. Two of the most innovative modern thinkers on the whole subject of punishment, Beccaria and Kafka came to the subject first through personal experience. Both had to cope with difficult fathers whom they accused of being tyrannical figures.

17. Beccaria, *On Crimes and Punishments, and Other Writings,* trans. Richard Davies (Cambridge: Cambridge University Press, 1995), 7. All further quotations of the work are from this edition and are cited in parenthetical references in the text.

18. See Richard Bellamy, introduction to Beccaria, *On Crimes and Punishments,* xxx.

19. Maestro, *Cesare Beccaria,* 34–37.

20. Francis Bacon, "On Friendship," in *The Essays or Counsels, Civil and Moral, of Francis Ld. Verulam, Viscount St. Albans* (Mount Vernon, N.Y.: Peter Pauper Press, 1948), 108. *The Essays* were first fully published in 1612. See also Bellamy, introduction to Beccaria, *On Crimes and Punishments,* xxx.

21. Only in the last two hundred years, under the influence of the Enlightenment, have human beings thought of happiness as an entitlement that is personally achievable here on earth. See generally Darrin M. McMahon, *Happiness: A History* (New York: Atlantic Monthly Press, 2006), 197–252; and see particularly Roy Porter, *Enlightenment: Britain and the Creation of the Modern World* (London: Penguin Books, 2000), 22. "The Enlightenment . . . translated the ultimate question 'How can I be saved?' into the pragmatic 'How can I be happy?'"

22. Quoted from Bellamy, introduction to Beccaria, *On Crimes and Punishments,* xvi–xvii.

23. J. S. Mill, "Bentham," in *J. S. Mill and Jeremy Bentham: Utilitarianism and Other Essays,* ed. Alan Ryan (New York: Penguin Books, 2004), 133, 139 (first published in 1838). Mill's father, James Mill, was a disciple of Bentham, and the two families spent time together throughout John Stuart Mill's childhood. John Stuart Mill served for a time as Bentham's secretary and research assistant. His own writings on utilitarianism popularized Bentham's ideas.

24. Jeremy Bentham, *The Rationale of Punishment,* ed. James T. McHugh (Amherst, N.Y.: Prometheus Books, 2009), 49–50; and McHugh, introduction, ibid., 12. All further quotations from this work will be noted by page number in parentheses in the text. See also Jeremy Bentham, "Cases Unmeet for Punishment," in *An Introduction to the Principles of Morals and Legislation,* ed. J. H. Burns and H. L. A. Hart (London: Athlone Press, 1970), 158.

25. Mill, "Bentham," 150.

26. Jeremy Bentham, "Of the Proportion between Punishment and Offences," in *Introduction to the Principles of Morals and Legislation,* 167–168.

27. Ibid., 167, 170. The quoted passages in the next paragraph are also from these pages. The emphases are Bentham's.

28. For an abstract account of this conflict, see Crane Brinton, "Adjustments and Amendments in the New Cosmology," in *The Shaping of the Modern Mind* (1950; New York: New American Library, 1959), 156–158.

29. Thomas Hobbes, *Leviathan,* ed. Richard Tuck (Cambridge: Cambridge University Press, 1996), 9. The high praise of *Leviathan* quoted in the text comes from John Rawls, *Justice as Fairness: A Restatement,* ed. Erin Kelly (Cambridge, Mass.: Harvard University Press, 2001), 1.

30. For a book-length treatment of this thesis, see Keally McBride, *Punishment and Political Order* (Ann Arbor: University of Michigan Press, 2007). McBride uses Hobbes and Locke as her controlling examples.

31. Anthony J. Sebok, *Legal Positivism in American Jurisprudence* (Cambridge: Cambridge University Press, 1998), 30.

32. See, for example, David Walker, "Positivism," in *The Oxford Companion to Law* (Oxford: Clarendon Press, 1980), 969–970; and, more generally, Jules Coleman and Scott Shapiro, eds., *The Oxford Handbook of Jurisprudence and Philosophy of Law* (Oxford: Oxford University Press, 2002), 26–27, 116–123, 147–157.

33. H. L. A. Hart, *The Concept of Law,* 2nd ed. (Oxford: Oxford University Press, 1994), 87–91. (The first edition was published in 1961.)

34. H. L. A. Hart, "A Prolegomenon to the Principles of Punishment," in *Punishment and Responsibility,* 1.

35. Hart, *Punishment and Responsibility,* 1.

36. Ibid., 1, 75, 231–232.

37. Hart, "Postscript: Part 2: Retribution," in *Punishment and Responsibility,* 211, 231.

38. *Walton v. Tryon,* 21 English Reports 262 (1753); repr., English Reports, vol. 21, Chancery, sec. 1 (London: Stevens and Son, 1902), 262–263. Hardwicke, lord chancellor of England at the time, actually paraphrases an even more telling though less crisp version from Sir Edward Coke in *The First Part of the Institutes of the Laws of England* (London: J & W. T. Clarke, 1832), I:34: "The law doth delight in . . . certaintie, which is the mother of quiet and repose."

39. Hart, *Punishment and Responsibility,* 8.

40. Timothy A. O. Endicott, "Law and Language," in Coleman and Shapiro, *Oxford Handbook of Jurisprudence and Philosophy of Law,* 945. Endicott argues that Hart tries to resolve jurisprudential problems by reexamining basic self-conceptions. Hart's favorite word and strategy is "eluci-

date," which means to clarify how and why different sides think about a problem.

41. Hart, *Punishment and Responsibility,* 9.

42. Ibid., 167, 183.

43. Ibid., 167, 183, 170–171.

44. Herbert Morris, "Persons and Punishments," *Monist* 52 (October 1968): 475–501; reprinted in *On Guilt and Innocence: Essays in Legal Philosophy and Moral Psychology,* by Herbert Morris (Berkeley: University of California Press, 1976), 31–57. Further references will be to the reprint edition. Jeffrie G. Murphy writes that "this essay, one of the classics of twentieth-century jurisprudence, almost single-handedly rescued robust retributivism from obscurity and rendered it philosophically respectable again." Murphy, "Some Second Thoughts on Retributivism," in *Retributivism: Essays on Theory and Policy,* ed. Mark D. White (Oxford: Oxford University Press, 2011), 97.

45. James Q. Wilson, introduction to *Thinking About Crime* (New York: Basic Books, 1975), xiv–xvii, xix. Looking back in a new introduction to his revised edition of 1983, Wilson summarizes the meaning of the first edition: "Rehabilitation has not yet been shown to be a promising method for dealing with serious offenders, broad-gauge investments in social progress have little near-term effect on crime rates, punishment is not an unworthy objective for the criminal justice system of a free and liberal society to pursue . . . deterrence and incapacitation work." Wilson, *Thinking About Crime,* rev. ed. (New York: Basic Books, 1983), 5. *Thinking About Crime* made Wilson "the most articulate spokesperson for the conservative crime response program . . . over the past three decades," because "he preached to the public that a new and more punitive crime policy was morally the right path for the nation." Henry Ruth and Kevin R. Reitz, *The Challenge of Crime: Rethinking Our Response* (Cambridge, Mass.: Harvard University Press, 2003), 4, 81.

46. Morris, "Persons and Punishments," 32–34.

47. Ibid., 32, 34, 36, 41.

48. Wilson, *Thinking About Crime* (1975), 75. See also "Criminologists" (43–63), "The Police and Crime" (81–97), and "Courts and Corrections" (162–182).

49. Ibid., 32–35, 55, 164, 169, 175, 199, 208.

50. Ibid., 172.

51. Wilson, introduction to *Thinking About Crime,* rev. ed. (1983), 10.

52. Wilson, *Thinking About Crime,* 21, 175, 181.

53. Ibid., 81–182.

54. James Q. Wilson, "Broken Windows: The Police and Neighborhood Safety," in *Thinking About Crime,* rev. ed. (1983), 78–79.

55. Wilson, *Thinking About Crime,* 182.
56. Ibid., 208–209.
57. Morris matches Wilson in this regard by comparing a punishment regime, which respects the power of choice and hence the right to punishment, with a regime of therapy, which would still have been highly suspect in the mentality of the 1960s. "With this [therapeutic] view of man the institutions of social control respond not with punishment, but with either preventive detention, in the case of 'carriers,' or therapy in the case of those manifesting pathological symptoms." In the first case, the person to be punished is a subject to be respected for possessing the moral capacity to exercising choice. In the second, the person who has fallen ill is an object to be treated. See Morris, "Persons and Punishments," 38–43.
58. Michel Foucault, *Discipline and Punish: The Birth of the Prison,* trans. Alan Sheridan (New York: Vintage Books, 1979), 22. (Originally published as *Surveiller et punir: Naissance de la prison* in 1975.)
59. Ibid., 58.
60. Ibid., 256.
61. John Rawls, "The Subject of Justice" and "The Veil of Ignorance," in *A Theory of Justice* (Cambridge, Mass.: Harvard University Press, 1971), 8, 136–137, 141, 245.
62. Rawls, "The Good of the Sense of Justice," "Legitimate Expectations and Moral Desert," and "The Concept of a Well-Ordered Society," in *Theory of Justice,* 577, 575, 315, 453–462. The subject of punishment does not appear at all in Rawls's restatement of his philosophy, *Justice as Fairness.* For other signs of Rawls's obvious reluctance to discuss punishment, see *Theory of Justice,* 241, 314.
63. The best of the efforts to use Rawls more intensively in a theory of punishment is that of Sharon Dolovich, "Legitimate Punishment in Liberal Democracy," *Buffalo Criminal Law Journal* 7 (2003–2004): 310–442. My quotations from her article are from pages 322 and 350. Dolovich identifies others who have used Rawls on theories of punishment (322n34). They include contributions from David A. Hoekema, Samuel J. M. Donnelly, Jeffrie G. Murphy, Bonnie Honig, and Samuel Scheffler. For Rawls's clear acknowledgment of his indebtedness to Hart for his Benthamite principles, see Rawls, *Theory of Justice,* 241, 314–315.
64. Dolovich, "Legitimate Punishment in Liberal Democracy," 394–399.
65. Rawls, *Theory of Justice,* 576.
66. Ibid., 244, 315.
67. Fyodor Dostoevsky, "Rebellion" and "The Grand Inquisitor," in *The Brothers Karamazov: A Novel in Four Parts with Epilogue,* trans. Richard Pevear

and Larissa Volokhonsky (New York: Vintage Books, 1991), 242–264, All quotations of these chapters in the following paragraphs are from this edition and are noted by page number in the text. All the ellipses in the quotations from "The Grand Inquisitor" are Dostoevsky's.

68. Proof of Dostoevsky's strong retributivist orientation comes from none other than H. L. A. Hart, *Punishment and Responsibility,* 158–159. Hart uses the novel *Crime and Punishment* to demonstrate that "Dostoyevsky passionately believed that society was morally justified in punishing people simply because they had done wrong" and that the novelist "hated and feared" utilitarian alternatives as Western forms of decadence.

69. The annotated version of the novel used here recovers the actual source of the story that Dostoevsky knew from three years before the publication of the novel in 1880: "Memoirs of a Serf," *Russian Herald,* no. 9 (1877). See *Brothers Karamazov,* 785n8.

70. Robert Cover famously describes the whole process of "jurisgenesis," the creation of legal meaning, as "world-creating" through aspiration (*"paideic"*) and "world maintaining" through enforcement ("imperial"). The Inquisitor is all enforcement. See Cover, "Nomos and Narrative," *Harvard Law Review* 97 (1983): 4ff. Quoted from the original and reprinted in *Narrative, Violence, and the Law: The Essays of Robert Cover,* ed. Martha Minow, Michael Ryan, and Austin Sarat (Ann Arbor: University of Michigan Press, 1992), 107–108.

71. For Dostoevsky's designation of Alyosha as the hero of his novel, see "From the Author," "The Third Son, Alyosha," and "Elders," in *Brothers Karamazov,* 3, 18–22, 25–27.

72. Matthew 7:14; 25:30, 41, 46.

73. See "Notes," in *Brothers Karamazov,* 786–787.

3. The Mixed Signs in Suffering

1. "Pain" and "Punish," in *The Compact Edition of the Oxford English Dictionary* (New York: Oxford University Press, 1971), 2054, 2360.

2. What the doctor who asks the question really wants to know is whether the pain is intolerable.

3. Virginia Woolf, "On Being Ill," *New Criterion,* January 1926, quoted here from Woolf, *On Being Ill* (Ashfield, Mass.: Paris Press, 2002), 6–7.

4. In *Graham v. Florida,* 560 U.S. 48 (2010), the court held that the cruel and unusual punishments clause of the Eighth Amendment does not permit a juvenile offender to be automatically sentenced to life imprisonment without parole for a crime less than homicide. *Roper v. Simmons,* 543 U.S. 551 (2005), abolished the death penalty for juvenile offenders.

5. For the quotations in this paragraph and the next, see John Locke, *An Essay Concerning Human Understanding,* ed. Roger Woolhouse (New York: Penguin Books, 1997), 130, 216, 316 (2.7.4; 2:20.1; 2.28.5).

6. Ibid., 252 (2.21.64). See also Edmund Wilson, *The Wound and the Bow: Seven Studies in Literature* (New York: Oxford University Press, 1965). All seven studies make the point, but see "Philoctetes: The Wound and the Bow," 223–242, especially 230, 235–237.

7. Pierre Grimal, *A Concise Dictionary of Classical Mythology,* trans. A. R. Maxwell-Hyslop (London: Blackwell, 1990), 89–90, 96, 306–308, 376. See also Sophocles, *Philoctetes,* in *Sophocles,* vol. 2, *Ajax, Electra, Trachiniae, Philoctetes,* trans. F. Storr, Loeb Classical Library (Cambridge, Mass.: Harvard University Press, 1967), 489.

8. John 3:16.

9. John 19:31–33. For commentary on the Roman punishment of death by crucifixion in this and the next paragraph, I rely on Jim Bishop, *The Day Christ Died* (New York: Harper Brothers, 1957), 308–324.

10. See, for example, *Baze v. Rees,* 553 U.S. 35 (2008) in which the Supreme Court held on April 16, 2008, that the possibility of unintended and unnoticed pain in administering an execution with lethal objection will not bar the use of it. The challenge to the practice was that the common sequence of three drugs used to sedate and then kill a condemned person "posed an unconstitutional risk that a condemned inmate would suffer acute yet undetectable pain." Linda Greenhouse, "Justices Uphold Lethal Injection in Kentucky Case," *New York Times,* April 17, 2008, A1, A26.

11. Elaine Scarry, *The Body in Pain: The Making and Unmaking of the World* (New York: Oxford University Press, 1985), 4–5, 14–15. Note that it is only awkwardly that "pain" works as a transitive verb—as in "Your behavior pains me"—while "to punish" is unavoidably transitive and all about the relationship between agent and object.

12. Genesis 3:16. For details of the medical controversies over anesthesia, see Martin S. Pernick, *A Calculus of Suffering: Pain, Professionalism, and Anesthesia in Nineteenth-Century America* (New York: Columbia University Press, 1985), 9, 19, 42–57, 152.

13. Victor Robinson, *Victory over Pain: A History of Anesthesia* (New York: Henry Schuman, 1946), 320.

14. Anemona Hartocollis, "Hard Choice for a Comfortable Death: Sedation," *New York Times,* December 27, 2009, A1, A24–25.

15. Adams, "Chaos (1870)," in *The Education of Henry Adams: An Autobiography* (Boston: Houghton Mifflin, 1961), 287–288. (Originally published in 1918.)

16. See, for example, Alan A. Stone, *Law, Psychiatry, and Morality: Essays and Analysis* (Washington, D.C.: American Psychiatric Press, 1984); B. F. Skinner, *About Behaviorism* (New York: Vintage Books, 1974); Joseph LeDoux, *The Emotional Brain: The Mysterious Underpinnings of Emotional Life* (New York: Simon and Schuster, 1996); Antonio Damasio, *The Feeling of What Happens: Body and Emotion in the Making of Consciousness* (New York: Harcourt, 1999); and Andrew Gluck, *Damasio's Error and Descartes' Truth: An Inquiry into Epistemology, Metaphysics, and Consciousness* (Scranton, Pa.: University of Scranton Press, 2007). All these works present limitations on free will except that by Gluck, who uses "consciousness studies" to try to reclaim the hegemony of rational thought in human behavior.

17. I paraphrase from "Negligence," "Pain and Suffering," and "Tort," in *Black's Law Dictionary*, 6th ed. (St. Paul, Minn.: West, 1990), 1032–1034, 1109, 1489.

18. Louis L. Jaffe, "Damages for Personal Injury: The Impact of Insurance," *Law and Contemporary Problems* 18 (1953): 222, 234.

19. The leading case in these controversies is *Seffert v. Los Angeles Transit Lines,* 364 P.2d 337 (Cal. 1961), where the leading jurist Roger Traynor dissented in frustration over an award of $314,000 for permanent foot injuries incurred in a streetcar accident while quoting from yet another case. "No rational being would change places with the injured man for an amount of gold that would fill the room of the court, yet no lawyer would contend that such is the legal measure of damages." Said Traynor, "It would hardly be possible ever to compensate a person fully for pain and suffering" (at 345–346). The previous case is *Zibbel v. Southern Pacific Co.,* 160 Cal. 237, 255 (1911).

20. Anthony J. Sebok, "Translating the Immeasurable: Thinking about Pain and Suffering Comparatively," *DePaul Law Review* 55 (2006): 383–384.

21. Mark A. Geistfeld, "Due Process and the Determination of Pain and Suffering Tort Damages," *DePaul Law Review* 55 (2006): 332; and Robert L. Rabin, "Pain and Suffering and Beyond: Some Thoughts on Recovery for Intangible Loss," *DePaul Law Review* 55 (2006): 360–362.

22. Richard Abel, "General Damages Are Incoherent, Incalculable, Incommensurable, and Inegalitarian (But Otherwise a Great Idea)," *DePaul Law Review* 55 (2006): 253, 258.

23. *Kwasny v. United States,* 823 F.2d 194, 197, and 194 (7th Cir. 1987).

24. Stephen D. Sugarman, "A Comparative Law Look at Pain and Suffering Awards," *DePaul Law Review* 55 (2006): 401, 434.

25. California Jury Instructions: Civil §14.13 (2005).

26. *McDougald v. Garber,* 536 N.E.2d 372, 374–375 (N.Y. 1989).

27. For the quotations in this paragraph and the next, see *Farmer v. Brennan,* 114 S. Ct. 1970, 1970, 1972–1973, 1990 (1994).

28. The quotations in this paragraph and the next are from *Rhodes v. Chapman,* 101 S. Ct. 2392, 2399, 2440, 2441 (1981).

29. Ibid. at 2396.

30. James J. Park, "Redefining Eighth Amendment Punishments: A New Standard for Determining the Liability of Prison Officials for Failing to Protect Inmates from Serious Harm," *Quinnipiac Law Review* 20 (2001): 410, 410n16.

31. This sentence first appears in the majority opinion of *Rhodes v. Chapman,* 101 S. Ct. at 2400. It is then repeated in the majority opinion of *Farmer v. Brennan,* 114 S. Ct. at 1976. Justice Souter, by repeating it, makes it his own and gives it greater authority as an established precedent, which is further confirmed because it is made on a greater form of abuse, not overcrowding with two in a prison cell but prison rape.

32. Anthony F. Granucci, " 'Nor Cruel and Unusual Punishments Inflicted': The Original Meaning," *California Law Review* 57 (1969): 840–842, 852, 862. Unless indicated otherwise, the historical origins of the amendment and early attitudes toward it here and in the next paragraphs are taken from this source. See also William Blackstone, *Commentaries on the Laws of England,* 4 vols. (1765–1769; repr., Chicago: University of Chicago Press, 1979), 4:369–372.

33. Granucci, " 'Nor Cruel and Unusual Punishments Inflicted,' " 855–856.

34. *Annals of Congress* 1:782–783 (1789). See also David P. Currie, *The Constitution in Congress: The Federalist Period, 1789–1801* (Chicago: University of Chicago Press, 1997), 94–96.

35. "Eighth Amendment claims were rare during the Court's first 175 years— the clause was discussed in only nine cases prior to its incorporation into the due process clause of the fourteenth amendment in 1962." (Incorporation came in *Robinson v. California,* 370 U.S. 660 (1962).) Margaret Jane Radin, "The Jurisprudence of Death: Evolving Standards for the Cruel and Unusual Punishments Clause," *University of Pennsylvania Law Review* 126 (1978): 997.

36. *Trop v. Dulles,* 356 U.S. 86, 101 (1958).

37. I quote and paraphrase here from Jack Rakove, *The Annotated U.S. Constitution and Declaration of Independence* (Cambridge, Mass.: Harvard University Press, 2009), 238–240.

38. For a good quick account of the debate on rules versus standards, see John C. Coffee Jr., "Principles versus Rules," in *Sesquicentennial Essays of the Faculty of Columbia Law School: 1858–2008* (New York City: Columbia Law School, 2008), 48–50.

39. I paraphrase from Judge Easterbrook throughout this paragraph; see Frank H. Easterbrook, "Abstraction and Authority," in *The Bill of Rights in*

the Modern State, ed. Geoffrey R. Stone, Richard A. Epstein, and Cass R. Sunstein (Chicago: University of Chicago Press, 1992), 353–354.

40. David A. Strauss, "Afterword: The Role of a Bill of Rights," in Stone, Epstein, and Sunstein, *Bill of Rights in the Modern State,* 550.

41. For the quotations in this paragraph and the next, see *Weems v. United States,* 217 U.S. 349, 366–367 (1910). See also *Coker v. Georgia,* 433 U.S. 584 (1987), which holds that state legislation authorizing execution of rapists violates the cruel and unusual punishments clause of the Eighth Amendment, and *Solem v. Helm,* 463 U.S. 277 (1983), which overturns a decision giving a defendant life without parole after passing a bad check, his seventh nonviolent felony, on the grounds of disproportionality for relatively minor criminal conduct.

42. *Harmelin v. Michigan,* 111 S. Ct. 2680, 2682, 2692, 2701–2702, 2709, 2720 (1991).

43. For a more complete rendering of how divided the court was in *Harmelin* and other cases, on which I rely, see Easterbrook, "Abstraction and Authority," 353–357.

44. For the best detailed account of the Supreme Court's inability to implement "an effective process for interpreting the Cruel and Unusual Punishment Clause" in death-penalty cases after *Furman v. Georgia,* 408 U.S. 238 (1972), led to a de facto moratorium on death-penalty cases in 1972 based on the Eighth Amendment and after *Gregg v. Georgia,* 428 U.S. 153 (1976), set forth procedural outlines that could overcome the prohibition of cruel and unusual punishments in 1976, see James S. Liebman, "Slow Dancing with Death: The Supreme Court and Capital Punishment, 1963–2006," *Columbia Law Review* 107 (2007): 1–130.

45. *Harmelin v. Michigan,* 111 S. Ct. at 2701.

46. For the facts surrounding the case, I rely on Linda Greenhouse, "Justices Uphold Lethal Injection in Kentucky Case"; and Adam Liptak, "Moratorium May Be Over, but Hardly the Challenges," *New York Times,* April 17, 2008, A1, A26.

47. "Opinion of Roberts, C. J.," *Baze v. Rees,* 553 U.S. 35, 61 (emphasis added).

48. *Baze v. Rees,* 553 U.S. at 50, 64, 67 (emphasis added).

49. The quotations in this paragraph and the next are from *Baze v. Rees,* 553 U.S. at 71–72, 78 (Stevens, J., concurring in judgment).

50. *Baze v. Rees,* 553 U.S. at 92 (Scalia, J., concurring in judgment).

51. Liebman, "Slow Dancing with Death," 121, 125. No one emerged from *Baze v. Rees* happily, and expert commentators, as well as some members of the court itself, immediately complained that the main impact of the decision would be more litigation with ever greater intricacy of interpretation. See Liptak, "Moratorium May Be Over, but Hardly the Challenges," A26.

52. Henry Ruth and Kevin R. Reitz, *The Challenge of Crime: Rethinking Our Response* (Cambridge, Mass.: Harvard University Press, 2003), 12, 69 (emphasis in the original). More generally, see Lynne H. Henderson, "The Wrongs of Victim's Rights," *Stanford Law Review* 37 (1985): 937–1021; and Robert A. Ferguson, "The Victim," in *The Trial in American Life* (Chicago: University of Chicago Press, 2007), 62–67.

53. See in general Leroy L. Lamborn, "Victim Participation in the Criminal Justice Process: The Proposals for a Constitutional Amendment," *Wayne Law Review* 34 (1987): 125–219. The Sixth Amendment currently describes the rights of only "the accused." It reads, "In all criminal prosecutions, the accused shall enjoy the right to a speedy and public trial, by an impartial jury of the State and district wherein the crime shall have been committed, which district shall have been previously ascertained by law, and to be informed of the nature and cause of the accusation; to be confronted with the witnesses against him; to have compulsory process for obtaining witnesses in his favor, and to have the Assistance of Counsel for his defence."

54. 42 U.S.C. § 10606a and 10606b (1990) and 18 U.S.C.A. § 3510 (1997). See also Carrie Mulholland, "Sentencing Criminals: The Constitutionality of Victim Impact Statements," *Missouri Law Review* 60 (1995): 731, 742; and William Glaberson, "Court Backs Statements by Survivors," *New York Times,* June 29, 1996, L9.

55. The kidnappings and murders of twelve-year-old Polly Klaas from a slumber party at her northern California home in 1993 and of seven-year-old Megan Kanka from next to her house in Hamilton Township, New Jersey, in 1994 became "part of the national psyche," with extensive media coverage of the victims and their families, and led dozens of states and the federal government to pass laws that require the registration of sex offenders. See "Jury Recommends Death for Killer of Polly Klaas," *New York Times,* August 6, 1996, A8; "At Center of 'Megan's Law' Case, a Man the System Couldn't Reach," *New York Times*, May 28, 1996, A1, B6; and "Study Says Megan Slaying Fits Pattern for Such Cases," *New York Times,* June 23, 1997, B5. For the heavy emphasis on victims during the trial of Timothy McVeigh, see "Bomb Jury Hears Testimony in Sentencing Phase of Case," *New York Times,* December 30, 1997, A12; Michael J. Sandel, "The Hard Questions: Crying for Justice," *New Republic,* July 7, 1997, 25; and Jason F. Cole, "Voices Crying in the Wilderness: The Role of Victims in the American Trial; A Study of the Oklahoma City Bombing Trials" (seminar paper, Columbia Law School, December 9, 1998).

56. *Payne v. Tennessee,* 501 U.S. 808, 826–827, 834 (1991).

57. I take the term "melodramatic imagination" and its implications from Peter Brooks, *The Melodramatic Imagination: Balzac, Henry James, Melo-*

drama, and the Mode of Excess (New Haven, Conn.: Yale University Press, 1976), 1–23.

58. These are definitions 2a and 2b in *Compact Edition of the Oxford English Dictionary*, 3626. Definition 1a applies to the Latin *victima*, "a living creature killed or offered as a sacrifice to some deity or supernatural power."

59. Leslie Fiedler, *An End to Innocence: Essays on Culture and Politics* (1948; repr., Boston: Beacon Press, 1955), 21.

60. *Payne v. Tennessee*, 501 U.S. at 856, 859, 863, 865, 867. Justice Stevens is not alone in these arguments. Chief Justice Robert N. Wilentz of the New Jersey Supreme Court also warns that allowing victims to address jurors could prompt them to base decisions about life or death on emotion. "Victim-impact evidence has no place in a rationally conducted sentencing proceeding," he writes. "It is a throwback, at least potentially, to the days when the death penalty could be imposed arbitrarily, without reason, much like being struck by lightning." Quoted from Glaberson, "Court Backs Statements by Survivors," L9.

61. Brent Staples, "When Grieving 'Victims' Can Sway the Courts: Americans Join the Culture of Revenge," *New York Times*, September 22, 1997, A26. (The writer's brother was murdered while begging for his life.)

62. Barry Glassner, *The Culture of Fear: Why Americans Are Afraid of the Wrong Things*, 10th anniversary ed. (New York: Basic Books, 2009), 230 (emphasis in the original).

63. The swing in attention from defendants to newly empowered victims is also helped by the frequent exercise by a defendant of the right to remain silent at trial; thus only the victim speaks directly about the crime in question and does so free from the customary restraints on testimony that pertain earlier in the trial process.

64. For the nature of these debates, see John Yoo, *War by Other Means: An Insider's Account of the War on Terror* (New York: Atlantic Monthly Press, 2006), on the side of the Bush administration; and Sanford Levinson, ed., *Torture: A Collection* (New York: Oxford University Press, 2004), covering the range of criticisms.

65. John H. Langbein, "The Legal History of Torture," in Levinson, *Torture*, 101. Langbein is also the author of the leading larger study on the subject, *Torture and the Law of Proof: Europe and England in the Ancien Régime* (Chicago: University of Chicago Press, 2006).

66. U.S.C.A., Title 18. Crimes and Criminal Procedure, Part I, Chapter 113C. Torture (18 U.S.C.A. § 2340).

67. See "Memorandum for William H. Haynes II, General Counsel of the Department of Defense (March 14, 2003) from Office of Legal Counsel, Office of the Deputy Assistant Attorney General, re: *Military Interrogation of*

Alien Unlawful Combatants Held outside the United States," https://www
.aclu.org/sites/default/files/pdfs/safefree/yoo_army_torture_memo.pdf.
See also John Yoo, "Interrogation," in *War by Other Means,* 165–203. For
the full record of available government documents that attempt to evade
the law of torture, see Karen J. Greenberg and Joshua L. Dratel, eds., *The
Torture Papers: The Road to Abu Ghraib* (Cambridge: Cambridge University Press, 2005).

68. See, for example, Vesla M. Weaver, "Frontlash: Race and the Develop-
    ment of Punitive Crime Policy," *Studies in American Political Development*
    21 (Fall 2007); 230–265; and, more generally, Michelle Alexander, *The
    New Jim Crow: Mass Incarceration in the Age of Colorblindness,* rev. ed. (New
    York: New Press, 2012).

69. Yoo, "Interrogation," in *War by Other Means,* 171–175, 187.

70. 18 U.S.C.A. § 2340A.

71. Quoted in Harold H. Bruff, *Bad Advice: Bush's Lawyers in the War on Ter-
    ror* (Lawrence: University Press of Kansas, 2009), 236.

72. The quotations in this paragraph and the next are from Scott Shane, "U.S.
    Practiced Torture after 9/11, Nonpartisan Review Concludes," *New York
    Times,* April 16, 2013, A1, A8. See also "Indisputable Torture: A New Non-
    partisan Study Confronts the Legacy of Brutality from the Bush Years,"
    New York Times, April 17, 2013, A22.

73. Thus a memorandum from the Office of the Attorney General to Presi-
    dent Bush on August 1, 2002, could argue that "even if the defendant
    [inflicting punishment] knows that severe pain will result from his ac-
    tions, if causing such harm is not his objective, he lacks the requisite
    specific intent" to be labeled a torturer. Similarly, the requisite degree of
    "severe pain" to qualify as torture entails "ailments that are likely to result
    in permanent and serious physical damage in the absence of immediate
    medical treatment. Such damage must rise to the level of death, organ
    failure, or the permanent impairment of a significant body function."
    Standards of Conduct for Interrogation under 18 U.S.C. §§ 2340–2340A,
    quoted in full in Greenberg and Dratel, *Torture Papers,* 175–176.

74. I paraphrase from Bruff, *Bad Advice,* 228. The quotation is from Chris
    Mackey and Greg Miller, *The Interrogators: Inside the Secret War against Al
    Qaeda* (Boston: Little, Brown, 2004), 471.

75. *Farmer v. Brennan,* 114 S. Ct. at 1976. Jeremy Waldron makes the argu-
    ment about the dangers in an assumption of a captive's discomfort. No
    guarantee of comfort in a prisoner can lead easily to "a continuum of
    discomfort" in which torture is present without being recognized. It is
    better not to think in terms of allowable discomfort, he suggests, and to
    accept instead that "torture is a crime of specific intent." Waldron, "Tor-

ture and Positive Law: Jurisprudence for the White House," *Columbia Law Review* 105 (2005): 1697, 1703.

76. Judee Norton, "Norton #59900," in *Doing Time: 25 Years of Prison Writing,* ed. Bell Gale Chevigny (New York: Arcade Publishing, 2011), 228–235; and Victor Hugo, *The Last Day of a Condemned Man,* trans. Christopher Moncrieff (Surrey, Eng.: Oneworld Classics, 2009). All quotations in the following paragraphs will be from these editions and will be noted by page number parenthetically in the text.

77. Kenneth Lantz, *The Dostoevsky Encyclopedia* (Westport, Conn.: Greenwood Press, 2004), 191. See also "A Chronology of Dostoevsky's Life," in Feodor Dostoevsky, *Crime and Punishment,* ed. George Gibian (New York: W. W. Norton, 1964), 691.

78. Frank Newport, "Sixty-Nine Percent of Americans Support Death Penalty," Gallup News Service, October 12, 2007, 1–8. The figures regarding percentages in favor of the death penalty in the next paragraph are also from this source. There is some thought that new factors may finally be reducing the consistent percentage in favor. The extraordinary cost of executions is changing the minds of some former champions of the penalty. Accounts through DNA evidence that some on death row are innocent and news that homicide rates have dropped are also mentioned as indicators. See Adam Nagourney, "Seeking End to Execution Law They Championed," *New York Times,* April 6, 2012, A1; and Wendy Ruderman, "414 Homicides a Record Low for New York," *New York Times,* December 29, 2012, A1, A3.

79. When Bernard Madoff was sentenced to 150 years in prison on eleven counts to be served consecutively, a number of the victims who spoke at the sentencing hearing wanted Madoff to experience real physical pain and degradation. Commentary spoke conventionally of Madoff "rotting" in prison. See *United States v. Madoff,* No. 09-CR-213 (DC) (S.D.N.Y. June 29, 2009); and Diana B. Henriques, "Madoff, Apologizing, Is Given 150 Years," *New York Times,* June 30, 2009), A1, B4. See also " 'Firebug' Killer to Rot," *New York Post,* April 5, 2013, 8.

4. The Legal Punishers

1. Eliot takes the title from chapter 16 of *Our Mutual Friend,* Charles Dickens's last finished novel, completed in 1865.

2. Michel Foucault describes how prisons have achieved virtually unlimited "punitive sovereignty" through separation from the juridical aspect of law. Prisons have become "the darkest region in the apparatus of justice . . . the place where the power to punish, which no longer dares to manifest itself

openly, silently organizes a field of objectivity." Foucault, "Complete and Austere Institutions," in *Discipline and Punish: The Birth of the Prison*, trans. Alan Sheridan (New York: Vintage Books, 1979), 244–256. For an expository account of the separate parts of the legal process, see Robert A. Ferguson, "Inside the Courtroom," in *The Trial in American Life* (Chicago: University of Chicago Press, 2007), 29–74.

3. Spending on corrections by the states (not including federal prison spending, but including federal funding to states) in fiscal year 2011 was estimated to be $51.7 billion. In 2010 it was $51.1 billion. See National Association of State Budget Officers, *State Expenditure Report, Examining Fiscal 2009–2011 State Spending* (2011), 52, http://www.nasbo.org/sites/default /files/2010%20State%20Expenditure%20Report.pdf. In 2011 the federal prison system spent just under $6.4 billion. See *Budget of the United States Government, Fiscal Year 2013* (2012), 140, http:///www.whitehouse.gov /sites/default/files/omb/budget/fy2013/assets/justice.pdf. For more sources and figures see note 26 in Chapter 1.

4. To the more than two million in prison must be added another five million who are monitored on probation or parole. See Todd R. Clear and James Austin, "Reducing Mass Incarceration: Implications of the Iron Law of Prison Populations," *Harvard Law and Policy Review* 3 (2009): 320.

5. James Gould Cozzens, *The Just and The Unjust* (New York: Harcourt, Brace, 1942), 338, 297. This awkward management of feelings in dealing with others is endemic. For other examples, see 94, 101, 213, 216, and 385.

6. On these issues, see Ian Weinstein, "The Adjudication of Minor Offenses in New York City," *Fordham Urban Law Journal* 31 (2004): 1157–1181.

7. The phrase and the quotations are from Eve Kosofsky Sedgwick, "Privilege of Unknowing: Diderot's *The Nun*," in *Tendencies* (Durham, N.C: Duke University Press, 1993), 23–25. Sedgwick uses the term to discuss sexual repression, but it is also used in theological discourse on the issue of theodicy by Jean-Luc Marion, "*Mihi magna quaestio factus sum*: The Privilege of Unknowing," *Journal of Religion* 85, no. 1 (2005): 1–24.

8. For the taboo structures and consensual controls that apply in institutional thinking, see Mary Douglas, "Institutions Confer Identity" and "Institutions Remember and Forget," in *How Institutions Think* (Syracuse, N.Y.: Syracuse University Press, 1986), 55–80. For a parallel example, see also Stuart Firestein, "A Short View of Ignorance," in *Ignorance: How It Drives Science* (New York: Oxford University Press, 2012), 10–30.

9. Anthony M. Kennedy, "Speech at the American Bar Association Annual Meeting, August 9, 2003: An Address by Anthony M. Kennedy, Associate Justice, Supreme Court of the United States," 2–3, http://www.supreme court.gov/publicinfo/speeches/viewspeeches.aspx?Filename=sp_08-09 -03.html.zdh.

10. See, for example, *Florence v. Board of Chosen Freeholders of County of Burlington*, 132 S.Ct. 1510, 1517–1518, 1520–1521 (2012); see also *ibid.* at 1526–1527 (Breyer, J., dissenting). The case is about lawful strip searches of persons held in prison, but it first includes arrests that lead to imprisonment for "driving with a noisy muffler" or "with an inoperable headlight," "failing to use a turn signal," or "riding a bicycle without an audible bell." The power of the police becomes even greater immediately after arrest. "While American police no longer rely on the third degree to elicit confessions, they continue to enjoy a virtual monopoly of unchecked power in the interrogation room." Richard A. Leo, *Police Interrogation and American Justice* (Cambridge, Mass.: Harvard University Press, 2008), 322.

11. In the words of one experienced litigator, "When a judge doesn't like what you're doing, you're not going to prevail." Mark Baker, *D.A.: Prosecutors in Their Own Words* (New York: Simon and Schuster, 1999), 245.

12. In interviews, the police often raise the need to strike first in a potentially hostile situation. See Mark Baker, *Cops: Their Lives in Their Own Words* (New York: Pocket Books, 1985), 21, 42, 67–68, 91, 252, 286, 291.

13. Robert Bell in New York City sought unspecified damages in the summer of 2012 for his arrest after giving "the middle-digit salute" to three police officers, "noting that his arrest record could deny him admission to 'the law school(s) of his choice.' " Bruce Golding, " 'Bird' Man Suing City," *New York Post,* July 12, 2012, 5.

14. For a brief account of the added discretion and power given to police officers by the weakening of *Mapp v. Ohio*, 367 U.S. 643 (1961), and *Miranda v. Arizona*, 384 U.S. 436 (1966), Supreme Court decisions that held the police to strict account for unlawful seizures of evidence and failure to safeguard a suspect's right to counsel, in more recent Supreme Court decisions, such as *Herring v. United States,* 555 U.S. 135 (2009), and *Montejo v. Louisiana*, 556 U.S. 788 (2009), see Candace McCoy, "2011: Fifty Years Later," in *Justice without Trial: Law Enforcement in Democratic Society,* 4th ed., ed. Jerome H. Skolnick (New Orleans, La.: Quid Pro Books, 2011), ii–iii. Professor McCoy concludes, "Police today, unlike those of 1962, are mostly unconstrained by the laws of criminal procedure." For the rearrangement in "division of labor" in recent years that has given "extraordinary power to prosecutors," see Judge Nancy Gertner, "A Short History of American Sentencing: Too Little Law, Too Much Law, or Just Right," *Journal of Criminal Law and Criminology* 100 (2010): 702–704. Judge Gertner is a federal district judge for the District of Massachusetts.

15. See John A. Eterno, "Policing by the Numbers," *New York Times,* June 18, 2012, A23. Eterno, a retired New York City police captain, writes that the "Compstat system of data driven crime fighting" has produced "a performance culture" with "strict daily quotas" that mean "needless summonses

for minor violations (putting one's feet on subway seats, playing chess in a park, failing to wear seat belts) and other quota-driven activity." "Today local commanders and patrol officers are allowed so little [discretion] that their work is no longer problem solving but bean counting."

16. See Thomas L. Haskell, ed., *The Authority of Experts* (Bloomington: Indiana University Press, 1984), 2, 10, 19, 23, 181, 218.

17. Stanley Milgram, "Behavioral Study of Obedience," *Journal of Abnormal and Social Psychology* 67 (1963): 371–378. Milgram's classic analysis of the innate potential for cruelty in a punisher has been verified over and over again in other ways. For an account of appalling cruelty in punishment across the twentieth century, see Jonathan Glover, *Humanity: A Moral History of the Twentieth Century* (New Haven, Conn.: Yale University Press, 1999).

18. William J. Stuntz, "The Pathological Politics of Criminal Law," *Michigan Law Review* 100 (2001): 508, 508n.

19. John S. Baker, "Revisiting the Explosive Growth of Federal Crimes" (Heritage Foundation Legal Memorandum No. 26, June 16, 2008), 1. http://www.heritage.org/research/reports/2008/06/revisiting-the -explosive-growth-of-federal crimes.

20. Paul J. Larkin, "Overcriminalization: The Legislative Side of the Problem" (Heritage Foundation Legal Memorandum No. 75, December 13, 2011), 1–3, http://www.heritage.org/research/reports/2011/12/overcrimi nalization-the-legislative-side-of-the- problem; and Erik Luna, "The Overcriminalization Phenomenon," *American University Law Review* 54 (2005): 704, 712–729.

21. Wendy Kaminer, *It's All the Rage: Crime and Culture* (Reading, Mass.: Addison-Wesley, 1995), 6, 179. "In the 1990s, fear of crime reached an all-time high. In August 1994, a Gallup poll found that 52 percent of a nationwide sample stated that crime was the most important problem facing the nation." Sara Sun Beale, "What's Law Got to Do with It? The Political, Social, Psychological and Other Non-legal Factors Influencing the Development of (Federal) Criminal Law," *Buffalo Criminal Law Review* 1 (1997): 44.

22. Franklin E. Zimring and David T. Johnson, "Public Opinion and the Governance of Punishment in Democratic Political Systems," *Annals of the American Academy of Political and Social Science* 605 (2006): 267.

23. I take these statistics and observations from Marc Mauer, "Why Are Tough Crime Policies So Popular?," *Stanford Law and Policy Review* 11 (1999): 10–11.

24. Harry A. Chernoff, Christopher M. Kelly, and John R. Kroger, "The Politics of Crime," *Harvard Journal of Legislation* 33 (Summer 1996): 577.

25. Clear and Austin, "Reducing Mass Incarceration," 308, 318–319.

26. Ibid., 324.

27. This may be the one thing that the *Dirty Harry* movies get right about police work.

28. "Anyone attempting to construct a workable definition of the police role will typically come away with old images shattered and with a new-found appreciation for the intricacies of police work." Debra Livingston, "Police, Community Caretaking, and the Fourth Amendment," *University of Chicago Legal Forum,* 1998, 261. See also Carl B. Klockars and Stephen D. Mastrofski, "Images and Expectations," in *Thinking about Police: Contemporary Readings,* 2nd ed., ed. Carl B. Klockars and Stephen D. Mastrofski (Boston: McGraw-Hill, 1991), 1–2. "Everyone we know who teaches about the police complains about the problem of where to begin. . . . Almost nothing worth saying about police can be said without also saying something about something else."

29. Charles E. Silberman, "The Wisdom of Solomon, the Patience of Job: What the Police Do—and Don't Do," in *Criminal Violence, Criminal Justice* (New York: Vintage Books, 1980), 269–273.

30. The officer who knees a man in the groin when that man continues to make abusive remarks about the officer in front of a crowd argues that he is maintaining the respect he needs to do his job in that community. Mark Baker, *Cops: Their Lives in Their Own Words,* 21.

31. Egon Bittner, "The Functions of Police in Modern Society," in Klockars and Mastrofski, *Thinking about Police,* 36, 42–44, 48. Bittner's full definition of the role of the police is *"a mechanism for the distribution of non-negotiably coercive force employed in accordance with the dictates of an intuitive grasp of situational exigencies,"* and he supports the definition by showing how it accords with communal expectations, with the actual allocation of police manpower, and with conflict resolution at the heart of most police activity.

32. "The police are almost always treated as a breed apart." David Alan Sklansky, *Democracy and the Police* (Stanford, Calif.: Stanford University Press, 2008), 8. In the words of one analyst, " 'Hermetically sealed' might be a more accurate description" of "the closed society" that police officers construct. Mark Baker, *Cops,* 3.

33. "Police investigators tend to be skeptical about many things. They tend to assume that rules of criminal procedure unduly restrict their discretion and authority. They tend to assume that the rules are unfairly stacked against them in favor of the suspect." Leo, *Police Interrogation and American Justice,* 20; see also Mark Baker, *Cops,* 239, 297–300.

34. Mark Baker, *Cops,* 239, 297–300.

35. For the information in this paragraph and the next two, see Kate Taylor, "Stop-and-Frisk Policy 'Saves Lives,' Mayor Tells Black Congregation,"

New York Times, June 11, 2012, A14; Ray Kelly, "Courts again Put NYers' Safety Last," *New York Post,* June 28, 2012, 6; David Seifman, Erik Kriss, and Dan Mangan, "Mike Rips Frisk Ruling 'Insanity,'" *New York Post,* June 29, 2012, 5; Andrea Peyser, "The Court of Lawlessness," *New York Post,* July 9, 2012, 15; Russ Buettner and William Glaberson, "Courts Putting Stop-and-Frisk Policy on Trial," *New York Times,* July 11, 2012, A1, A3; and Erica Goode, "Philadelphia Defends Policy on Frisking, with Limits," *New York Times,* July 12, 2012, A11, A14.

36. Mark Baker, *Cops,* 210. "'Nobody understands but another cop.' Police officers work under hazardous, stressful conditions, and this draws them together into a kind of brotherhood."

37. Cozzens, *Just and The Unjust,* 411, 265. All further quotations from this source will be noted parenthetically by page number in the text.

38. Mark Baker, *Cops,* 11–13, 33, 72.

39. Ibid., 253. The same source offers an example. "I've seen guys brought in and the entire outgoing platoon—who have no idea what's going on except that a cop has a guy in a back room and he's beating him up—and the entire platoon, forty guys, go in and take a shot. Everybody wants a piece. The guy's half dead. What'd he do? Well, he spit on a cop. He doesn't deserve six months in the hospital for spitting on a cop" (252).

40. Bittner, "Functions of Police in Modern Society," 37.

41. The cruelty of predators is frequently mentioned by the police along with the pejorative terms noted that are often used to describe them. Again in the words of one, "If all you deal with for eight hours a day is the assholes of society, you do get a little prejudiced." Mark Baker, *Cops,* 298, 182, 265.

42. Ibid., 18–19.

43. Mark Baker, *D.A.,* 24.

44. Ibid., 46, 78, 83, 157.

45. Paul B. Wice, *Chaos in the Courthouse: The Inner Workings of the Urban Criminal Courts* (New York: Praeger, 1985), 20. "Most of the judges within the criminal courts have prosecutorial inclinations (and in many instances, prosecutorial experience as well)." For the classic decision from a former prosecutor that gives prosecutors leeway in presenting a case, see Associate Justice David Souter's opinion in *Old Chief v. United States,* 519 U.S. 172, 187–188 (1997). Here a prosecutor is allowed to move beyond the formal definition of an offense to tell "a colorful story with descriptive richness," with the right "as much to tell a story of guiltiness as to support an inference of guilt."

46. Tracy L. Meares, "Rewards for Good Behavior: Influencing Prosecutorial Discretion and Conduct with Financial Incentives," *Fordham Law Review* 64 (1995): 854.

47. Peter Krug, "Prosecutorial Discretion and Its Limits," *American Journal of Comparative Law* 50 (Fall 2002): 643. See also Daniel Richman, "Prosecutors and Their Agents, Agents and Their Prosecutors," *Columbia Law Review* 103 (May 2003): 750–751.

48. "Prosecutorial Discretion: Thirty-Second Annual Review of Criminal Procedure," *Georgetown Law Journal* 91 (May 2003): 187.

49. The quotations are contained in an article by Barry Coburn, "The Prosecution Should Give It a Rest," *New York Times,* December 13, 2008, 13. The court quotation comes from the United States Court of Appeals for the Ninth Circuit.

50. Jackson's comments in this and the immediately following paragraphs are all from Robert H. Jackson, "The Federal Prosecutor," *Journal of the American Institute of Criminal Law and Criminology* 31 (May–June 1940): 3–6. Jackson delivered these remarks at the Second Annual Conference of United States Attorneys in Washington, D.C., on April 1, 1940. See also John Jay Douglass, ed., *Ethical Considerations in Prosecution* (Houston: National College of District Attorneys, College of Law, University of Houston, 1977), 3.

51. Mark Baker, *D.A.,* 230, 253.

52. For the quotations in this paragraph and the next, see ibid., 47, 77, 153, 230.

53. Ibid., 47, 139, 224–226.

54. Ibid.

55. See *Lafler v. Cooper,* 132 S. Ct. 1376, 1388-1389 (2012).

56. For the quotations in this paragraph and the next, see Oren Bar-Gill and Omri Ben-Shahar, "The Prisoners' (Plea Bargain) Dilemma," *Journal of Legal Analysis* 1 (Summer 2009): 737–738, 769–770. If there are five defendants, each defendant must gamble on which one of them will go to trial against the plea-bargained testimony of the others.

57. Rachel Barkow, "Separation of Powers and the Criminal Law," *Stanford Law Review* 58 (2006): 1034.

58. *Missouri v. Frye,* 132 S. Ct. 1399, 1406-1407 (2012).

59. Jonathan Haidt, "The Emotional Dog and Its Rational Tail: A Social Intuitionist Approach to Moral Judgment," *Psychological Review* 108 (2001): 814, 817, 819–820, 827. Haidt, a psychologist, is particularly valuable for explaining the history of joint understanding in his "intuitionist model" through a variety of disciplines: cognitive studies, philosophy, neuroscience, studies in social behavior, history, and evolutionary biology.

60. For this and related arguments, see Stuntz, "Pathological Politics of Criminal Law," 533–539.

61. John Gastil, E. Pierre Deess, Philip J. Weiser, and Cindy Simmons, *The Jury and Democracy: How Jury Deliberation Promotes Civic Engagement and Political Participation* (New York: Oxford University Press, 2010), 191, 9.

62. For how the local knowledge that gives competence to the juror "as neighbor and peer" also can destroy "the impartiality of the juror as neutral arbiter of events," see Jeffrey Abramson, "Juries and Local Justice," in *We, The Jury: The Ideal System and the Ideal of Democracy* (Cambridge, Mass.: Harvard University Press, 2000), 18 and, more generally, 17–55.

63. For a fuller account of the jury system and its history, see Robert A. Ferguson, "The Jury," in *Trial in American Life*, 52–56, 350–351.

64. Thomas Paine, "Of the Origin and Design of Government in General: With Concise Remarks on the English Constitution," in *Common Sense*, in *The Complete Writings of Thomas Paine*, ed. Philip S. Foner, 2 vols. (New York: Citadel Press, 1945), 1:4; Henry David Thoreau, "Resistance to Civil Government," in *Reform Papers: The Writings of Henry D. Thoreau*, ed. Wendell Glick (Princeton, N.J.: Princeton University Press, 1973), 63.

65. I quote and paraphrase from Stuntz, "Pathological Politics of Criminal Law," 533–534.

66. Harry Kalven Jr. and Hans Zeisel, *The American Jury* (Chicago: University of Chicago, 1966), 59, 494–497; Abramson, *We, The Jury*, 253–254.

67. See Judge James S. Gwin, "Juror Sentiment on Just Punishment: Do the Federal Sentencing Guidelines Reflect Community Values?," *Harvard Law and Policy Review* 4 (2010): 173–200. Judge Gwin's article is based on both empirical research and anecdotal information, and he discovers that in sentencing under the federal guidelines, his sentence "was almost five times higher than the average of the jurors' sentence recommendations." Ibid., 173.

68. Kate Stith and José A. Cabranes, *Fear of Judging: Sentencing Guidelines in the Federal Courts* (Chicago: University of Chicago Press, 1998), 78.

69. See generally William J. Stuntz, *The Collapse of American Criminal Justice* (Cambridge, Mass.: Harvard University Press, 2011). For commentary on the lost role of juries in the current system, in part because of "the quick-and-dirty character" of plea bargains, see 7, 32, 39, 137, and 302.

70. I paraphrase from Ronald Dworkin, *Law's Empire* (Cambridge, Mass.: Harvard University Press, 1996), 407. "The courts are the capitals of law's empire, and judges are its princes."

71. I take these categories and the recognition of changeableness based on a judge's prior personal history and political convictions from Richard A. Posner, *How Judges Think* (Cambridge, Mass.: Harvard University Press, 2008), 7–13, 40–42, 70–72. Posner also addresses how easily some judges are influenced by circumstances in the surrounding community.

72. This was not just a conservative issue in the mid-1970s. For a liberal perspective in the period that wanted limitations on discretion but also stressed rehabilitation and warned against the harshness of sanctions that

limiting discretion might bring, see James Vorenberg, "Narrowing the Discretion of Criminal Justice Officials," *Duke Law Journal* 1976 (1976): 651–697.

73. For the best short analysis of the shift toward punitiveness and the reasons for it, see Gertner, "Short History of American Sentencing," 691–707.

74. James Q. Wilson, "Courts and Corrections," in *Thinking About Crime* (New York: Basic Books, 1975), 163, 166.

75. Ibid., 163–165.

76. See, for examples, Ashley Nellis, "Throwing Away the Key: The Expansion of Life without Parole Sentences in the United States," *Federal Sentencing Reporter* 23 (October 2010): 29.

77. Gertner, "Short History of American Sentencing," 699, 704–706. See also *United States v. Booker,* 543 U.S. 220 (2005); and Beale, "What's Law Got to Do with It?," 49–51.

78. American Bar Association, Public Educational Division, ed., *Law and the Courts: A Handbook of Courtroom Procedures with a Glossary of Legal Terms* (Chicago: ABA Press, 1987), 24. See also Gerard E. Lynch, "Our Administrative System of Criminal Justice," *Fordham Law Review* 66 (1998): 2118–2119.

79. In this paragraph and all later paragraphs on the Madoff case, I rely on and paraphrase from three long articles: Diana B. Henriques, "Madoff Is Sentenced to 150 Years for Ponzi Scheme," *New York Times,* June 29, 2009, A1; Benjamin Weiser, "Judge Explains 150-Year Sentence for Madoff," *New York Times,* June 29, 2011, A1; and Benjamin Weiser, "Madoff Says Judge Made Him a 'Human Piñata,'" *New York Times,* June 29, 2011, A20. Judge Chin has since been elevated to the United States Court of Appeals for the Second Circuit.

80. *United States v. Madoff,* No. 09-CR-213 (DC) (S.D.N.Y. June 29, 2009) (96TJ-MADF), 46–49. In the parts of Judge Chin's sentencing statement, retribution applied to Madoff, whom Judge Chin "did not believe . . . was genuinely remorseful" or fully cooperative with further investigations. Deterrence addressed other financial speculators with the warning that punishment of them would be severe at a time at which the nation was experiencing one financial scandal after another. Justice for the victims sought to help those swindled "in some small measure" to heal and regain some trust in governmental concern, surveillance, and punishment of investment fraud.

81. Ibid. at 46–47.

82. Ibid. at 47–48. Of the widow's plight and its relation to a general "sense of betrayal," Judge Chin says, "I was particularly struck by one story that I read in the letters," and he proceeds to tell the story of how Bernard Madoff gave her particular, very personal assurances.

83. Harold J. Rothwax, *Guilty: The Collapse of Criminal Justice* (New York: Random House, 1996), 130–132.

84. David Gergen and Judge Harold Rothwax, "The Collapse of Criminal Justice," *Newshour Online,* February 14, 1996, http://www.pbs.org.news hour/gergen.rothwax.html.

85. Rothwax, *Guilty,* 7.

86. Gergen and Rothwax, "Collapse of Criminal Justice."

87. *United States v. Madoff* at 50.

88. Michel Foucault, "Complete and Austere Institutions," in *Discipline and Punish: The Birth of the Prison,* trans. Alan Sheridan (New York: Vintage Books, 1979), 246–247 and, more generally, 231–256.

89. As one prison guard notes, "This is the job I landed, not the job of my dreams." Quoted in Joe Domanick, "Anatomy of a Prison," *Los Angeles Magazine,* September 14, 2009, http://www.lamag.com/features/Story .aspx?ID=1335100.

90. "Many [officers] feel they are perceived, and come to perceive themselves, as occupying the lowest rung of the law enforcement pecking order." C. M. Brodsky, "Work Stress in Correctional Institutions," *Journal of Prison and Jail Health* 2 (1982): 74–102. See, more generally, Peter Finn, "Correctional Office Stress: A Cause for Concern and Additional Help," *Federal Probation* 62 (1998): 69.

91. Guards are particularly fond of picking on inmates convicted of sexual crimes or crimes against children. In this they ape and condone the predatory behavior of prisoners.

92. These practices are used in what are called "extractions" from a jail cell. See Lena Kurki and Norval Morris, "The Purposes, Practices, and Problems of Supermax Prisons," *Crime and Justice* 28 (2001): 399–400.

93. Finn, "Correctional Officer Stress," 65–74.

94. U.S. Bureau of Labor Statistics, " "Summary," in *Correctional Officers: Occupational Outlook Handbook,* April 26, 2012, http://www.bls.gov/ooh /protective-service/print/correctional-officers.htm.

95. Finn, "Correctional Officer Stress," 65–66.

96. Yoshiaki Nohara, "Prison Guard in Training: On the Job, behind Bars," *Herald* (Everett, Wash.), April 6, 2008, http://www.heraldnet.com/apps /pbcs.dll/article?AID=/20080406N.

97. "Summary," in *Correctional Officers.*

98. Ibid.; and Adam Liptak, "U.S. Imprisons One in 100 Adults, Report Finds," *New York Times,* February 29, 2008, http://www.nytimes.com/2008/02/29 /us/29prison.html?ref=prisonsandprisoners.

99. I paraphrase from Joshua Page, *The Toughest Beat: Politics, Punishment, and the Prison Officers Union in California* (New York: Oxford University Press, 2011), 5–7.

100. I paraphrase and quote from Domanick, "Anatomy of a Prison."

101. Quoted from Carol J. Williams, "Justice Kennedy Laments the State of Prisons in California, U.S.," *Los Angeles Times,* February 4, 2010, http://articles.latimes.com/2010/feb/04/local/la-me-kennedy4–2010feb04. More generally, Justice Kennedy, speaking before a group of Los Angeles lawyers, "expressed obvious dismay over the state of corrections and rehabilitation in the country."

102. See Max Weber, *The Protestant Ethic and the Spirit of Capitalism,* trans. Talcott Parsons (New York: Scribner's, 1974). Weber first published the book in German in 1905, and Parsons's first translation is from 1930. Weber saw Protestantism as encouraging capitalism by attaching the duty of vocation to the successful pursuit of gain as a sign of God's favor.

103. Page, *Toughest Beat,* 139.

104. One of the two largest private prison companies, Corrections Corporation of America, openly admits these elements of profit and warns its investors to protect them. "The demand for our facilities and services could be adversely affected by the relaxation of enforcement efforts, leniency in conviction or parole standards and sentencing practices or through the decriminalization of certain activities that are currently proscribed by our criminal laws. For instance, any changes with respect to drugs and controlled substances or illegal immigration could affect the number of persons arrested, convicted, and sentences, thereby reducing demand for correctional facilities to house them." Corrections Corporation, *Risk Related to Our Business Industry* (the corporation's annual report for 2010). Quoted from Katherine Gorman, "Private Prisons, Public Price: Evaluating the Costs of the Private Prison Industry" (seminar paper, Columbia Law School, April 29, 2013), 14.

105. Ethan Bronner, "Judge in Alabama Halts Private Probation," *New York Times,* July 14, 2012, A13.

106. "Return of Debtors' Prisons," *New York Times,* July 14, 2012, A16.

107. All the information in this and the next paragraphs on the Louisiana system are from an eight-part series published by the *Times Picayune* of New Orleans in May 2012. The quotations are from Cindy Chang, "Louisiana Incarcerated: How We Built the World's Prison Capital [Part One]," *Times Picayune,* May 13, 2012, A1, A6; and Cindy Chang, "Louisiana Incarcerated: How We Built the World's Prison Capital [Part Two]," *Times Picayune,* May 14, 2012, A1, A4.

108. Chang, "Louisiana Incarcerated [Part One]," A7, A8.

109. Ibid.

110. For the quotations and figures in this paragraph and the next, see Sam Dolnick, "As Escapees Stream Out, a Penal Business Thrives," *New York Times,* June 17, 2012, A1, A16–A17.

111. Ibid.; Sam Dolnick, "Poorly Staffed, a Penal Center Mired in Chaos," *New York Times,* June 18, 2012, A1, A19; Dolnick, "At Penal Unit, a Volatile Mix Fuels a Murder," *New York Times,* June 19, 2012, A1, A18, A19.

112. Stephen J. Rackmill, "The Trouble with Halfway Houses," *New York Times,* June 23, 2012, A18. Rackmill is also a retired chief United States probation officer for the Eastern District of New York.

113. Dolnick, "As Escapees Stream Out, a Penal Business Thrives," A1, A16–17.

114. For a more detailed explanation, see David Garland, "The Commercialization of Justice," in *The Culture of Control: Crime and Social Order in Contemporary Society* (Chicago: University of Chicago Press, 2001), 116–117.

115. For an overview of the rise of private prisons and the reasons for them, see Judith A. Greene, "Entrepreneurial Corrections: Incarceration as a Business Opportunity," in *Invisible Punishment: The Collateral Consequences of Mass Imprisonment,* ed. Marc Mauer and Meda Chesney-Lind (New York: New Press, 2003), 95–113.

116. Dolnick, "As Escapees Stream Out, a Penal Business Thrives," A16.

117. A number of criminologists trace the harshness of American punishment to the legacy of slavery. For a good reading of this influence, see James Q. Whitman, *Harsh Justice: Criminal Punishment and the Widening Divide between America and Europe* (New York: Oxford University Press, 2003), 22–23, 30–31, 172–178, 198–199.

118. Patricia Williams, "On Being the Object of Property (a Gift of Intelligent Rage)," in *The Alchemy of Race and Rights* (Cambridge, Mass.: Harvard University Press, 1991), 217, 220.

119. U.S. Const. amend. XIII (emphasis added).

5. The Legally Punished

1. Jonathan Simon, "Project Exile: Race, the War on Crime, and Mass Imprisonment," in *Governing through Crime: How the War on Crime Transformed American Democracy and Created a Culture of Fear* (New York: Oxford University Press, 2007), 141–142.

2. Ibid., 141.

3. "Minorities are gravely over-represented in every stage of the criminal process—from pedestrian and automobile stops, to searches and seizures, to arrests and convictions, to incarceration and capital punishment." Erik Luna, "Race, Crime, and Institutional Design," *Law and Contemporary Problems* 66 (Summer 2003): 183.

4. The U.S. Sentencing Commission found that under obligatory sentencing the difference between sentences for blacks and others had leveled off by 2002, but after *United States v. Booker* in 2005 made sentencing advisory,

"those differences appear to have been increasing steadily." See Marisa Taylor, "Racial Disparities in Sentencing Rise after Guidelines Are Loosened," *McClatchy Washington Bureau,* March 12, 2010, http://www.mc clatchydc.com/2010/03/12/v-print/90316/racial-disparities-in-sentenc ing.html.

5. Charles Dickens, "Covering a Multitude of Sins" and "Mr. Bucket," in *Bleak House* (New York: W. W. Norton, 1977), 99–101, 277–284.

6. See Jack Henry Abbott, *In the Belly of the Beast* (New York: Vintage Books, 1991), 120, 6–7 (first published by Random House in 1981). All further quotations from the book will be cited in parenthetical references in the text. Emphases in quotations are Abbott's. In and out of foster care from the moment of his birth, Jack Henry Abbott (1944–2002) first entered juvenile detention centers at the age of nine. At age twelve, he was sent to the Utah Industrial School for Boys. Released as an adult at age eighteen, he was soon given an indeterminate sentence of up to five years for forgery (passing bad checks), but three to twenty years were added to that sentence when he killed another prisoner, he claimed in self-defense. Writing *In the Belly of the Beast* at thirty-seven, he observed that "since age twelve I have been free the sum total of nine and a half months." Six weeks after being released on parole in 1981, largely on the strength of his book, Abbott killed the son-in-law of the owner of a small café in Manhattan during a quarrel over whether the restroom was restricted to staff use only. See also Mark Gado, "Jack Abbott, From the Belly of the Beast," http://www.crimelibrary.com/notorious_murders/celebrity/jack_abbott /index.html.

7. The legal scholar and sociologist James Jacobs devotes an entire essay to the problem, including the following comment from an irate prisoner as subject: "Instead of doing your bull shit research from an armchair, why didn't you come in as an inmate so you could find out what it's all about, you phony cock sucker." See Jacobs, "Appendix 1: Participant Observer among Prisoners," in *Stateville: The Penitentiary in Mass Society* (Chicago: University of Chicago Press, 1977), 215–229. The full and far more abusive version of the above quotation is from page 223.

8. Michael Wayne Hunter, "Sam," in *Doing Time: 25 Years of Prison Writing,* ed. Bell Gale Chevigny (New York: Arcade Publishing, 2011), 197. (Originally published in 1999.)

9. Adam Gopnik, "The Caging of America," *New Yorker,* January 30, 2012, 72.

10. Abbott was an autodidact who never got past the sixth grade in formal education. Part of his need to be a consistent rebel prevented him from taking advantage of any educational programs while he was in prison. All his power as an intellectual came from solitary reading, from which he

notes that he did not know how to pronounce 90 percent of the words he mastered. See *In the Belly of the Beast,* 18–19.

11. "Conditions of confinement are not punishment in any recognized sense of the term, unless imposed as part of the sentence." Justice Clarence Thomas in *Farmer v. Brennan,* 114 S.Ct. 1970, 1990 (1994) (Thomas, J., concurring in the judgment).

12. National Prison Rape Elimination Act Commission, "The Prison Rape Elimination Act Commission, Testimony: Testimony of Tom Cahill" (Washington, D.C., June 14, 2005), http://www.justdetention.org/en /NPREC/tomcahill.aspx (archive website of the hearings of the National Prison Rape Elimination Commission). Cahill was repeatedly raped and tortured by other prisoners after a prison guard falsely told them that Cahill was a child molester and that they would receive extra rations if they "took care of me." The guards "wanted to make sure I learned my lesson."

13. Ibid.

14. Abbott's words about the sudden danger that every new prisoner faces are confirmed in every collection of prison narratives.

15. *OZ, Internet Movie Database,* http://www.imdb.com/title/tt018421. The use of rape as an organizing device and the corruption this implies in *OZ* are so pervasive that the narrator of the program from inside prison begins the series by announcing, "They call this the penal system, but it's really the penis system." "Season 1, Episode 1, The Routine." See also Joe Wlodarz, "Maximum Insecurity: Genre Trouble and the Closet Erotics in and out of HBO's *Oz,*" *Camera Obscura* 20 (2005): 58, 73.

16. See Marisa Guthre, " 'The Wire' Fears HBO May Snip It," *New York Daily News,* December 15, 2004, http://www.nydailynews.com/archives/enter tainment/wire-fears-hbo-snip-article-1.608149. See also J. M. Tyree, "Review of *The Wire:* The Complete Fourth Season," *Film Quarterly* 61 (2008): 38 ("*The Wire* is in the business of telling America truths about itself that would be unbearable even if it were interested in hearing them"). For how *The Wire* shows "systemic dysfunction" in law enforcement, and for how "harm is done, day in and day out, by regular people trying to do and keep their jobs," see Susan A. Bandes, "And All the Pieces Matter: Thoughts on *The Wire* and the Criminal Justice System," *Ohio State Journal of Criminal Law* 8 (2010–2011): 438; David Alan Sklansky, "Confined, Crammed, and Inextricable: What *The Wire* Gets Right," *Ohio State Journal of Criminal Law* 8 (2010–2011): 473–479; and Frank Rudy Cooper, "Hyper-incarceration as a Multidimensional Attack: Replying to Angela Harris through *The Wire,*" *Washington University Journal of Law and Policy* 37 (2011): 67–88.

17. Titus Reid, "A Rebuttal to the Attack on the Indeterminate Sentence," *Washington Law Review* 51 (1975–1976): 565–566. See also Jeremy Travis, "Invisible Punishment: An Instrument of Social Exclusion," in *Invisible Punishment: The Collateral Consequences of Mass Imprisonment*, ed. Marc Mauer and Meda Chesney-Lind (New York: New Press, 2003), 30.

18. Kathleen Dean Moore, *Justice, Mercy, and the Public Interest* (New York: Oxford University Press, 1989), 70. See also Alan Dershowitz, "Indeterminate Confinement: Letting the Therapy Fit the Harm," *University of Pennsylvania Law Review* 123 (1974): 302–304.

19. See Susan Greene, *The Gray Box: An Investigative Look at Solitary Confinement*, Dart Society Reports (Spring 2012), http://www.ochbergsociety.org /magazine/2012/01/the-gray-box-an-original-investigation/.

20. Atul Gawande, "Hellhole: Annals of Human Rights," *New Yorker*, March 30, 2009, 41. This article finds the same totally debilitating result in prisoners of war and other victims held in isolation as it does in prisoners held in solitary confinement, and it does not matter whether the person held has a great deal of inner resourcefulness to call on.

21. Jeremy Bentham, *The Rationale of Punishment* (Amherst, N.Y.: Prometheus Books, 2006), 129–130. (First published in French in 1818 and in English in 1830.)

22. Many authorities quote Charles Dickens's horrified reaction in 1840 to "the secret punishment" of solitary confinement when he visited the Eastern State Penitentiary in Philadelphia, a so-called model prison: "Very few men are capable of estimating the immense amount of torture and agony which this dreadful punishment, prolonged for years, inflicts upon the sufferers. . . . I hold this slow and daily tampering with the mysteries of the brain, to be immeasurably worse than any torture of the body." For perhaps the most complete, readily available quotation, see Gopnik, "Caging of America," 74.

23. *In re Medley*, 134 U.S. 160, 168 (1890).

24. In June 2006 a bipartisan national task force, the Commission on Safety and Abuse in American Prisons, found that anything beyond ten days of solitary confinement held no benefits, created serious harm to an inmate, and made it "highly likely" that an inmate would "commit more crimes" when released into a general prison population. Comparable research on prisoners of war shows that identity remains strong only when an isolated prisoner fights back. Identity becomes "rooted in thwarting prison control." Gawande, "Hellhole," 40, 44. See also Greene, *Gray Box*, 5. Greene shows how "defiance" is a way to "kill time in solitary."

25. When levels of solitary confinement were reduced dramatically in 2007, suicides, stabbings, and killings in prison also dropped in a

supermaximum-security prison in Parchman, Mississippi. When the California State Prison in Los Angeles County experimented with relaxed levels of control and greater inmate and guard cooperation for a unit of its most serious offenders in 2009, the same thing happened. The level of violence also dropped in Maine's supermax state prison in 2011 when the numbers in solitary confinement were reduced and more cooperative patterns of surveillance were put in place. All three experiments concluded that high levels of solitary confinement simply did not work well for a prison population. See, in order, Erica Goode, "Rethinking Solitary Confinement," *New York Times,* March 11, 2012, A1; Joe Domanick, "Anatomy of a Prison," *Los Angeles Magazine,* September 14, 2009, 7, http://www.la mag.com/features/Story.aspix?ID=1335100; and Lance Tapley, "Reducing Solitary Confinement," *Portland Phoenix,* November 2, 2011, http://port land.thephoenix.com/news/129316-reducing-solitary-confinement/.

26. Edgar Allan Poe, "The Pit and the Pendulum," in *Collected Works of Edgar Allan Poe,* ed. Thomas Olive Mabbott, 3 vols. (Cambridge, Mass.: Harvard University Press, 1978), 2:681–700. (Poe wrote this story in 1842.) See also the comparable descriptions of how prisoners try to pass time in solitary confinement in Abbott, *In the Belly of the Beast,* 32–33; and Greene, *Gray Box,* 4–9.

27. See European Commission for the Prevention of Torture and Inhuman or Degrading Treatment or Punishment (CPT), *The CPT Standards: "Substantive" Sections of the CPT's General Reports,* CPT Annual General Reports, CPT/Inf/E (2002), http://www.cpt.coe.int/en/documents/eng-stan dards-prn.pdf; and United Nations Commission against Torture, *Consideration of Reports Submitted by States Parties under Article 19 of the Convention: Switzerland,* ¶ 133, U.N. Doc. CAT/A/49/44 (April 20, 1994). For a good general account of objections to solitary confinement in international law, on which I rely, see Jules Lobel, "Prolonged Solitary Confinement and the Constitution," *University of Pennsylvania Journal of Constitutional Law* 11 (2008): 122–124.

28. In 2006 the Commission on Safety and Abuse in America's Prisons noted with alarm that between 1995 and 2000 "the growth rate in the number of people housed in segregation far outpaced the growth rate of the prison population overall." John J. Gibbons and Nicholas de B. Katzenbach, "Summary Findings," in *Confronting Confinement: A Report of the Commission on Safety and Abuse in America's Prisons* (New York: Vera Institute of Justice, 2006), 14, http://www.vera.org/pubs/confronting-confinement.

29. James Ridgeway and Jean Casella, "Fortresses of Solitude, Part 1: The Alcatraz of the Rockies; Solitary Watch" (February 28, 2011), 1, 3–4, http://solitarywatch.com/about/fortresses-of-solitude-part-1/.

30. Lobel, "Prolonged Solitary Confinement and the Constitution," 115.
31. The facts in this paragraph are all taken from Leena Kurki and Norval Morris, "The Purposes, Practices, and Problems of Supermax Prisons," *Crime and Justice* 28 (2001): 385–396.
32. Ibid., 400, 404, 415.
33. Robert Hood on "Supermax: A Clean Version of Hell," *60 Minutes* (CBS television broadcast, October 14, 2007), http://www.cbsnews.com/stories /2007/10/11/60minutes/main3357727.shtml?source=RSSattr=60minutes _3357727.
34. Prison Litigation Reform Act of 1995, Public Law No. 104-134, §803(d), 110 Stat. 1321 (1996), codified at 42 U.S.C. § 1997e(e).
35. Lobel, "Prolonged Solitary Confinement and the Constitution," 134. The cases in question, in order, are *Harper v. Showers,* 174 F.3d 716, 717–720 (5th Cir. 1999); *Watts v. Gaston,* No. 97-0114-CB-M U.S. Dist. LEXIS 6593 (S.D. Ala. Apr. 1, 1999); and *Fackler v. Dillard,* No. 06-10466, 2006 WL 2404498 (E.D. Mich. July 7, 2006).
36. *Harris v. Garner,* 190 F.3d 1279, 1282 (11th Cir. 1999).
37. Debbie A. Mukamal and Paul N. Samuels, "Statutory Limitations on Civil Rights of People with Criminal Records," *Fordham Urban Law Journal* 30 (2002–2003): 1501. See also 18 U.S.C. §922(g), the federal law placing various limits on anyone "who has been convicted in any court of a crime punishable by imprisonment for a term exceeding one year."
38. Solomon Moore, "Number of Life Terms Hits Record," *New York Times,* July 23, 2009, A24. "In the past 20 years, the average life term served has grown from 21 years to 29 years before parole." "From 1992 to 2008, the number in prison for life without parole tripled from 12,453 to 41,095." "The Misuse of Life without Parole," *New York Times,* September 13, 2011, A30.
39. Consider the explanation of a thirty-six-year-old prisoner serving a life term begun when he was twenty-two when he rips up the family photographs sent to him. "After 14 years, these people are strangers to me; as I must be to them. My parents will be dust if/when I ever get out of prison. My three sisters will be in their mid-70's to late 60's. So what was I doing holding on to photos of moments I was not a part of, or know nothing about?" Greene, *Gray Box,* 1, 7. See also Serge F. Kovaleski, "Killers' Families Left to Confront Fear and Shame," *New York Times,* February 4, 2012, A1.
40. *Turner v. Safley,* 482 U.S. 78, 84–85 (1987). The decision gives prison officials discretionary power to prevent correspondence between prisoners in different prisons, but it goes much further in indicating that the court in general will not apply its highest standards of review ("strict scrutiny") to the complaints that inmates bring against prison authorities for the

violation of the minimal rights they might retain. The court hedges in this case only to the extent of requiring that prison authorities must have a very good reason on the separate issue of preventing a marriage between inmates. The decision is later qualified in the standard to be applied from defense of a "legitimate penological interest" to the requirement of a "compelling government interest," but not in the presumed deference that the decision requires in recognition that "running a prison is an inordinately difficult undertaking." See *Warsoldier v. Woodford,* 418 F.3d 989, 994 (2005). The Supreme Court has continued to cite *Turner v. Safley* as law in later cases.

41. *Hudson v. Palmer,* 104 S. Ct. 3194, 3195–3198, 3208 (1984).

42. Ibid. at 3198, 3200, 3202.

43. Ibid. at 3200, 3202 (emphasis added).

44. Ibid. at 3196, 3199–3201.

45. Ibid.

46. *Farmer v. Brennan,* 114 S. Ct. at 1975.

47. "Several courts have held that 'the bare allegation of sexual assault' does not constitute a physical injury under the statute [Section 1997e(e) of the Prison Litigation Reform Act of 1995 requiring a prior showing of physical injury for a civil action]." Quoted from Lobel, "Prolonged Solitary Confinement and the Constitution," 133–134. The cases cited are *Hancock v. Payne,* No. Civ.A.1.03CV671JMRJMR, 2006 WL 21751, at *3 (S.D. Miss. Jan. 4, 2006); and *Smith v. Shady,* No. 3: CV-05-2663, 2006 WL 314514, at *2 (M.D. Pa. Feb. 9, 2006).

48. See *McGill v. Duckworth,* 944 F.2d 344, 345, 348, 353 (7th Cir. 1991). A diminutive prisoner was raped in the shower while in protective custody, and the court decided that the victim's "decision to accept the risk [of taking the shower] precludes blaming the guards and higher-ups in the prison system."

49. In *In the Belly of the Beast,* heavily reviewed in the popular press in 1981 and 1982, Abbott claims that "something like ninety percent" of male prisoners "express sexual interest in their own sex" and carry it out through force or other means of intimidation (68, 79–81).

50. *Farmer v. Brennan,* 114 S. Ct. at 1975. Quotations from this source in the next paragraphs will be by page number in parenthetical references in the text.

51. *McGill v. Duckworth,* 944 F.2d at 345, 349. Part of the court's rejection of recovery is blamed on deteriorating conditions beyond prison-authority control. "Crowding is endemic, as taxpayers reluctant to foot the bill for increased space also clamor for longer sentences that may increase the prison population." Even so, "No matter how deplorable, prison conditions that are undesired are not 'punishment.'"

52. *Hudson v. Palmer,* 104 S. Ct. at 3200.

53. *Farmer v. Brennan,* 114 S. Ct. at 1986.

54. *Whitnack v. Douglas County,* 16 F.3d 954, 956–959 (8th Cir. 1994).

55. Ibid.

56. *Wilson v. Wright,* 998 F. Supp. 650, 652, 655, 657 (E.D. Va. 1998).

57. Ibid. at 654–657.

58. *Hall v. Terrell,* No. 08-CV-00999-DME-MEH (2009).

59. *Green v. Floyd County, Ky.,* 803 F. Supp. 2d 652, 653, 655 (E.D. Ky. 2011).

60. Ibid.

61. *DeLee v. White,* 2011 WL 7415124 (W.D.N.Y.), 1–7, 15, 20 (emphasis added).

62. See *Farmer v. Brennan,* 114 S. Ct. at 1984. See also Marjorie Rifkin, "*Farmer v. Brennan:* Spotlight on an Obvious Risk of Rape in a Hidden World," *Columbia Human Rights Law Review* 26 (Winter 1995), 305. Rifkin exposes "the Court's unrealistic view concerning both the extent of due process afforded prisoners and the state of prison life and violence."

63. *Turner v. Safley,* 482 U.S. at 84.

64. To take just one example, the number of Americans either serving time or awaiting trial for a drug offense jumped from 40,000 in 1980 to "nearly half a million" by 2002, a tenfold increase. See Marc Mauer and Meda Chesney-Lind, introduction to Mauer and Chesney-Lind, *Invisible Punishment,* 6. In the California prison system under court review, there are 140,000 prisoners in facilities made for 80,000, and the reduction ordered by the court still leaves the facilities at 137.5 percent of the system's capacity. See Adam Liptak, "Justices Order California to Shed 30,000 Prisoners," *New York Times,* May 23, 2011, A1.

65. *Brown v. Plata,* 131 S. Ct. 1910, 1951 (2011) (Scalia, J. dissenting).

66. *Brown v. Plata,* 131 S. Ct. at 1924. For the photograph of the "dry cages" see Appendix C. Ibid at 1950. Citations of the court's majority opinion in the next paragraphs will be given at the end of each paragraph in the text by page number in parentheses.

67. Eric Schlosser, "The Prison-Industrial Complex," *Atlantic* (December 1998), http://www.theatlantic.com/magazine/print/1998/12/the-prison-industrial-complex/304669/.

68. *Farmer v. Brennan,* 114 S. Ct. at 1979. "The Eighth Amendment does not outlaw cruel and unusual 'conditions'; it outlaws cruel and unusual 'punishments.'"

69. *Brown v. Plata,* 131 S. Ct. at 1953 (Scalia, J. dissenting). For commentary on Scalia's "pungent and combative" manner and the quotation in oral dissent, see Liptak, "Justices Order California to Shed 30,000 Prisoners," A1.

70. *Brown v. Plata,* 131 S. Ct. at 1968 (Alito, J. dissenting).

71. Albert Sabbaté, "Overall California Crime Drops amid Prison Realignment," January 9, 2013, http://abcnews.go.com/ABC_Univision/News

/crime-drops-california-economy-early-release-inmates/story?id=18167411; but see Grant Scott-Goforth, "Officials: Spike in Property Crimes Coincides with Prison Realignment," *Eureka Times-Standard,* February 18, 2013, http://www.times-standard.com/localnews/ci_22609469/officials-spike -property-crimes-coincides-prison.

72. Quoted in "California's Overcrowded Prisons: The Challenges of 'Re-alignment,'" *Economist,* May 19, 2012, http://www.economist.com/node /21555611/print.

73. The quotations are from Doran Larson, "Fourth City: The Prison in America" (unpublished manuscript of prison narratives with the assistance of Olivia Wolfgang-Smith and Rory Pavach), 32–33. Larson, associate professor of English at Hamilton College, has conducted classes and collected prison stories in the Attica Correctional Facility, a maximum-security prison in Attica, New York, for many years. He holds the most complete current record of prison accounts that we have, and a version of it will be published by Michigan State University Press in 2014.

74. The quotations in this paragraph are all from Patricia McConnel's fictionalized accounts based on her own life in prison. She says that "ninety percent of the events described in this book actually occurred." See McConnel, *Sing Soft, Sing Loud* (Flagstaff, Ariz.: Logoria, 1995), 6–8, 13, 18, 61, 239.

75. Chevigny, *Doing Time,* 2.

76. McConnel, *Sing Soft, Sing Loud,* 133–134.

77. Victor Hassine, "How I Became a Convict," in Chevigny, *Doing Time,* 20–21. See also 1 and 366. The irony in Hassine's death lies in the fact that it was the sight of an earlier suicidal inmate that turned him into a successful writer in prison.

78. Daniel Roseboom, "The Night the Owl Interrupted," in Chevigny, *Doing Time,* 68–70.

79. J. R. Grindlay, "Myths of Darkness: The Toledo Madman and the Ultimate Freedom," and Richard Stratton, "Skyline Turkey," in *Doing Time,* 42–46, 80–85. These stories exemplify that aspect of the genre. The Toledo Madman bewilders the guards by assuming a benevolent passive resistance against every form of coercion. Skyline Turkey climbs a tower and refuses to come down because he wants to be given a work permit.

80. Susan Rosenberg, "Lee's Time," in Chevigny, *Doing Time,* 206–216.

81. Scott A. Antworth, "The Tower Pig," and Michael Wayne Hunter, "Sam," in Chevigny, *Doing Time,* 58–67, 196–205.

82. Paul St. John, "Behind the Mirror's Face," in Chevigny, *Doing Time,* 121–123.

83. Ibid., 121.

84. Hassine, "How I Became a Convict," 19–20.

85. Jean-Paul Sartre, *No Exit,* in *No Exit and Three Other Plays* (New York: Random House, 1976), 45. (Huis Clos—No Exit—was first performed at the Théâtre du Vieux-Colombier in Paris in 1944.)

86. Jimmy Santiago Baca, "Coming into Language," in Chevigny, *Doing Time,* 106.

87. Moore, "Number of Life Terms Hits Records," A24.

6. The Punitive Impulse in American Society

1. James Q. Whitman, *Harsh Justice: Criminal Punishment and the Widening Divide between America and Europe* (New York: Oxford University Press, 2003), 207. Whitman pins his hopes on the thought that reform in the United States has been "essentially religious." His own relative pessimism may lie in the fact that we live in an increasingly secular age.

2. Criminologists generally find an uptick in the politics of crime in the late twentieth century with greater percentages of imprisonment, but several studies identify regular trends of harshness in earlier periods of American history. For examples, see V. F. Nourse, "Rethinking Crime Legislation: History and Harshness," *Tulsa Law Review* 39 (Summer 2004): 925–938.

3. Baron de Montesquieu, *The Spirit of Laws,* trans. Thomas Nugent (London: Collier Macmillan, 1949), 1:81, 83, 84–93 (6:9–21). The leading theorists in the formation of the Constitution of the United States and the new nation—James Wilson, James Madison, and Alexander Hamilton, for example—referred approvingly to "the celebrated Montesquieu" as a prime authority on virtue in government during the Federal Convention of 1787. See Max Farrand, ed., *The Records of the Federal Convention of 1787,* 4 vols. (New Haven, Conn.: Yale University Press, 1966), 1:71, 308, 391, 485, 497, 580; 2:34, 530; 3:109, 197.

4. See Marc Mauer, "Why Are Tough on Crime Policies So Popular?," *Stanford Law and Policy Review* 11 (Winter 1999): 9–17.

5. Numerous sources in the literature of criminology support these claims. A good summary, relied on here and in the next paragraph, can be found in Sara Sun Beale, "What's Law Got to Do with It? The Political, Social, Psychological and Other Non-legal Factors Influencing the Development of (Federal) Criminal Law," *Buffalo Criminal Law Review* 1 (1997): 25, 40–44.

6. "The relative ineffectiveness of more and longer prison sentences in reducing crime is well known among criminologists and practitioners in the field of criminal practice." Mauer, "Why Are Tough on Crime Policies So Popular?," 13.

7. I take this understanding of gridlock from Michael Heller, *The Gridlock Economy: How Too Much Ownership Wrecks Markets, Stops Innovation, and Costs Lives* (New York: Basic Books, 2008).

8. On the subject of intractability, I rely in part on an earlier publication, Robert A. Ferguson, "The Immigrant Plight / Immigration Law: A Study in Intractability," *Columbia Journal of Race and Law* 2 (Spring 2012): 241–243.

9. For an excellent source on the pervading nostalgia in American understandings, see David Lowenthal, *The Past Is a Foreign Country* (New York: Cambridge University Press, 1985), 369–371, 383, 389–391, 397. See also Stephanie Coontz, *The Way We Never Were: American Families and the Nostalgia Trap* (New York: Basic Books, 1992).

10. John R. Searle, *The Construction of Social Reality* (New York: Free Press, 1995), 23, 33, 129.

11. Pierre Bourdieu, *In Other Words: Essays towards a Reflexive Sociology,* trans. Matthew Adamson (Stanford, Calif.: Stanford University Press, 1990), 11–13, 76

12. Pierre Bourdieu, *The Logic of Practice,* trans. Richard Nice (Stanford, Calif.: Stanford University Press, 1990), 269.

13. Bourdieu, *In Other Words,* 11–13.

14. Steven Pinker, *The Stuff of Thought: Language as a Window into Human Nature* (New York: Penguin Books, 2007), 3.

15. See, for example, Barry Glassner, *The Culture of Fear: Why Americans Are Afraid of the Wrong Things* (New York: Basic Books, 2009), now in its tenth-anniversary edition; Frank Furedi, *Culture of Fear Revisited: Risk-Taking and the Morality of Low Expectations,* 4th ed. (1997; repr., New York: Continuum, 2007); and Peter N. Stearns, *American Fear: The Causes and Consequences of High Anxiety* (New York: Routledge, 2006).

16. John B. Thompson, *Studies in the Theory of Ideology* (Berkeley: University of California Press, 1984), 4, 11.

17. Georg Simmel, *Conflict and the Web of Group-Affiliations* (New York: Free Press, 1955), 101.

18. Erica Goode, "U.S. Prison Populations Decline, Reflecting New Approach to Crime," *New York Times,* July 26, 2013, A11, A16.

19. For supporting evidence that judges who are elected are influenced by harsh communal attitudes when they sentence, see Stephen B. Bright and Patrick J. Keenan, "Judges and the Politics of Death: Deciding between the Bill of Rights and the Next Election in Capital Cases," *Boston University Law Review* 75 (May 1995): 759–835; Paul Brace and Brent D. Boyea, "State Public Opinion, the Death Penalty, and the Practice of Electing Judges," *American Journal of Political Science* 52 (April 2008): 360–372;

and Equal Justice Initiative, "The Death Penalty in Alabama: Judge Override," *Equal Justice Initiative,* July 2011, 1–30, http://www.eji.org/files /Override_Report.pdf. See also Justice John Paul Stevens's comment in dissent in *Harris v. Alabama,* 513 U.S. 504, 519 (1995): "Present-day capital judges may be 'too responsive' [to] a political climate in which judges who covet higher office—or who merely wish to remain judges—must constantly profess their fealty to the death penalty."

20. For the quotations and a good reading of this phenomenon, see Joseph F. Kennedy, "Monstrous Offenders and the Search for Solidarity through Modern Punishment," *Hastings Law Journal* 51 (July 2000): 830.

21. The term and its definition come from Peter Brooks, *The Melodramatic Imagination: Balzac, Henry James, Melodrama, and the Mode of Excess* (New York: Columbia University Press, 1984), 1–23.

22. The archetype in movie crime is the *Dirty Harry* movies, in which Clint Eastwood is an honest cop chasing serial killers and rapists who manipulate officialdom enough to continue crime sprees. In the first and best-known movie in the series, Harry Callahan overcomes official obstacles to kill the serial killer Scorpio. See *Dirty Harry* (1971), *Magnum Force* (1973), *The Enforcer* (1976), *Sudden Impact* (1983), and *The Dead Pool* (1988).

23. The popular series *Law and Order* ran for twenty years, from September 12, 1990, to May 24, 2010, "an eternity in network years," and it continues to be watched in reruns everywhere because of its formulaic way of fusing violence to the formal definition of it in court. See Alessandra Stanley, "The TV Watch: 'Law & Order': Soon to Be Gone but Not Forgotten," *New York Times,* May 17, 2010, C1.

24. Stephen Prince, "Graphic Violence in the Cinema: Origins, Aesthetic Design, and Social Effects," in *Screening Violence,* ed. Stephen Prince (New Brunswick, N.J.: Rutgers University Press, 2000), 6, 22–23.

25. Ibid., 22–23. As early as 1931, Francis "Two Gun" Crowley said that movies inspired him to go around "bumping off cops." Aspects of his life were then used in Howard Hughes's famous film *Scarface* in 1932. See J. David Slocum, *Violence and American Cinema* (New York: Routledge Press, 2001), 117–118. See also R. Lance Holbert, Dhavan V. Shah, and Nojin Kwak, "Fear, Authority, and Justice: Crime-Related TV Viewing and Endorsements of Capital Punishment and Gun Ownership," *Journalism and Mass Communication Quarterly* 81 (2004): 343–363 (the authors conclude that TV viewing predicts fear of crime in audience members); and Kenneth Dowler, "Media Consumption and Public Attitudes toward Crime and Justice: The Relationship between Fear of Crime, Punitive Attitudes, and Perceived Police Effectiveness," *Journal of Criminal Justice and Popular Culture* 10 (2003): 109–126. Dowler also concludes that

"respondents who are regular viewers of crime drama are more likely to fear crime."

26. Commentary on how the *Godfather* movies have influenced behavior of actual gangsters is voluminous. "Real mobsters . . . emulate what were in many ways idealized versions of themselves." Jon Lewis, *The Godfather* (New York: Palgrave Macmillan, 2010), 72. Lewis goes on to say "*la via vecchio* (the old way) was not something they learned from their parents in the family business but from the gangsters they so identified with on the screen." See also Alessandro Camon, "*The Godfather* and the Mythology of Mafia," in *Francis Ford Coppola's "Godfather" Trilogy,* ed. Nick Browne (New York: Cambridge University Press, 2000), 57, 70–71; and Peter Biskind, "Life Copies Art," in *The Godfather Companion: Everything You Ever Wanted to Know about All Three "Godfather" Films* (New York: Harper Perennial, 1990), 61.

27. Chris Sullentrop, "Americana at Its Most Felonious," *New York Times,* November 10, 2012, C1, C7.

28. See Ronald Weitzer and Charis E. Kubrin, "Breaking News: How Local TV News and Real-World Conditions Affect Fear of Crime," *Justice Quarterly* 21 (2004): 497–519.

29. Matt Delisi, "Extreme Career Criminals," *American Journal of Criminal Justice* 25 (2001): 239, 248. "Extreme career criminals are intractably bad. There is simply no hope of rehabilitating or transforming these predators into law-abiding citizens."

30. Lonnie H. Athens, *The Creation of Dangerous Violent Criminals* (New York: Routledge Press, 1989), 80–81, 96–97. On risk and its relation to dangerous offenders and why "the menace of such dangerous offenders" has become "so powerful an icon in modern Western societies," see Mark Brown and John Pratt, introduction to *Dangerous Offenders: Punishment and Social Order,* ed. Mark Brown and John Pratt (London: Routledge, 2000), 1. See more generally 1–13.

31. The anthropologist Mary Douglas explains, "To invoke very low probabilities of a particular dangerous event makes surprisingly little difference to the understanding of a choice. This is not because the public does not understand the sums, but because many other objectives which it cares about have been left out of the risk calculation." Mary Douglas, "Risk and Danger," in *Risk and Blame* (London: Routledge, 1992), 40.

32. For the problems that law faces because of exceptionalism, see Harold Koh, "On American Exceptionalism," *Stanford Law Review* 55 (May 2003): 1479–1527. See also Scott Shane, "The Opiate of Exceptionalism," *New York Times,* October 21, 2012, SR6. "Imagine a presidential candidate who spoke with blunt honesty about American problems. . . . The candidate

might try to stir up his audience by flipping a familiar campaign trope: the United States is indeed No. 1, he might declare—in locking its citizens up, with an incarceration rate far higher than that of the likes of Russia, Cuba, Iran or China. . . . How far would this truth-telling candidate get? Nowhere fast."

33. The airplane attacks on the World Trade Center in New York and the Pentagon in Washington, D.C., on September 11, 2001, followed by President George W. Bush's announcement of a long-term "War on Terror" and the development of the Department of Homeland Security, have immeasurably reinforced acceptance of a combined foreign and domestic threat to national security in current American thought.

34. No amount of security stops the United States from accounting for 41 percent of all world military spending, with the next-largest spender, China, coming in at a bare 8 percent, one-fifth the U.S. total. A whopping 4.7 percent of American gross domestic product goes to defense, far above the percentages of other countries in the world. See Stockholm International Peace Research Institute (SIPRI), "Background Paper on SIPRI Military Expenditure Data, 2011," (April 17, 2012), 2, 5, http://www.sipri.org /research/armanemtns/milex/sipri-factsheet-on-military-expenditure -2011.pdf.

35. Jeffrey M. Jones, "Americans Most Confident in Military, Least in Congress" (June 23, 2011), 1–4, http://www.gallup.com/poll/148163/americans-confi dent-military-least-congress.aspx?version=print.

36. A Showtime television series, *Homeland,* first aired in 2011 and continues to run. It seized on precisely this element of suspense, closing the gap between foreign and domestic threats, to attract close to two million viewers in its first season and more than that in its second. Showtime, *Homeland,* http:///www/sho.com/sho/homeland/home. See also Scott Collins, " 'Homeland' Season Finale Hunts Down Ratings Record for Showtime," *Los Angeles Times,* December 17, 2012, http://articles.latimes.com /2012/dec/17/entertainment/la-et-st-homeland-season-finale-hunts-down -ratings-record-for-showtime-20121217.

37. Both presidential candidates, Mitt Romney and Barack Obama, stepped gingerly around any thought of a direct ban on assault rifles in their debate on October 16, 2012, when they were asked directly what they would actively do to get those weapons out of civilian hands, and both mentioned the right to keep weapons to defend the home.

38. The trial of George Zimmerman in July 2013 for pursuing and then killing a young black teenager on his way home on the night of February 26, 2012, illustrated many of these problems. Zimmerman beat all charges, from second-degree murder to manslaughter, under these laws even

though he sought the confrontation with Trayvon Martin well away from his own home. See Adam Nagourney, "Prayer, Protests and Anger Greet Florida Verdict," *New York Times,* July 15, 2013, A1, A8; Lizette Alvarez, "Self-Defense Hard to Topple," *New York Times,* July 15, 2013, A1, A9; and "Trayvon Martin's Legacy," *New York Times,* July 15, 2013, A16.

39. Jonathan Safran Foer, "Some People Love Guns. Why Should the Rest of Us Be Targets?," *Washington Post,* April 22, 2007, http://www/washington post.com/wp-dyn/content/article/2007/04/20AR2007042001980.html.

40. *McDonald v. Chicago,* 130 S. Ct. 3025, 3027 (2010). The decision effectively extended the right to all individuals to "keep and bear arms" by announcing that the due process clause of the Fourteenth Amendment incorporates the Second Amendment, with the Second Amendment now applying to all state law. The decision made most gun-control statutes in the states unconstitutional.

41. Philip Alpers, Amélie Rossetti, Marcus Wilson, and Quentin Royet, "Guns in the United States, Facts, Figures, and Firearm Law," *GunPolicy.org* (last accessed September 20, 2013), http://www.gunpolicy.org/firearms/region /united-states.

42. I take these figures and paraphrase from Glassner, *Culture of Fear,* 44, 232.

43. Foer, "Some People Love Guns."

44. "[The United States'] overall homicide rate is seven times that of England and Wales, its murder rate for young men is a staggering 52 times higher." Jock Young, "The American Experiment," in *The Exclusive Society: Social Exclusion, Crime and Difference in Late Modernity* (London: Sage Publications, 1999), 146.

45. Every law student learns in first-year criminal law that a gun in the house is most likely to be used on an occupant there or on an acquaintance through anger or accident.

46. Thompson, *Studies in the Theory of Ideology,* 24.

47. Benjamin Franklin, *Autobiography,* ed. Joyce E. Chaplin (New York: W. W. Norton, 2012), 77. These words come just before Franklin's secular plan of moral perfection. They were written in 1784.

48. "Young black and Latino males (especially if unemployed) are subject to particularly harsh sentencing compared to other offender populations. . . . Black and Latino defendants tend to be sentenced more severely than comparably situated white defendants for less serious crimes." Tushar Kansal, *Racial Disparity in Sentencing: A Review of the Literature,* ed. Marc Mauer (Washington, D.C.: Sentencing Project, 2005), 1–2, www.sentenc ingproject.org. "Minorities were 60 percent of all inmates in U.S. prisons in 2004 (black inmates were an estimated 41 percent of all inmates, whites were 34 percent and Hispanics, 19 percent)." Katherine J. Rosich,

Race, Ethnicity, and the Criminal Justice System (Washington, D.C.: American Sociological Association, 2007), 17, http://asanet.org.

49. "Black and Hispanic men are more likely to receive longer prison sentences than their white counterparts since the Supreme Court loosened federal sentencing rules [in *United States v. Booker,* 543 U.S. 220 (2005)], a government study has concluded." Maris Taylor, *McClatchy Newspapers,* March 12, 2010, http://www.mcclatchydc.com/2010/03/12/v-print/90316/racial-disparities-in-sentencing.html.

50. Robert N. Bellah, Richard Madson, William M. Sullivan, Ann Swidler, and Steven M. Tipton, *Habits of the Heart: Individualism and Commitment in American Life* (Berkeley: University of California Press, 1985), viii, 37, 275, 312n28. Habits of the heart include "consciousness, culture, and the daily practices of life."

51. For an argument that exceptionalism holds absolute sway on issues of punishment, see the claim of Associate Justice Antonin Scalia in *Stanford v. Kentucky,* 492 U.S. 361, 369n1 (1989). Here, in answer to restrictions on the death penalty elsewhere, Scalia insists that "it is American conceptions of decency that are dispositive."

52. Nicole Perlroth, "How to Devise Passwords That Drive Hackers Away," *New York Times,* November 8, 2012, B8.

53. Bellah et al., *Habits of the Heart,* 147. See also Yehoshua Arieli, *Individualism and Nationalism in American Ideology* (Cambridge, Mass.: Harvard University Press, 1964), 183–210, 246–276; and Alexis de Tocqueville, *Democracy in America,* trans. George Lawrence, ed., J. P. Mayer (New York: Doubleday, 1969), vol. 2, pt. 1, chaps. 1 and 2.

54. See Bernice Lott, "Cognitive and Behavioral Distancing from the Poor," *American Psychologist* 57 (February 2002): 100–110; Chris L. Coryn, "Antecedents of Attitudes toward the Poor" (2002), http://www/iusb.edu/~journal/2002/coryn/coryn.html, and Catherine Cozzarellli, Anna V. Wilkinson, and Michael J. Tagler, "Attitudes toward the Poor and Attributions of Poverty," *Journal of Social Issues* 57 (2001): 207–227. Lott shows how the well-off use "cognitive distancing" to exclude, devalue, and discriminate against the poor. Coryn uses regression analysis to demonstrate that the happier people are with their world, the more likely they are to blame the poor for their situation. Cozzarelli, Wilkinson, and Tagler prove that stereotypes of the well-off about the poor are significantly more negative than stereotypes about the middle class. All three studies also claim that studies of this problem are relatively rare.

55. James Lincoln Collier, *The Rise of Selfishness in America* (Lincoln, Nebr.: Authors Guild Backinprint, 2005) (originally published by Oxford University Press in 1991); Jock Young, "The Criminology of Intolerance:

Zero-Tolerance Policing and the American Prison Experiment," in *Exclusive Society*, 121–147; and Daniel Dorling, *Injustice: Why Social Inequality Persists* (Bristol, U.K.: Policy Press, 2010).

56. John G. Cawelti, *Apostles of the Self-Made Man* (Chicago: University of Chicago Press, 1965), 42–44.

57. In this paragraph and the next, I borrow terminology from Charles Tilly, *Durable Inequality* (Berkeley: University of California Press, 1998), 7–9, 225. See also Peter Edelman, "Poverty in America: Why Can't We End It?," *New York Times,* July 29, 2012, SR5. Edelman notes that "the wealth and income of the top 1 percent grows at the expense of everyone else. Money breeds power and power breeds more money. It is a truly vicious circle."

58. Erving Goffman, *Stigma: Notions on the Management of Spoiled Identity* (New York: Simon and Schuster, 1963), 3, 131.

59. Peter Edelman is again on the mark here when he writes, "As long as people in the middle identify more with the top than the bottom, we are doomed [to enormous levels of poverty]." "Poverty in America," SR5.

60. Loïc Wacquant, "The Criminalization of Poverty in the Post–Civil Rights Era," in *Punishing the Poor: The Neoliberal Government of Social Insecurity* (Durham, N.C.: Duke University Press, 2009), 41. See generally 41–75.

61. See Joseph E. Stiglitz, "America's 1 Percent Problem," in *The Price of Inequality: How Today's Divided Society Endangers Our Future* (New York: W. W. Norton, 2012), 1–20; and Pew Economic Mobility Project, *Economic Mobility and the American Dream: Where Do We Stand in the Wake of the Great Recession?* (Washington, D.C.: Pew Charitable Trusts, 2011), http://www/economicmobility.org/poll2011.

62. Quoted from Edelman, "Poverty in America," SR5. See more generally Peter Edelman, *So Rich, So Poor: Why It's So Hard to End Poverty in America* (New York: New Press, 2012).

63. Dan Fromkin, "Half of American Households Hold 1 Percent of Wealth" (July 19, 2012), fromkin@huffingtonpost.com, http://www.huffingtonpost.com/2012/07/19/households-wealth-american-1-percent_n_1687015.html. These figures are based on "Congress's nonpartisan research services" and "the Federal Reserve's latest Survey of Consumer Finances." Fromkin observes, "The rich have so much that the average net worth in the U.S. is actually 6.5 times that of a typical American family."

64. *Dragnet,* one of the first phenomenally popular television crime shows, running originally from January 3, 1952, to August 23, 1959, always ended with the face of the culprit receiving an announced sentence. The device, though, is used everywhere, now often with a last vignette of the legal figures who made it happen.

65. "Jailbird: a person who is or who *has been confined* in jail" (emphasis added). *Webster's Third New International Dictionary of the English Language Unabridged* (Springfield, Mass.: Merriam-Webster, 1993), 1208.

66. Compare Ruth Benedict, *The Chrysanthemum and the Sword: Patterns in Japanese Culture* (Cleveland, Ohio: Meridian Books, 1967), 222–224; and Clifford Geertz, "Person, Time, and Conduct in Bali," in *The Interpretation of Cultures: Selected Essays* (New York: Basic Books, 1973), 401. Benedict argues that shame cultures rely on external sanctions for good behavior, while true guilt cultures rely on an internalized conviction of sin. Geertz sees more of an interaction between the two concepts, and I accept that understanding here. For the separate "prevailing criterion" for distinguishing shame and guilt by external and internal sanctions, and the idea that no culture can be formed without one or the other, see Gerhart Piers and Milton B. Singer, *Shame and Guilt: A Psychoanalytic and a Cultural Study* (Springfield, Ill.: Charles C. Thomas, 1953), 37, 48.

67. The historian Daniel Boorstin may be credited with first identifying the extent to which the United States has become an image culture back in 1961 in *The Image; or, What Happened to the American Dream* (New York: Athenaeum, 1961). Coming to a fuller understanding of the possibilities, Boorstin changed the title in the twenty-fifth anniversary edition in 1987 to *The Image: A Guide to Pseudo-events in America.*

68. Scott Sayare, Maïa De La Baume, and Robert Mackey, "French Shocked by I.M.F. Chief's 'Perp Walk,'" *New York Times Lede Blog* (May 16, 2011), http://thelede.blogs.nytimes.com/2011/05/16/french-shocked-by-i-m-f-chiefs-perp-walk.

69. "CUFF LINKS!," *New York Post,* August 28, 2012, 1 (the ellipsis in the quotation in the text is the *Post*'s).

70. "Lindsay Lohan Jailed When Judge Revokes Bail," *New York Post,* October 20, 2011, 1; "Former NYPD Commissioner Bernie Kerik in Shackles: THE FALLEN MIGHTY," *New York Post,* October 16, 2012, 1.

71. I take all these carefully documented court-ordered examples from Stephen P. Garvey, "Can Shaming Punishments Educate?" (Cornell Law Faculty Publications, Paper 277, July 1, 1998), http://scholarship.law.cornell.edu/facpub/277.

72. See Graeme Newman, *Just and Painful: A Case for the Corporal Punishment of Criminals,* 2nd ed. (New York: Harrow and Heston, 1995).

73. The main defender of shaming for many years was leading scholar Dan M. Kahan, "What Do Alternative Sanctions Mean?," *University of Chicago Law Review* 63 (1996): 591–653. Kahan recanted a decade later, but only after dozens of articles took up the subject. See Kahan, "What's Really Wrong with Shaming," *Texas Law Review* 84 (2006): 2075–2095. For

another supporter, see Aaron S. Book, "Shame on You: An Analysis of Modern Shame Punishment as an Alternative to Incarceration," *William and Mary Law Review* 40 (1999): 653–686. A major early opponent of shaming in these debates has been Toni M. Massaro, "Shame, Culture, and American Criminal Law," *Michigan Law Review* 89 (1992): 1880–1943. For a good summary of the overall debate, its participants, and its theoretical implications, see Dan Markel, "Are Shaming Punishments Beautifully Retributive? Retribution and the Implications for the Alternative Sanctions Debate," *Vanderbilt Law Review* 54 (2001): 2157–2242.

74. The quotations in this paragraph and the next are from James Q. Whitman, "What Is Wrong with Inflicting Shame Sanctions?," *Yale Law Journal* 107 (1998): 1062, 1088, 1092.

75. Thomas J. Scheff, "Shame and Conformity: The Deference-Emotion System," *American Sociological Review* 53 (1988): 395, 397, 400, 405. See, more generally, Martha C. Nussbaum, *Hiding from Humanity: Disgust, Shame, and the Law* (Princeton, N.J.: Princeton University Press, 2004).

76. Glassner, *Culture of Fear,* xi–xvii, xxv, 238. One of Glassner's major themes is that "atypical tragedies grab our attention while widespread problems go unaddressed." For other leading studies in this genre, see Peter N. Stearns, *American Fear: The Causes and Consequences of High Anxiety* (New York: Routledge, 2006); Furedi, *Culture of Fear Revisited;* David L. Altheide, *Terrorism and the Politics of Fear* (New York: AltaMira Press, 2006); and Mark Siegel, *False Alarm: The Truth about the Epidemic of Fear* (Hoboken, N.J.: John Wiley and Sons, 2005).

77. Francis Bacon, "Of Suspicion," in *The Essays or Counsels, Civil and Moral, of Francis Ld. Verulam, Viscount St. Albans* (Mount Vernon, N.Y.: Peter Pauper Press, 1948), 29–30. (*The Essays* date from 1625.)

78. Montaigne, "Of Fear," in *The Complete Essays of Montaigne,* trans. Donald M. Frame (Stanford, Calif.: Stanford University Press, 1948), 52–53. See also Judith N. Shklar, "Putting Cruelty First," in *Ordinary Vices* (Cambridge, Mass.: Harvard University Press, 1984), 23.

79. Jeffrey A. Gray, *The Psychology of Fear and Stress* (New York: McGraw-Hill, 1971), 10–11, 15–20. The innate fears from stimuli are three, "loud noise, sudden loss of support, and pain," but even acquired fears take on an innate quality through four general principles, "intensity, novelty, 'special evolutionary dangers' . . . and stimuli arising from social interaction." The most common fears—of the dark, of snakes, of heights—come through maturation or through classical conditioning in a species that has experienced devastation from them.

80. Arthur L. Stinchcombe, Rebecca Adams, Carol A. Heimer, Kim Lane Scheppele, Tom W. Smith, and D. Garth Taylor, *Crime and Punishment—Changing Attitudes in America* (San Francisco: Jossey-Bass, 1985), 37–47, 67–73, 100.

81. William J. Stuntz, *The Collapse of American Criminal Justice* (Cambridge, Mass.: Harvard University Press, 2011), 22.

82. Erik Luna, "Race, Crime, and Institutional Design," *Law and Contemporary Problems* 66 (2003): 183.

83. See, for example, *Whren v. United States,* 517 U.S. 806 (1996), a unanimous Supreme Court decision that gives the police the widest possible latitude in stopping any car when they feel that any legal infraction has taken place. The subsequent racial profiling and low-grade harassment of minority owners of automobiles parallel frequent stop-and-frisk procedures of walkers in ghetto neighborhoods. See David A. Harris, "'Driving While Black' and All Other Traffic Offenses: The Supreme Court and Pretextual Traffic Stops," *Journal of Criminal Law and Criminology* 87 (1997): 544–557.

84. I quote and paraphrase here from one of the best extended treatments of discrimination against minorities by the criminal justice system, Michael Tonry, *Malign Neglect—Race, Crime, and Punishment in America* (New York: Oxford University Press, 1995), xii. More recently, see Bruce Western, *Punishment and Inequality in America* (New York: Russell Sage Foundation, 2006).

85. This frequent mantra is often reversed: "If you can't do the time, don't do the crime." I take it from a publication that examines the treatment of juveniles as adult offenders: Nicholas W. Bakken, *You Do the Crime, You Do the Time* (Tampa, Fla.: International Foundation for Protection Officers, 2007), 1–14.

86. The sources of information about the Rikers prison homicide in this paragraph and the next five paragraphs are Al Baker, "Indictments Are Expected in Killing of Inmate," *New York Times,* January 22, 2009, A30; John Eligon, "Correction Officers Accused of Letting Inmates Run Rikers Island Jail," *New York Times,* January 23, 2009, A20; "Editorial: Rikers Horror Story," *New York Times,* January 29, 2009, A26; Benjamin Weiser, "Lawsuits Suggest Pattern of Rikers Guards Looking Other Way," *New York Times,* February 4, 2009, A21; Russ Buettner, "Rikers Extortions Noted before Death," *New York Times,* March 16, 2009, A17; Elizabeth A. Harris, "Correction Officers Plead Guilty in Assault Case," *New York Times,* October 22, 2011, A14; Colin Moynihan, "Two Officers Sentenced in Rikers Island Assault Case," *New York Times,* January 18, 2012, A17; and "City Pays $2 Million in Case of Inmate Killed at Rikers," *New York Times,* June 9, 2012, A18. See also Geoffrey Gray, "The Lords of Rikers," *New York Magazine,* January 30, 2011, http://nymag.com/print/?/news/features/70978.

87. I take this terminology and its implications from Luc Boltanski, "The Metaphysics of Justice," in *Distant Suffering: Morality, Media and Politics* (Cambridge: Cambridge University Press, 1979), 67–70.

88. Susan Opotow, "Moral Exclusion and Injustice: An Introduction," *Journal of Social Issues* 46 (1990): 1 (emphasis in the original).

89. Quoted by Fritz Stern, "The Goldhagen Controversy: One Nation, One Controversy, One Theory," *Foreign Affairs,* November/December 1996, 128–129; and Richard Powers, "Book Review," *Journal of American History* 89 (2002): 726–727.

90. John Rawls, *A Theory of Justice* (Cambridge, Mass.: Harvard University Press, 1971), 597–598, 606.

91. For the quotations in this paragraph and the next, see ibid., 439.

92. No one cares about the old lifer who dies in prison, but when Richard Ramirez, whom media sources named the "Night Stalker," died in prison after killing fourteen women under the sign of Satan in the 1980s, he was worth four columns and a photograph in the obituary section of the *New York Times* a quarter of a century after his arrest. Douglas Martin, "Richard Ramirez, the 'Night Stalker' Killer, Dies at 53," *New York Times,* June 8, 2013, D8. Murder is common and worth a comment; it is the gunman who says, "Killing people" is "what I like doing best," who receives extensive coverage. Liz Robbins and Joseph Goldstein, "Gunman's Note Said 'Killing People' Was What He Liked Best," *New York Times,* December 26, 2012, A20.

93. Writing later, Rawls implies that injustice is a failure in fundamental consensus through the idea that "political justice" refers to "what we may call an 'overlapping consensus,'" which must remain "more or less stable." He emphasizes the problems in achieving justice but not the obviously less coherent (because it is unstable) condition of injustice. Injustice again appears as simply the lack of justice. John Rawls, "Justice as Fairness: Political Not Metaphysical," *Philosophy and Public Affairs* 14 (1985): 225, 251.

94. Judith Shklar, *The Faces of Injustice* (New Haven, Conn.: Yale University Press, 1990), 2–3, 15.

95. Kennedy delivered this comment in a press conference on March 21, 1962. See Theodore C. Sorensen, *Kennedy* (New York: Harper and Row, 1965), 42; and Robert Dallek, *An Unfinished Life: John F. Kennedy, 1917–1963* (Boston: Little, Brown, 2003), 504. Shklar, *Faces of Injustice,* 3.

96. Shklar, *Faces of Justice,* 22, 104. See also Cicero, *De officiis,* trans. Walter Miller (Cambridge, Mass.: Harvard University Press, 1921), 24–38 (1:7–11); and for the extensive iconography of the figure of justice and the nature of blindness attached to it, Dennis E. Curtis and Judith Resnik, "Images of Justice," *Yale Law Journal* 96 (1987): 1727–1772.

97. *Riggs v. California,* 119 S. Ct. 890, 890–891 (1999). See also Linda Greenhouse, "Three Strikes Challenge Fails, but Others Are Invited," *New York Times,* January 20, 1999, A12.

98. Shklar, *Faces of Injustice,* 29.

99. For one of the clearest analyses of the point that "only where there is justice is there injustice," see Agnes Heller, *Beyond Justice* (New York: Basil Blackwell, 1987), 222–229.

7. The Law against Itself

1. See Michael C. Campbell and Heather Schoenfeld, "The Transformation of America's Penal Order: A Historicized Political Sociology of Punishment," *American Journal of Sociology* 118 (March 2013): 1375–1423. The average increase in state incarceration rates in that period was 285 percent. See Paige Harrison, "Incarceration Rates for Prisoners under State or Federal Jurisdiction, per 100,000 Residents," Bureau of Justice Statistics, Washington, D.C. (2011), http://bjs.ojp.usdoj.gov/content/data/cor pop25.csv.

2. Stephanos Bibas, *The Morality of Criminal Justice* (New York: Oxford University Press, 2012), xvi. Bibas concludes, with plenty of justification, "Our procedures are too hidden, too insular, and too deaf to the range of needs people have." Ibid., 165. For a study that shows how little the public actually knows about criminal justice, see Julian V. Roberts, "Public Opinion, Crime, and Criminal Justice," *Crime and Justice* 16 (1992): 99–180.

3. For an interesting discussion of how the capacity for autonomy determines legal understanding, see David A. J. Richards, "Rights, Utility, and Crime," *Crime and Justice* 3 (1981): 262–265.

4. Projections from the census of 2010 put the population of Rhode Island at 1,050,292 and that of New Hampshire at 1,320,718 in 2012. For the Rhode Island figures, see United States Census Bureau, "State & County QuickFacts: Rhode Island," (June 27, 2013), http://quickfacts.census.gov /qfd/states/44000.html; and for the New Hampshire figures, see United States Census Bureau, "State & County QuickFacts: New Hampshire" (June 27, 2013), http://quickfacts.census.gov/qfd/states/33000.html.

5. For perhaps the best nonlegal and certainly the most interesting definition of the rule of law on these terms as "transactional mode of association," see Michael Oakeshott, "The Rule of Law," in *On History and Other Essays,* ed. Timothy Fuller (Indianapolis: Liberty Fund, 1999), 129–178. (Originally published in 1983.) See specifically 131–135, 144, 148–151, and 174.

6. Lon Fuller, *The Law in Quest of Itself* (Chicago: Foundation Press, 1940), 5 (emphases in the original).

7. Ibid., 16–17, 55–56.

8. Ibid., 99.

9. Ronald Dworkin, *Taking Rights Seriously* (Cambridge, Mass.: Harvard University Press, 1977), 17, 22, 24.

10. Susan Neiman, *Moral Clarity: A Guide for Grown-up Idealists* (New York: Harcourt, 2008), 81.

11. See Robert A. Ferguson, "The Curves of Justice: Spatial Metaphors in the Courtroom Novel," *English Language Notes* 48 (Fall/Winter 2010): 129–141.

12. Richard Henry Dana Jr. in *Two Years before the Mast* (1840) first popularized the reform movement against corporal punishment aboard American ships, and four of Herman Melville's novels, *Typee* (1846), *Redburn: His First Voyage* (1849), *White-Jacket; or, The World in a Man-of-War* (1850), and *Moby-Dick; or, The Whale* (1851), are all critical of a captain's absolute authority and forms of punishment while at sea. Daniel Webster's famous speech "Constitution and Union" on March 7, 1850, in defense of the Compromise of 1850 ends with his warning about the foundering ship of state: "I am looking out for no fragment upon which to float away from the wreck." See James W. McIntyre, ed., *The Writings and Speeches of Daniel Webster,* 18 vols. (Boston: Little, Brown, 1903), 10:57. Webster's scene is also one that Herman Melville turned into highest art in 1851 in the apocalyptic conclusion of *Moby-Dick.* Then there is Henry Wadsworth Longfellow's equally famous earlier poem "The Building of the Ship" in its 1849 version, when it is more popularly known as "O Ship of State!" because the ship is named "the UNION," as noted in the following lines: "Sail on, O Ship of State! / Sail on, O UNION, strong and great! / Humanity with all its fears, / With all the hopes of future years / Is hanging breathless on thy fate!" Henry Wadsworth Longfellow, *Poems* (New York: Dutton, 1970), 340. This well-known poem by Longfellow, then America's leading poet, may have influenced both Webster and Melville.

13. For a different analysis that discusses Melville's interest in the state of law in the United States and notes his concern over the rejection of natural law, see Charles A. Reich, "The Tragedy of Justice in *Billy Budd*," *Yale Review* 56 (Spring 1967): 368–389.

14. Herman Melville, *Billy Budd, Sailor (An Inside Narrative),* ed. Harrison Hayford and Merton M. Sealts Jr. (Chicago: University of Chicago Press, 1962), 43. Future quotations of *Billy Budd* will be from this definitive edition of the novella and will be cited in parentheses in the text. For the nature of legal combinations in the early Republic, see Robert A. Ferguson, *The American Enlightenment, 1750–1820* (Cambridge, Mass.: Harvard University Press, 1997). For the loss of this combination in modern society, see R. Evan Davis, "An Allegory of America in Melville's *Billy Budd*," *Journal of Narrative Theory* 14 (Fall 1984): 178–180.

15. Most critics have long agreed with William V. Spanos in his book-length analysis of *Billy Budd* that Melville's capacious use of an eighteenth-

century European event actually constructs "a cautionary tale addressed to an American public" of Melville's day and that it remains relevant in our own. See Spanos, *The Exceptionalist State and the State of Exception: Herman Melville's "Billy Budd"* (Baltimore: Johns Hopkins University Press, 2011), 136–140.

16. Melville, like other intellectuals of his day, rejected the rigidities in law over labor issues in the Gilded Age and deplored, among other things, the manifestly unjust legal determinations and executions of four radical labor organizers in the Haymarket Riot cases of 1887. See Michael Paul Rogin, *Subversive Genealogy: The Politics and Art of Herman Melville* (1979; repr., Berkeley: University of California Press, 1985), 284; Alan Trachtenberg, *The Incorporation of America: Culture and Society in the Gilded Age* (New York: Hill and Wang, 1982), 201–207; and Andrew Delbanco, *Melville: His World and Work* (New York: Knopf, 2005), 297–322. For an account of widespread denunciation of the Haymarket trials among American literati, see Robert A. Ferguson, "Traitors in Name Only: The Haymarket Defendants," in *The Trial in American Life* (Chicago: University of Chicago, 2007), 191–231.

17. For the classic misreading of blame that targets Captain Vere, see Richard H. Weisberg, "Accepting the Inside Narrator's Challenge: *Billy Budd* and the 'Legalistic Reader,'" *Cardozo Studies in Law and Literature* 1 (Spring 1989): 27–48. Numerous critics in the symposium featured in this issue of the journal effectively challenge this view from different interpretive directions, including Brook Thomas (49–70), Richard A. Posner (71–82), Steven Mailloux (83–88), and Walter Benn Michaels (89–96).

18. Readers, in the sympathy they are asked to feel for Billy Budd, often forget that he is a loaded cannon ready to strike with dangerous force whenever he is directly challenged, which he already has done aboard *The Rights of Man*. See Melville, *Billy Budd, Sailor*, 47.

19. Many critics simply assume that the narrative and authorial voices are the same. For a critical analysis that explicitly claims that "the voice of the narrator seems throughout interchangeable with Melville's own," see Edwin M. Yoder Jr., "Melville's Billy Budd and the Trials of Captain Vere," *Saint Louis University Law Journal* 45 (2001): 1116.

20. Debates about what kind of testament Melville leaves in this last word of the writer have been sharp. For a full account of those debates, see Robert Milder, introduction to *Critical Essays on Herman Melville's "Billy Budd,"* ed. Robert Milder (Boston: G. K. Hall, 1989), 3–18. The honor of the exact wording "last will and testament" may belong to John B. Noone Jr., who opens his analysis with the claim in "*Billy Budd:* Two Concepts of Nature," *American Literature* 29 (1957): 249, but Noone follows E. L. Grant

Watson, "Melville's Testament of Acceptance," *New England Quarterly* 6 (1933): 319–327. For "virtually a consensus that the work constituted Melville's 'testament' " early on, see Harrison Hayford and Merton M. Sealts Jr., preface to Melville, *Billy Budd, Sailor,* v.

21. The manuscript lay ignored with other loose materials in a japanned tin bread box until 1919, when Raymond Weaver, a graduate student at Columbia University, was "set to work on Melville by [Professor] Carl Van Doren." Weaver recognized its importance and arranged for the first publication of *Billy Budd* in 1924. Hershel Parker, *Reading "Billy Budd"* (Evanston, Ill.: Northwestern University Press, 1990), 42–46.

22. For a critical insistence on just this technique in the proper approach to literature, see J. M. Lotman, "Point of View in a Text," *New Literary History* 6 (Winter 1975): 339–350.

23. John Masefield, *Sea Life in Nelson's Time,* 2nd ed. (London: Methuen & Co., 1920), 213. A sailor who struck an officer was "fairly certain to be hanged or flogged through the fleet." One who had also been accused of mutiny and who had actually killed a superior officer would undoubtedly have received a worse and more visible punishment. Keelhauling involved dragging its victim beneath the bottoms of wooden ships encrusted with barnacles that tore the skin off. A very painful death would have been the result whatever its form. Under the reigning Articles of War at the time, "If any Officer, Mariner, Soldier or other person in the Fleet, shall strike any of his Superior Officers . . . on any Pretense whatsoever, every such Person being convicted of any Offense, by the Sentence of a Court Martial, shall suffer death." 22 George II, c. 33, II, 22 (1749). Death would certainly have been fully suffered in this case.

24. Nathaniel Hawthorne to James T. Fields, November 3, 1850, in *The Letters, 1843–1853,* vol. 16 of *The Centenary Edition of the Works of Nathaniel Hawthorne,* ed. Thomas Woolson et al. (Columbus: Ohio State University Press, 1987), 371.

25. Nathaniel Hawthorne, "The Custom-House," in *The Scarlet Letter,* in *Centennial Edition of the Works of Nathaniel Hawthorne,* 1:35–36.

26. Hawthorne, "The Scowl and Smile" and "Clifford's Chamber," in *The House of the Seven Gables,* in *Centennial Edition of the Works of Nathaniel Hawthorne,* 2:237, 249–252.

27. For a parallel analysis of these changes that uses the term "formalism" where I refer to "legal positivism," see Brook Thomas, "*Billy Budd* and the Untold Story of the Law," *Cardozo Studies in Law and Literature* 1 (Spring 1989): 57–60. Thomas also comes to the conclusion that there is little room to blame Captain Vere for the decisions made aboard the *Bellipotent.*

28. Daniel Webster, "The Salem Trial Murder, 1830," in *The Papers of Daniel Webster: Speeches and Formal Writings*, ed. Charles M. Wiltse and Alan R. Berolzheimer, vol. 1, *1800–1833* (Hanover, N.H.: University Press of New England, 1986), 398, 401, 445.

29. Ibid., 401, 445. The last quotation is from Abraham Lincoln's second inaugural address, March 4, 1865, in which God appears to will "the mighty scourge of war" until "every drop of blood drawn with the lash shall be paid by another drawn with the sword." "Second Inaugural Address, March 4, 1865," in Philip Van Doren, ed., *The Life and Writings of Abraham Lincoln* (New York: Random House, 1999), 841.

30. I paraphrase and quote in this paragraph from a powerful contemporary analysis of the distinctions between natural law and legal positivism, that of Lloyd Weinreb, *Natural Law and Justice* (Cambridge, Mass.: Harvard University Press, 1987), 125.

31. The judge in question is C. Roger Vinson, senior federal judge of the United States District Court for the Northern District of Florida. See John Tierney, "For Lesser Crimes, Rethinking Life behind Bars," *New York Times*, December 12, 2012, A1, A28–A29. The quotations in the next paragraph are from the same article and involve, in order, the following federal district judges: J. Phil Gilbert, Philip G. Reinhard, Ronald E. Longstaff, and Howard Sachs.

32. Ibid., A28.

33. See Sir William Craigie and James R. Hulbert, eds., *A Dictionary of American English on Historical Principles*, 4 vols. (Chicago: University of Chicago Press, 1936), 3:1404.

34. Franklin D. Roosevelt, "Presidential Address to Congress of December 8, 1941," often known as the "date which will live in infamy" speech. *Declaration of a State of War with Japan, Germany, and Italy*, Serial Set Vol. No. 10575, Session Vol. No. 15, 77th Cong., 1st Sess., S. Doc. No. 77-148, at 8 (1941).

35. Jeffrey M. Jones, "Americans Most Confident in Military, Least in Congress," *Gallup Poll* (June 23, 2011), 1–4, http://www.gallup.com/poll/148163/americans-confident-military-least-congress.aspx?version=print. See the discussion of American self-definition through superpower status and military might in Chapter 6.

36. George Kateb, *Human Dignity* (Cambridge, Mass.: Harvard University Press, 2011), 64, 109, 155–156.

37. This paragraph and the next two make use of and paraphrase the approach of Michael J. Sandel, "Justice and the Good Life," in *Justice: What's the Right Thing to Do?* (New York: Farrar, Straus and Giroux, 2009), 260–261. Interpolation of the Pledge of Allegiance to illustrate Sandel's approach is my own.

38. The two most famous opinions in which the Supreme Court has directly countered a majority interest at the time are *Brown v. Board of Education,* 347 U.S. 483 (1954), in which the court ruled that de jure racial segregation in schools violated the equal protection clause of the Fourteenth Amendment, and *Loving v. Virginia,* 388 U.S. 1 (1967), in which the court ruled that the absolute right of an adult to marry excluded all race-based legal restrictions on marriage.

39. *Washington v. Glucksberg,* 521 U.S. 702, 720–721 (1997). Intervening citations have been omitted. Chief Justice Rehnquist regularly conflates "fundamental rights" with "fundamental liberties" in this opinion. Scholars dispute the "objectivity" of this standard, finding only "judicial alchemy," but generally point to the standard of "deeply rooted in this Nation's history and tradition" as ruling doctrine. See Paul Brest, "The Fundamental Rights Controversy: The Essential Contradictions of Normative Constitutional Scholarship," *Yale Law Journal* 90 (April 1981): 1063–1109; and David Crump, "How Do the Courts Really Discover Unenumerated Fundamental Rights? Cataloguing the Methods of Judicial Alchemy," *Harvard Journal of Law and Public Policy* 19 (Spring 1996): 795–916.

40. For the history of neglect of prisoner rights in America, see Caleb Smith, *The Prison and the American Imagination* (New Haven, Conn.: Yale University Press, 2009).

41. This question is the subtitle of Sandel, *Justice: What's the Right Thing to Do?*

42. *Address of the President of the United States Delivered before a Joint Session of the Two Houses of Congress, January 6, 1941,* Serial Set Vol. No. 10598, Session Vol. No. 21, 77th Cong., 1st Sess., H.R. Doc. No. 77-1 (1941).

43. Of the 625,000 soldiers who died in the American Civil War, only one, Captain Henry Wirz, was tried, convicted, and executed for war crimes. His crime was allowing 12,900 Union prisoners under his command to die of starvation, malnutrition, and related causes in Andersonville Prison. See Drew Gilpin Faust, *This Republic of Suffering: Death and the American Civil War* (New York: Knopf, 2008), 215; and, more generally, William Marvel, *Andersonville: The Last Depot* (Chapel Hill: University of North Carolina Press, 1994).

44. The dangers of a literal legal positivism have long been recognized. "If one were to judge from the notions apparently underlying many judicial opinions, and the overt language even of some of them, the solution of the puzzle is simply that a crime is anything which is *called* a crime, and a criminal penalty is simply the penalty provided for doing anything which has been given that name. So vacant a concept is a betrayal of intellectual bankruptcy." Henry M. Hart Jr., "The Aims of the Criminal Law," *Law and Contemporary Problems* 23 (Summer 1958): 404.

45. "How to Cut Prison Costs," *New York Times,* November 11, 2012, SR 12.

46. Giorgio Del Vecchio, "Justice and Legality. The Respect for Legality and the Struggle for Justice," in *Justice: An Historical and Philosophical Essay,* ed. A. H. Campbell, trans. Lady Guthrie (Edinburgh: Edinburgh University Press, 1956), 155, 158 (first published in Italian in 1924). Del Vecchio wrote in parlous political times. Benito Mussolini ruled Italy through a coalition of Fascists and Nationalists starting in 1922. Del Vecchio mounts a direct challenge to legal positivism in this chapter as a derivative form, "the 'historical precipitate' of the idea of justice." He outlines the situations in which a higher appeal might guide "the struggle against written laws in the name of the 'unwritten,' the revindication of natural law against the positive law that denies it."

47. Ibid., 155, 157–158 (emphasis in the original).

48. *Brown v. Plata,* 131 S. Ct. 1910 (2011).

49. Daniel Dorling, *Injustice: Why Social Inequality Persists* (Bristol, U.K: Policy Press, 2010), 1, 13. Dozens of ordinary psychological defense mechanisms also allow injustice to thrive. See Susan Opotow, "Moral Exclusion and Injustice: An Introduction," *Journal of Social Issues* 46 (1990): 10–11, 13. Opotow provides an exhaustive list of twenty-six "manifestations in moral exclusion" that help create injustice. They include such entries as "biased evaluation of groups," "dehumanization," "fear of contamination," "blaming the victim," "self-righteous comparisons," "groupthink," "condescension," "unflattering comparisons," "double standards," "euphemisms," "diffusing responsibility," and "normalizing violence."

50. The prosperity of prison-guard unions and private prisons shows how "big money is corrupting the nation's criminal-justice system, replacing notions of public service with a drive for higher profits." Eric Schlosser, "The Prison-Industrial Complex," *Atlantic* (December 1998), 1, 4, http://www.theatlantic.com/magazine/print/1998/12/the-prison-industrial-complex/304669/.

51. Ibid., 2–3. See also Brian Resnick, "Chart: One Year of Prison Costs More than One Year at Princeton," *Atlantic Monthly* (November 2011), 5, http://www.theatlantic.com/national/archive/archive/2011/11/chart-one-year-of-prison-costs-more-than-one-year-at-princeton247629.

52. Katherine Beckett and Theodore Sasson, *The Politics of Injustice: Crime and Punishment in America* (Thousand Oaks, Calif.: Pine Forge Press, 2000), 186. See also The Pew Center on the States, "Time Served: The High Cost, Low Return of Longer Prison Sentences" (June 2012), 1, http://www.pewtrusts.org/uploadedFiles/wwwpewtrustsorg/Reports/sentencing_and_corrections/Prison_Time_Served.pdf.

53. Amnesty International, "Violation in Prisons and Jails: Needless Brutality," in *United States of America—Rights for All* (1998), 55, http://www.amnesty

.org/en/library/asset/AMR51/035/1998/en/fd3d. Also quoted at greater length in Beckett and Sasson, *Politics of Injustice,* 187.

54. Todd R. Clear and James Austin, "Reducing Mass Incarceration: Implications of the Iron Law of Prison Populations," *Harvard Law and Policy Review* 3 (2009): 307–334.

55. Christian Henrichson and Ruth Delaney, "The Price of Prisons: What Incarceration Costs Taxpayers" (Vera Institute of Justice: Center on Sentencing and Corrections, July 2012), 9, http://www.vera.org/sites/default/files /resources/downloads/Price_of_Prisons_updated_version_072512.pdf.

56. Ashley Nellis, "Throwing Away the Key: The Expansion of Life without Parole Sentences in the United States," *Federal Sentencing Reporter* 23 (October 2010): 30.

57. See Michel de Certeau, " 'Making Do': Uses and Tactics," in *The Practice of Everyday Life,* trans. Steven Rendall (Berkeley: University of California Press, 1984), 29–42. Certeau argues that transgressive responses naturally go up when impositions become strict. People will find a way around restrictions and repression in creative but often transgressive ways: "Sly as a fox and twice as quick: there are countless ways of 'making do.' "

58. For virtually all these recommendations, see Richard L. Lippke, *Rethinking Imprisonment* (Oxford: Oxford University Press, 2007), 105–176. Lippke is a retributivist, but theorists of other persuasions do not disagree with these proposals, and most would support them ardently.

59. The quotations and assumptions in this paragraph are taken from Francis T. Cullen, Jennifer A. Pealer, Bonnie S. Fisher, Brandon K. Applegate, and Shannon A. Santana, "Public Support for Correctional Rehabilitation in America: Change or Consistency," in *Changing Attitudes to Punishment: Public Opinion, Crime, and Justice,* ed. Julian V. Roberts and Mike Hough (Cullompton, Devon: Willan, 2002), 128–132.

60. *United States v. Bailey,* 444 U.S. 394, 421 (1980) (said in dissent). A prisoner could not claim that duress (sexual assault and threat of death) could justify an escape "unless and until he demonstrates that, given imminence of the threat, violation of the escape statute was his only reasonable alternative."

61. Human Rights Watch, "U.S. Federal Statistics Show Widespread Prison Rape" (December 16, 2007), http:/www.hrw.org/news/2007/12/15/us -federal-statistics-show-widespread-prison-rape.

62. Chief Justice Warren Burger, "No Man Is an Island" (address to the American Bar Foundation), *American Bar Association Journal* 56 (April 1970): 326.

63. John Donne, "Meditation XVII," in *Devotions upon Emergent Occasions,* in *The Works of John Donne,* ed. Henry Alford (London: John W. Parker,

1839), 3:574–575. This meditation on lack of separation was written in 1624, four years after the *Mayflower* sailed across a previously boundless ocean to establish a hitherto impossibly distant English community in what was already called the New World.

64. See, for example, the John Jay College of Criminal Justice's Prison-to-College Pipeline program (P2CP) through its Prisoner Reentry Institute: "Spurring Innovation, Improving Practice," http://johnjayresearch.org/pri /projects/nys-prison-to-college-pipeline/; and Susan Sturm, Kate Skolnick, and Tina Wu, *Report: Building Pathways of Possibility from Criminal Justice to College: College Initiative as a Catalyst Linking Individual and Systemic Change* (New York: Center for Institutional and Social Change, Columbia Law School, October 13, 2011), 1–38.

65. For all these characteristics in a good overview, see Gerald G. Gaes, "The Impact of Prison Education Programs on Post-release Outcomes," *Reentry Roundtable on Education* (March 31 and April 1, 2008), 1, 11–12, http:// www.jjay.cuny.edu/GaesTheEffectivenessofPrisonEducationPrograms.pdf.

66. Paula Smith and Myrinda Schweitzer, "The Therapeutic Prison," *Journal of Contemporary Criminal Justice* 28 (2012): 7–8, 11–14.

67. Nigel Walker, *Why Punish?* (Oxford: Oxford University Press, 1991), 1–3.

68. By less, I mean that we might have to dismantle some of the precedents that use rights talk to protect the punisher in order to recognize the rights of the punished.

69. Excess in punishment also runs directly against the notion that dignity depends on the presence of self-control. See Michael J. Meyer, "Dignity, Rights, and Self-Control," *Ethics* 99 (April 1989): 520–534, particularly 533–534.

70. I paraphrase and quote in this paragraph from Ruth W. Grant, "The Ethics of Incentives: Historical Origins and Contemporary Understandings," *Economics and Philosophy* 18 (April 2002): 111–112, 114–115, 130, 133–135 (emphasis in the original).

71. Alfred Adler, quoted in *The Individual Psychology of Alfred Adler*, ed. H. L. Ansbacher and R. R. Ansbacher (New York: Basic Books, 1956), 96. Adler made the point in 1914.

72. *Webster's Third New International Dictionary of the English Language Unabridged* (Springfield, Mass.: Merriam-Webster, 1993), 1089. The dictionary gives both noun and verb forms in that order.

73. John Dewey, *The Middle Works of John Dewey*, vol. 12, *Reconstruction in Philosophy* (Carbondale: Southern Illinois University Press, 1982), 181. For a postmodern take on this subject, on which I rely in part, and for Russell's comment, see Richard Rorty, *Philosophy and Social Hope* (New York: Penguin Books, 1999), 23.

74. The great advantage of private initiatives in prison reform is that they can depend on a voluntary basis in proceeding.

75. In New York State correctional officers receive a twelve-month program that boils down to just eight weeks of formal training at the Correctional Services Training Academy, where they receive "academic courses in such areas as emergency response procedures, interpersonal communications, legal rights and responsibilities, security procedures, and concepts and issues in corrections" along with "rigorous physical training to develop fitness, strength and stamina." New York State Department of Corrections and Community Supervision, "Correctional Officer" (last visited September 20, 2013), http://www.doccs.ny.gov/Jobs/CorrectionOfficer.html. The website shows its real purpose with the logo of a hand holding a key next to the words "the key to a secure future." Being a correctional officer in the United States is generally understood to be a position without much vocational prestige. In Norway, in contrast, prospective correctional officers enter a three-year training program with courses in psychology and social relations to go with a general program. Those who complete the program hold positions honored within Norwegian society. See Erwin James, "The Norwegian Prison Where Inmates are Treated Like People," *The Guardian*, Februry 24, 2013, G2-9, http://www.guardian.co.uk/society/2013/feb/25/norwegian-prison-inmates-treated-like-people. The Norwegian model might be one to follow in proposed restoration programs. I am indebted to Christina Helburn, "Unusual, but Not Cruel, Punishment: A Study of Bastoy Prison in Norway" (seminar paper, Columbia Law School, spring semester 2013), for the references on Norway's incarceration arrangements.

76. For one of many efforts to reconcile retribution and rehabilitation, see R. A. Duff, "Punishment and Rehabilitation—or Punishment as Rehabilitation," *CJM: Criminal Justice Matters* 60 (2005): 18–19.

77. For commentary on these reentry issues, see Jeremy Travis, "'What Works' for Successful Prisoner Reentry," *Testimony before the U.S. House of Representatives Committee on Appropriations Subcommittee on Commerce, Justice, Science and Related Agencies* (Washington, D.C., March 12, 2009). Travis has been president of John Jay College of Criminal Justice since 2004.

78. For a study that hopes to find a scientific basis for distinguishing serial criminals, see Adrian Raine, *An Anatomy of Violence: The Biological Roots of Crime* (New York: Pantheon Books, 2013). But even if such designations could be made, could a fair justice system make distinctions on this basis?

79. The Second Chance Act in 2008 and guidelines issued by the U.S. Equal Employment Opportunity Commission using Title VII of the Civil Rights Act of 1964 as amended are supposed to prevent employers from dis-

criminating against released inmates who apply for employment, but the laws apply only in certain situations and are easily avoided in other ways. Finding employment on return to a ghetto community is a hopeless prospect for most convicted felons who are later released.

80. Shawn Bushway, "Employment Dimensions of Reentry: Understanding the Nexus between Prison Reentry and Work" (Urban Institute Reentry Roundtable Discussion Paper, New York University Law School, May 19–20, 2003), 4, http://www.urban.org/UploadedPDF/410853_bushway .pdf.

81. Emily S. Sanford, "The Propriety and Constitutionality of Chain Gangs," *Georgia State University Law Review* 13 (1997): 1171–1173.

82. Julie Creswell, "Pay Stretching to 10 Figures: Hedge Fund Titans Get Mixed Returns and Lavish Paydays," *New York Times,* April 15, 2013, B1, B9.

83. "There will be fierce resistance to paid prison labor from some quarters so long as there are free laborers who remain unemployed," and "Resentment toward paid prison labor is apt to be greatest where the state is most active in its facilitation." Richard L. Lippke, "Prison Labor: Its Control, Facilitation, and Terms," *Law and Philosophy* 17 (1998): 556.

84. Aristotle, "Justice," in *Nichomachean Ethics,* 2nd ed., trans. Terence Irwin (Indianapolis: Hackett, 1999), 71–74 (5.3.10–20).

85. Aristotle, *On Rhetoric: A Theory of Civic Discourse,* trans. George A. Kennedy (New York: Oxford University Press, 2007), 63 (1.6.20.1363a).

86. Morris R. Cohen, "Moral Aspects of the Criminal Law," *Yale Law Journal* 49 (April 1940): 997.

87. H. L. A. Hart, *Punishment and Responsibility: Essays in the Philosophy of Law,* 2nd ed. (New York: Oxford University Press, 2008), 27.

88. Neiman, *Moral Clarity,* 422.

89. For a full account of current prison conditions in California, see Ruth Wilson Gilmore, *Golden Gulag: Prisons, Surplus, Crisis, and Opposition in Globalizing California* (Berkeley: University of California Press, 2007).

90. Wilbert Rideau, "When Prisoners Protest," *New York Times,* Wednesday, July 17, 2013, A25. Rideau served nearly forty-four years for manslaughter, mostly in one of the worst systems in the country, the Louisiana State Penitentiary.

91. Jennifer Medina, "Hunger Strike by California Inmates, Already Large, Is Expected to Be Long," *New York Times,* July 11, 2013, A10. Carol Strickman, a lawyer with Legal Services for Prisoners with Children, adds to her other comments, "There have been so many problems for decades, and now they are being forced to deal with them all at once."

92. Donald L. Barlett and James B. Steele, *America: What Went Wrong?* (Kansas City: Andrews and McMeel, 1992). I paraphrase from the ten chapter

titles. Literally dozens of books since this one have identified the same problems in various ways.

93. Paul C. Vitz and Susan M. Felch, eds., *The Self: Beyond the Postmodern Crisis* (Wilmington, Del.: ISI Books, 2006), 3, 23, 83–84, 107–108, 122, 153–155, 124.

94. Michael Schudson, *The Good Citizen: A History of American Civic Life* (New York: Free Press, 1998), 313.

95. Daniel Kahneman, *Thinking, Fast and Slow* (New York: Farrar, Straus and Giroux, 2011), 307–308.

96. Thomas Nagel, *Equality and Partiality* (New York: Oxford University Press, 1991), 83–84, 100–102.

97. Jürgen Habermas, *Moral Consciousness and Communicative Action,* trans. Christian Lenhardt and Shierry Weber Nicholsen (Cambridge, Mass.: MIT Press, 1990), 13 (emphasis in the original).

98. Amartya Sen, *The Idea of Justice* (Cambridge, Mass.: Harvard University Press, 2009), xi, 4–5, 46. Sen warns here, in taking a swipe at conventional legal thought, that "avoidance of reasoned justification often comes not from indignant protestors but from placid guardians of order and justice."

99. Charles Taylor, *The Ethics of Authenticity* (Cambridge, Mass.: Harvard University Press, 1991), 15, 75.

100. Ibid., 15, 75–77.

101. Ibid., 52.

102. Robert D. Putnam, *Bowling Alone: The Collapse and Revival of American Community* (New York: Simon and Schuster, 2000), 28.

103. Robert D. Putnam, "*E Pluribus Unum*: Diversity and Community in the Twenty-First Century; The 2006 Johan Skytte Prize Lecture," *Scandinavian Political Studies* 30 (2007): 137–141. See, more generally, Robert D. Putnam and Lewis M. Felstein, *Better Together: Restoring the American Community* (New York: Simon and Schuster, 2003), 2–4, 271, 282–285.

104. See Richard Hofstadter, *Anti-intellectualism in American Life* (New York: Vintage Books, 1963); Robert N. Bellah, *The Broken Covenant: American Civil Religion in Time of Trial* (New York: Seabury Press, 1975); and Richard Sennett, *The Fall of Public Man* (New York: Random House, 1974).

105. Ursula K. Le Guin, "The Ones Who Walk away from Omelas," in *The Wind's Twelve Quarters* (1976; New York: Harper Perennial, 2004), 275–284. All further references to passages from the story and Le Guin's comments about it will be given in the text by page number in this edition. The story first appeared in the science-fiction anthology *New Dimensions* in 1973. The allegorical parallels are numerous, starting with the name: Salem, O[regon], backwards.

106. For a debate over just how harsh the nature of this bargain should be understood to be, compare Michele Alexander, *The New Jim Crow: Mass In-*

carceration in the Age of Colorblindness, rev. ed. (New York: New Press, 2012); and James Forman Jr., "Racial Critiques of Mass Incarceration: Beyond the New Jim Crow," *New York University Law Review* 87 (April 2012): 101–146. See also James Forman Jr., "Harm's Way: Understanding Race and Punishment," *Boston Review* 36 (January/February 2011), http://bostonreview.net/BR36.1/forman.php.

107. Tennessee Williams, "Scene Ten," in *A Streetcar Named Desire,* in *Tennessee Williams: Plays, 1937–1955,* ed. Mel Gussow and Kenneth Holdich (New York: Library of America, 2000), 552. The play, from 1947, won the Pulitzer Prize for Drama in 1948.

Coda

1. *Inferno,* 32:9–14. For purposes of analysis I have used Dante Alighieri, *The Divine Comedy of Dante Alighieri,* trans. John D. Sinclair, 3 vols. (New York: Oxford University Press, 1961). All further citations of *Inferno* and *Purgatorio* will be from this prose translation in parenthetical references in the text by location, canto, and line. References to Sinclair's notes will be by page in footnotes. Another advantage of Sinclair's translation is that it allows the original Italian to be checked on pages that face the English translation.

2. Dante justified his decision to write his poem in Italian as a choice, not a necessity, by giving his strongest and most extended claim for the vernacular Italian in Latin to demonstrate his mastery of both in *De Vulgari Eloquentia,* written in 1304/1305, shortly before he began work on the *Commedia.* For a modern translation of that work from Latin into English, see Dante, *De Vulgari Eloquentia,* ed. and trans. Steven Botterill (Cambridge: Cambridge University Press, 1996).

3. Recognition of the realism in the poem is first made in Eric Auerbach, *Dante: Poet of the Secular World,* trans. Ralph Manheim (New York: New York Review of Books, 1961), ix, 110, 114 (first published in 1929), from which the quotations are taken. More recently, see Teodolinda Barolini, *The Undivine Comedy: Detheologizing Dante* (Princeton, N.J.: Princeton University Press, 1992), 14, 146. Barolini shows how Dante's "narrative realism" and "empiricism" serve a larger mysticism but can be treated analytically on their own.

4. Dante was one of the six priors ruling Florence in 1300. He was banished for being on the losing side of a civil war.

5. For examples of Dante's explicit approval of God's punishments, see *Inf.* 11:88–90; 14:16–18; 24:119–120.

6. Much debate revolves around Dante's use and understanding of the concept *contrapasso.* He uses the term only once (*Inf.* 28:142), in a passage

where Bertran de Born describes how his crimes of sowing discord and separating family members from one another have led to the punishment of separating his head from his body in hell. One might also look to the punishment of false diviners in *Inf.* 20:37–39, where those who prophesied falsely have been left in hell with their heads facing backward instead of forward. In canto 10 of *Purgatorio,* those filled with pride must bend down and face the ground, where lessons of humility are waiting for them. In canto 13, the envious have their eyes stitched so as not to see and covet what others have. Dante is not always consistent about the exact nature of the countering device, but the punishment is always made to fit the crime in some way. The controlling difference is that punishments in hell are permanent, while those in Purgatory are temporary, no matter for how long. For a good account of debates over Dante's use of the term, see Francesco Mazzoni, "Dante's Contrapasso: Context and Texts," *Italian Studies* 55 (2000): 1–19.

7. "Abandon every hope, ye that enter." God has placed this inscription on the gates of hell (*Inf.* 3:9).

8. For example, in the second round of the seventh circle, Dante idly breaks a branch of the suicides who are encased in trees to find out where they are. "Why manglest thou me?" cries the bleeding victim, Piero delle Vigne. "Hast thou no spirit of pity? We were men and now are turned into stocks" (*Inf.* 13:30–39).

9. Scholars have worked hard to trace faint biographical parallels. For analogies between the poem and Dante's life, see John A. Scott, "Dante and His Contemporary World," in *Understanding Dante* (Notre Dame, Ind.: University of Notre Dame Press, 2004), 314–336.

10. Fra Alberigo, in canto 33, is in this category of punishment in hell before he dies. In murdering his brother and his brother's son through an invitation to dinner, he has betrayed both family and guest. Divine justice has separated his soul from his body and sent it to hell, leaving the living body with a demon in its place. This way, the sinner immediately suffers in both places, with no possibility of an intervening forgiveness through prayer or conversion while alive.

11. Here Cato, the classical symbol of virtue and action, rebukes Virgil with the words "there is no need of fair words." Virgil himself admits, "Foolish is he who hopes our reason can trace the infinite ways taken by one Substance in three Persons."

12. For one explanation of the distinctions in punishment between hell and purgatory, see Marc Cogan, "Delight, Punishment, and the Justice of God in the *Divina Commedia*," *Dante Studies, with the Annual Report of the Dante Society* 111 (1993): 40.

13. Dante turns the act of embracing the spirits of the dead into an amusing story. In canto 2 of *Purgatorio,* he tries to embrace a spirit in the figure of Casella, a Florentine musician and friend in life, only to find it impossible to hold a spirit. "O empty shades, except in semblance," he cries and ends up holding only himself (*Pur.* 2:77–80).

14. The self-love that takes the form of envy is thus turned into kindness toward others in canto 13 of *Purgatorio.*

15. Several parts of the *Commedia* present the tragic and absolute separation of close members of families between the realms of hell and purgatory and between hell and those still living. Isolation is especially dreadful in the *Commedia* because medieval culture lacked a modern sense of independence in individualism; identity came through communal ties.

16. I rely in this paragraph and the next on Isabel Moreira, *Heaven's Purge: Purgatory in Late Antiquity* (New York: Oxford University Press, 2010), 4–7, 207–211. See also Paula Fredriksen, *Sin: The Early History of an Idea* (Princeton, N.J.: Princeton University Press, 2012), 1–5; and Peter Brown, "The Risks of Being Christian," *New York Review of Books,* December 20, 2012, 70–76.

17. See Sinclair's notes in Dante, *Divine Comedy,* 1:51, 54–55. In one of several examples of divided families, Manfred's father, Frederick II, is in hell.

18. Sinclair elaborates on the joke by pointing out that Dante and Forese had made fun of Forese's wife in epistolary exchanges. Dante is righting a youthful wrong here. See ibid., 2: 306–307.

19. Here Dante exclaims, "Italy enslaved, hostel of misery, ship without pilot in great tempest, no princess among the provinces but a brothel!" He adds, "All the cities of Italy are full of tyrants."

20. Again I follow the work of Barolini, *Undivine Comedy.*

21. "Of the three otherworldly kingdoms which the *Divina Commedia* represents, Purgatory is Dante's most original creation. Hell and Paradise were already well-established places within the medieval imagination." Jeffrey T. Schnapp, "Introduction to *Purgatorio,*" in *The Cambridge Companion to Dante,* 2nd ed., ed. Rachel Jacoff (Cambridge: Cambridge University Press, 2007), 91.

Cases Cited

Baze v. Rees, 553 U.S. 35 (2008)

Brown v. Board of Education, 347 U.S. 483 (1954)

Brown v. Plata, 131 S. Ct. 1910 (2011)

Coker v. Georgia, 433 U.S. 584 (1987)

DeLee v. White, 2011 WL 7415124 (W.D.N.Y. 2011)

Fackler v. Dillard, No. 06-10466, 2006 WL 2404498 (E.D. Mich. July 7, 2006)

Farmer v. Brennan, 114 S. Ct. 1970 (1994)

Florence v. Board of Chosen Freeholders of country of Burlington, 132 S. Ct. 1510 (2012)

Furman v. Georgia, 408 U.S. 238 (1972)

Graham v. Florida, 560 U.S. 48 (2010)

Green v. Floyd County, Ky., 803 F. Supp. 2d 652 (E.D. Ky. 2011)

Gregg v. Georgia, 428 U.S. 153 (1976)

Hall v. Terrell, No. 08-CV-00999-DME-MEH (2009)

Hancock v. Payne, No. Civ.A.03CV671JMRJMR, 2006 WL 21751 (S.D. Miss. Jan. 4, 2006)

Harmelin v. Michigan, 111 S. Ct. 2680 (1991)

Harper v. Showers, 174 F.3d 716 (5th Cir. 1999)

Harris v. Alabama, 513 U.S. 504 (1995)

Harris v. Garner, 190 F.3d 1279 (11th Cir. 1999)

Herring v. United States, 555 U.S. 135 (2009)

Hudson v. Palmer, 104 S. Ct. 3194 (1984)

In re Medley, 134 U.S. 160 (1890)

Kwasny v. United States, 823 F.2d 194 (7th Cir. 1987)

Lafler v. Cooper, 132 S. Ct. 1376 (2012)

Loving v. Virginia, 388 U.S. 1 (1967)

Mapp v. Ohio, 367 U.S. 643 (1961)

McDonald v. Chicago, 130 S.Ct. 3025 (2010)

McDougald v. Garber, 536 N.E.2d 372 (N.Y. 1989)

McGill v. Duckworth, 944 F.2d 344 (7th Cir. 1991)

Miranda v. Arizona, 384 U.S. 436 (1966)

Missouri v. Frye, 132 S. Ct. 1399 (2012)

Montejo v. Louisiana, 556 U.S. 788 (2009)

Nunez v. City of New York, No. 11-CV-5845(LTS)(THK) (S.D.N.Y May 24, 2012)

Old Chief v. United States, 519 U.S. 172 (1997)

Payne v. Tennessee, 501 U.S. 808 (1991)

Rhodes v. Chapman, 101 S. Ct. 2392 (1981)

Riggs v. California, 119 S. Ct. 890 (1999)

Robinson v. California, 370 U.S. 660 (1962)

Roper v. Simmons, 543 U.S. 551 (2005)

Seffert v. Los Angeles Transit Lines, 364 P.2d 337 (Cal. 1961)

Smith v. Shady, No. 3: CV-05-2663, 2006 WL 314514 (M.D. Pa.) (Feb. 9, 2006)

Solem v. Helm, 463 U.S. 277 (1983)

Stanford v. Kentucky, 492 U.S. 361 (1989)

Trop v. Dulles, 356 U.S. 86 (1958)

Turner v. Safley, 482 U.S. 78 (1987)

United States v. Bailey, 444 U.S. 394 (1980)

United States v. Booker, 543 U.S. 220 (2005)

United States v. Madoff, No. 09-CR-213 (DC) (S.D.N.Y. June 29, 2009)

Walton v. Tryon, 21 English Reports 262 (1753); repr., English Reports, vol. 21, Chancery, sec.. 1 (London: Stevens and Son, 1902), 262–263

Warsoldier v. Woodford, 418 F.3d 989 (2005)

Washington v. Glucksberg, 521 U.S. 702 (1997)

Watts v. Gaston, No. 97-0114-CB-M U.S. Dist. LEXIS 6593 (S.D. Ala. April 1, 1999)

Weems v. United States, 217 U.S. 349 (1910)

Whitnack v. Douglas County, 16 F.3d 954 (8th Cir. 1994)

Whren v. United States, 517 U.S. 806 (1996)

Wilson v. Wright, 998 F. Supp. 650 (E.D. Va. 1998)

Zibbel v. Southern Pacific Co., 160 Cal. 237 (1911)

Further Reading

Theoretical Works

Aristotle. *Nicomachean Ethics*. Translated by Terence Irwin. 2nd ed. Indianapolis: Hackett, 1999.

Beccaria, Cesare. *On Crimes and Punishments and Other Writings* [1764]. Translated by Richard Davies. Cambridge: Cambridge University Press, 1995.

Bentham, Jeremy. *An Introduction to the Principles of Morals and Legislation* [1780]. Edited by J. H. Burns and H. L. A. Hart. London: Athlone Press, 1970.

———. *The Rationale of Punishment* [1830]. Edited by James T. McHugh. Amherst, N.Y.: Prometheus Books, 2006.

Calvin, John. *Institutes of the Christian Religion* [1536]. Edited by John T. McNeill. 2 vols. Louisville, Ky.: Westminster John Knox Press, 1960.

Foucault, Michel. *Discipline and Punish: The Birth of the Prison* [1977]. Translated by Alan Sheridan. New York: Vintage Books, 1979.

Fuller, Lon. *The Law in Quest of Itself*. Chicago: Foundation Press, 1940.

Hart, H. L. A. *Punishment and Responsibility* [1967]. 2nd ed. Oxford: Oxford University Press, 2008.

Hobbes, Thomas. *Leviathan* [1651]. Edited by Richard Tuck. Cambridge: Cambridge University Press, 1996.

Kant, Immanuel. *The Metaphysics of Morals* [1797]. In Kant: Political Writings. Translated by H. B. Nisbet. Cambridge: Cambridge University Press, 1970.

Locke, John. *Two Treatises of Government* [1680 and 1690]. Edited by Peter Laslett. Cambridge: Cambridge University Press, 1960.

Mill, John Stuart. *Utilitarianism* [1861]. Edited by George Sher. 2nd ed. Indianapolis: Hackett, 2001.

Nietzsche, Friedrich. *On the Genealogy of Morals* [1887] and Ecco Homo [1908]. Translated by Walter Kaufmann. New York: Vintage Books, 1989.

Rawls, John. *Justice as Fairness: A Restatement*. Cambridge, Mass.: Harvard University Press, 2001.

———. *A Theory of Justice*. Cambridge, Mass.: Harvard University Press, 1971.

Ricoeur, Paul. *The Symbolism of Evil*. Translated by Emerson Buchanan. Boston: Beacon Press, 1967.

Schmitt, Carl. *Political Theology: Four Chapters on the Concept of Sovereignty* [1933]. Translated by George Schwab. Chicago: University of Chicago Press, 2005.

Critical Works

Banks, Cyndi. *Punishment in America: A Reference Handbook*. Santa Barbara, Calif.: ABC-CLIO, 2005.

Bender, John. *Imagining the Penitentiary: Fiction and the Architecture of Mind in Eighteenth-Century England*. Chicago: University of Chicago Press, 1987.

Berns, Walter. *For Capital Punishment: Crime and the Morality of the Death Penalty*. New York: Basic Books, 1970.

Bibas, Stephanos. *The Machinery of Criminal Justice*. New York: Oxford University Press, 2012.

Braithwaite, John. *Crime, Shame, and Reintegration*. Cambridge: Cambridge University Press, 1989.

Brooks, Peter. *Troubling Confessions: Speaking Guilt in Law and Literature*. Chicago: University of Chicago Press, 2000.

Chevigny, Bell Gale, ed. *Doing Time: 25 Years of Prison Writing* [1999]. New York: Arcade Publishing, 2011.

Dubber, Markus D., and Lindsay Farmer, eds. *Modern Histories of Crime and Punishment*. Stanford, Calif.: Stanford University Press, 2007.

Feeley, Malcom M., and Edward L. Rubin. *Judicial Policy Making and the Modern State*. New York: Cambridge University Press, 1999.

Franklin, H. Bruce, ed. *Prison Writing in 20th-Century America*. New York: Penguin Books, 1998.

Garland, David. *The Culture of Control: Crime and Social Order in Contemporary Society*. Chicago: University of Chicago Press, 2001.

———. *Punishment and Modern Society: A Study in Social Theory*. Chicago: University of Chicago Press, 1990.

Gottschalk, Marie. *The Prison and the Gallows: The Politics of Mass Incarceration in America*. Cambridge: Cambridge University Press, 2006.

Hay, Douglas, Peter Linebaugh, John G. Rule, E. P. Thompson, and Cal Winslow. *Albion's Fatal Tree: Crime and Society in Eighteenth-Century England*. New York: Pantheon Books, 1975.

Jacobs, James B. *Stateville: The Penitentiary in Mass Society*. Chicago: University of Chicago Press, 1977.

Kappeler, Victor E., and Gary W. Potter. *The Mythology of Crime and Criminal Justice*. 4th ed. Long Grove, Ill.: Waveland Press, 2005.

Lacey, Nichola. *The Prisoner's Dilemma: Political Economy and Punishment in Contemporary Democracies*. Cambridge: Cambridge University Press, 2008.

Langbein, John H. *Torture and the Law of Proof: Europe and England in the Ancien Régime*. Chicago: University of Chicago Press, 2006.

MacNeil, William P. *Novel Judgements: Legal Theory as Fiction*. London: Routledge, 2012.

Mandery, Evan J. *A Wild Justice: The Death and Resurrection of Capital Punishment in America*. New York: W. W. Norton, 2013.

Mauer, Marc. *Race to Incarcerate*. 2nd ed. New York: New Press, 2006.

McBride, Keally. *Punishment and Political Order*. Ann Arbor: University of Michigan Press, 2007.

McConnel, Patricia. *Sing Soft, Sing Loud*. Flagstaff, Ariz.: Logoria, 1995.

Menninger, Karl. *The Crime of Punishment*. New York: Viking Press, 1966.

Miethe, Terence D., and Hong Lu. *Punishment: A Comparative Historical Perspective*. Cambridge: Cambridge University Press, 2005.

Morris, Herbert. *On Guilt and Innocence: Essays in Legal Philosophy and Moral Psychology*. Berkeley: University of California Press, 1976.

Murphy, Jeffrie G. *Punishment and the Moral Emotions: Essays in Law, Morality, and Religion*. Oxford: Oxford University Press, 2012.

Newman, Graeme. *Just and Painful: A Case for the Corporal Punishment of Criminals*. 2nd ed. New York: Harrow and Heston, 1995.

Osborough, W. N. *Literature, Judges, and the Law*. Dublin: Four Courts Press, 2008.

Raine, Adrian. *The Anatomy of Violence: The Biological Roots of Crime*. New York: Pantheon Books, 2013.

Reiff, Mark R. *Punishment, Compensation, and Law: A Theory of Enforceability*. Cambridge: Cambridge University Press, 2005.

Ruth, Henry, and Kevin R. Reitz. *The Challenge of Crime: Rethinking Our Response*. Cambridge, Mass.: Harvard University Press, 2003.

Sarat, Austin, Lawrence Douglas, and Martha Merrill Umphrey, eds. *Law's Madness*. Ann Arbor: University of Michigan Press, 2006.

Silberman, Charles E. *Criminal Violence, Criminal Justice*. New York: Vintage Books, 1978.

Simon, Jonathan. *Governing through Crime: How the War on Crime Transformed American Democracy and Created a Culture of Fear*. New York: Oxford University Press, 2007.

Singer, Michael, *Prison Rape: An American Institution?* Santa Barbara, Calif.: Praeger, 2013.

Stuntz, William J. *The Collapse of American Criminal Justice*. Cambridge, Mass.: Harvard University Press, 2011.

Ten, C. L. *Crime, Guilt, and Punishment: A Philosophical Introduction*. Oxford: Clarendon Press, 1987.

Tonry, Michael. *Crime, Punishment, and Politics in Comparative Perspective.* Chicago: University of Chicago Press, 2007.

————. *Malign Neglect—Race, Crime, and Punishment in America.* New York: Oxford University Press, 1995.

————, ed. *Why Punish? How Much? A Reader on Punishment.* New York: Oxford University Press, 2011.

Walker, Nigel. *Punishment, Danger and Stigma: The Morality of Criminal Justice.* Oxford: Basil Blackwell, 1980.

————. *Why Punish?* Oxford: Oxford University Press, 1991.

Western, Bruce. *Punishment and Inequality in America.* New York: Russell Sage Foundation, 2006.

White, Mark D., ed. *Retributivism: Essays on Theory and Policy.* Oxford: Oxford University Press, 2011.

Whitman, James Q. *Harsh Justice: Criminal Punishment and the Widening Divide between America and Europe.* New York: Oxford University Press, 2003.

Wilson, James Q. *Thinking About Crime.* New York: Basic Books, 1975.

Zimring, Franklin E., and Gordon Hawkins. *The Scale of Imprisonment.* Chicago: University of Chicago Press, 1991.

Zimring, Franklin E., Gordon Hawkins, and Sam Kamin. *Punishment and Democracy: Three Strikes and You're Out in California.* New York: Oxford University Press, 2001.

Credits

Permission to quote in epigraphs has been granted for the following works: from Tennessee Williams, *A Streetcar Named Desire*, © 1947 by The University of the South, reprinted by permission of New Directions Publishing Corp., by permission of Georges Borchardt, Inc., for the Estate of Tennessee Williams, all rights reserved; from Morris R. Cohen, "Moral Aspects of the Criminal Law," *Yale Law Journal* 49 (April 1940): 1025, by The Yale Law Journal Company, Inc.; from Erich Fromm, "Mechanism of Escape," in *Escape from Freedom* (1941; repr., New York: Henry Holt for Avon Books, 1969), 158, by Henry Holt and Company; from Alexander Bickel, "The Infirm Glory of the Positive Hour," in *The Least Dangerous Branch: The Supreme Court at the Bar of Politics* (New Haven, Conn.: Yale University Press, 1986), by Yale University Press; from Dante Alighieri, "Canto 16," in *Purgatorio, The Divine Comedy,* trans. John D. Sinclair (1939 by the Bodley Head), 213, reprinted here by permission of the Random House Group Limited, and from H. L. A. Hart, *Punishment and Responsibility: Essays in the Philosophy of Law,* 2nd ed. (New York: Oxford University Press, 2008), 172, by Oxford University Press.

Index

Abbott, Jack Henry: as author of *In the Belly of the Beast,* 139–140, 141; on time, 140, 167; on prison conditions, 142–144, 155, 161; on abuse, 143, 159; on rape, 144; on indeterminate sentencing, 145; on solitary confinement, 146–147; forms of punishment experienced by, 148; on degradation, 150; on effects of prison conditions, 164–165, 168–169; suicide of, 169

Abu Ghraib, 85, 87

Abuse: on Rikers Island, 26, 190–192; types of, 26–27; deliberate indifference doctrine, 74, 151, 153–155; *Farmer v. Brennan,* 74, 75, 89, 144, 151, 153–156; *Rhodes v. Chapman,* 74–75; refusal to recognize, 75; standard of official knowledge of, 75; by guards, 128–129, 191–192; stress as a factor in, 129; Abbott's description of, 143, 159; lack of punishment of, 143–144, 151, 158–159, 192; *Hudson v. Palmer,* 151–153, 155; *Turner v. Safley,* 151, 155, 159–160; *DeLee v. White,* 158–159; justification of, 159; reliance on internal remedies in, 159; deference to prison authorities in, 159–160; recognition of, 218–219; acceptance of, 219. *See also* Rape, in prison

Acceptance, of punishment, 21

Accountability: definition of, 5, 7–8; applications of, 29, 38, 119, 175, 181

Activism, judges accused of, 120. *See also* Leniency

Adams, Henry, 70

Adjustment hearings, 226

Adler, Alfred, 223

African Americans, 16, 86–87, 138–139, 189. *See also* Minorities, ethnic

Alito, Samuel, 81, 162, 163

America. *See* United States

American Bar Association: Kennedy's address to, 17–19; Burger's address to, 219

American Bar Association's Model Rules of Professional Conduct, The, 110

American exceptionalism, 141, 175, 178, 182

America: What Went Wrong? (Barlett and Steele), 233

Amnesty International, 216

Anesthesia and pain, 66, 69

Antiquity, punishment in, 32–34

Arendt, Hannah, 19

Armed forces, 175, 179–180

Arrest, ongoing effects of, 98. *See also* Conviction

Ashcroft, John, 88

Athens, Greece, 33

Authorities, prison, 156–157

Authority, to punish, 11, 50, 131

Auto-da-fé, 61

Bacon, Francis, 40, 188, 189

"Bad man," theory of, 193

Baze v. Rees, 79–81

Beatings, of prisoners. *See* Abuse

Beccaria, Cesare, 30, 39–44, 45. 81

Bellah, Robert, 181, 182

Bentham, Jeremy, 4, 9, 24–25, 30, 44–50, 52–54, 146, 148

Betterment, as invidious distinction, 182–183

Bible, brutality in, 33–34

Biester, Edward G., 96

Billy Budd, Sailor (Melville), 199–208, 209, 210

Blackmun, Harry, 156, 218, 219, 221

Bleak House (Dickens), 139

Bloomberg, Michael, 107

Boredom, in prison, 140, 165, 223

Bourdieu, Pierre, 173–174

condemned, 92; support for, 93; vs. life
sentence, 93
Debtors' prison, 132
Degradation, unacceptable, 149–150
Deity. *See* God
DeLee v. White, 158–159
Deliberate indifference doctrine, 74, 151,
153–155
De Officiis (Cicero), 194
Deprivation, as theory of punishment, 19,
100, 102, 144, 147–149, 150, 165, 238
Deterrence, as theory of punishment, 12,
14, 49, 50, 51, 55, 57, 58, 123
Dewey, John, 224
Dickens, Charles, 139, 146
Difference, in punitive impulse, 181.
See also African Americans; Minorities,
ethnic
Dignity, as control on punishment, 29, 80,
127, 162–164, 181, 186, 196, 210, 221, 238
Discipline: as correction, 3, 35, 127, 132,
145, 213, 228, 238, 248; as field of study,
4–5, 96, 173–175, 199.
Discipline and Punish (Foucault), 57–58
Discrimination, 139, 236–237
Disease, in prisons, 161
Divine Comedy, The (Dante), 239–249
Dostoevsky, Fyodor, 6, 60–64, 91
Drama, of crime: in fiction, 19–25, 60–64,
96, 139, 199–208, 236–238; in crime
shows, 144–145. 176–177, 185, 218; in
prison narratives, 165–168; in reportage,
183–187, 190–192; in poetry, 239–249
Drug laws, 208–209, 225–226. *See also*
Sentences
Dry cages, 160–161
Due process clause, 211, 212
Dworkin, Ronald, 198

Easterbrook, Frank H., 77–78
Education, 12, 99, 127, 129, 130, 217, 219,
226, 228, 229
Education of Henry Adams, The (Adams), 70
Egalitarianism, 181–183
Eighth Amendment, 71, 74, 75–80, 84, 86,
117, 153, 154–155, 159, 162
Emotion: in punishment, 11–12, 45;
Bentham's unawareness of, 46; in debates
about pain, 69; and victim impact

statements, 84; in prison rules, 90–91,
166
Employment, 227, 228–230. *See also*
Productivity
Enlightenment, 32, 37–44, 200
Entertainment: prison conditions as,
144–145, 218; crime in, 176–177
Equality and Partiality (Nagel), 234
Escape from Alcatraz (film), 144
Essay Concerning Human Understanding, An
(Locke), 66–67
Ethics, separation of law from, 198
Ethics of Authenticity, The (Taylor), 234–235
Evil, 12, 29, 43, 45, 47, 48, 67, 108, 116, 123,
142, 145, 177, 202, 210, 221, 231
"Evil man," 193
Exceptionalism, American, 141, 175, 178, 182
Execution: in England, 76; for treason, 76;
pain in, 79–82; witnesses to, 80, 81–82,
92–93. *See also* Death penalty
Eye for an eye, 28, 37. See also *Lex talionis*

Faces of Injustice, The (Shklar), 193–195
Failure: in punishment, 21, 29; in mercy,
33; in spirit, 63–64; in institutional
coordination, 99–101, 135; as social sin,
141–142; in prison administration, 162,
212, 238; in communal understanding,
172–173; against success, 183–184; in
rehabilitation, 224, 226
Fairness: and limits on punisher, 11; and
length of sentence, 14; and separation of
punishment functions, 98; in decision
making, 234
Farmer, Dee, 74, 153–155
Farmer v. Brennan, 74, 75, 89, 144, 151,
153–156
Fatalism: in tort doctrine 72; over
intractability 172; over injustice 194;
over judgment, 201; over prison abuse,
219; 225; over unsolved communal
problems, 233–234
Fear: Wilson's use of, 56–57; of police, 106;
and jury trials, 116; culture of, 175,
176–177, 179; levels of, 175; in punitive
impulse, 175, 176–177, 188–190; created
by media, 177; and gun ownership,
179–180; response to, 189; freedom from,
212–213